"This is political biography at its best. By reviewing the careers (and self-reflections) of politicians who devoted themselves to advance LGBT rights from around the world, Reynolds illustrates the idea that the struggle for LGBT rights faces universal as well context-specific challenges. Reynolds's central claim is that gay rights don't emerge by themselves. They require the courage, astuteness, and perseverance of dedicated politicians to make them happen."
—Javier Corrales, Professor of Political Science, Amherst College

"A must read in an era of relativism and complacency. In *The Children of Harvey Milk*, Andrew Reynolds reveals the political heroes and the personal journeys who contributed and are contributing to a radical shift in public attitudes on LGBT rights in parts of the World. Reynolds sensibly paints the way LGBTI leaders excel in turning their personal hardship in the precursor to beauty and triumph. More importantly, Children of Harvey Milk identifies ingredients of a recipe for a much-needed global social change starting with political participation and representation of LGBTI people."
—Fabrice Houdart, Human Rights Officer
at the United Nations Human Rights Office

"Andrew Reynolds tells inspiring stories of people—some familiar, some not—who were courageous enough to say 'this is who I am' and fight for a place at the table. They helped bring a community out of the shadows and into the light in ways both large and small."
—Jim Obergefell, co-author of *Love Wins* and named plaintiff of
the marriage equality decision Obergefell v. Hodges

"Andrew Reynolds' *The Children of Harvey Milk* is a compelling work of LGBTQ history and at the same time a clarion call for queer people to resist, to reform—and to get involved in politics. The book's true heart and soul are the stories of the army of LGBTQ politicians who have transformed our world in the decade's since Milks' assassination. A must read for anyone interested in how social change happens."
—Steven Petrow, Columnist, *USA Today*, and Former President,
National Lesbian & Gay Journalists Association

"It takes many players, many methodologies, and many contributions to achieve transformative change such as our winning the freedom to marry in 25 countries so far (up from zero when we started). By collecting for the first time such a broad sweep of the emerging group of openly LGBT elected officials, Andrew Reynolds gives us their perspectives on the ways in which they make it into office, figure out how to use their voices and votes, work with activists (and sometimes butt heads with them), influence their colleagues, balance the pressures and expectations on them (both typical and singular), represent their own communities, find the courage to lead, and, sometimes, prove pivotal."

—Evan Wolfson, Founder, Freedom to Marry

"Andrew Reynolds tells moving stories of politicians whose openness about being LGBT is reshaping laws and policies. Some led us out of the closet, while others had to be led—but all have helped create a more welcoming world. Reynolds links the stories with social science research to create a convincing picture of the past and the future of change."

—M. V. Lee Badgett, Prof of Economics,
University of Massachusetts Amherst

"Mandatory reading for all of those interested social justice movements, *The Children of Harvey Milk* is smart, educational, and entertaining. Reynolds draws his readers in by humanizing a movement that is all but exclusively politicized. Not only does this book fill a giant gap in the academic literature, it also manages to remain engaging and accessible to both academic and non academic readers alike. I can't recommend it any more highly."

—Melody Moezzi, Author of *Haldol and Hyacinths:*
A Bipolar Life and *War on Error:*
Real Stories of American Muslims

The Children of Harvey Milk

The Children of Harvey Milk

How LGBTQ Politicians Changed the World

ANDREW REYNOLDS

OXFORD
UNIVERSITY PRESS

OXFORD
UNIVERSITY PRESS

Oxford University Press is a department of the University of Oxford. It furthers
the University's objective of excellence in research, scholarship, and education
by publishing worldwide. Oxford is a registered trade mark of Oxford University
Press in the UK and certain other countries.

Published in the United States of America by Oxford University Press
198 Madison Avenue, New York, NY 10016, United States of America.

Library of Congress Cataloging-in-Publication Data
Names: Reynolds, Andrew, 1967– author.
Title: The children of Harvey Milk : how LGBTQ politicians changed the world / Andrew Reynolds.
Description: New York, NY : Oxford University Press, [2019] |
Includes bibliographical references.
Identifiers: LCCN 2018005204 (print) | LCCN 2018007708 (ebook) |
ISBN 9780190460969 (updf) | ISBN 9780190460976 (ebook) | ISBN 9780190460952 (hardcover)
Subjects: LCSH: Gay rights—History. | Gay politicians—History. |
Sexual minority politicians—History. | Gays—Political activity—History. |
Sexual minorities—Political activity—History.
Classification: LCC HQ76.5 (ebook) | LCC HQ76.5 .R49 2019 (print) |
DDC 323.3/26409—dc23
LC record available at https://lccn.loc.gov/2018005204

1 3 5 7 9 8 6 4 2

Printed by Sheridan Books, Inc., United States of America

for

Atticus, Scout, Cecilia, Tess, and Owen

my children

CONTENTS

ACKNOWLEDGMENTS

This book has been a decade-long journey made with a handful of trusted companions. My Sancho Panza, Ali Stoyan: we tilted at windmills across the globe and no one could wish for a finer collaborator and travel companion. Leah Elliott, who picked up the reins and drove forward. Ines Blaesius, who joined for the final lap and pushed me over the line.

Pete Lesser gave great advice in the early days of conceptualizing the book and Kathleen Kearns helped me evolve the story structure. Dave McBride was my enthusiastic and patient editor at Oxford, ably assisted by Emily Mackenzie.

I cannot thank enough all the individuals who gave of their time and thoughts in interviews (listed in the appendix). Many others contributed along the way: Chad Blair, Javier Corrales, Christian Correa, Andrew Flores, Tanner Glenn, Charles Gossett, Rob Hayward, Andrew Hollingsworth, Olivia Jackson-Jordan, Kaitlyn Karcher, Caroline Kennedy, Anna Kirey, Maricka Klawitter, Mary Koenig, Dennis Mumby, Georges Nzongola-Ntalaja, Harry Prance, Tom Tuner, Sarah Pedersen, Marc Solomon, and Tana Stamper.

The manuscript was mostly written at Enzo's (thank you, Heinz); Brown Bear Bakery (thank you, David and Lee); the public library on Orcas Island, Washington state; and Café Driade and the Open Eye (thank you, Scott and Elizabeth) in Chapel Hill, North Carolina; and wrapped up in Berlin at the Hertie School of Governance (thank you, Mark). Thank you also to Morgan, Erin, Jeff, Mary, Emma, and Annie on Orcas for making life fun.

This book is for *my* children, but of course every day is for Layna ("have you finished yet?") Mosley.

PROLOGUE

Gilbert and Harvey, San Francisco 1978

Gilbert Baker was nineteen when he was enlisted into the Army to go to Vietnam. But it turned out he was not a fighter. Rather than being discharged, he was transferred to San Francisco to be an Army nurse. Gilbert appreciated this—San Francisco in the 1970s was gay Nirvana. After leaving the Army, Gilbert stayed on and became a fixture of the Castro. He taught himself to sew. He dressed up. He had fun. A couple of days before the June 25, 1978, Gay Freedom parade the Mayor of Castro Street called him on the phone. "Gilbert," Harvey said. "We need a logo, a symbol. We need a positive image that can unite us." Gilbert thought, I sew my own dresses, so why not a flag? Gilbert was twenty-seven. Harvey had just turned forty-eight. Five months later Harvey Milk was dead. The flag Gilbert created would live and grow.

In 1978 it was a rebel flag. The rainbow frightened people. The flag began with eight stripes, but Gilbert ran out of hot pink dye. What sort of gay man runs out of hot pink dye? Then they decided to hang the flags vertically on the lampposts of San Francisco, but it only worked if there was an even number of colors, so Gilbert changed the flag to six stripes. Indigo was out. To most straight people the rainbow flag symbolized queer things, unknown things, sparked uncomfortable thoughts and conversations, gave rise to images of isolation and shame, and then, disease.

Forty years later the pride flag is everywhere—it makes people smile inside, feel warm, happier. Gay pride flags are given to children to wave. It is flown for head of state visits and above government buildings. It is the symbol of every pride parade in the world. A mile-long pride flag was flown in New York to celebrate twenty-five years of the gay rights movement; it was the largest flag ever made. The White House transformed its façade into a facsimile of Gilbert's flag on the occasion of marriage equality coming to all of America in June 2015. In December 2016 when Vice President–elect Mike Pence moved into the Chevy Chase neighborhood outside of Washington, DC, before taking residence at the vice president's house, his neighbors blanketed the streets with rainbow flags. "We want to make clear how we feel about how other people should be treated," one neighbor told CBS News. "I think he's a man who can use a little reminder of American values, so I think that's a good gesture," said another.

The history of Gilbert Baker's flag is much like the history of openly gay elected officials. Not everyone embraces them, but a lot more people do than they did forty years ago. In 1978 the flags were rare and exotic. There were a few on the streets of San Francisco and in urban gay enclaves, but not many. Likewise, there were very few openly gay elected officials anywhere in the world. By 1980 there had been Harvey Milk in San Francisco; Elaine Noble in Massachusetts; Nancy Wechsler, Jerry DeGrieck, and Kathy Kozachenko in Michigan, Alan Spear in Minnesota; Coos Huijsen in the Netherlands and Angelo Pezzana in Italy, but very few others. Today the rainbow flag is flown over large swaths of the globe where thousands of gay, lesbian, bisexual and transgender elected officials hold office—from Brazil to Belgium, Cape Town to Canberra. The flag that spurred hate now is the universal symbol for love. The rainbow still symbolizes queer things, but queer is not so frightening anymore.

In Charles Dickens's novel Betsy Trotwood warns the young David Copperfield that "it is in vain to recall the past, unless it works some influence upon the present." But who determines history, the lessons of the past? Individuals write it, but the big picture is painted with brushes way beyond the scope of one pair of hands. Humanity floats along on a pulsating tide of economic imperatives and social transformation. But the stories in this book demonstrate that individuals can change the flow of history. They divert the current, build tiny dams, and imperceptibly cause the river to take a slightly different course. At different places and in different times, leaders take on different tasks. While most politicians appear to revel in the darker sides of their personalities, a minority rise to the task. The legendary biographer Robert Caro notes that power doesn't always corrupt; sometimes it cleanses, but what power always does is reveal. Some leaders scrape away at the edges of long-welded-shut windows, while others continue the job by prizing open the frames to let fresh air force out the stale, giving the next generation the courage to jump through.

As individuals we adapt remarkably quickly—on a one-to-one basis we cook for each other, go to one another's birthday parties, our children have play dates, we work together, sing together, and increasingly love across boundaries: we interact. But as groups we have a propensity to retreat to our silos. The herd is more risk-averse than the individual. The gay rights movement became successful when it became personal, about people. When it became about Fred, not the gay person. When people saw Chloe, not the faceless transgender woman, they had a reference point. With visibility gay people became the neighbor and not an abstract, disconcertingly aberrant other.

The treatment of gay men and lesbians around the world still dominates the headlines on a daily basis. In Europe and the Americas, it has become the issue that exemplifies how dramatic social and legal change can happen, and happen at a dizzying pace. It is the issue on which law and popular opinion have moved more substantively, and more quickly, than any other issue of the last century. In much of the world, gay people can now marry, serve, lead, and are welcome at the tables of their straight neighbors. Gay rights continue to spread globally—on the heels of the introduction of same-sex marriage in Australia, Austria, Belgium, Germany, Iceland, Ireland, Scotland, and the United States, marriage equality is being discussed in surprising places around the world. At the start of 2018 over one billion people lived in countries where they could marry someone of the same sex: twenty-five nation-states and forty-three other jurisdictions.

But the brightening dawn for many contrasts with an ominous darkness cloaking large swaths of the world with re-energized homophobia. Laws designed to intimidate and invalidate have emboldened thugs to kill, maim, and drive underground gay Africans, Russians, and West Indians. Hope and despair have rarely been more vividly juxtaposed. Nearly three billion people live in countries where just being gay is a crime.

How do gay rights become a reality? Why do people change their view on whether homosexuality is acceptable and homosexuals are deserving of respect and legal equality? The answers lie in a compelling web of deeply personal stories of individual gay men and women transforming the views and votes of those around them. Many of these men and women were—and are—advocates, activists, teachers, entertainers, athletes, and journalists. But some of the most important figures have been politicians. In the 1970s Harvey Milk justified his run for office in San Francisco with the mantra that for gay people to be treated equally they must have a seat at the table. Visible gay leaders, out of their closets, needed to run for and be elected to public office to shatter the fear generated by the myths swirling around their invisibility.

Fast-forward from San Francisco in the 1970s to Carson City, Nevada, in 2013. The Nevada State Senate was considering same-sex marriage. Up until the very last minute the vote was too close to call. Though Nevada's unofficial tagline is "What happens in Vegas, stays in Vegas," the state has long been much more conservative than this would suggest. In 2002 voters amended the state constitution to ban same-sex marriage with nearly 70 percent of the vote. In 2009 the legislature introduced civil unions for gay couples, but only after overriding a Republican governor's veto. Approving full marriage equality was always going to be an uphill battle. With its large Democratic majority, the Nevada

Assembly was unlikely to be the roadblock to gay marriage, but the Senate, where the Democrats held a wafer-thin 11 to 10 majority, was going to be difficult. In the run-up to the vote Mormon and Catholic Democrats, in alliance with Republicans, were seen as likely to give the no vote the edge. But midway through the debate Senator Kelvin Atkinson of Las Vegas slowly got to his feet. He began tentatively: "I'm forty-four years old. I have a daughter. I'm black." There he paused. His eyes scanned the room; he took a deep breath and said, "I'm gay." Atkinson took a moment before continuing, "I know for some of you it's the first time you're hearing me say that . . . that I am a black gay male." Atkinson had not planned to come out so publicly that day, but he was moved to do so as the debate challenged the essence of who he was as a man. A few hours later, when it came to the vote, one Republican, Ben Kieckhefer of Reno, joined all eleven Democrats, including the Democratic doubters, Ruben Kihuen (an observant Catholic) and Justin Jones (a Mormon), in voting yes. A new tone had been set. By February 2014 neither the Republican governor nor the Democratic attorney general of Nevada would seek to defend the state's gay marriage ban in federal court, effectively signing the death knell of opposition to marriage equality. On October 9 Atkinson and his partner, Sherwood Howard, were the first same-sex couple to marry in the state.

It is no shock to learn that knowing someone who is gay affects the way people think about homosexuality and gay rights. Indeed, the number of Americans who support same-sex marriage in the United States has tracked closely with the number of people who say they know a gay person. As more and more people say they have a family member, close friend, or coworker who is gay, support for marriage equality and other gay rights increases. Still, openly gay or lesbian elected officials have a surprisingly large effect on legislation and attitudes. This is surprising given that politicians today, of every stripe, have such a poor reputation for doing anything much of any good at all.

It is true that growing numbers of women in office change the way we think about gender and politics, while ethnic minority legislators give a face and a voice to marginalized communities. However, the direct link between *descriptive* representation and policy change for these groups is often murky and tenuous. But there is powerful evidence to show that openly gay representatives—members of Parliament, senators, state legislators, mayors, and councilors—have a dramatic impact on the progress on gay rights in their countries, states, and towns. The effect of these elected officials is bigger than any other comparable group. The connection between having even a single out gay representative and policy change—from Washington to London, Mexico City to Kathmandu—is bold and irrefutable. Other things matter as well. Social norms and values change, countries become more democratic and developed, positive role models become more common in the spaces where we live our lives: at school and work, on TV and in movies, music and sport; advocates for change become more savvy and strategic. But in this mix, the payoff of a few nationally recognized political leaders, who happen to be gay and open about it, is huge.

A note: I use the abbreviation LGBTQ to refer to the lesbian, gay, bisexual, transgender, and queer community. This is a wide lens, including those who identify as gender nonconforming, nonbinary, intersex, and queer. On occasion, the abbreviation LGB is used when the focus is sexual orientation and not on issues of gender identity. LGBT refers to both sexual orientation and gender identity.

Figure 1.1 Louisa Wall, Tau Henare, and Metiria Turei, marriage equality vote, April 17, 2013. Credit: Stuff/DominionPost New Zealand.

The Milk Principle

A Māori Love Song

On April 17, 2013, the parliament of New Zealand met in the modernist dome of a parliamentary building, affectionately known as the Beehive, in the capital Wellington, to debate and vote on the final reading of the Definition of Marriage Amendment Bill. The law to open up the institution of marriage to same-sex couples had gone through months of review, public submissions, and campaigning; the issue had percolated through New Zealand society for years. As the votes were counted, Louisa Wall, the Labour MP for the working-class suburb of Manurewa in Auckland, made her way to the well of the chamber. The public gallery overhanging them was heaving. Before reading out the result of the vote, Lindsay Tisch, the National Party representative in the speaker's chair, reminded the spectators that parliamentary rules forbade them from commenting on the announcement. The dignity of parliament was to be respected with silence.

Wall is many things: a woman, a Māori, a Member of Parliament, a black fern (a member of New Zealand's world champion rugby team), and a professional health researcher. Louisa Wall is also a lesbian. In May 2012, on her second attempt, she was able to submit her bill to open the institution of marriage to all New Zealanders. Some gay rights were introduced comparatively early on in New Zealand. Sex between men was decriminalized in 1986, a Human Rights Act covered sexual orientation and gender identity in 1993, and same-sex civil unions were introduced in 2005. But it took twenty years since the first out elected representative, and a host of failed bills, to reach that day in Wellington in April 2013.

As Speaker Tisch read out the vote on marriage equality on that autumn day in Wellington:—"members, the ayes are seventy-seven, the nos are forty-four"—cheers and applause filled the Beehive. Metiria Turei, the leader of the Greens, wearing an elaborate pink hat topped with a long feather, presented a huge bouquet of flowers to Wall. As she did, a single male voice broke into song;

in turn the entire gallery harmonized in a moving rendition of the Māori love song *Pokarekare Ana,* which was popularized by Māori soldiers in training before embarking for the war in Europe in 1914. As the parliamentarians looked upward some sang along with the gallery, some cried, while others filed down to congratulate Wall. Tau Henare, a Māori representing the conservative National Party, was the first to embrace her. Turei presented flowers to all the reps in the chamber who happened to be gay. Wall rubbed noses with the Māori Party figure Te Ururoa Flavell. Nobody who saw that moment felt that the dignity of parliament had been diminished: it had been enriched.

The New Zealand story—out gay elected officials transforming views and votes—is one that has been replicated across the world in national legislatures, state houses, and local town halls countless times. Angela Eagle was the first out lesbian Member of Parliament in the United Kingdom, and has held the highest party and government positions over her quarter-century career. She was a government minister under Prime Minister Gordon Brown and was the first to challenge Jeremy Corbyn's Labour Party leadership in the summer of 2016. We spoke in her Palace of Westminster office next to Big Ben, looking out over the Thames, Westminster Bridge, the London Eye, and the sweeping history that is central London. When I mention the New Zealand gallery's *Pokarekare Ana* song Eagle welled up, her eyes reddened as she fought back tears, overtaken by the emotion of what that moment meant not just to Kiwis but to people the world over.

A week later, when describing the moment in Eagle's office to Lord Ray Collins, I offhandedly mentioned that I could understand why she had begun crying. Collins, who had been a high-ranking openly gay trade union official in Britain before his elevation to the Lords, fixed me with his eyes and softly said, "Can you . . . can you really?" I knew instinctively in my gut what he was saying was true. I said I understood Eagle's reaction because I myself cannot watch the video of the singing gallery in New Zealand without tearing up, but I could never understand what she had gone through as a one-of-a-kind for over fifteen years: by far most prominent lesbian in British politics. A woman who had in equal parts been vilified, interrogated, mistrusted, and underestimated simply because of her sexual orientation. All humans have stories, but the stories told by the children of Harvey Milk change hearts and minds in a powerful way. Sometimes just being in the room is more powerful than any argument, spreadsheet, analysis, or ideology.

Louisa Wall first entered parliament in 2008 when she replaced a retiring representative from the Labour Party list, avoiding the spotlight of a district election. But three years later she won her Manurewa district with a margin 10 percent larger than her predecessor's. At the time marriage equality was passed she was one of six openly gay members of the New Zealand Parliament, representing all four main parties and very different parts of the island nation. Three men, three women. New Zealand has always been on the cutting edge of diversity—the first nation to enfranchise women in 1893 and in 1999 electing Georgina Beyer, the first-ever transgender politician in office, who was re-elected twice before stepping down in 2007.

Wall brings so many colors to the conversation: a Māori, sports star, health professional, lesbian. Unlike countries such as France and Spain, where legislation to enact gay marriage was introduced and shepherded by straight allies, in New Zealand Louisa and her gay colleagues led the charge. They were able and willing to make the debate very personal. All were in the chamber for the final debate and were among the representatives who spoke. Kevin Hague, the Green MP, reflected on the twenty-eight-year journey he and his partner had taken to that date. "When we got together our relationship was against the law. We were outsiders. We did not belong," he said. After describing the letters he had received detailing how gay men in his country had lived in fear and shame and at greater risk of suicide, depression, and disease, Hague said: "That is why this bill is so much more than achieving equality under the law. It is about saying these lives matter. Our society is big enough for all. You belong unequivocally and without having to compromise who you are." He closed by relating the words of a young girl named Alicia. "Imagine you are me for a second, or any other queer teenager in New Zealand . . . starting to come to grips with who you are. All around you, your family and religious community, perhaps even your friends, are buzzing with talk about a bill, which affects you more than you dare let on. What they say makes it clear that if they knew what you were, what you really are, they would not accept you. There is a reason so many of us have considered suicide as an acceptable way out at some point, and this is it." Alicia told Hague: "What your support of this bill has meant is immeasurable."

To succeed, Louisa Wall and her gay colleagues needed to make alliances with straight representatives. There were just five gay MPs alongside Wall and to win, they needed at least sixty votes. Traditional allies on the Left could be relied upon, but the key was to win over the socially conservatives representing parties and places slow to come to terms with new worldviews. To do this they were aided by politicians like Maurice Williamson from the conservative National party, whose comedic speech mocking those who thought gay marriage was the end of times went viral on the web. Intermingled with the jokes, Williamson poignantly expressed that he wanted loving sex-same couples to be able to feel the joy of adopting children, as he had done with his three. The Green MP Mojo Mathers, who is deaf, spoke in emotional terms about what this law meant to her lesbian daughter. "For me, one of the highlights of being a mother is when my daughter snuggles up to me on the sofa and shares with me her hopes, her dreams, her aspirations for her future. Like countless other young women, she hopes for love, marriage, children, a good job, and a house with a white picket fence. All of these options are available to her older sister. When this bill passes tonight, which I hope it does, it will give both my daughters the equal opportunity to marry the person they love. No mother could be more proud of her daughters than I am, and to see them have equal rights before the law is very important to me." Mathers's remarks echoed the core strategic ethos of the equality campaign, centering on traditional values of "love, family, and commitment."

Louisa Wall also marshaled groups outside of Parliament to lobby, such as Legalise Love and the Campaign for Marriage Equality, along with local groups in the cities and university. The public made 21,533 submissions made on the bill, with 60 percent in favor of the legislation. As a Māori, Wall also brought her indigenousness to the table. She told me that had had no more important ally in her cross-party working group on marriage equality than the Māori Party MP Te Ururoa Flavell. Wall notes that Māori culture is not predisposed to discriminate on the basis of identity. Indeed, she argues that homophobia in New Zealand was a colonial import: "Pre-colonization we didn't discriminate against any members of our tribe or clan."

Elizabeth Kerekere writes that pre-colonial Māori were sexually experimental people who openly accepted gender and sexual fluidity. Anyone who didn't fit into heterosexuality was considered takatāpui, meaning "devoted partner of the same sex." "Takatāpui were part of the whanau [community], we were not separate, we were not put down, we were not vilified for just being who we are. Sex was a normal part of life. There was a lot of pride in skill. If you wanted to have sex you should be good at it," Kerekere notes. But she also notes that "colonization changed everything—our expression of sexuality, women having control of their own body, female leadership. We lost all of that, having fluidity, being polyamorous . . . our sexuality was stolen."

In his speech on the marriage equality bill, Te Ururoa Flavell noted that in 1888 the English had made customary Māori marriages illegal and rendered children illegitimate. "So when opponents of this bill criticize a change to the definition of marriage as contravening our sacred tradition, I would have to say, 'Whose traditions are we talking about?' "

To Wall passing marriage equality was the touchstone, if not the endpoint. She said that passing the bill was like winning a World Cup final (an experience she knows well) and as momentous as the Treaty of Waitangi, which had given Māori the rights of British subjects in New Zealand in the mid-nineteenth century. I asked her about the proximate triggers to the final push for legal equality. She mentioned events in America and how Kiwis watch the other side of the globe. (This is ironic, given that the LGBT rights movement was spurred in large part in response to the Māori academic Ngahuia Te Awekotuku being barred from entry to the United States for being a lesbian in 1972.) But Wall says that

President Barack Obama coming out for gay marriage started a "global conversation," and the 2012 Macklemore song "Same Love" gave the hip-hop crowd validation of same-sex love, family, and commitment. Wall credits two LGBT leaders who came before her as paving the way: Chris Carter, the first out gay man in the New Zealand Parliament serving between 1993 and 2011, and Georgina Beyer, the groundbreaking Māori and first transgender elected MP in history.

For Wall, presence in politics is the intimacy of reducing the degrees of separation between LGBT to straight. Over twenty religious ministers asked her personally to withdraw the bill but instead she met them, talked through the issues that were important to them, and brought many of them around. The joyful singing in the Beehive caused tears far beyond the South Pacific. "Did you know the song was coming?" I asked. She smiles. She also sees that moment in New Zealand's history as wrapped up with the state's attempts to reconcile with their indigenous population. The equality law not only showed respect for LGBT Kiwis, but also the relevance of indigenous culture. "There was so much love in the room," she tells me, "in contrast with France when their bill went through. For me it was about respect, tolerance, and the ability to move on."

Australia Joins the Duet

Four years after the New Zealand Parliament erupted into song, Australia joined the duet. The gallery in Canberra sang, *"We are one, but we are many. And from all the lands on earth we come. We'll share a dream and sing with one voice. I am, you are, we are Australian."* With only four MPs voting against—which was unrepresentative of the conflict and trauma it took to get there—Australia had marriage equality. As in New Zealand, the change had been led by out LGBT Australians in alliance with passionate allies. The New South Wales State Sydney MP Alex Greenwich was the public face of the marriage equality campaign, and the newly minted federal out gay MPs (Trevor Evans, Trent Zimmerman, Tim Wilson, and Julian Hill) made the vote personal in the Senate and House.

While the lower house only saw its first out MP elected in 2015, Penny Wong had been in the Senate for fifteen years and a minister in the governments of Labour Prime Ministers Kevin Rudd and Julia Gillard. For Wong, the moment was a powerfully emotional validation of her career. The first out gay Liberal Party Senator, Dean Smith, had the honor of introducing the bill in the upper house, and the Green Party Senator Janet Rice spoke about how marriage equality would make her own marriage whole. When Rice's partner Penny transitioned they "went from being a perfect family in the eyes of others, to being weird." They stopped holding each other's hands in public because of the "blatant transphobia" and the omnipresent fear of violence. The MP for

Goldstein-Melbourne, Tim Wilson, made the Milk principle manifest in the debate on marriage equality in the House of Representatives. He spoke of his partner Ryan Bolger and noted, "This debate has been the soundtrack to our relationship. In my first speech, I defined our bond by the ring that sits on both of our left hands, and that they are the answers to questions we cannot ask." With that, he proposed to Bolger, who was sitting in the gallery. Bolger shouted "yes" and the Speaker asked for it to be recorded in Hansard. "That was a 'yes,' a resounding 'yes,' " said the Speaker. "Congratulations, well done mate."

As the Liberal Party MP Andrew Wallace spoke, the first out gay MP, his party colleague Trent Zimmerman, sat directly behind him—framed on Wallace's shoulder on the television screen. Wallace noted that he was a devout Catholic who had been taught that homosexual behavior was wrong and that marriage was only between a man and a woman. At nineteen he joined a monastery, and while that proved not to be his calling, his faith remained his center. "You can humiliate me, you can take away my personal belongings, my wife could leave me, my children could leave me, but at the end of the day all I have that you can't take away from me is my faith," he told ABC News. But a few years earlier his daughter had come out to him, and parental love made him reconsider what was important. He recalled that as he struggled to come to terms with the new reality his daughter said, "Dad, in the years to come, my generation will look back and judge your generation about how you deal with the issue of homosexuality in the same way that your generation considered your parents' generation in the way that they dealt with our indigenous people." He understood her, and despite his faith, was voting for the bill.

There was the incongruous site of the senior straight white conservative MP, Warren Entsch, being embraced as the law was agreed. He had campaigned for marriage equality for twenty years, often defying his own Liberal Party to such a degree that he was sometimes assumed to be gay. In 2006 he told the LGBT paper *The Pink Broad*, "I would think that if I was a gay activist, people would say 'Oh, just another bloody fairy out there trying to push his own agenda,' but because of my background, people are a little bit puzzled by it and sitting up and listening . . . and in fact I'm getting a lot of people that are not gay coming up to me and saying to me 'Hey, you know, we've got gay friends and family too.'" One of the actual gay parliamentarians, Dean Smith, said the bill was "more Warren's than anyone's, we simply walk in the track he has laid." As the cheers subsided the opposition Labour MP Linda Burney flung herself into Entsch's arms. The only aboriginal MP, Burney had lost her thirty-three-year-old son Binni to suicide six weeks earlier. Burney told Parliament, "I support marriage equality as someone who has, and has had, loved ones who identify as LGBTIQ. [Burney includes the intersex community.] To them, marriage equality would mean so much . . . I honor these people. In particular my late son,

Binni." Australian aboriginals mirror the Māori in New Zealand. Allen Clarke of Buzzfeed notes that "homophobic attitudes within the Indigenous community can be largely attributed to Christian missionaries who forbade Aboriginal and Torres Strait Islanders living under the church's care, under government orders, from practicing traditional culture. It was from this period that the idea of homosexuality being sinful became a common view within the Indigenous community—one that still prevails today."

The Australian Parliament had only held its legislative vote after a national referendum had focused the minds of the voters on whether they were ready to make all citizens equal. While the principle of putting basic human rights to a referendum is deeply flawed, the massive majority in Australia laid to rest any lingering unease that the people were being dragged into modernity against their will. With 133 Australian electorates voting for equality, only seventeen did not. Overall the yes's beat the no's, 62 percent to 38 percent. It was a vote for the future, by the future. The overall turnout was 80 percent, and even eighteen-year-olds turned out by 80 percent.

You Can't Hate Us If You Know Us

The stories that weave through this book pose a question: How do these elected officials actually drive legal progress and engender social acceptance? We know there is a relationship between presence and change, but what is the mechanism? Harvey Milk saw in his candidacy as something much bigger than just him or his impact on the politics of San Francisco. The symbolic importance of being in the room, a room of community leaders, legitimized by popular vote, was crucial. In his standard stump "Hope" speech, which he honed throughout his campaigns for public office in San Francisco in the 1970s, Milk would lock eyes with the audience and build to a well-rehearsed crescendo: "Like every other group, we must be judged by our leaders and by those who are themselves gay, those who are visible. For invisible, we remain in limbo—a myth, a person with no parents, no brothers, no sisters, no friends who are straight, no important positions in employment . . . a gay person in office can set a tone, can command respect not only from the larger community, but from the young people in our own community who need both examples and hope."

Four decades of practice have proved Harvey Milk correct. There is a battery of evidence that simple presence and visibility matters hugely in determining attitudes toward gay people. Familiarity breeds acceptance far more often than backlash. Out elected officials are legislative entrepreneurs; they set agendas, persuade colleagues to vote for equality laws (or at least get colleagues predisposed to be hostile to abstain), and they win victories by building gay–straight alliances. But beyond all of that, just being there, as a gay man or woman, seems to have a significant effect on the psychology of colleagues and institutions. The visible gay leader need not be an advocate, a trailblazer, or trumpet their sexual orientation. Just being in the room, at the table and around the water cooler, seems to grow support for equality and lessen distrust. In a 2011 article Greg Lewis, a professor of public management at Georgia State University, found that "people who know lesbians and gays are much more likely to support gay rights even after controlling for demographic, political and religious variables and the effect holds for every issue, in every year, for every type of relationship, and for every demographic, religious and political subgroup."

In her book *Good Neighbors: The Democracy of Everyday Life in America*, Nancy Rosenblum argues that we live in two democracies: a political democracy as citizens and voters, and a democracy of everyday life where we function as neighbors. Politics is abstract, but neighbors are practical and concrete: flesh and bone. Neighborly interactions, good and bad, hinge on apolitical reciprocation, likes, shared interests, and tasks. It's not impossible to break the apolitical ties and demonize a family you once carpooled with, but it's a higher emotional bar. Here is why the act of coming out and being visible is such a powerful driver of change—it's an apolitical act that removes sexual orientation from being a political statement. And while the two dads who live down the street may make you less likely to vote for homophobic laws or the candidates who advocate them, the gay son, daughter, cousin, or uncle packs an exponentially more powerful punch. The "other" is now more powerful than even the friendly gay neighbor— the other is now part of you, so you are the other. How can I be hateful to my own flesh and blood? The growth in numbers of Britons and Americans supporting gay rights over time tracks the growing number who say they have a close friend or family member who is gay. The Pew Research Center found that Americans saying they personally knew someone who was gay or lesbian had increased to 87 percent in May 2013, a 26 percent rise over 1993. Sixty-seven percent said they knew more than one or two gay people. Nearly 50 perent of people in 2013 said they had a close family member or friend who was gay. Simultaneously, the number of Americans who had a favorable opinion of gay men rose to 54 percent, and of lesbians 58 percent. Evan Wolfson, the founder and driving force behind the Freedom to Marry campaign, points out that the story is slightly more nuanced. Values change not merely because straight people know someone who is gay; change comes through meaningful conversations with the gay people they know. Sons and daughters, uncles and aunts have those conversations face-to-face around the kitchen table. While out elected officials are mostly limited to having those conversations with individual voters through the media, they can be equally meaningful.

The International Lesbian and Gay Association conducted a huge attitude survey in 2017, reaching 116,000 people in seventy-seven countries. The findings were overwhelming: when respondents knew an LGBT person they were much more likely (73%) to support their equal rights and protections. But only 44 percent of those who said they did not know an LGBT person agreed. The problem was visibility. Only 41 percent of respondents said they knew someone who was romantically or sexually attracted to people of the same sex; 40 percent said they didn't know anyone, and 19 percent did not know if they knew such a person. The figures were unsurprisingly lower for gender identity: 35 percent said they knew someone who dresses, acts, or identifies as another sex than that which they were born; 45 percent said they didn't, and 20 percent did not know. Again, familiarity drove support for equality: 81 percent of those surveyed who said they were comfortable socializing with someone of a gender minority were in favor of granting legal gender recognition, while 63 percent of those who were uncomfortable socializing disagreed. There is no visibility without LGBTQ people coming out. National Coming Out Day was started in 1988 by Jean O'Leary and Rob Eichberg. They asked their friend Karen Ocamb to help them make a video to launch their idea. "This is the silliest idea I ever heard," Karen told Jean. "Do you think that everybody who's been in the closet is just all of a sudden going to one day come out because you said to come out?" And Jean said, "Yes!" So Karen helped them. It was a success, and Karen said to Jean, "I take back everything I said! I always underestimate you." Ocamb reflects, "Now it's almost passé. But at the time, it was a major commitment. People really felt emotional about it. They talked with their friends about whether to do it or not. Now it's so much easier than it was then." In the 1980s the average age to come out was between nineteen and twenty-three; in 2017 it was sixteen. Jean O'Leary went on to die of cancer, Rob Eichberg of AIDS.

On the LGBTQ&A podcast hosted by Jeffrey Masters in 2017, Harvey Milk's friend and the originator of the AIDS quilt, Cleve Jones, bemoaned the fact that the political act of coming out seems to have lost some of its sparkle despite losing none of its power. "Once the haters know that they have queer and trans people in their families, in their workplace, in their neighborhood, on their block, in their congregation, in their school, it becomes very difficult for them to continue to hate us. More difficult for them to vote against us or harm us. Coming out has always been an essential part of this movement. It was articulated very powerfully by Harvey Milk during his campaigns in San Francisco . . . It was the rallying cry: We have to come out, we have to come out. It seems so simplistic but it's a powerful notion and a big part of why we have come as far as we have within my lifetime. Because ordinary people made that bold decision to say 'Mom, Dad . . . this is who I am.' It was real bravery." In 2017 nine of every ten

LGBT youth said they were out to close friends, though only 64 percent were out to their classmates.

What is it about contact and visibility that moves hearts? Value change is rarely driven by altruism or argument; it is driven by empathy, and empathy is driven by specificity. You don't become passionate about gay rights because it's illogical that lovers cannot visit their partners in the hospital; you care when you see the desperation and fear on the face of your friend Bill when he is not allowed to be with his boyfriend Larry on the cancer ward. You don't get passionate about bullying in school because high numbers of queer teens are bullied in secondary school; you get upset because your cousin Julie cries in her room every day after school because the kids call her faggot girl while shoving her in the toilet stall by the playground. What changes society are names and faces and the stories of real people with eyes you can look into and feelings you can empathize with. When you ask most homophobes why they oppose gay rights they will tell you that homosexuality is wrong, perverse, or against their religion. But ask them about Jack's son Danny who lives on their street and they might say, "Well, Danny is different. He's a nice kid. He's not one of those Hollywood gays. I've never seen him in make-up. What he does on his own time is no business of mine."

Contact with the "other"—however it is defined—has measurable positive effects. Matt Lowe, a PhD student at MIT, set up an experiment in India. He recruited over 1,200 young Indian men from different castes and randomly assigned them to teams playing in a month-long cricket league, alongside a control group. Some were assigned to teams of one caste, while others played on mixed-caste teams. Some teams played against their own caste, others against different castes, and others against mixed-caste teams. Lowe found that players on mixed-caste teams were more likely to develop friendships across caste after the experiment. After a month, such collaborative contact reduced caste bias in a voting exercise by up to 33 percent. As Lowe suggests, "participants are not just changing their minds about those they directly interact with, but also about the caste group in general." Players were probably influenced by material benefits of mixed-caste collaboration, which increased the predicted win probability of a team by 4 percent.

Thus, when it comes to normalizing the role of LGBTQ people in politics, visibility is almost everything. The long-serving Chancellor of Germany, Angela Merkel, was steadfast in her opposition to marriage equality for twelve years of her premiership despite the fact that by 2017 about 80 percent of Germans believed that marriage equality should be law. For years Merkel said she was not persuaded that same-sex couples could successfully raise children. As late as 2015 the chancellor reiterated that while she was against state discrimination, "for me, personally, marriage is a man and a woman living together." But on the eve of the 2017 national elections Merkel shocked Germans by reversing her view and saying that a free vote should be held on the issue in the Bundestag. Allowing a free vote was tantamount to guaranteeing equality would quickly become law. What had happened to Merkel to cause what *Stern* magazine called this "bomb-shell . . . that shattered one of the pillars of German conservatism"? She told a live audience at a *Brigitte Magazine* conference in Berlin in September that she had a "life-changing experience" when having dinner with a lesbian foster couple who were raising many children in her Baltic Sea constituency. "If the youth welfare service entrusts a lesbian couple with eight foster children, then the state could no longer use child welfare as an argument against adoptions," she said. Ironically, Merkel had worked closely with her foreign minister, the openly gay Guido Westerwelle, for four years, and spoke at his funeral. But Westerwelle and his partner did not have children. Some saw Merkel's conversion as more expediency than sincerity, or as the *Economist* said, "the chancellor has honed the art of u-turning in style." Sincere or calculated, the fact that Merkel used a story of breaking bread with gay people as the cause of her change illustrates that personal contact resonates with voters.

The *contact hypothesis* has long been a staple of how psychologists understand the mechanics of social change. As Jesse Singal describes the theory, "it's the simple, inspiring idea that when members of different groups—even groups that historically dislike one another—interact in meaningful ways, trust and compassion bloom naturally as a result, and prejudice falls by the wayside." In 1943 Robin Williams published his classic text *The Reduction of Intergroup Tensions*, which speculated that "personal contacts between members of different groups are generally most effective in producing friendly relations when the individuals are of the same, or nearly the same, economic and social status and share similar interests and tastes." A sweet spot for straight–LGBTQ interactions is where class and tastes are often shared. In 1954 Gordon Allport reiterated the heightened power of contact if there was no power imbalance between the groups or individuals. In essence, slave-owners having contact with slaves does not necessarily produce empathy, but a gay member of congress interacting with straight member of congress might. In 2006 Linda Tropp and Thomas Pettigrew published a meta-analysis of five hundred past studies and concluded that there was overwhelming evidence that contact under the right conditions had strong effects. Crucially, visible LGBTQ people in the real world provide a porthole into a community through which empathy can pass and connect straight and gay. Their lives—highs and lows—are relatable, and thus the person and group become humanized. In his book *Your Brain on Music*, Daniel Levitin describes how we effectively extend our musical tastes and start to like "new" music by finding a piece that confirms some expectations and confounds others. It has elements of familiarity (relatability) and surprise (newness). "The way our brain deals with standards situations," Levitin writes, "is that it extracts those elements

that are common to multiple situations and creates a framework within which
to place them . . . a schema." But "the songs that we keep coming back to for
years play around with our expectations just enough that they are always at least
a little bit surprising." For example, Freddie Mercury and Queen's "Bohemian
Rhapsody" acts as a gateway drug between Cosi fan Tutti and Kate Bush (or vice
versa). Farrokh Bulsara (Freddie Mercury's birth name) was something of a cultural gateway himself.

The positive effects of LGBTQ presence on the majority (straight) group
often leads to the creation of allies who go on to cheerlead for the rights of the
minority. As LGBTQ politicians are almost never in the majority, they rely on
straight allies to enhance and guarantee the community's rights. Singal gets to
the heart of what we know about personal contact: "When you have close, meaningful relationships with members of another group, it's simply much harder to
embrace negative stereotypes about members of that group, or to look the other
way when their members are mistreated."

Dustin Lance Black, the Oscar-winning screenwriter of the movie *Milk*,
argued in a speech to the Dublin Law Society that "you can't change minds
by arguing the truths, by arguing the law, by arguing the science and the facts.
The thing that changes hearts and mind, is story." The transformative effects of
knowing a gay person stretch to the world of fiction. As viewers become attached
to gay characters on TV, for example, they start to develop the values found in
people who have close gay family members or friends. Ellen DeGeneres has
led the charm offensive on television since her coming out in 1998. In his 2012
book *The Storytelling Animal: How Stories Make Us Human*, Jonathan Gottschall
noted that "when we are absorbed in fiction, we form judgments about the
characters exactly as we do with real people, and extend those judgments to
the generalizations we make about groups. When straight viewers watch likable
gay characters on shows like *Will and Grace*, *Modern Family*, *Glee*, and *Six Feet
Under* they come to root for them, to empathize with them—and this seems
to shape their attitudes toward homosexuality in the real world. Studies indicate that watching television with gay-friendly themes lessens viewer prejudice,
with stronger effects for more prejudiced viewers." Awareness and support for
transgender Americans and their rights has been given a huge boost by the
high visibility of Sophia, the character Laverne Cox plays on the popular HBO
series *Orange Is the New Black*, and the HBO series *Transparent*, produced by
the dynamic trans duo of Zackary Drucker and Rhys Ernst. Laverne Cox was
featured on the front cover of *Time* magazine in May 2014. In a 2017 journal
article, Tracy Gillig and her coauthors found that an episode of *Royal Pains*
featuring a trans character had a more powerfully positive effect on attitudes to
trans people than concurrent news reports, and seeing two or more transgender
storylines across shows like *Transparent* and *Orange Is the New Black* reduced the

association between viewers' political ideology and their attitudes toward transgender people by half. Gillig's coauthor Erica Rosenthal said that "watching TV shows with nuanced transgender characters can break down ideological biases in a way that news stories may not. This is especially true when the stories inspire hope or when viewers can relate to the characters."

The modern heart-shifters in Britain include some of the most well-loved television personalities, the humorists and presenters: Sandy Toksvig, Stephen Fry, Sue Perkins, and Clare Balding. Sports stars include the diver Tom Daley, the Welsh national rugby player Gareth Thomas, top referee Nigel Owens, the boxer Nicola Adams, and the football player Casey Stoney.

Helpfully, LGBTQ people are often particularly good at presenting themselves after a lifetime of training that seems to produce muscle memory in every generation. In *Breaking Down the Walls of Heartache: How Music Came Out*, Martin Aston writes that many of the most successful managers of rock stars of the 1960s, 1970s and 1980s—for groups such as the Beatles, the Who, Cream, Bee Gees, Yardbirds, Rod Stewart, Marc Bolan, David Bowie, Cat Stevens, James Taylor, Iggy Pop, and the Ramones—were gay men who were genius at presenting their clients in the most broadly attractive way possible. "Gay men at the time would be judged almost entirely on how they looked. It wasn't like there were lots of nice places to go and have lovely conversations. It was all communicated through cruising." As a result, Aston says that gay men were skilled with the "art of being seen" much more so than straights, who felt at sea. Gay men dominated both production and consumption; *Rolling Stone*'s dynamic cofounder was Jann Wenner.

As a policy issue, marriage is much easier to personalize for elite gay leaders than employment discrimination, homelessness, or health insurance, because the inequality affects them directly and their friends and colleagues can see that up close and personal. As Louisa Wall says, presence "creates a level of intimacy." The former US congressman Barney Frank says that legislating is a very personal thing—it is based on relationships, reciprocation, friendships, and shared goals.

The presence of leaders who look like you also can have a dramatic effect on the self-worth and achievement of the young members of the out group. The University of Chicago psychologist Sian Beilock describes the "Obama effect" in her book *Choke*. This was a phenomenon in which immediately after the presidential election of 2008, there was a closing in the racial achievement gap: African American high school students, presented with this prominent role model who defied racial stereotypes about intelligence, were finally performing up to their potential in the SATs. Similarly, the Johns Hopkins University economist Nicholas Papageorge followed over 1,000 black children entering third grade in North Carolina. Thirteen percent dropped out before graduating, and less than half even looked into going to college. But Papageorge found that if they had just a single black teacher in third, fourth, or fifth grade they were not only less likely to drop out of high school, but were much more interested in going to college. The effects were magnified for low-income black boys. Papageorge's team later replicated the results in Tennessee. The role-modeling effects were dramatic: "If having a teacher with high expectations for you matters in high school, imagine how much it matters in third grade. Many of these kids can't imagine being an educated person, and perhaps that's because they have never seen one that looks like them. Then they get to spend a whole year with one. This one black teacher can change a student's entire future outlook."

Adam Glynn and Maya Sen studied how judges makes decisions. Alongside confirming the conventional wisdom that they base their decisions on law and ideology, Sen and Glynn found that personal experiences also matter. "Having at least one daughter corresponds to a 7% increase in the proportion of cases in which a judge will vote in a feminist direction." In 2003 Chief Justice Rehnquist surprised the Supreme Court by denouncing "stereotypes about women's domestic roles." During the term he wrote the opinion, he sometimes left early to pick up his granddaughters from school; his daughter had been recently divorced and he was playing a larger role in their lives. The phenomenon has deep antecedents. By August 1920, thirty-five states had passed constitutional amendments that would allow women to vote, but ratification needed thirty-six. Of the holdouts, only the State of Tennessee would even call a special session. But the 19th Amendment was being blocked in their House of Representatives: it was a 48–48 tie. Harry Burn, a twenty-four-year-old representative from McMinn County, was opposed to women's suffrage and wore a red rose to make his position clear to all. But on the day of the vote his mother wrote to him saying, "Don't forget to be a good boy . . . vote for suffrage and don't keep them in doubt!" With the letter clenched in his fist, Burn cast the vote that was to enfranchise women in America. Defending himself against enraged anti-suffragists the following day, Harry said, "I know that a mother's advice is always safest for her boy to follow . . . and my mother wanted me to vote for ratification."

Stereotypes are enduring, pernicious, and imbibed early on in life. In a 2017 paper published in *Science,* Lin Bian, Sarah-Jane Leslie, and Andrei Cimpian found that at age five, children seemed not to differentiate between boys and girls in expectations of who was "really, really smart"—childhood's version of adult brilliance. But by age six, girls were prepared to lump more boys into the "really, really smart" category and to steer themselves away from games intended for those in that category. The authors noted that "these stereotypes discourage women's pursuit of many prestigious careers; that is, women are underrepresented in fields whose members cherish brilliance (such as physics and philosophy)." Expectations are reinforced by the culture that is visible around you. In their 2017 paper "Who Becomes an Innovator in America: The Importance of

Exposure to Innovation," Alex Bell, Raj Chetty, Xavier Jaravel, Neviana Petkova, and John Van Reenen found that exposure mattered in a very gender-specific way: "Women are more likely to invent in a given technology class if they grew up in an area with many female inventors in that technology class. Growing up around male inventors has no impact on women's propensity to innovate."

The growing number of women in elective office has had a measurable effect. Sarah Kliff summarized the evidence in *Vox*, noting that "women legislators are more likely to introduce legislation that specifically benefits women. They're better at bringing funding back to their home districts. And, to put it bluntly, they just get more shit done: a woman legislator, on average, passed twice as many bills as a male legislator in one recent session of Congress." Michele Swers at Georgetown University notes that "women in Congress are just more likely to prioritize issues that have a direct connection to women—violence against women, family leave policy, those kind of things." Women in office are also just as strong role models for the next generation as minority or LGBTQ office holders are. David Campbell and Christina Wolbrecht find evidence that the presence of high-profile women politicians inspires adolescent girls to become engaged in politics.

There are visceral impacts and life-changing consequences when one's existence is validated by symbolic representation. When society chants over and over that you are not worthy, not equal, and not wanted, the mere fact that you see a person like you in a position of prestige and power is both inspiring and reassuring. The effect is particularly powerful on vulnerable LGBTQ teenagers and young adults, but also has considerable effect on the grown and fully formed. We know more about the effects of a community being demonized—for example, the horrific mental health consequences to transgender children when they are invalidated—but there is also a correlation between social validation and a decline in group health. Julia Raifman and her colleagues at Johns Hopkins University found that in the thirty-two states that enacted same-sex marriage laws between 1999 and 2015, suicide attempts dropped 7 percent among all students and by twice as much among gay kids after the laws were passed. There was no change in suicide attempts in states without those laws. The survey of 26,000 kids illustrated dramatic baseline differences—about 29 percent of LGB teens reported attempting suicide at some point, compared with just 6 percent of straight teens.

Visibility has just as much power in the corporate world. Paul Zahra, the CEO of the clothing chain David Jones, told the financial journalist Fiona Smith that when he started on the corporate ladder, "most gay people were being portrayed in sitcoms as being effeminate and flimsy and certainly not as CEOs of a company. And, so, there was nothing to aspire to." He spent his time passing as heterosexual. Other powerful out CEOs have begun to be more comfortable with their role-model status: Inga Beale of Lloyd's of London, Stephen Clarke of WH Smiths, Jason Grenfell-Gardner at IGI Laboratories, Anthony Watson of Uphold, Martine Rothblatt of United Therapeutics, Antonio Simoes at HSBC, Christopher Bailey of Burberry, the Egyptian-Australian head of SBS Michael Ebeid, Quantas CEO Alan Joyce. Lord John Browne, former head of BP, embraced the role as a gay role model after being outed in difficult circumstances in 2007. Tim Cook was circumspect about his public presentation for three years after succeeding Steve Jobs at the helm of Apple, but then in 2014 he wrote a coming-out piece for *Bloomberg Business*:

> For years, I've been open with many people about my sexual orientation. Plenty of colleagues at Apple know I'm gay, and it doesn't seem to make a difference in the way they treat me. Of course, I've had the good fortune to work at a company that loves creativity and innovation and knows it can only flourish when you embrace people's differences. Not everyone is so lucky. While I have never denied my sexuality, I haven't publicly acknowledged it either, until now. So let me be clear: I'm proud to be gay, and I consider being gay among the greatest gifts God has given me. Being gay has given me a deeper understanding of what it means to be in the minority and provided a window into the challenges that people in other minority groups deal with every day. It's made me more empathetic, which has led to a richer life. It's been tough and uncomfortable at times, but it has given me the confidence to be myself, to follow my own path, and to rise above adversity and bigotry. It's also given me the skin of a rhinoceros, which comes in handy when you're the CEO of Apple.
>
> I don't consider myself an activist, but I realize how much I've benefited from the sacrifice of others. So if hearing that the CEO of Apple is gay can help someone struggling to come to terms with who he or she is, or bring comfort to anyone who feels alone, or inspire people to insist on their equality, then it's worth the trade-off with my own privacy.

There are also numerous examples of Wall Street CEOs seeing the light when their kids come out as gay. Morgan Stanley and Credit Suisse First Boston CEO John Mack changed his views when his son Stephen told him he was gay in 1997. Paul Singer of the Elliott Management Group went on to become the biggest Republican donor to gay rights causes after his son Andrew came out in 1998.

One of the notable characteristics of the forces driving progress toward equality is that they are overwhelmingly mutually reinforcing and symbiotic in their action. Positive change is clearly not only driven by the descriptive representation of lesbian and gays in public office. There exists a virtuous circle, of which descriptive representation is one key part. LGBTQ representation also normalizes LGBTQ people so that voters are less inclined to discriminate, and judges, reading public opinion, are more inclined to rule that discriminatory laws are unconstitutional. Likewise, judges ruling in favor of equality spur voters to reconsider their preconceived notions, which in turn heightens the public's propensity to support marriage equality and to elect openly gay political candidates. The US Supreme Court's decision in *Obergefell v. Hodges* in 2015 was the product of substantial social, political, and legal momentum in favor of gay rights, but that momentum only took hold at the turn of the millennium. Between 1973 and 1990, the percentage of adults who believed homosexuality was not wrong only rose from 11 percent to 13 percent. The momentum after 2000 was built in large part on the states that introduced same-sex marriage legislation, and that progress rested in no small part on the out lesbian and gay state legislators who had led those legislative battles. Advocacy organizations have been able to use these openings to change the tone of the debate over gay rights, and, as judges and legislatures promote the equality laws the organizations demand, money and attention gathers around the advocacy campaigns, increasing their scope and effectiveness. Success breeds success, while waning enthusiasm to discriminate is contagious.

In 2013 I found that having out LGBT national parliamentarians enhanced a nation's gay-friendly law score by up to 20 percent. The presence of even a small number of openly gay legislators was associated significantly with the future passage of enhanced gay rights, even after including controls for social values, democracy, government ideology, and electoral system design. Once openly gay legislators are in office they have a transformative effect on the views and voting behavior of their straight colleagues. The impact that out gay elected officials have on the voting behavior of their colleagues and resulting public policy may be higher than that of female and minority MPs precisely because their visibility in office is such a new, and in some cases jarring, phenomenon. Newfound legislative presence and political viability feeds into a climate of transformation of values. Individual legislators can nurture familiarity and acceptance from their straight colleagues. As noted earlier, there is strong evidence that in general, heterosexuals become more supportive of gay rights when they know someone who is gay. Globally there are billions of people who do not realize that they know someone who is gay: perhaps a family member, friend, or colleague at work. Furthermore, gay elected representatives work as legislative entrepreneurs advocating, setting agendas, and building alliances with straight legislators to put equality issues on agendas and marshal majorities in favor.

This "familiarity through presence" effect is echoed in studies of American state legislatures and levels of social tolerance of homosexuality in the population at large. A cohort of scholars led by Donald Haider-Markel has shown that increased LGB representation is associated with the adoption of policies that benefit LGB people. Even a small number of openly gay legislators had a positive effect on the adoption of domestic partner benefits. This effect persists above and beyond those of ideology, interest-group strength, and public opinion. While the presence of LGBs in public office can heighten a legislative backlash against gay rights, the presence of openly gay legislators produced a positive net result for the LGB community overall. Haider-Markel also found out legislators playing leading roles in promoting and advocating for bills that advance LGB civil rights. They were as much educators as policymakers: "Even controlling for other factors, such as state and legislative characteristics, higher LGB representation in state legislatures does lead to greater substantive representation in terms of LGB related bills introduced and adopted."

There are a myriad of factors driving progress in LGBTQ rights. But the visible presence of out gay and transgender people in public office seems to carry more weight and power than any other explanation. The characters of this book are the vanguard of that change.

Figure 2.1 Peter Tatchell and Simon Hughes, election declaration, Bermondsey, February 20, 1983. Credit: Homer Sykes.

2

The Ballad of Peter and Simon

A black-and-white photograph taken in the wee hours of the morning on February 24, 1983, encapsulates three decades of postwar British politics: the incongruous and simultaneous successes of homophobia and progressivism. The faces of two men fill the frame; from that moment their life trajectories would divulge, and they would remain inextricably entwined. The square-jawed man in a pin-striped suit looks upward to the heavens as he receives the cheers of his supporters. An outsized orange rosette pinned to his lapel, he is in his element. Behind his left shoulder is a man of the same age, who gazes downward on the crowd wistfully. His mismatched checked shirt and tweed jacket are an uneasy nod to convention rather than an embrace. He sports no party rosette. It is the moment when Simon Hughes won and Peter Tatchell lost the most famous by-election in British history. Both men look resolute. In Hughes's eyes you can see the man arriving at his destination—his destiny. In Tatchell's he is already imagining the next battle front, and perhaps one can make out a touch of relief that it is all over and he will not be strapped into the straitjacket of legislative office.

Peter Tatchell and Simon Hughes are brothers of history rather than blood. Like many brothers their relationship has been tumultuous, fraught with anger and resentments, but in later life a creeping mutual respect, and even guarded affection, bonds them beyond the old newspaper clippings. The Battle of Bermondsey is not remembered primarily as a party political affair—Liberal versus Labour—but rather it has always been "Peter and Simon." The twists of their lives over three decades have brought them closer together.

Their battlegrounds were the housing estates of the London borough of Southwark—laboring Londoners in working docklands across the River Thames from ornate Westminster, St. Paul's Cathedral, and the theater district. It was the urban village where in 1835 James Pratt and John Smith had been the last men in Britain hung for the "abominable crime of buggery." After a fruitless day hunting for work on the south side of the river Pratt had met Smith and an older man, William Bonill, at a local pub and returned to Bonill's flat in George Street to continue their merriment. George Street is eight hundred yards from the house in which Simon Hughes has lived for the last thirty-five years. Bonill's landlords, Mr. and Mrs. Berkshire, were troubled by the procession of men visiting his flat during the day, so when Bonill left the room, Jane Berkshire attempted to see what Pratt and Smith were up to by spying through the keyhole. She later told the police she had seen the men engage in the "appearance" of sex. The law against buggery had been enacted in 1533. It was still on the books when Tatchell and Hughes fought their election in 1983. It was not repealed until 2003. Judge Barron Gurney sentenced Pratt and Smith to death in September 1835 and gave William Bonill fourteen years in the penal colony of Tasmania, where he died six years later. Despite a clemency campaign by Pratt's friends, family, and even the accusing Jane and George Berkshire, James Pratt and John Smith were hung on November 27. Charles Dickens visited the men in prison and wrote that they "had nothing to expect from the mercy of the crown, their doom was sealed." Some 150 years later a gay man was not going to be hung in Bermondsey, but he also was not going to be particularly welcome. It was a working-class Labour sanctuary.

Simon Hughes and Peter Tatchell grew up in different worlds, separated by much more than the ten thousand miles between the mountains of Snowdonia and the beaches of Melbourne. One was the veritable easy chair of rural Wales, the other the hardscrabble existence of working-class Australia. But both developed a passion for the human rights of the marginalized and oppressed. Peter Tatchell was born in West Melbourne in 1952 to a father who worked as a factory lathe operator and a mother who packed biscuits. His parents split when he was four and his new stepfather worked as a gardener, cleaner, and taxi driver. Like most Christian evangelicals of the time, his parents saw homosexuality as an abomination. Chronic asthma left his mother often unable to work, placing an extra burden on Peter to help with the three younger children. He sold newspapers—a penny for six—collected old drinks bottles and recycled paper.

Peter ran to escape. At Mount Waverley High School he ran cross country for Frank McMahon, who followed the new training methods of his friend, the famed Australian running guru Percy Cerutty, who would coach Ron Clarke to seventeen world records. There was speed in Peter's genes. His cousin, Merv Lincoln, broke the mile world record when Peter was six, running the remarkable time of 3:55.9. Roger Bannister had broken the four-minute mile barrier only four years before. Lincoln's time was over a second faster than the world record, but unfortunately Merv finished second to his compatriot Herb Elliott, who ran 3:54.5 in the same race. Merv Lincoln's obituary in May 2016 was titled: "Merv Lincoln, Miler Who Was Always Second Best, Dies at 82."

When Peter was four, Ron Clarke, ran in the Australian national mile at the Olympic park in Melbourne, a few miles from the Tatchell house. Just past the halfway stage of the race Clarke tripped on the heels of a runner ahead of him, and as he hit the cinders John Landy attempted to hurdle Clarke's flailing body but was unable to avoid scraping Clarke's outstretched arm with his spikes. Landy stopped mid-race and went back to Clarke, apologized, and pulled him to his feet. He then embarked on the impossible task of catching the runners who had sprinted past. With the gathering roars of 22,000 spectators Landy ran down the field and won the race in a time of 4:04:2. It was estimated that Landy's sportsmanship cost him about seven seconds. At the time the mile world record was 3:58 (which Landy himself had held since 1954, being the second man to break the four-minute mile). The following day the *Melbourne Sun News-Pictorial* sports editor, Harry Gordon, published an open letter to Landy: "Yours was a classic sporting gesture. It was a senseless piece of chivalry—but it will be remembered as one of the finest actions in the history of sport. In a nutshell, you sacrificed your chance of a world record to go to the aid of a fallen rival. And in pulling up, trotting back to Ron Clarke, muttering 'sorry' and deciding to chase the field, you achieved much more than any world record."

Despite living fifty years in Britain, Tatchell retains his soft Australian accent. "I knew about the incident where John Landy stopped to help the fallen Ron Clarke. Both men were personal heroes," he says. Running for the Waverley Amateur Athletic Club, young Peter achieved some success. Like his cousin Lincoln he was fast, but the teenager had damaged lungs, possibly from working with asbestos when helping his uncle build houses. This meant that he reached a certain level but could improve no further. If Peter Tatchell's life had to be summed up in a fortune cookie proverb it would be "it is more important to stop to pull up a man who has fallen, than win."

On the morning of Sunday September 11, 1963, when Peter was eleven, the Ku Klux Klan placed sixteen sticks of dynamite under the front steps of the 16th Street Baptist Church on the other side of the world in Birmingham, Alabama, killing four little black girls. He was horrified: "How could anyone kill another human being, let alone four young girls?" Tatchell's empathy gene was tripped. Despite having to leave school to earn money at sixteen, he read voraciously. He struggled with the realization that he was gay but soon embraced it, along with a number of progressive causes. He threw himself into anti-Vietnam war organizing and agitating for Aboriginal Australian rights and education. By the end of the 1960s, like many other conscientious objectors to conscription in Australia, he was faced with either a two-year prison term or absconding from the country. That is what brought Tatchell to London in 1971.

Simon Hughes's grandfather, Henry, was a peripatetic Welsh-speaking adventurer from the picturesque seaside town of Portmadoc in North Wales, on the edge of the Snowdonia National Park. At various times he was a brewer, pharmacist, sailor, and writer. Henry's only son James was born in Twickenham, London, in 1905 and took on his father's profession as a brewer. Sylvia Ward married James on Christmas Eve in 1946, and in May 1951 Simon was born, the third of four boys. The family fluttered around the Welsh-English border—Cheshire, Glamorgan, and Herefordshire—spending each summer in sylvan Tan-y-Bwlch in the heart of Snowdonia, the mountainous land of their ancestors.

Hughes's family tree had dabbled in politics—a distant cousin had stood for Parliament as a Liberal and lost—but it was not the family business. Henry and Sylvia were Tories until Thatcher came along. Simon recalls being shocked at John F. Kennedy's assassination as a twelve-year-old in 1963, and excited by a close-fought 1964 British election—a battle royale between the Conservatives and Labour. At the time he was head boy of the Cathedral School at Llandaff, north of Cardiff, the Welsh capital, a place where boys in black blazers and maroon ties were educated in the shadows of the twelfth-century Anglican cathedral. As head boy Simon sought to remove the school class system, which gave hot water to the older boys and cold to the young and allowed the prefects to dole out punishments. The school was the font of fantastic tales. Forty years earlier one student—the eight-year-old Roald Dahl—had placed a dead mouse in a jar of gobstoppers in the sweet shop of the despised local witch, Mrs. Pratchett. What became known as "the Great Mouse Plot of 1924" led to Dahl being caned by the headmaster. While Hughes was head boy, the local MP Thomas George Thomas came to speak. Thomas became Secretary of State for Wales and then one of the most famous Speakers of the House of Commons while simultaneously being blackmailed for being homosexual. After his death he was investigated for sexually abusing children.

In 1966, the fifteen-year-old Simon wrote to all the political party branches in the Welsh Pontypridd constituency where his family was living. Remarkably they all replied, sending manifestos to the precocious teen. Hughes read the Liberal pamphlet and said, "Yes. That's the one for me." "As a teenager I was about equality at home, against apartheid in South Africa, and for justice for the Palestinians," he tells me over tea on the river terrace at Westminster. (I have known Simon since I was a teenager when I became politically active in high school, and then in university around many of the issues we were both passionate about; my life in politics became an academic one that took me to America via South Africa. But we stayed in touch over the years.) In the late 1960s and 1970s being a Liberal was not the strategic path to a career in politics. The party had only six seats in Parliament, and there wasn't even a Liberal candidate in the London constituency of Bermondsey in 1970.

Simon Hughes had an unwavering ambition from primary school to be a lawyer, specifically a barrister. Henry Hughes said it was acceptable for his sons not to become brewers, but told them they could not be teetotal. After three years at Selwyn College, Cambridge, Hughes moved to London to attend the Inns of Court School of Law. A three-year stint practicing law on the continent was capped by a return to legal practice in London. In 1977 Simon and two young colleagues cycled around London looking for a place to live. They moved into a flat on the Old Kent Road in Camberwell, south of the Thames. At the time the Liberal Party higher-ups wanted to resurrect derelict seats and were scratching around for energetic young candidates who were happy to pour in their sweat and tears for no greater reward than saving their deposits. There was no hope of winning. In August 1980 Hughes tried to join the local Camberwell and Peckham Liberal Party, but "they were so incompetent I couldn't even find them to join. I managed to find the Bermondsey party first." Hughes was member number six—hardly a mass movement. The party had never elected anyone locally. At least the border of the Bermondsey constituency was across the road; Hughes could see it. When the ramshackle Camberwell Liberal branch discovered they had a willing sacrificial lamb in their midst they pleaded with Hughes to join them. "Too late—I've joined the party across the road," he said.

Bermondsey was the antithesis of natural Liberal territory. Hughes stood and lost to Labour in the London Council elections of 1981, winning only 2,900 votes (around 16 percent). Hughes lost not just to the Labour Party candidate but to the young left-wing rebel George Nicholson, who had been selected by the grassroots insurgents led by Peter Tatchell as the candidate replacing the old Labour incumbent of thirty-four years. The following year Simon tried again, and his 636 votes in the smaller Riverside ward of Southwark Council was enough to place fourth (in a three-member ward), but still no victory. His younger brother Jamie came fourth in the Abbey ward. Eventually three of the Hughes sons would stand for election: Simon and Richard as Liberals and Jamie for the Social Democratic Party. There was zero chance that the Liberals would take Bermondsey in the general election in 1983. But then the sitting MP resigned, triggering the most infamous by-election in British history.

The Liberal candidate in Bermondsey in 1979, Joe Taylor, scored 7 percent and his vote had been declining over each election he contested in the 1970s. But he wanted to stand again. Simon liked Joe and felt he had earned the right to contest Bermondsey again, but Simon allowed his name go forward anyway. But he did not canvass to be selected as the parliamentary candidate. The selection meeting was held on the night of an important England football match and therefore leaned toward the older, rather than younger, members. Taylor won the nomination by a single vote. But then the Liberals and new Social Democratic Party formed an electoral alliance and all parliamentary constituency boundaries were updated. Because of this each local party was offered the chance to redo its candidate selection. This time Simon made an effort, and he was selected as the candidate in September 1982.

Once Peter Tatchell arrived in London he devoted himself to exploring a world far removed from his childhood in Australia. "I devoured books on philosophy, politics, and psychology. I went to night school to do a degree in sociology. I experimented with LSD. I walked and hitchhiked around Morocco, East Africa, and the South Pacific islands, mostly sleeping rough in trees, cemeteries, roadside verges, beaches, and church yards. I got dysentery in the Sahara, which nearly killed me. I wrote reports exposing Indonesia's brutal occupation of West Papua, the feisty independence movement in the New Hebrides, and the scandalous labor conditions on British-owned tea estates in Malawi," he says. By the early 1970s he was a mainstay of the new Gay Liberation Front (GLF), staging sit-ins at pubs that banned gays and making common cause with the women's movement, black, Irish, working-class, and anti-colonial groups. The GLF saw direct action theater as an essential tactic to raise awareness and ruffle feathers.

In 1972 the German-born psychologist Hans Eysenck advocated electric shock aversion therapy to cure homosexuality during a public talk at St. Thomas's hospital opposite the palace of Westminster. Eysenck also believed in the "overwhelming importance of genetic factors in producing the great variety of intellectual differences which we observe in our culture, and much of the difference observed between certain racial groups." Tatchell challenged Eysenck from the audience and was roughly thrown out of the room. "Many of us saw ourselves as not just gay but also as part of the broad anti-capitalist, anti-imperialist movement, striving for the emancipation of all humankind," Peter says. His radicalism was a direct challenge to the traditional British left. "Our message was 'innovate, don't assimilate.'" The Labour Party would rather gays be seen and not heard, if seen at all. Like Hughes, for Tatchell simply joining the local Labour Party was a challenge. In 1972 he tried to join his local Hammersmith Labour Party branch, but he received no reply to his application. Six years later he tried again, got a response from the Hornsey Labour Party, and was accepted. After he moved to a single-person flat on the Rockingham Estate in Elephant and Castle in the Bermondsey constituency he applied to have his party membership transferred, but again it took multiple attempts. "New members were seemingly not welcome," he remembers. We talk in the very same flat as I move a stack of papers teetering on a chair and sit on an island surrounded by the paraphernalia of a life of protest: *Outrage!* posters in one corner, binders strewn across what might have once been a bed, and placards propped against walls.

Peter and Simon's paths were set for a collision.

The Infamous Bermondsey Bi-Election

If Simon's selection to be the candidate for Bermondsey was plain sailing, Peter's was the polar opposite. The incumbent Labour Member of Parliament, Bob Mellish, had run the constituency and local party as a personal fiefdom since being elected in 1946. The constituency was the epitome of a safe Labour seat. In the previous general election Mellish had won over two and a half times the votes of his closest rival, the Conservative candidate, and had a majority of nearly 12,000 votes. The Liberals were a very distant third with only 2,000 votes. Mellish's right-hand man was the Southwark Labour leader John O'Grady, who had run the council with an iron fist since 1968.

By 1979 Mellish and O'Grady were feeling threatened by an influx of new members, in part led by Tatchell, who were attempting to democratize the local party and radicalize its political views. The young radicals quite openly wanted to wrest power away from the Right and select a new parliamentary candidate in place of Mellish. The insurgency group was demonized as being part of the extreme-left Militant tendency (although Tatchell's leftist ideology was of a quite different brand). Being a strong promoter of gay rights was another strike against Tatchell. He describes the local party of the time as a "mixture of union men who lived the patriarchy and socialists who saw homosexuality as a bourgeois perversion."

The first stage of the takeover campaign was completed in 1980 when Tatchell was elected secretary of the local party and his allies took every other position. In July of the following year Mellish announced he would not seek re-election, and a candidate selection meeting was scheduled for the end of the year. Tatchell felt he didn't have the experience to stand, but he was prevailed upon to carry the banner of the new Left after it became apparent no one else was willing to do it. He still expected to lose. However, in November 1981 he was selected as the prospective parliamentary candidate for Bermondsey over the former MP, Arthur Latham, who had lost Paddington by 106 votes in 1979. The selection vote was Tatchell 37, and 30 for Latham.

Tatchell then became the pawn in a much greater battle over the soul of the Labour Party. The relatively new leader of the national party, Michael Foot, and Bob Mellish were oceans apart politically but on good personal terms, and Foot decided to use Bermondsey to stamp his authority and cauterize the hard-left entryism into the party. On December 3, 1981, Michael Foot responded to a question in the House of Commons about Tatchell being the Labour candidate for Bermondsey by stating unequivocally "can I say Mr Speaker, that the individual concerned is not an endorsed member of the Labour Party, and as far as I am concerned, never will be." The national press were relentless in their onslaught against Tatchell and what they thought he represented. He recalls that almost every mention of his name was affixed with "Australian-born," "draft-dodger," "gay-rights supporter," "extreme left-winger," and "militant." "I was a foreigner, deserter, political extremist and by innuendo, homosexual," he says.

However, by August 1982 another senior Labour figure, Tony Benn, had persuaded the Labour National Executive Committee to soften its line and not

stand in the way of Tatchell if he was reselected as the candidate. In a tearful interview to *Thames News*, Bob Mellish's hatred of Tatchell brimmed over: "I got
news for Mr. Tatchell and all that shower down in Bermondsey," he said, choking
up. "The moment he is endorsed I shall resign." He was true to his word: he
resigned from the Labour Party and in November from his seat, forcing the by-
election. Mellish could have waited for Margaret Thatcher to call a general election, but he was intent on maximizing the chances of Tatchell losing the seat
in the glare of a by-election. Was there something deeper prompting Mellish's
vitriolic fear of being challenged? Was someone questioning the emperor's new
clothes?

In the by-election Tatchell was facing multiple battle fronts. He says it was
"like living through a low-level civil war." In retrospect, the Liberals turned out
to be only the third most culpable culprits in the homophobic campaign. First
came the national press, who vilified Tatchell on a daily basis. Second, the Labour
movement sought to sabotage the campaign, both from within and without. It
all started badly when the Labour hierarchy ordered that 25,000 leaflets had to
be pulped because they were produced at printers associated with Militant tendency. The press had a field day, and the wasted costs counted against overall election expense limits. John O'Grady stood in the election as a Real Bermondsey
Labour candidate with the active backing of former MP Mellish. The *Daily
Mirror* framed the race as between two Labour candidates: "Only a Labour man
can win but which one?" The centrality of homophobia to O'Grady's campaign
was unvarnished. In the last week of the campaign he sang from the back of a
traditional horse and trap:

> Tatchell is a poppet, as pretty as can be;
> But he must be slow if he don't know that he won't be your MP.
> Tatchell is an Aussie, he lives in a council flat;
> He wears his trousers back to front because he doesn't know this
>   from that.

If that wasn't enough to deal with, the support of the national party ranged from
unenthusiastic to bordering on sabotage. The leadership may have conceded
that Tatchell was going to be the official candidate, but their support was lukewarm in the extreme. Headquarters committed a fraction of the workers that
they normally would for a by-election. The *Times of London* noted that "there
is no doubt at Westminster that several Labour figures would like to see Mr.
Tatchell defeated, if only as a signal to the party's hard left."

Nevertheless, the Liberals were far from blameless. When the climate is so
ripe for abuse one has to take a conscious decision between the high and the

low road; it takes some effort to stay out of the gutter when the road slopes in that direction. A few Liberal canvassers took it upon themselves to wear badges saying "I've been kissed by Peter Tatchell," and Tatchell claims that others reminded voters that they should not hold against him the fact that he was a left-wing extremist, Australian homosexual. Most controversially, the Liberals distributed the infamous "It's a straight choice leaflet" that contrasted the "divided and declining Labour Party" with the "Liberal/SDP Alliance candidate Simon Hughes . . . he's the only one to beat Tatchell!"

Thirty-two years later I wound up discussing the leaflet with Andrew Ellis, who at the time had been the chief executive of the Liberal Party. It was a surreal debate, for at the time we were trapped in a safe house in the capital of Yemen, Sana'a, as the booming sounds of rockets and gunfire signaled the advance of the Houthi fighters into the city. Andrew, who I regard as a decent and honest man and a friend, maintained that there was nothing consciously homophobic about the leaflet and that the language of a two-horse race—a straight choice—was lifted from the playbook of countless earlier by-elections. And it is true that the Liberals used the phrase on leaflets in other by-elections. But suffice it to say, it is an interpretation upon which we disagree.

The climate of homophobia spurred significant threats to Tatchell. During the by-election Peter recalls that he "received several hundred hate letters, two bullets, and thirty threats to kill me and petrol-bomb my flat." One letter he received was emblematic of many:

> Dear Peter,
> It should now be clear to you that the people of Bermondsey have no intention of electing a cock-sucking, arse-fucking communist poof as their MP. You should therefor confine yourself to do what you appear to be good at. You may be excellent at pulling cocks but you certainly cannot pull the votes. I have been a life long member of the Labour Party but I resigned when I heard that trash like you can become official candidates. For the sake of the Labour movement—fuck off—we don't want fairies.

Thirty-five years later I asked Peter if he had been surprised by the viciousness of the campaign. "I thought I'd get some flack, but nothing on the scale that I received," he told me.

Added to the chips stacked against him was the naïvéty of the Labour campaign. Tatchell struggled with how to present his sexual orientation. It was no great secret that he was gay, but he was persuaded not to speak openly about the fact during the campaign. In his campaign memoir *The Battle for Bermondsey*,

Tatchell noted that his sexual orientation was well-known among party members when selected, however:

> In our hearts, most of us felt that to be open and honest about my sexually was ideally the best policy. We were not in an ideal situation. I was a left-wing socialist, loathed by the media and the Right, and facing a critical by-election where the incumbent was most likely to campaign against me. From discussions with journalists, it was clear that as soon as I put my sexuality on public record, it would then become in the eyes of Fleet Street a matter of legitimate public interest and justification for them to publish the most intimate details about my private life . . . Reluctantly, and after considerable soul-searching, we decided that while refusing to discuss my sexuality with the media, I should continue to reiterate my strong support for homosexual equality.

Six days before polling day the *Daily Mail* published a poll headlined "Tumbling Tatchell" that had Tatchell at 34 percent, Hughes at 28 percent, O'Grady at 24 percent, and the Tory candidate at 11 percent. Michael Foot's continuing Labour leadership had become entwined with the party's performance in its safe inner London heartland, and thus many anti-Labour voters saw voting for Simon, now the front-runner to defeat Peter, as the best way to bloody Labour's nose. On the weekend before the Thursday vote an anonymous leaflet was circulated featuring the drawing of Queen Elizabeth II and a lipsticked Tatchell, titled "Which Queen Will You Vote For?" It accused Peter of being a "traitor to Queen and country" and printed his telephone number and home address. A stream of obscene calls followed and Tatchell requested police protection, which was turned down. By the Monday Tatchell's own election agent, David Fryer, was telling the press that he predicted the result would be very close between Labour and Liberal—an unintended invitation for disgruntled Labour and Tory voters to tactically switch to Simon Hughes. On the Tuesday a Thames Television poll had Peter and Simon tied at 30 percent. "Up until the last week I thought it would be a two-horse race between Peter and O'Grady," Simon told me. "I had no idea until the day before, that I might win." Around midnight Simon called his agent, Peter Bray, who was already at the count at the Geoffrey Chaucer School, and asked, "Did we manage to win?" Bray replied with calculated understatement, "Simon, I think there maybe a couple of votes to spare."

In the early hours of Friday, February 25, the returning officer for the Bermondsey constituency stood on a low stage and announced the totals for the sixteen candidates. The school sits a mile south of Shakespeare's Globe Theatre—equidistant between Peter's flat and Simon's house. (Twenty-five years later its name was changed to the Globe Academy.) Simon's votes were the seventh to be read out, just before the humbled Tory, who had been beaten down into fourth place: "Simon Henry Ward Hughes, seventeen thousand and seventeen votes." The Liberals erupted in rapturous celebration. There were six more candidates to be announced, prolonging Tatchell's agony on stage. John O'Grady had taken 2,200 votes from Tatchell. After an eternity the returning officer reached the official Labour candidate. "Peter Gary Tatchell. Seven thousand, six hundred and ninety-eight." The Liberals cheered again. It was an abject humiliation for Labour: the swing to the Liberals was over 44 percent. Even today it remains the largest swing in British electoral history.

Over thirty years later, those six weeks in the spring of 1983 still smart. Tatchell maintains that "the Bermondsey by-election was the most homophobic, violent, and smear-ridden campaign in British history." *Gay News* described it as the "greatest public vilification of a gay figure since Oscar Wilde." Chris Smith, who was to come out as the first gay MP the following year, reflects that the by-election hit the embryonic gay rights movement hard: "We were dealt a savage blow by Bermondsey," he says. The moment impacted both the winners and losers. The insidious campaign homophobia made manifest the perception that gays had no seat at table. But Tatchell notes that the outcome was also a wake-up call.

It is important to stress the idiosyncracies of British by-elections: the intensity of focus and national attention, and the fact that they are overvested in importance and significance. The extremes are exaggerated in the cauldron of a by-election that would not happen in the case of over six hundred seats in a mass general election. Tatchell believes that "if I fought a general election I might have won"; most observers would change his "might" to "would have." Hughes reflects that "winning the seat was extraordinary—an iconic moment. But that was me being in right place at right time. A virtue of circumstances as much as of me." Referring to the ugliness of the campaign, "I would have wanted things to happen differently if I could have done. I'm still trying to heal some of the wounds. I apologize again." Hughes believes that the way in which he was first elected may have even enhanced his desire to always do the right thing: "The circumstances of the by-election have made me even more conscious of my responsibilities than I otherwise might have been."

Over the next thirty years, as the gay rights movement in Britain underwent highs and lows, Peter's and Simon's lives would continue to intersect.

Simon in the House, Peter in the Streets

In Parliament, Simon Hughes quickly established himself as the charismatic pied piper of the Liberal Left. In the 1980s the Liberal Party was riven between a radical Left centered around the youth movement and a moderate centrist party leadership. The Liberal leader, David Steel, had wedded himself to David Owen and the new Social Democratic Party (SDP), which was a home to former right-wing Labour Party MPs. The Young Liberals despised Owen and the SDP and their anti-progressive outlook. Matters came to a head over the issue of Britain's independent nuclear deterrent at the party's conference in Eastbourne in 1986. The SDP had itself been established in 1981 by breakaway senior Labour Party figures unhappy, in part, about Labour's new commitment to unilateral nuclear disarmament. Steel saw the Eastbourne vote as a test of loyalty to him and commitment to the Liberal–SDP alliance. But after an impassioned speech by Hughes against the leadership line, the party members voted 652 to 625 to do away with an independent nuclear deterrent. Steel was embarrassed, Owen was furious, and Simon Hughes's mantle as the hero of the Left was forever cemented. Hughes reflects that the whole affair "put me on the political map."

Nevertheless, the relationship between the Liberals and the right-of-center SDP grew closer until a marriage was proposed in 1987 and consummated in 1988. The compromised birth of the Liberal Democrats led Hughes to his only flirtation with another party when he seriously considered defecting to the fledgling Green Party and becoming its first, and only, MP.

Nevertheless, he chose to stay in the fold became a folk hero of the rank and file. In 2000 Hughes came within 6,000 votes of being elected leader of the national party. In a five-candidate race he was the runner-up to Scottish MP Charles Kennedy, who went on to lead the party for seven years and, in 2005, to its best electoral performance since 1923. As Hughes recalls, "Charles was clever and the favored candidate of the establishment. He had a head start in the election which was testament to my lack of ambition and focus. Charles in the end was successful as leader, with an unusual style." But both men were keeping secrets that would ultimately prove their undoing: "Issues that in the end tripped both of us up," Simon confesses. Kennedy's deepening alcoholism gave his colleagues serious worry, and his functional decline led to a parliamentary putsch in January 2006 where he was unceremoniously forced to stand down.

It looked like the party leadership was finally within Simon's grasp. As the popular president of the party and the doyen of the grassroots, he was the obvious favorite to succeed Kennedy. He even had Tatchell's backing. Twenty years after the Battle for Bermondsey, Peter told *Pink News*: "Simon Hughes is the best of the Lib Dem leadership candidates. If I was a party member, he'd get my vote . . . I don't hold grudges, I want to see the party give a stronger lead on social justice and green issues. Simon is the contender most likely to move the Liberal Democrats in that direction." In late January Hughes had a 62–18 percent lead over Ming Campbell among Liberal Democrat voters who expressed a preference.

Then came the sting.

Reaching its peak in 2005–2006, the British tabloid newspaper *The Sun* engaged in the widespread illegal hacking of phone calls and records of prominent celebrities and politicians. Two weeks after the leadership race began, *Sun* journalist Trevor Kavanagh told Hughes that they had evidence that he had called the gay chat line *Man Talk*. On January 26, 2006, they printed a front-page story: "A Second Limp-Dem Confesses: I'm Gay Too." Being gay was something Simon had to "confess" to, and he was transformed from the "muscular strong-jawed Christian" to a limp, effeminate pansy. This was followed by a cascade of sensational headlines in the British press, exemplified by the *Daily Mail's* "I'm Gay Too: Shock Admission by Hughes" and the *Evening Standard's* "LibDem Hopeful admits Homosexual Affairs after Two Denials."

The *Sun's* outing came not only in the midst of the leadership race but only days after Hughes had denied he was gay in interviews with the *Daily Telegraph*, *The Guardian*, and the *Independent*. After the *Sun's* story Hughes made it clear to both the BBC and *Pink News* that he identified as bisexual, having had relationships with both men and women, but there was a sense that the real sin was that he had been disingenuous about his sexuality. Simon has no doubts: "I would have won if not for the story."

We sit on the terrace of Westminster looking across the Thames to the South Bank as the sun sets behind the bridge. Ming Campbell went on to win that 2006 leadership election—and, after a year being caretaker, handed over the leadership to a young MP from Sheffield, Nick Clegg. In 2010 Clegg led the Liberal Democrats into a coalition government with David Cameron's Conservatives, condemning the party to electoral oblivion in 2015. "How would UK politics have been different if you had won the leadership in 2006?" I ask quietly. Simon looks across at St. Thomas's Hospital looming on the other side of the gray water and ponders the question. "I was fired up to be the leader of a radical party," he begins. "We would have had a very different style in 2010—far more progressive. Even if we *had* done a deal with the Tories, it would have been a different deal. It wouldn't have looked like a coalition of two parties that were the same. I would have made sure that some of the things that gave us grief wouldn't have happened." But along with the regret there is introspection. "Being a party leader places enormous pressure on your private life today—I'm not certain that I had all the skills to do that," he says.

After his shattering election loss and vilification in 1983, Peter Tatchell chose the extra-parliamentary route. In 1990 he helped establish *Outrage!*, which used direct action, protest performance art, and threats to out prominent and hypocritical politicians and bishops. The Stonewall campaign had been founded a year earlier. If *Outrage!* was the rebellious teenager, Stonewall was the responsible adult. Tatchell describes *Outrage!* and Stonewall as analogous to the suffragists and suffragettes. "Stonewall were the respectable, suited, small-c conservative face of LGBT activism. *Outrage!* were the outsiders who confronted and shamed the establishment." He conceded that "you need both: people on the inside to negotiate solutions and on outside to shake things up." Tatchell looks back on their early activities with pride. "Our strategy was to force the issue on the public agenda. Protests every other week for years. To get LGBT discrimination reported, raise public awareness, put the authorities under pressure to respond." An *Outrage!* action often led to Stonewall being invited into the corridors of power. "First, you are ignored. Then you are damned as evil, beyond the pale. In the third phase you are dismissed as impractical. By the fourth phase, people engage. Then there is grudging acceptance. Finally you and your campaign is embraced," Peter tells me. "Indeed, many would say at that stage you become the establishment," I reply.

One of *Outrage!*'s most controversial tactics was the threat of outing public figures who were in the closet and voting against gay rights. The group released the names of ten gay Church of England bishops in 1994, to widespread condemnation in the press. Ultimately, one of those named came out. The following January the group delivered a letter to David Hope, the bishop of London, urging him to come out. Three months later he told the press that his sexuality was a "grey area." *Outrage!* then moved the focus on to politicians. "In 1996 we sent letters to twenty MPs warning them that if they continued to support anti-gay legislation then we would expose them," Peter tells me. "As a result most of them stopped voting against equality." None came out at the time, although the Tory MP Alan Duncan did later. "We weren't asking them to come out. The threat secured 80 percent of the objective." Writing in 1995, Tatchell defended the tactic: "Outing is queer self-defence. Lesbians and gay men have a right, and a duty, to expose hypocrites and homophobes. Outing is a shock tactic. We make no apology for that. No movement for social justice has ever won equality without being provocative." Tatchell argues that it remains a valid strategy, but one to be used sparingly. Indeed, the tactic was fraught. After letters were received by the MPs, the *Belfast Telegraph* led with a front-page story that one of the twenty was an Irish MP from Ulster, Sir James Kilfedder. As Nicholas Whyte noted, "Kilfedder's homosexuality was one of the most public secrets in Northern Ireland politics," but he had consistently voted against gay rights. It is not clear whether Kilfedder had the paper in his hands at the time, but he died of a heart attack on the train to Parliament from Gatwick Airport that day. Former US Representative Barney Frank has a similar outing rule to Tatchell's. "It goes back to John Locke: the rulers need to be governed by the rules that they set. That is a major protection against arbitrary government. Legislating against homosexuality and then practicing it is a fundamental violation of democratic principles," he told me.

Led by Tatchell, *Outrage!* returned to haunt the clergy when the group interrupted the Archbishop of Canterbury's Easter Sermon in Canterbury Cathedral in
1998. This led to Tatchell's only conviction for protesting, under the Ecclesiastical
Courts Jurisdiction Act of 1860. Tatchell asserts that *Outrage!* were the true
parents of same-sex marriage in the United Kingdom. "In 1992 we had five same-
sex couples file suit in the Marylebone Court." But the group had serious ambivalence about the institution itself. "We don't support marriage—it is a patriarchal
heterosexist institution. But on the other hand the ban on same-sex marriage is
homophobic," he says. "To me it was a lightning-rod issue. The one institution that
the hetero-supremacists believed that was theirs alone. They would fight hardest to
protect it." *Outrage!* launched an Equal Love campaign in 2010. Tatchell aims fire
on the big sister in the gay rights family: "Stonewall opposed equal marriage since
1992 onwards. They actively sought to sabotage the campaign."

Peter reveals that at the time of the Bermondsey by-election he was enjoying
a "secret romance" with the London-born British footballer Justin Fashanu,
whose parents hailed from Nigeria and Guyana but who had been raised by
white foster parents in rural Norfolk. While playing for the greatest team in the
history of football, Norwich City, Fashanu would become known for scoring
the BBC "goal of the season" against Liverpool in 1980. After he had spun and
rifled a volley past the England goalkeeper Ray Clemence, he simply walked
away with his index finger raised in a powerfully understated celebration. But
more famously he was the first—and to date only—professional footballer in
Britain to come out as gay, in 1990 at the tail end of his career. But in the early
1980s, at the height of his celebrity, Fashanu was struggling in the closet and his
assignations with Peter had to be arranged with cloak-and-dagger secrecy. In a
commemoration written after Fashanu had committed suicide in 1998 at the age
of thirty-seven, Peter recalled:

> Justin and I met at the London gay night-club Heaven in 1981, soon
> after he realized he was gay. I had just been selected as the Labour can-
> didate for Bermondsey, and he had recently transferred from Norwich
> to Nottingham Forest. He had considerable difficulty in accepting his
> sexual orientation, but through our talks—often late at night on the
> phone from his hotel in Nottingham—he began to feel good about his
> gayness. Despite the evident risk of his own exposure by association,
> Fashanu thought nothing of going out with me to night-clubs, parties,
> family celebrations, and high-profile events where he was the guest of
> honor. He knew journalists and photographers would be there. It was
> almost as if he wanted to be outed by the press to end the pretense and
> pressure of leading a secretive double life. All this was happening in
> the run-up to the Bermondsey by-election in 1983. I, too, was in the

media spotlight. I was often tailed by tabloid journalists eager for a scoop on my private life. Justin was, to his great credit, determined that our friendship would not be compromised by the threat of newspaper exposure. I was more cautious and protective. So, when we planned a night out together, I resorted to devious means to lose the tabloid reporters that often trailed me. They never did catch us.

One can understand the attraction Fashanu would have to Tatchell. Peter was unusually willing to put himself on the line for his beliefs.

By the mid-1990s Zimbabwean president (and former prime minister) Robert Mugabe was casting around for scapegoats to blame for the failures of his ailing administration. The Irish Catholic missionary-school-educated man turned anti-colonial mastermind began to target the tiny out gay and lesbian Zimbabwean community in the most vitriolic and violent way. Zimbabwe's state-sponsored homophobia was extreme even on a continent where homosexuality was almost exclusively illegal. In 1999 Tatchell engaged in one of his most risky acts of direct action theater. *Outrage!* activists stopped Mugabe's car on a London street. Tatchell grabbed the president's arm and said, "President Mugabe, you're under arrest: torture is a crime under international law, I am now summoning the police." Peter says that the dictator "shrunk back in the seat like a frightened little boy." After the incident Mugabe took to referring to Tatchell as a "gay gangster." Two years later the sequel left Tatchell badly injured. He attempted a second citizen's arrest in Brussels and Mugabe's bodyguards knocked him unconscious, damaging his right eye and leaving persistent neurological issues. Over the following decade, Peter went on to confront Mike Tyson and Prime Minister Tony Blair, and march in the Moscow gay pride celebration.

Simon Hughes also turned his gaze on international LGBT rights after the disappointment of the leadership election defeat. Soon after being outed in 2006 Hughes fought hard to stop one of his constituents, Mehdi Kazemi, from being deported to his homeland of Iran, which had already executed Kazemi's boyfriend for homosexuality. Like many other LGBT figures who come from the dominant ethnic group, Hughes believes that his "sexual orientation gives me empathy for [the] marginalized side of people not part of the minority."

Torn Labels

Simon Hughes is one of only six men who have been elected to national office to identify as bisexual; as of January 2018 there have been eight women, elected in seven wealthy Western countries. That's fourteen total over time (only 3% of the total of all LGBT representatives) and five currently in office (again 3% of the total). There are only two out bisexual men in office anywhere in the world today (Sweden and Britain), both Conservatives. In the United States there is (and has only ever been) a single out self-identifying bisexual congressperson, Kyrsten Sinema, and a lone governor, Kate Brown of Oregon. There have been eleven bisexual US state legislators in history, but only five in office as of 2017. This consistent share of the LGBT cohort—a tiny number—sits jarringly with the fact that the majority of LGBTQ people today (where we have good data) identify as bisexual. In 2011 Gary Gates at the Williams Institute found that over half of LGB Americans self-identified as bisexual (52%). Gay men accounted for 31 percent and lesbians for 17 percent. Indeed, the largest individual group within the umbrella were women who identified as bisexual (33%), and bisexual men (19%) outnumbered lesbians.

In 1948 Alfred Kinsey found that 13 percent of the men he studied were either mostly or exclusively homosexual for at least three years between the ages of sixteen and fifty-five. A further 25 percent had significant same-sex experience. He found similar results for women five years later. At the time Kinsey's results were disparaged as wild exaggerations. The US General Social Survey found that 4.5 percent of American males reported a same-sex partner in 1990, but 8.2 percent did in 2014. For women, 3.6 percent reported at least one female sexual partner in 1990, and that had more than doubled to 8.7 percent by 2014. The UK National Survey of Sexual Attitudes and Lifestyles in 2000 found that 9 percent of Brits self-reported that they had same-sex experiences. By 2014 YouGov found that 19 percent said they would identify as bisexual, and among eighteen to twenty-four-year-olds the figure was 49 percent.

There is every reason to believe that the same reality is true worldwide. Young people are much more likely to identify as bisexual, pansexual, or queer, or to reject labeling of any type. If the elected representatives of the LGBTQ community actually mirrored the community they would be far more likely to be bisexual and of color. Some say the future is fluid, with labels torn asunder. The much-loved British TV presenter and *Bake Off* star Sue Perkins told *Pink News*, "I laugh and get hugely cheered by the fact my goddaughter is fourteen and some of her friends identify as pansexual," she said. "It's just like, 'Good for you.' I've always thought it was a spectrum and I've been slightly dumbfounded and made furious by the fact that I was forced to make a binary choice because it's always about the person." Peter Tatchell has long argued that in the future "more people are likely to have gay sex but less people will identify as gay or straight. This is because the absence of homophobia will make the need to assert and affirm gayness (and heterosexuality) irrelevant and redundant. They won't feel the need to label themselves (or others) as gay or straight. In a nonhomophobic culture, no one will care who loves who. That's true queer liberation." The *New York Times* columnist Charles M. Blow wrote, "attraction is simply more nuanced for more people than some of us want to admit, sometimes even to ourselves." Blow identifies as bisexual because simply "in addition to being attracted to women, I could also be attracted to men . . . That attraction may never manifest as physical intimacy, nor does it have to, but denying that it exists creates a false, naïve, and ultimately destructive sense of what is normal and possible. I don't feel in any way defective or isolated in my identity. If fact, I feel liberated or and even enlightened by it." As Kinsey wrote in "Sexual Behavior in the Human Male" seventy years ago, "The world is not to be divided into sheep and goats. Not all things are black, nor all things white. It is a fundamental taxonomy that nature rarely deals with discrete categories. Only the human mind invents categories and tries to force facts into separated pigeon-holes. The living world is a continuum in each and every one of its aspects."

The lack of visible representatives of bisexual people in politics impoverishes democracy. The largest section of the LGBT community may be bisexual women, but they have virtually no political voice. Bisexual and pansexual people are not the stereotypical rich pampered dilettantes who can pass and avoid prejudice. Bisexual Americans are much more likely to be in poverty than lesbians, gays, and straights; they also suffer from higher rates of poor health, depression, and workplace discrimination. Bisexual women are more likely to experience interpersonal partner domestic violence and are three times as likely to be on the receiving end of police violence. Shockingly, a study found that while straight women have a 17 percent chance of being raped and lesbians have a 13 percent chance, bisexual women have a 46 percent chance of being raped. In the *Journal of Bisexuality*, researcher Nicole Johnson and MaryBeth Grove found that 50 percent of bisexual women in America had experienced rape, with 75 percent being victims of sexual violence. Bisexuals also have the worst experiences with formal support resources. In Britain, bisexual people are 80 percent more likely to feel anxiety than the average person. Thus it is no surprise that bisexuals are the most likely of any group to attempt suicide—by a significant margin.

It does not help that those bisexuals who are visible often have a bad reputation. Historically, the known bisexuals in public office have been married men who were caught with their pants down, giving credence to the prejudice that they are conniving, untrustworthy, and suspect. The Labour Party Welsh Secretary Ron Davis had a moment of madness on Clapham Common in 1998, and Bob Mellish's workingman's homophobia was a cover for his own closet. Even the bisexuality of fictional politician Frank Underwood in the American version of *House of Cards* is not used to demonstrate his modernity—it shows his duplicity and narcissism.

One high-profile case involved Labour MP Keith Vaz, who was outed in a salacious tabloid sting: a swirling mess of gay sex, eastern European rent boys, drugs, nom de plumes, and farcical alter-egos. One can only imagine the steepness of

Keith Vaz's nursery slope. Born in Aden, Yemen, to Catholic Indian parents from Goa with a father who was a correspondent for the *Times of India*, Vaz moved to England at the age of nine, eventually making his way to Cambridge. The youngest Labour MP elected in 1987 at thirty-one, Vaz was the focus of British-Asian pride. He married an up-and-coming female lawyer six years later, and they had two children. How did his nascent sexuality have a chance?

I ask Lord Michael Cashman why more people do not come out. "For some it's a lack of self-worth," he says. For others it is "a nursery slope you get on. Imagine, you are from a tough east-end family, a girl on your side for show. Pressure to get married. Then you find yourself with a life you didn't imagine and don't know how to change. You create a façade and you become so vulnerable. The more secrets you have the weaker you become and the more vulnerable you become." He concludes, "I was able to come out because of Paul [Cottingham, Cashman's partner]." Upon his elevation to the Lords, Cashman told John Rentoul of *The Independent*, "We're all like fruits on a tree. Only if the ones on the outside get the sunlight first, and come to fruition and drop, can the rest on the inside develop and be picked or drop into a gentle basket. We each come out in our own way and in our own time."

The way I explain the situation to my students is that when the LGBTQ community has a family reunion, the lesbians and gays sit at the adult table while the bisexuals sit at a card table in the corner that has been repurposed as the kids' table. They are seen and not heard, but they get to listen to the grown-ups. In years past the transgenders would be relegated to serving the food and then told to leave, but now they at least get to sit at the kids' table with the bisexuals.

It's not even a given that bisexuality is a "real" thing. Carrie Bradshaw's throwaway line in *Sex in the City*, "I'm not even sure bisexuality exists. I think it's just a layover on the way to Gay Town," wasn't a joke. When Christy Holstege was campaigning for election to the Palm Springs City Council, some attacked her for playing the "bisexual card" for gain because she was married to a cisgender man. Councilor Roberts told Frank Bruni that "social media started to trash her. They were saying she's not really bi, maybe she had an experience in college, and now she wants to sweep up gay dollars and gay votes. So I called her up one day and said: 'Christy, I'm making the weirdest call I've ever made in my entire life. You're being accused of being fake gay, fake bi. This is a whole new world for me. This is a parallel universe.' "

Figure 3.1 Panti Bliss. Credit: Conor Horgan.

Figure 3.2 Rory O'Neill. Credit: Conor Horgan.

3

I Have Quite a Powerful
and Carrying Voice

David and Patrice, Leopoldville,
the Belgian Congo

David was born into the heat, dust, and chaos of Leopoldville in the heart of Africa. He first breathed air in the Belgian Congo, although he was not of there; he was not African or even Belgian. He was a little round-faced Anglo-Irish boy dressed in a linen cloth cap to ward off the sweltering sun. As he rested in the sweaty arms of his nanny on the bottom step of the ornate post office with its wrap-around veranda, he looked up into the angular face of a young postal clerk who was skipping down the steps, package tucked under his arm. Élias Okit'Asombo's khaki uniform was baggy on his thin frame, but his pencil mustache and sliver of black goatee made his nanny think of the suave matinee idols she had seen on the movie posters at the Apollo Palace Theatre.

Élias was born at Onalua, a village near the Methodist mission at Wembo-Nyama, in the southern, savannah portion of Katako Kombe territory. His people, the Tetela, believed a child has two descents, that of the father and the mother. Having studied at both Protestant and Catholic schools, he had garnered two sets of names: Elias Okit'Asombo was his Protestant name, from the Old Testament, meaning "heir of the cursed." That name was prescient. Patrice was his Catholic name, Patrice Lumumba in full. Patrice would not escape the curse of his Congolese fathers.

Both Patrice and David were outsiders, and always would be. Patrice the quick-witted of four brothers, a Catholic who attended Protestant school for the few years that his farmer father could afford. David, the effervescent and sensitive child, would lose his father as a little boy and return to Dublin to be raised by his mother and aunt. Trading the searing heat for bone-chilling rain, the oppressive sun for depressive clouds, he would be the Protestant boy surrounded by Catholics. But Élias and David were outsiders in a much greater sense. Patrice Lumumba would break free of the straitjacket of colonization to lead his nation to independence—but he would only live seven months free. David Norris was an outsider because he happened to like men—after a seven-decade battle he would liberate his nation from the straitjacket of state-sanctioned homophobia.

Norris had always feet in two worlds. While his father was an English war hero, his mother was descended from Irish Kings. Aida Margaret FitzPatrick was born in Mountrath, County Laois, in 1901. The county of Laois is the center of Ireland—double landlocked—and Mountrath is the tiny market town in the center of Laois, known as the "fort of the bog." They were Irish, but not Republicans. David's mother was a southern unionist—indeed, almost all of Norris's Irish ancestors were Anglican unionists, meaning that they valued the Crown over independence.

David Norris is one of the few people who truly warrant the description "larger than life." He is actor, performer, poet, and firebrand: Joyce and Wilde, Parnell with Milk. An hour in his company is a front-row seat to the best one-man show in town. We slowly walk to the parliamentary tea room as his walking stick thumps the tiled floor. The ornate rooms are all fraying red velvet and gold threads. In the middle of our conversation he jerks his head toward the door as a lamp flickers. "Who's feckin' around with the lights!" he booms to no one in particular. He is Falstaff, without the drink.

Being gay and young in 1960s Ireland was the equivalent of one of Dante's rings of hell, and David retreated into books. "I learnt that being gay could be dangerous, so I internalized it for a time and it became a source of great difficulty," he writes in his memoir, *A Kick at the Pricks*. There was no question of a political life in the Republic. Ireland, the idiosyncratic island where minority Protestants are as devout as majority Catholics, came late to the enlightenment. The law against sodomy did not extend to Ireland for technical reasons until the 1630s, but then the nation embraced its fear of the other with open arms. As Norris wrote, "I was born a criminal; from the moment of my arrival on this planet, my essential nature defined me as such." Indeed, Irish identity was as much a curse for straight as gay. For centuries all Irish men and women were born into repression and second-class citizenship under the British occupation. Liberation and self-determination was a matter for both national pride and personal realization. There were always important gay people in Ireland, from the heralded like Oscar Wilde to the closeted Easter uprising saints: Padraig Pearse, Roger Casement, Dr. Kathleen Lynn, and her partner Madeleine Ffrench-Mullen.

David told his mother Aida he was gay when he was twenty, just before she passed away. "I remember she was in the garden of our house in Ballsbridge, cutting the roses with secateurs, and she turned and said something like, 'Oh, that's nice.' She wasn't given to the very deep emotional things, though she was a very good, kind, and wonderful mother; terribly witty and entertaining. But there was an element of the stiff upper lip there."

Norris could not pursue politics because he "wasn't real—only people who got married and had children were real," he tells me as he sips his tea from a chipped china cup. "I met my first love in the first-ever Wimpy hamburger restaurant in Dublin in the 1960s. He said 'I love you but I can't marry you.' We were living in a glass cylinder—we could be seen but not touched." David lives as much with his literary characters as he does in the real world. "No one is telling the full truth—from Forster, to Bronte, to Dickens," he explains. "They shy away from telling the truth when describing relationships. Perhaps they don't know the truth. But Joyce broke taboos and told the truth. You can hear him turning into a pig—dirty postcards, an encounter with a prostitute—really little piggy paragraphs." Norris crouches, eyes wide, and morphs into a chubby, spluttering, ravenous schoolboy to perform Joyce. "Pig stuff—pepper flower fat and sauce—stuff it into his belly," he smacks his lips. "It's ruthless honestly," he continues. "Joyce showed that it was possible to construct a morality apart from convention."

In the 1960s, like most "ho-mo-sex-uals"—Norris draws out the word for comic effect—he felt alone. "I thought I was the only one. Then I saw an advert in the *Observer*—WRITE TO 28A KENNEDY STREET, MANCHESTER to join the CAMPAIGN FOR HOMOSEXUAL EQUALITY." He wrote away but found out the CHE was entirely focused on Britain, so he founded the Campaign for Homosexual Law Reform in Dublin. Their first pride march attracted seven people. In 1975 he was the first openly gay man to appear on Irish television. "David, are homosexuals sick people?" asked the presenter. "No, indeed they are not. We are neither sick, ill, pathological, neurotic nor any of these emotive terms that are occasionally used by people who are not well-informed on the subject, to conceal their own prejudices," replied Norris. "People might wonder could the state of homosexuality be cured, as it were?" the presenter continued. David grunted: "We're not ill, so we don't require a cure."

The overwhelming task was to challenge the criminalization of homosexuality in Ireland. Norris offered himself as the plaintiff in 1977. The time was ripe. His parents had died; his employer, Trinity College, was sympathetic; and he had a psychiatric report from 1966 saying he was of sound mind. He went to New York to enlist international experts in November 1978. No one was there to meet him at the airport; Harvey Milk had just been shot dead. Back in Ireland he wanted to lift the veil of silence. "I wanted something more theatrical—lay out all the evidence in vivid color—mental capacity, sexuality, statistics, organization." The case was finally heard in 1980. Norris's argument was that the anti-homosexuality laws of 1861 and 1885 were rescinded by the equality clauses of the Irish Constitution of 1937. Judge McWilliams's summary began like a manifesto of gay rights: the gay population was surprising large, they weren't less intelligent, and they weren't attracted to children. But Norris relates that at the very end McWilliams took a swerve: despite all the evidence, the law against homosexuality was in line with the "Christian and democratic nature of the Constitution." An appeal failed in 1982 and the case went to the European Human Rights Commission. They ruled in Norris's favor by a single vote, but the Irish government ignored the finding. The next step was the European Court of Human Rights. Norris won again, but it took until 1993 for a new government to decriminalize homosexuality in the Republic. The boy from Leopoldville and Laois went on to lead the charge for civil partnerships, which took another eighteen years, and finally the hugely meaningful enactment of marriage equality by popular referendum in 2015.

As he crusaded, Norris not only challenged homophobic law but transformed attitudes toward gay people. He made manifest and human a community in the eyes of a sheaf of Irish men and women who went on to become significant opinion shapers. In 1969 the twenty-five-year-old Mary Bourke asked Norris to help her run for the Trinity College Senate seat. She had to overcome being young, female, and Catholic, but she won. For the legal case against the Irish anti-homosexuality law in 1977 David enlisted Mary (now Robinson) as junior counsel. To better understand the case, Robinson asked Norris to write down what it is like growing up gay in Ireland. When she read the letter, written in longhand, she cried. David wanted the case to be full of drama and color—of life and love, in a loud and carrying voice. When the case went to the European Court of Human Rights, Mary Robinson was chief counsel. In 1990 Robinson was elected the first-ever female president of Ireland and remains one of the most revered heads of state. When Norris founded the Campaign for Homosexual Law Reform another young law professor, Mary McAleese, agreed to be cochair. McAleese succeeded Robinson as the second female president of Ireland.

In the 1970s David Bernard Norris and Harvey Bernard Milk concluded that for change to happen gay people needed to be visible in public life. It took Milk four elections over four years until he was finally victorious; it took Norris six elections and a decade. David first threw his hat into the ring for the Senate elections at Trinity College in 1977. Three senators were elected by the 11,000 graduates of the leading university in Ireland—a veritable who's who of movers and shakers. The state paid for a candidate's manifesto to be posted to all electors. Norris thought it would be a terrific way to get his ideas out to the shapers of public opinion, and couldn't see how he could lose. "My ideas were so clear, so advanced, so right I wouldn't be surprised if I topped the poll!" he recalls. "I was crushed with only 220 votes," he reveals. Over three elections in the early 1980s he went from a vote of 336 to 392 to 850—still a long way from victory.

Finally, in 1987, he won over 2,000 votes and was elected, alongside his friend Mary Robinson.

When he first walked into the Senate, Norris says the "paint nearly came off the ceilings," but he set about building personal relationships and destroying the notion that he was a one-trick pony. He had no objection to being seen as a gay politician interested in gay rights, but "it was not my only repertoire. I would touch the untouchable areas," he says. "Abortion. I established the first foreign affairs committee, I held the first debate on AIDS." David Norris stops midsentence.

> "You're not eating your biscuit?" he stares at me. "Eat your biscuit," he
>   commands.
> I attempt to speak.
> "Are you going to eat your biscuit?"
> "No?"
> Norris grabs it off my plate and eats it.
> Clearly I did not move quickly enough.

Friends began to approach Norris about running for the presidency at the end of Mary Robinson's term in 1997, but it took another fourteen years for him to get in the race. The portents looked good—he was seen as something of a feisty national treasure, and the Irish presidency is more symbolic than substantial. Electing Norris felt like a statement about Ireland becoming modern and inclusive. With the presidential election of 2011 four months away, the *Irish Independent* led with the news: "Norris holds 37 percent of the vote, almost three times as much support as his two closest rivals." Every poll predicted Norris would be the "first gay President of Ireland"; even the mainstream parties expected him to win.

The fall from grace was swift and devastating.

Katherine and Ann Louise: Surprised by Love

Long before Katherine and Ann Louise fell for each other they fell for god. In their memoir *Our Lives Out Loud* Katherine wrote that as a six-year-old, "I literally experienced an affective relationship with transcendence. It was at the center of my little heart." A lifetime later Ann Louise recalled the pure love of headmistress Mother Imelda's hug given to each child as she entered school every morning. Katherine Zappone's life has revolved around alternating spaces. For the first twenty-two years of her life she alternated between the two poles of the northwest American state of Washington: Spokane, the conservative hub of the flatlands east of the Cascade Mountains, and Seattle, the progressive mecca of the coast with Mount Ranier looming on the horizon. As an adult Katherine bounced between America and Ireland: the church and heresy, social ostracism and embrace. She has spent a life managing to embrace and synthesize opposites. Progressive and Catholic, feminist and family.

Ann Louise Gilligan did not oscillate. Hers was a straight line: God, teaching, and Ireland. As a young girl she would gather children in the park and bring them back for her lessons at the family's dining room table. In 1963, at the age of eighteen, Ann Louise began her training as a nun in Loreto Abbey, Rathfarnham, on the outskirts of Dublin. Animated by the credo of its seventeenth-century founder Mary Ward—"Truth, Freedom, Justice, Sincerity and Joy"—after three years she moved to a new religious teaching college but was uneasy with the human isolation of orders and, needing engagement with people and poverty, she decided to leave the religious life. This led to a master's degree in Paris in 1974 and "the opportunity to meet my footnotes," as she puts it, attending lectures by Simone de Beauvior, Yves Congar, and Abbe Pierre.

While Ann Louise was deeply immersed in Catholicism at Loreto Abbey, Katherine was with the Jesuits at Gonzaga College back in her hometown of Spokane. The radical transformation of tone, if not substance, of the 21st Council of the Catholic Church in 1962 captivated both young women. *Aggiornamento*—"to-day-ing," or the act of inserting faith into day-to-day life—became a mantra for both. Upon returning from Paris, Ann Louise took a position at St. Patrick's College in Drumcondra—the place that would become her professional home for most of her life. At Gonzaga, Katherine wrote an essay on St. Paul's Letter to the Romans, which so impressed her professor, Fr. Vincent Beuzer, that he encouraged her to switch from medicine to theology. She did. After Spokane came Washington, DC, and the Catholic University of America, and visits to her girlfriend Katie and Dorothy Day's mission in the Bowery in Lower Manhattan, New York.

Katherine met Katie when she was fifteen—their love was secret but endured from childhood to adulthood, high school to college and beyond, from Spokane to Seattle and then New York—for thirteen years. This is a lifetime when you fall for each other as teens—even more remarkable when you are illegal and living in the shadows. They invented a parallel world to survive, but that world ran its course. In 1981, suffering the pain of the end of their affair, Katherine found escape in Boston and the doctoral program in theology at Boston College; she wanted a town where she knew no one. In contrast, Ann Louise lived as a nun both literally and figuratively, "innocent, if not ignorant, about my sexual iden-tity." Her vow of chastity was confirming rather than confounding.

There were to be just two PhD students in theology starting at Boston College in September 1981: one from the West of America, the other from the East of Ireland. Katherine told the *Irish Independent* that she "thought Ann

Louise was gorgeous, but I couldn't dare hope she would be attracted to me. She looked so straight. But I don't know what that looks like, maybe I did, too." Ann Louise wrote, "I've often said that I was surprised by love when I met Katherine. I didn't know I was a lesbian, although I had no doubt that I fell in love when I was with her. There was no indecision, no trauma or anxiety when it came to coming out, because it was the most wonderful thing that had happened in my life." They were theologians in love with god—but god was swirling in a wind tunnel of new ideas. In the papers of Pauli Murray, housed at Harvard, there is a photograph of Carter Heyward and four other women offering themselves for ordination to Bishop Paul Moore at the Cathedral of St. John the Divine in Manhattan in 1973. Less than a decade after Heyward's radical challenge to orthodoxy, Katherine and Ann Louise adopted her as their mentor as they worked on their doctorates in divinity at Boston College. Zappone says Carter Heyward was a "fiery, inspiring, courageous and creative feminist theologian." It also did not escape their notice that she was an out lesbian. At the same time Ann Louise became Paulo Freire's graduate assistant— the same man who would inspire another immigrant, Margaret Marshall, in her passion for liberation education. Marshall would go on to play a crucial cameo part in gay rights progress a quarter-century later.

As they grew together in Massachusetts, Katherine and Ann Louise shied away from the spotlight. They hid in the shadows, only coming out to close friends and allies. They admired the small cohort of out lesbians they interacted with professionally, but remained very private and hid away on the coast of Cape Cod. "A layer of silence was slowly erecting itself around our public lives," says Katherine. Even when they held a commitment ceremony in 1982 they still shied away from coming out to their parents. But a few years later, Katherine received a letter from her sister saying that their youngest brother, Mark, had come out to their parents. This prompted her, at the age of thirty-three, to write a letter of her own across the Atlantic. "I told them that I was very happy with Ann Louise and happy to share the relationship with them. Then I sat and waited for a response. My parents soon rang us to tell us that it was fine and they loved me . . . Then my father wrote this extraordinary letter that started with: 'Dear daughters . . . 'I didn't wonder if they would still love me—of course they would—but I did wonder if my relationship would put a distance between me and them."

In the midst of writing up their dissertations, Katherine and Ann Louise moved to Dublin and Ann Louise returned to work at St. Patrick's. It soon became clear that the effective head of St. Pat's, the Catholic Archbishop of Dublin, was not predisposed to a lesbian in his midst. In 1984 she was offered the position of head of the Department of Religious Studies. The archbishop vetoed the appointment, and successive heads of the Irish Catholic Church blocked her advance.

The same year Katherine and Ann Louise watched the one openly gay activist, David Norris, battle alone on the national stage. Ireland was a nation stuck in time, very far from how it is today. Only 30 percent of women worked outside the home and only 17 percent of married women did so. Nor was politics a place for women, let alone lesbians. There were only fourteen women in the Irish Parliament. The following year, in 1985, using the money from the sale of her father's pubs in Dawson and Wexford, Ann Louise and Katherine bought their spiritual home, a tumble-down hunting lodge built by an English major in 1889. They named their house "the Shanty," and it was to become the heart of their community outreach work for the next thirty years. The house was in the tiny village of Brittas, just down the road from the depressed and forlorn housing estates of Tallaght in the southwest of Dublin. Some 30,000 poor Irish men and women had been relocated to "abandoned building sites with nothing but endless monotonous rows of small, grey concrete houses," Katherine says. "No description could capture the sense of desolation that marked this place in the mid-1980s." Unemployment was as high as 70 percent; women suffered inordinate poverty, domestic abuse, and health problems. There were no day care centers to enable mothers to work—in fact, there were only nine workplace child care centers in all of Ireland.

As Katherine and Ann Louise developed their networks of communal welfare, they faced the challenges that all families face. Ann Louise's parents died of cancer within a few years of each other, and then, in 1992, Ann Louise herself found a small lump in her breast. She was forty-seven. She had surgery, treatment, and after a long period of anxious recuperation, regained her strength and vivaciousness.

In 1994 Katherine Zappone was granted Irish citizenship—not based on her partnership with Ann Louise, but on the fact that she had an Irish-born great-grandmother. This at least ended a decade of anxiety they faced every time they left Ireland as to whether Katherine would be allowed to return. Katherine was angry: "Had we been a married couple, acquiring citizenship would have been a matter of simply filling in a few forms." A trip to Chile in 2001 prompted them to revisit their will. The Shanty was in both their names, but they were informed that as they were not considered a married couple, if one of them passed away the survivor would have to sell the house to pay the death taxes. The house was their financial security. In the dignified language of a theologian, Katherine told the *Irish Independent* that this state of affairs was "out-fucking-rageous." After a decade of avoiding participating in any form of lesbian and gay activism they had an epiphany: embodying change was the role they had been chosen for. "Most of our lives we had advocated for justice for others, but it wasn't until the case that we were looking for justice for ourselves," Katherine tells me. Their love was so strong, so pure, so unimpeachable, that if they were a visible testimony to the good of same-sex relationships, they could be a powerful force of change. As Katherine says, that "personal empathy—the ability to feel the emotions of another—is a prime and necessary ingredient in any agency for systematic change." They left the church and joined the world. *Zappone and Gilligan v. Revenue Commissioners* became one of the two most important gay rights cases in Irish history. The stakes were high in both general and personal terms. Either woman could be fired by their respective employers for their sexual orientation without redress, and the costs of the legal case were estimated to be a quarter of a million Irish pounds.

In the midst of the case Katherine's brother Mark traveled to Canada to Vancouver, to attend one of the first gay weddings in the world. Ann Moore, a British Columbia commissioner of oaths, was marrying couples in her house overlooking Vancouver Bay. Ever since their commitment ceremony in Rockport, Massachusetts, in 1982, Katherine and Ann Louise had been looking for something formal and traditional. They were married just a few months later, in Vancouver on September 13, 2003—to their knowledge, the first same-sex Irish couple to be married. They became the poster couple for gay rights in their home country, with all the related support and approbation. In 2005 the *Irish Times* led with the headline "State to Challenge Lesbian Couple's Legal Action." The judgment took five years in the making and Katherine and Ann Louise lost twice: they did not have the right to marry under the constitution and their Canadian marriage was not valid in Ireland, plus they were told they had to pay their court costs. But in a much greater sense they won everything. They turned the tide in favor of equality and laid the bridge that would allow Ireland to cross to modernity by ratifying by referendum marriage equality a decade later. First came the Civil Partnerships in 2010 and then the 34th Amendment of the Irish Constitution, which allowed for the Marriage Act 2015. Indeed, the embrace that Ireland gave the couple was as much personal as legal. In 2011 Prime Minister Enda Kenny chose to use one of his appointments to the Senate to bring Katherine Zappone inside the barrel: the first out lesbian parliamentarian in Ireland's history.

Katherine tells me that she was appointed because she had a long background in human rights work and community uplift, but also because Kenny wanted to flag up his government's support for marriage equality. Indeed, in a private aside the Taoiseach told her, "we've just had a meeting on *your* referendum," the *your* being the same-sex marriage referendum. Katherine Zappone and Ann Louise Gilligan are unique in being integrally seen as a couple in the public's mind. Virtually every LGBTQ politician has been an individual presence. They may have had a partner, even a husband or wife, but the focus was on the one, not the other. Katherine and Ann Louise broke all their barriers as a couple, a partnership, and a demonstration of love. LGBT leaders marched for marriage equality to be allowed to prove that it could enrich the institution, but Katherine and Ann Louise had been proving that for decades.

"We had thousands of people in our home and in our lives for ten years—people loved us as a couple," says Katherine. I sit with the senator in Dublin Castle on a cold rainy day in October 2014, and she is overcome with emotion in the middle of our interview. "I have an extraordinary relationship with Ann Louise. Our love relationship is an exceptional blessing on both our sides. We also happen to have the gifts of communicating about that." This is what has allowed them to redefine the norm. Irish television featured Katherine and Ann Louise's house remodel on the daytime show *Room to Improve*—classic light entertainment for regular people. Viewers were presented with a lesbian kitchen, lesbian landscaping, lesbian rugs, and even a lesbian master bedroom, but they saw just a house and a married couple. It was the most popular show of the season.

In the spring of 2013 Ann Louise suffered her first brain hemorrhage. She was very ill, and the bleeding caused her to permanently lose some of her sight. Katherine had to juggle her responsibilities in the Senate with being a caregiver to the formerly entirely independent Ann Louise. The events at a dinner a few days before I talked with Katherine touched her deeply. A stream of parliamentarians from all parties and parts of the country trooped over to their table to embrace Ann Louise and check on her health. They talked about the home improvement TV show and seamlessly engaged Katherine and Ann Louise as a couple. "Jesus, isn't that a gorgeous home," they said. The two women felt the love of powerful politicians who had checkered histories on supporting their love. Since the court case both women are stopped on the street by strangers—often young gay men and women, who thank them for giving them courage and hope. "It is extraordinary," muses Katherine. "It pulls on our hearts . . . it helps us keep on keeping on." Katherine's place in the Senate also has affected the nation's legislators. Before becoming a senator, Rónán Mullen was the spokesperson for Cardinal Desmond Connell, who was found to have covered up numerous instances of child sex abuse. He used his position in the Senate to push extremist religious views and led opposition to marriage equality in Ireland. Katherine tells me that there is "a little dance he continues to do . . . constantly affirming me but afraid of debating me because I know his [theological] ground." Indeed, the only time I see a flash of anger in her eyes is when she talks about her own experience of homophobia in Ireland: "I lost my profession as a theologian."

She had more productive relationships with colleagues like Feargal Quinn, one of Ireland's most successful businesspeople. Quinn became a senator in 1993 and was a very active and successful member of the upper house. In 2013 he and Katherine spearheaded the campaign to keep the Senead, against the prime minister's wishes. Their bill to democratize the way the Senate was elected was seen as key to persuading the public that reform was preferable to abolition.

Her presence was particularly important when seeking the ear of Finance Minister Michael Noonan. "I use that opportunity," she told me, "when it comes to LGBT rights in revenue and taxes, finance bills, seeking full equivalency, even immigration." In a conversation with Noonan on same-sex couple taxation, she was able to say, "You recall that case *Zappone and Gilligan versus the State*? I am Zappone."

Despite serving effectively at the grace of Enda Kenny, Senator Katherine Zappone remained an unabashed independent and helped lead opposition to a Senate reform measure being pushed hard by the prime minister. Knowing that after biting the hand that fed her reappointment to the Senate was all but dead, she decided to run for the lower house in her home district in the general election of February 2016.

No out lesbian had ever been elected to the Irish Dail. It would be the greatest test of whether Ireland had truly changed.

The Importance of Being Earnest

In the summer of 2011 David Norris's presidential campaign in Ireland was reeling. "The media decided to do me in," says Norris. "They spent the entire electoral period telling grotesque lies to the public—which did not turn the public against me but it confused them. There was a news story every day that I was a tax fraud, welfare cheat, cocaine addict, blind, had abused the Senate to get passports for lovers, advocated parents having sex with their children." None of this was true. "It was unbearable, unbelievable." I ask if things are improving today. "No," says Norris. "The media is a nest of homophobia. They wouldn't know respect if it came up and pissed in their eye."

The initial blow to Norris's presidential ambitions came from an obscure interview conducted a decade earlier. In 2001 Norris had spoken to a restaurant critic, Helen Lucy Burke, for *Magill* magazine. The *Ireland on Sunday* newspaper dusted off the old interview with the salacious headlines: "Senator Backs Sex with Children." It was an outrageous misinterpretation of Norris's abstract musings on Plato's *Symposium* and clearly a calculated onslaught against his presidential ambitions. Burke later confessed that she'd been waiting for a moment to stick the knife in by using the age-old smear of linking homosexuality with pedophilia. Norris's ambitions were on the ropes, but he remained standing. Then, in July, a second major attack was launched. In the 1970s Norris had been in a relationship with Ezra Nawi, an Israeli human rights activist. Journalists discovered that Norris had written a letter asking for clemency from the Israeli judicial system for his friend in 1997. Unfortunately, the charge against Nawi was having sex with a minor, a fifteen-year-old to be precise. This second blow was too much for Norris to recover from; his team imploded, and he withdrew from the race on August 2.

Norris retreated for six weeks to his mountaintop hideaway in Cyprus to lick his wounds. But he was not done. Something urged him to return to the fray. Friends warned him against re-entering the race, saying it would be a "crucifixion," but Norris was looking for resurrection. On September 16 Norris began to seek nominations again: he had twelve days. To be a candidate one needed either the support of twenty members of Parliament (Norris could only gather eighteen at that late stage) or four local authorities. The polls still showed Norris ahead of all other candidates— Labour Party member Michael D. Higgins, Sinn Fein's Martin McGuiness, and a clutch of others. Higgins and Norris had been friends for years, and in a great act of decency Higgins actually encouraged his Labour colleagues on Dublin City Council to vote for Norris to allow him to secure his fourth council nomination and be a candidate. In Irish elections voters rank-order the candidates on their ballot papers. By a process of knocking out and redistributing the ballots of the weakest candidates, the system ultimately produces a winner with over half the votes. On Thursday, October 27, 2011, David Norris received 109,000 votes, coming in fifth on first preferences with 6.2 percent of the poll. Seventy percent of the second preferences of Michael D. Higgins's 700,000 votes went to Norris. Norris gave 60 percent to Higgins. They were clearly closely aligned.

"Why did the media single you out?" I ask. "It was payback time for what I did on the defamation bill," Norris says. "I put my head on the block. Irish politicians are gutless in the face of the media. I've won four libel actions so far; I will win the five pending." Norris does have some friends in the press. The *Irish Times*, for example, likened him to Oscar Wilde.

Like Simon Hughes and Peter Tatchell, the twists of history may have put Norris and Higgins in the places they were meant to be. Norris says that "in retrospect, the whole thing has shaken out beautifully, because we have got a superb president: an honorable man who will put his neck on the line for the marginalized and the vulnerable. And I am where I should be also, on the back benches of Seanad Eireann, saying the things that nobody else in this country is prepared to say." As a child, David's mother would always reproach him for jumping in puddles: "Don't stir mud," she would admonish. But that is ex-actly what delights Norris. The Irish American former mayor of Seattle, Ed Murray, told me that Norris has had an impact far beyond Ireland. "The best day of my life was when we passed marriage equality here in Washington. The role David played was similar to that. In many ways what the Irish did was even more affirming—it was about family, it was about my culture, which wasn't al-ways very affirming. David plays that role nationally and internationally to Irish Americans. He affirms something that we didn't think could happen in Ireland. With better political advice, David could have been elected president."

On May 22, 2015, a two-thousand-strong crowd gathered in the courtyard of Dublin Castle to witness the results of the marriage equality referendum. Tens of thousands of men and women, mostly young and straight, had returned to Ireland just to vote for equality. The hashtag #HomeToVote was used 72,000 times on Twitter on the day of the vote. The electoral register had swelled by 2 percent. The turnout was over 60 percent; the previous two national referendums had turnouts of 39 percent and 33 percent. The referendum had been spurred by the Irish Constitutional Convention (2012–2014), which combined 66 randomly selected citizens and 33 politicians—including four from the north. The convention was tasked with deliberating on eight specific issues, but marriage equality dominated. Leading Irish politics scholars Johan Elkink, David Farrell, Theresa Reidy, and Jane Suiter found that the referendum result reflected the enthusiasm of the young for a new Ireland and a broad shift in attitudes to homosexuality. One quarter of all voters had been personally canvassed by campaigners—87 percent of them by the Yes campaign and only 36 percent by the No campaign. In their opinion surveys Elkink and his colleagues found that conservative Ireland was dying, and voters under forty-four were massively (over 80%) in favor of marriage equality. An Irish voter who came of age in the year David Norris was first elected was forty-six at the time of the referendum. Ireland has changed across the board, and not just generationally: Elkink et al. note that "the balance of opinion along the liberal conservative cleavage has been transformed since the 1980s with a liberal majority in evidence across all social classes, regions and genders."

As the results poured in, it became clear that same-sex marriage would win by an overwhelming margin: 62–38 percent. Every one of the Republic's twenty-six counties, bar one, voted in favor. It was the first country in the world to pass gay marriage by popular referendum. The seventy-one-year-old Senator David Norris made his way to the front of the platform that had been erected in front of the rainbow flag-waving crowds—most of whom hadn't even been born when Norris began his lonely campaign for equality in the 1970s. There was no microphone, but that did not deter Norris from addressing the masses, "I have quite a powerful and carrying voice," he bellowed and punched the air with each word. "The message from this small independent Republic to the entire world is one of dignity, freedom, and tolerance: *liberté, égalité, fraternité*." The euphoria of the crowd shook the Parliament buildings.

Are You Coming Home for Christmas?

Ireland was once as much a theocracy as a state. The Catholic Church looked over the shoulder of every decision. I met all five out gay and lesbian members of the Irish Parliament back-to-back from 10 a.m. to 5 p.m. one day in October 2014 as wet skies enveloped Dublin Castle. First I spoke with Katherine Zappone, then Labour MPs John Lyons and Dominic Hannigan, newly out Cork Fine Gael MP Jerry Buttimer, and last David Norris. In my first meeting Zappone asked me if I was meeting the other five. "Other five?" I repeated, bemused. She looked at me . . . thinking . . . catching herself. "Four . . . yes, the other four," she said unconvincingly. John Lyons and Dominic Hannigan were elected for the Labour Party in their high-water-mark election of 2011. Despite being the first out candidates elected in Ireland, neither experienced outright homophobia in the campaign. Their journeys were far from smooth or easy, but when they ran as out candidates their party and people were solidly behind them.

The road was quite different for Jerry Buttimer, the Fine Gael MP for the southern city of Cork. This is the city that gave Ireland Michael Collins, who went on to sire Fine Gael—the party of the 1921 Anglo-Irish Treaty that Collins negotiated with Winston Churchill before he was sold down the river by his supposed ally Éamon de Valera. Cork's village of Cobh was the *Titanic*'s last port of call before it sank four days later in April 1912. Buttimer grew up one of four kids on the Benvoirlich Estate in the Bishopstown district of Cork. After high school he studied to be a priest for six years at the National Seminary for Ireland in Maynooth. But he chose not to be ordained, instead returning to his home town to be a schoolteacher. He was elected to the Cork city council in 2004 and three years later moved up to the Senate in Dublin. In 2011 he was elected as one of the five MPs for his home Cork South-Central constituency.

It is easy to see why Buttimer is one of the most popular parliamentarians. He instantly makes you feel like an old friend having a fireside chat: likable, honest, authentic. Was he nervous about coming out? "The honest answer is yes, a sense of trepidation," he says. "But you can't be governed and held captive by judgements of others." Like many politicians in the closet, Buttimer was in the hinterland of Don't Ask, Don't Tell: "People knew and I never denied," he tells me. He always voted for gay rights and was up front in his advocacy. On April 30, 2012, after being in Parliament for five years, he told a reporter from the *Irish Examiner*: "I am a MP who just happens to be gay—it is one little composition of the story that is me, and I will continue to be the politician I was yesterday."

"Why come out, then?" I ask. Jerry says there were a multitude of reasons that the timing was right. First, he had been appointed as a delegate to the constitutional convention that was to debate marriage equality. "If I was going to be authentic and be true to myself, and to members of convention, it was the right thing for me to come out." Second, he wanted to counter the public perception that Fine Gael was lukewarm on social progress and LGBT rights. Jerry met a few Fine Gael colleagues in a bar who were gay and suggested that they form an LGBT group in the party. That launch was quickly followed by Buttimer's coming out. The party needed to communicate inclusion and create a space where members could come out. Jerry says there were a "sizable number" of gay members throughout the party. But even in the glass closet there were many difficult coming-out conversations to navigate: his father, party colleagues, the public and friends he mingled with in the world of Irish sport. There is little doubt that Buttimer's coming out as the first Fine Gael parliamentarian opened up space for others. The new party group had a stall at the Fine Gael conference of 2013 and a series of members came up to offer thanks: some gay, but many more with children and relatives who happened to be gay or lesbian. He tells me the story of one woman who approached him. Her husband had struggled with his son being gay; like many young gay Irish men he had fled to Britain and became estranged from his father. The wife said that after Jerry came out her husband was able to ask his son whether he was coming home for Christmas. Though a city of over 100,000 people, Cork remains a village in spirit. "People know you and approach you," Jerry tells me. "I cherish that familiarity. I'm struck by the number of people who stop me to say 'you helped me coming out' or [you] 'made it easier to accept my child.'"

Jerry believes that gay rights are not just for LGBT people but enrich society as a whole. He suggests that legal equality is one of the missing puzzle pieces for the Irish people to complete the evolution of Mazlow's hierarchy of needs. In 1943 Abraham Mazlow proposed that humans strive to complete a series of needs for fulfillment, with the most basic, physiological needs forming the base of the pyramid. Next come safety, belonging and love, esteem, and self-actual-ization ("what a man can be, he must be"). Buttimer maintains that marriage equality is part of the higher tier of self-actualization, as it allows individuals and society to fulfill their potential. He also sees the arc of Irish history building to this point: a commonality in the fight for the self-determination of the state and the person, the freedom to be who you are, the right to live a life that embraces your sexuality. "Our 1916 proclamation says we cherish our children equally. The essence of a republic is the respect that the state holds for its citizens ability to be free," says Buttimer.

Jerry is a living commercial for contact theory. "If you want to have change you have to bring people with you on the journey. You cut the grass, take care of the house, go to work, pay the bills, and people say, 'that's my neighbor.'" Paudie Coffey is from rural Waterford and was the Fine Gael minister of state in the Department of Environment. Jerry and Paudie shared an office. "I told him I was gay and he said to me 'You're the only gay person I know.' When he went home to tell his wife that night and repeated that Buttimer was the only gay person he knew, his wife replied, 'no he's not.'" Jerry continues, "Paudie had been unsure of his position on gay rights, but he was my friend and we shared interests in sports, politics, outdoor pursuits. His journey was not a product of pounding aggression. It was interaction with people. 'What do these people want? They want to get married, have kids. They are no different to me.'" Buttimer was able to make three-dimensional the issues that his party colleagues had previously seen in only two dimensions. In a debate on homophobia in the Dail in 2014, he told his colleagues that he spent most of his life "struggling . . . in my country that I love," as he had been "beaten, spat at, chased, harassed, and mocked because of who I am."

In 2016 Buttimer's Cork constituency was downsized to four MPs instead of five, and Buttimer lost half his core vote areas in the north. This made it very tough for him to hold his seat. He had come fifth in first preferences in 2011. When we spoke 2014 he was candid in his expectations. "I'm conscious that I may not be back," he told me, "and that puts an onus on me to achieve as much as possible in these five years." In the 2016 elections, despite winning a higher proportion of first preferences than when first elected, he lost out in the final count to his colleague Simon Coveney. But a few months later he stood again for election to the Senate and was successful in the Labour panel, coming second overall in first preferences. Enda Kenny appointed him as leader of the Senate on June 8, 2016. Like others, Senator Buttimer credits David Norris with cutting a path for him and the others. "His campaigning zeal as a lone voice . . . I have tremendous admiration for what he achieved in face of what he endured. Because of him it's easier for people like me to be myself."

David Norris, then Katherine Zappone, and then Jerry Buttimer built a bridge that a young Fine Gael MP—the "fifth man" Katherine erringly referred to in our meeting—was able to cross a few months after I had spent the day with the out caucus. Leo Varadkar is the new Ireland: immigrant father from Bombay, a doctor, a Hindu, an outsider; Irish mother from Dungarvan in Waterford, a nurse, a Catholic, an insider. Varadkar is the golden boy. Often described as "a masterful political operator," the *Irish Times* called him a "man who rose to the top through years of preparation and carefully cultivated relationships." Journalists often say Leo is "an enigma," a "canny political operator," and "calculated." It is hard not to wonder whether the same distrustful adjectives would be applied to a straight man with ambition. Varadkar made it to the top tier of politics by the age of thirty-two. When he went on national radio to come out in January 2015 at thirty-six, just months before the marriage equality referendum, he was the minister for health, having previously held the portfolios of transport, tourism, and sport.

The Power of Panti

On May 22, 2015, Leo Varadkar, Jerry Buttimer, Katherine Zappone, and David Norris stood on the hastily erected stage in the courtyard of Dublin Castle waiting for the marriage equality referendum result. But one of the biggest cheers was reserved for Rory O'Neill—a.k.a. drag queen Panti Bliss—embracing Gerry Adams, the leader of Sinn Fein and former provisional IRA commander. There have been few more incongruous hugs in history. In a short space of time Panti had become as much of a national treasure as James Joyce, Seamus Heaney, and George Bernard Shaw.

O'Neill started performing in the early 1990s after growing up in the tiny market town of Ballinrobe on the far west coast of County Mayo. O'Neill is almost the most famous person to come out of Ballinrobe, but not quite. In the late nineteenth century Charles Boycott was an English land agent collecting rents, exploiting locals, and enforcing the will of his boss, John Crichton. Crichton, the Third Earl of Erne and bigwig of the Protestant Orange Order, was the archetypal absentee landlord. His agent, Boycott, was, by all historical evidence, a deeply unpleasant man who treated the people of Ballinrobe with petty contempt. In 1880 the locals had had enough and they started a campaign to ostracize Boycott—a strategy outlined by the famed nationalist leader Charles Parnell. Boycott lost his postal delivery, laundress, and blacksmith. The local shopkeepers refused to sell him food. His workers withdrew their labor. Boycott became a cause célèbre for being boycotted.

As a child Rory O'Neill would drive with his father, the town veterinarian, to Captain Boycott's house, Lough Mask, where the Daly family lived. A gay boy in Ireland in the 1970s was often made to feel as uncomfortable as Mr. Boycott had been, shunned and teased for a distinctiveness that couldn't be hidden. O'Neill testifies to a decent childhood within a loving family, but he had the "vague feeling of being on the outside." "I wasn't unhappy," he writes in his memoir *Women in the Making*. "I had friends, I painted pictures and made models out of plaster. I liked cycling down to the lake on hot days and diving into the dark bog water while the women of the town sat chest-high in the water, washed their hair and chatted. And yet I was lonely."

We chat in the afternoon in Rory's Pantibar in central Dublin. Our words are punctuated by the thump of beer barrels rolling up from the cellar. "When I was young the only gays were caricatures," he tells me. Then he recalls the thrill of seeing Boy George singing on the BBC's *Top of the Pops*. "We stood around the school yard arguing about it: was he a woman or not? The idea that he was just a big gay was unfathomable." In 1984 the band Bronski Beat, fronted by Jimmy Somerville, released their hit "Small Town Boy." "I remember walking down to the bus at Christmas listening to 'Small Town Boy,' bawling my eyes out, because it was me," O'Neill says. Because of this, he is deeply aware of the power of Panti. "When I was fourteen years old if I had seen this giant drag queen on TV it would have meant the world to me . . . I didn't meet a real live gay until I went to art college and there was only one . . . and he's still my best friend."

The Ballinrobe railway station had been closed for good eight years before O'Neill was born, but he grew up obsessed with trains—perhaps looking for romantic escape from the village of conformity. He fled eastward, station by station, first as far across the country as one could go, to art college in Dún Laoghaire, and then farther eastward to gay London. Then he went by rail across the world as far away from Ballinrobe as possible: Western Europe, Hungary, Russia, China. At the end of the line he spent five years in Japan. Finally, Panti came home—to Dublin, at least—and in 2007 opened the Pantibar, which quickly became a focal point for LGBTQ life in Ireland.

In 2014 Panti Bliss accidentally became the conscience of modern Ireland. In January O'Neill had called out homophobia in the Irish media and identified some journalists by name on a prime-time chat show. RTÉ, the national channel, balked and paid out €85,000 to those named. As few weeks later, as his alter ego, O'Neill was asked to give the Noble Call speech at the Abbey Theatre in Dublin. The speech was a ten-minute musing on external and internalized homophobia and about who owns the definition and pain. In the February 1 speech O'Neill, as Panti, said in part:

> Have you ever been standing at a pedestrian crossing when a car drives by and in it are a bunch of lads, and they lean out the window and they shout "Fag!" and throw a milk carton at you? Now it doesn't really hurt. It's just a wet carton and anyway they're right—I am a fag.
>
> But it feels oppressive.
>
> When it really does hurt, is afterwards. Afterwards I wonder and worry and obsess over what was it about me, what was it they saw in me? What was it that gave me away? And I hate myself for wondering that. It feels oppressive and the next time I'm at a pedestrian crossing I check myself to see what is it about me that "gives the gay away" and I check myself to make sure I'm not doing it this time.
>
> Have you ever turned on the computer and seen videos of people just like you in faraway countries, and countries not far away at all, being beaten and imprisoned and tortured and murdered because they are just like you?
>
> And that feels oppressive.
>
> And for the last three weeks I have been lectured by heterosexual people about what homophobia is and who should be allowed, identify it. Straight people—ministers, senators, lawyers, journalists— have lined up to tell me what homophobia is and what I am allowed to feel oppressed by. People who have never experienced homophobia in their lives, people who have never checked themselves at a pedestrian crossing, have told me that unless I am being thrown in prison or herded onto a cattle train, then it is not homophobia.

And that feels oppressive.

So now Irish gay people find ourselves in a ludicrous situation where not only are we not allowed to say publicly what we feel oppressed by, we are not even allowed to think it because our definition has been disallowed by our betters. I do, it is true, believe that almost all of you are probably homophobes. But I'm a homophobe. It would be incredible if we weren't. To grow up in a society that is overwhelmingly homophobic and to escape unscathed would be miraculous. So I don't hate you because you are homophobic. I actually admire you. I admire you because most of you are only a bit homophobic. Which all things considered is pretty good going. But I do sometimes hate myself. I hate myself because I fucking check myself while standing at pedestrian crossings.

And sometimes I hate you for doing that to me.

But not right now. Right now, I like you all very much for giving me a few moments of your time. And I thank you for it.

Ireland wanted to fall in love with their queer selves and Rory O'Neill gave them Panti—to date the speech has been viewed online by close to a million people. "We had reached a time in our history where we wanted to understand who we are," he says. For centuries Irish people had seen their nation and culture depicted as "bishops beating everyone with croziers and jangly music. We never felt ourselves as in the vanguard, as leaders, as progressives. Panti is the antithesis of all the things about Ireland that annoyed us. She is an avatar—both real and entirely created—which allows people to project onto her a lot of different meanings."

O'Neill argues that introducing marriage equality by referendum was not the way to do it, but the overwhelming popular vote turned out to be "incredibly powerful" putting the issue to bed and making it feel like "an entirely done conversation." He compares this to France, "where it remains a live issue because it was brought in by a political elite." The demonstrable impact of the vote was immediate. "We saw gay couples holding hands from day of referendum," he says. Crucially, regular ordinary people are very proud of the change. "It transformed, not just the queers, but how the whole country feels about themselves."

O'Neill says his emergence as the Irish conscience was "1,000 percent unplanned—I am *the* accidental activist." I asked him whether he sees Panti as a way into people's hearts. "More than I had anticipated," Rory says. "I was aware of power she could have over the years I performed on stage, but they were self-selected audiences. But after the Abbey Theatre I became very aware. The kid of drag queen she is—relatable—if you squint she could be your aunt. You think the drag would people off, but it doesn't, it's a way in." All the years of drag shows have taught Rory the way into people's hearts. "The first few minutes I'm say nothing—its silliness—just words." If you watch the Abbey Theatre speech you see that this is true. For the first few minutes the audience is trying to make sense of what is on stage ("Mary what's that . . . that's a fella"). But after they have gotten over the novelty of drag, Rory says, "they start hearing you."

A few months later O'Neill revealed on Irish radio that he had been diagnosed as HIV positive in 1995; while he was healthy, he endured the constant crushing fear felt by anyone diagnosed with the virus and lived the ostracism that left HIV/ AIDS Irish men and women more shunned than anyone else. On Christmas Day 2015 Panti Bliss delivered a parodic "Queen's Speech" on national television (beating the ratings of the actual Queen Elizabeth II, who was competing for attention on Irish TV). In November 2015 Trinity College awarded Rory O'Neill and David Norris honorary degrees of law for their monumental work on bringing LGBTQ rights to Ireland. Like Eddie Izzard in Britain and the American writer David Sedaris, Panti's brand of humor and warmth takes her out of the niche and into the mainstream. Through his tenacious existence over decades, Izzard has made gender nonconformity part of the fabric of life; Sedaris puts the voice of the sardonic gay man on the bedside tables of millions of straights. Rory O'Neill draws in the farmer from Mayo, the priest from Donegal, and the grandmother from Cork because his pretending comes from a place of deep authenticity. As O'Neill notes, Panti "is allowed to speak to power and occasionally prick it with a sharpened stiletto. Even in small ways, I am allowed to say in drag things I could never get away with out of drag." In that wonderful Irish turn of phrase, O'Neill is "your man Panti." Panti is a construct owned by the Irish, by design. Who is fooling who? Some might see these crossover successes as neutralizing the glorious weirdness of the queer, but O'Neill doesn't see it that way. He told the *Irish Times*, "I don't feel that I've been mainstreamed, I feel that the mainstream has made a little room for me." There is great power in making laugh the people who might be predisposed to distrust you.

Because of David Norris, Katherine Zappone, and Ann Louise Gilligan, Ireland is a different place today. I asked Senator Ivana Bacik, Norris's colleague from the Trinity constituency, what the three had meant to the movement for change. "It is important to acknowledge and celebrate the immense courage of those individual litigants whose decision to challenge injustice and inequality through the courts led in so many cases to the achievement of real and significant progressive social change in Ireland," she told me. Norris cut a path that allowed others to follow. Up until 2012 the only out Irish parliamentarians were either independents or from the Irish Labour Party; there were none from Fine Gael or Fianna Fáil, who had historically dominated government. It was perceived to be political suicide to come out as gay in Ireland. Pat Carey studied with Ann Louise at St. Patrick's and then went on to have a stellar career in government with Fianna Fáil as an MP, chief whip, government minister, a party grandee. It wasn't until he left politics at the age of sixty-five that he finally felt able to come out. "When I look back it's an awful pity I didn't feel able to do that. Nobody stopped me, but I wasn't sure how it would be received," he said. There has still never been an out Fianna Fáil member of Parliament.

Rory O'Neill is touched by the lives he sees changed by Panti. He tells me about a teenaged boy he met after a show in Donegal who had just lost his mother. His father brought him to the show because of the boy's love for Panti, and it was a healing moment. Thurles, in County Tipperary, is about as rural Irish as one can get. At a show there a mother and father brought up their fifteen-year-old son, in "a full face of make-up," to sign Panti's book that they had given him. "A happy kid, being flamingly gay at a drag show, that his parents have brought him to, in this small town," O'Neill says. That is the power of Panti—making it okay to be gay.

O'Neill feels something of a detachment from his famous creation. He tells me he is less affected by "the praise and attention when Panti is the conduit of it." And that is helpful. Rory says Panti is the "fun, drunk Aunt," while Rory is the "steady uncle who allows the drunk Aunt to be the fun one." Indeed, "I'm very used to performing as Panti. I'm much less comfortable doing it as Rory. I wouldn't have done the [Nobel Call] talk as Rory. Drag is a mask, armor, a superhero outfit. It is bigger, more colorful, more defined. Attention is drawn to this specialized version of you that is designed for that attention."

What is on the horizon for Panti? Rory believes that legal rights in Ireland are "kind of a done project, but one you have to keep an eye on." He is most impressed with the way in which the Irish gay rights movement has energized other rights issues in the country: waking the feminists, the repeal of the 8th movement (the constitutional provision against abortion), travelers' rights. "Their stories were always abstracted, and now real women have stood up and told their stories." O'Neill is enthused about spreading the gospel of equality to nations dragging behind: the Irish government has sent Panti to Sarajevo, Istanbul, and Saigon to bring her particular brand of evangelicalism. "And how about politics," I ask. "No. I'm no good at it." Rory is firm. "I hate conference rooms, meetings, and photocopies. I'm much better at being a lightning rod."

Panti is an avatar for love. As O'Neill notes, "it's very easy to hold prejudices against people you don't know; it's much harder to hold prejudices against people you know." He claims that his motivations "are always quite selfish—I was trying to change my world," but that is far from true. There are few people in history who have done more to make their nations kinder, more loving places.

Figure 4.1 Lord Waheed Alli. Credit: Theo Grzegorczyk.

4

I Have Never Come Across
a Homo in This House

Travel a mile down the river from Shakespeare's Globe Theatre in Bermondsey, go under the Thames by way of the Rotherhithe tunnel, and you are in Limehouse—Michael Cashman's birthplace in 1950. Limehouse is theatrical: it conjures the intrigue of sailors wandering gritty back lanes and the misty opium dens of the late nineteenth century, bustling docks of rippling men and heroically put-upon women. It is where Liberal Prime Minister David Lloyd George railed against the House of Lords in 1909, the seat of Labour Prime Minister Clement Atlee, and where the Social Democratic Party was founded by the gang of four in 1981. Cashman is a man of the stage, responding to my questions in crafted poetic stanzas. He became a star of the West End, but was raised in the rough-and-tumble of the East End. He was born three weeks early on account of his heavily pregnant mother stepping in to defend his dad, Johnny, in a street fight outside Stepney East train station. Like many working-class Londoners with fathers in the trade, Michael was registered soon after birth to be a docker. His mum was a cleaner. Half a century on we sit only a few miles to the west, but we could not be farther away from the docklands of the 1950s.

It was dangerous to be gay in the postwar world that Michael grew up in. The great men in the Palace of Westminster made that clear in 1952 when Alan Turing was convicted of homosexuality under the same gross indecency law that sent Oscar Wilde to prison in 1895. Turing was a genius and should have been a national hero—laying the foundations for computer science and artificial intelligence, he worked at the secret codebreaker house at Bletchley Park, where he cracked the German Enigma code machine, shortening the war by years. But all that was for naught if you were queer. In January 1952 Turing met a nineteen-year-old man from Manchester named Arnold Murray. A few weeks later an acquaintance of Murray's robbed Turing's flat. During the police investigation it came out that Murray and Turing were lovers. Alan Turing chose chemical castration over going to prison. It destroyed him. Turing was as theatrical as

Cashman. He loved the scene in *Snow White* where the Queen poisoned the apple. On June 7, 1954, he bit into an apple he had laced with cyanide. He was forty-one. Alan Turing was just one of over 100,000 gay British men—many jailed and tortured—who were convicted for homosexual offenses, including John Gielgud and Lord Montagu.

The former Tory MP Jerry Hayes dug into the debates on homosexual law reform in the 1950s. The quotes he found were emblematic of the times. Just before Turing committed suicide, the former Minister Lord Winterton ranted: "This nauseating subject. Fornication and adultery are evils . . . nothing does more evil or does more harm than the filthy, disgusting, unnatural vice of homosexuality." The Tory MP for Cheadle, William Shepherd, offered the eyebrow-raising comment "incest is a much more natural act than homosexuality." To which his colleague James Dance added, "it was the condoning of these offences which led to the fall of Nazi Germany." Sir Cyril Osborne saw just holding a debate as an affront: "The sponsors of this bill claim that there about one million 'homos' in this country . . . I do not believe that our country is as rotten as that. It is an awful slur on the good name of the country. I have never come across a homo in this house."

Michael says that the East End gave life color and flavor as a boy. Parental oversight was limited: "go to school and then come home," he was told. Other than that the children had the run of the docks. He sensed he was attracted to boys from about the age of seven, but he didn't know it was wrong. But the following year he was sexually abused by an eighteen-year-old docker, and he began to learn guilt. He told BBC Radio, "I thought maybe someone spotted this about me, maybe it is written on my forehead. And you know what, I never, ever told my mum and dad that that happened to me. It was made clear that you can't fancy boys." At the age of twelve Michael changed schools and appeared in the end-of-term school show. He was spotted by a talent agent and taken to audition for the lead role in *Oliver!*, Lionel Barts's iconic stage musical. When he got the part he began earning £3 a week more than his father, who told him, "I don't want my son to go on the stage—it's full of poofs and queers."

"I thought, yippee!" Michael tells me.

He was sent to stage school. He performed for Richard Nixon. The theater was a protective bubble, but the world outside of that was a very different climate. The year Michael starred as Oliver the *Sunday Mirror* ran the helpful feature: "How to Spot a Possible Homo." According to the article, "Basically, homos fall into two groups—the obvious, and the concealed. *Obvious*: Those who dye their hair, touch up their lips, and walk with a gay little wiggle could be spotted by a One-Eyed Jack on a foggy day in Blackwall Tunnel. *Concealed*: They wear silk suits and sit up at chi-chi bars with full bosomed ladies. Or they wear hair sports jackets and give their wives a black eye when they get back from the working men's club. They wrestle, play golf, ski and work up great knots of muscles lifting weights. They are married, have children." In an accidental fit of insight, *The Sunday Mirror* concluded that "they are everywhere and they can be anybody."

In 1967 Michael moved in with his boyfriend Lee, who was twenty-four, seven years his senior. Homosexuality was about to be decriminalized, but the age of consent was twenty-one. Two years later a local docker, whom Michael knew to be married with children, demanded sex. The teenaged Michael said no. "He dragged me by the hair, and I tried to talk him out of it, and he knocked me unconscious." Michael wanted to go to the police, but Lee noted it would be they who would be on trial: "Ask yourself: who will they believe? Two queers, or a straight guy?"

Michael's star rose in the mid-1960s with his move into television, which twenty-two years later would cement his place in LGBT history. The ground-breaking London-based soap opera *EastEnders* had been running eight months in 1985 when Michael first appeared as Colin Russell, a graphic designer who had moved into Albert Square. *EastEnders* had established a huge family of fans: 33 million watched the Christmas Day episode that year, two-thirds the population of Britain. The creators, Julia Smith and Tony Holland, warned Michael that the plotline was coming. "Colin was an ordinary guy," Cashman tells me. "We didn't know he was gay for three months." He notes that the plotline was groundbreaking in so many regards—not just because Colin was gay, but because he was out and had a rough working-class boyfriend who was under the legal age of consent. There was an episode about robbery and Colin and Barry's inability to go to the police because of their "illegality." This drew on Michael's own history. Colin and Barry (Gary Hailes) shared the first gay kiss on British television. It was hardly salacious. on the forehead, fully clothed, and not even in a bedroom. It would be another two years before Colin would be shown kissing a (new) boyfriend on the lips. But it shattered stereotypes: 17 million Britons saw their first representation of a same-sex kiss.

Michael Cashman's qualms about retribution for his visibility were borne out. The climate in the 1980s was deeply hostile, and gay-bashing seemed like a le-gitimate sport. A few months earlier the Chief Constable of Greater Manchester had raved, "God sent AIDS to us" and that homosexuals were "swirling in a human cesspit of their own making." After the kiss, the *Sun* newspaper led with the front-page headline "EASTBENDERS" and, referring to Colin and Barry, "yuppie poofs." The *News of the World* went further, outing Cashman's partner Paul Cottingham to the world with the headline "Secret Gay Love of AIDS scare *EastEnder*." Cashman recalls, "Our lives were displayed on the front pages in lurid details. I was linked with the gay plague." They printed Michael and Paul's address. A brick came through their window that afternoon. But Cashman kept two piles of correspondence in his dressing room. "Positive on one pile and negative on the other. The positive pile was always bigger."

After he had been on *EastEnders* for eighteen months Thatcher's government introduced Section 28, which banned the teaching of homosexuality in schools. Cashman says Section 28 woke him up. "The 60s were when we did some heavy lifting to pull the pendulum up to get some heavy momentum but it wasn't until the 70s that we got to swing with it. We had our clubs, bars, pubs, saunas," he says. The 1980s were when they started to fight back politically. Along with the actor Ian McKellen and health activist Lisa Power, Michael founded the pressure group Stonewall. They sought to persuade, cajole, and befriend the decision-makers, working with the establishment to make manifest the humanity of gays and lesbians. In the 1990s they began to gain momentum, and the election of Tony Blair's Labour government in 1997 really took them to a higher plateau. "Each of the things we won led us to be interested in the next hurdle," he tells me. Cashman was the only one of four sons to become an actor, and the only one to go into politics—the one passion he did inherit from his father. He was an elected member of the European Parliament for the West Midlands from 1999 until he stood down in 2014. Today Lord Cashman of Limehouse performs in the red velvet robes of the House of Lords.

The changes brought about by the Blair government allowed Michael and Paul to register as civil partners in 2006. (They had met in 1983.) To friends they appeared to be the model couple, the intensity of their love and partnership never waning. "Paul and I used to joke. Our lives are like library books. They may often be on the shelf but they are well thumbed," Michael says. In 2011 Paul was diagnosed with the very rare blood cancer angio sarcoma. When he passed away in 2014 Michael was devastated. He told the Lords, "I was absolutely clear that if my husband and partner was to die, I wanted to die with him." When Paul passed Michael was amazed by how respectful the media were. "Not a snipe, not a quip, nothing but respect and appreciation for his life. What a contrast to 1987."

In 2014 the Labour leader, Ed Miliband, appointed Cashman as the Labour Party's Czar for International LGBT rights—a new shadow cabinet position. In this new role Cashman hoped to move into government after the May 2015 election. That was not to happen, but he set about working with multinationals to leverage the power of global business to argue the economic benefits of equality and the negatives of discrimination. Is there too much normalization of gay people? I ask. "No!" Cashman replies passionately. "The equality agenda is all about being able to opt out. To celebrate difference," he says. He believes the gains will be hard to roll back: "Stepping back from equality is completely out of touch with the British electorate," he asserts, although one does not have to scratch very deep to find the homophobia. When another iconic soap opera, *Coronation Street*, featured a gay kiss between two vicars in July 2016 the BBC received sixty-seven complaints. That same month Cashman resigned from his LGBT Envoy position, along with all the other out shadow cabinet members, in protest at Jeremy Corbyn's leadership.

"What does visibility mean to you?" I ask him. Cashman gives an impromptu soliloquy. "The most powerful thing is visibility. Being able to give your view of the world in which you have lived, and the world in which you want to live and the world in which you want others to live, and you cannot do that if you are silent, you cannot do that if you are invisible. It's about destroying the stereotypes that ghettoize, diminish, and defame us."

When I ask him "When people come up to you and say you changed their lives how do you feel?", Michael surprises me with his answer. "The waste," he says. I raise my eyebrows. "The waste of people, all the pain and suffering. That it needed someone like me to make a change." He relates that he often hears variations of the story, comments such as "at the age of eight I saw you on TV and I knew I was not alone." He goes on, "I know what they mean and it is humbling. But I have no grand plan. My greatest motivation has always been: What if that were me?" As he narrates his life one feels as though the real validation he yearned for was from family. When his parents were still alive Cashman made a documentary investigating the treatment of lesbians and gay men. "The next morning my dad called me," he relates. "He said, 'I just wanted to tell you that I was in the pub last night. The guv'nor offered me a pint because of your program. I had a walk round the market square, then came back. I'm proud of you.'" Michael pauses to remind me what a "rough and tough relationship" he had with his father, and then returns to the occasion of their conversation. There was silence on the line, he tells me.

> "Yeah, yeah," Michael said.
> "No. I'm proud of you," his dad repeated.
> "I know, you said it last night, Dad."

Then Lord Cashman took a deep breath as his eyes filled up with tears.

> Then he said, "and I love you." It was at that moment I think that my father realized that if he'd been me and he'd been gay, he would have done everything—exactly every single step—the same way as me. Of his four sons I think I was the only one he ever said "I love you" to. That's the brilliance of being yourself.

Twenty-seven years later and a world apart, Lord Michael Cashman reprised his role as Colin in *EastEnders*. In a harrowing story line, Colin Russell returned to Albert Square in the midst of a funeral for a young man beaten to death for holding hands with his boyfriend. Colin wanted Dot, the matriarch who in 1989 had struggled to overcome her Christianity to be the first to accept Colin with love, to attend his wedding. But Dot was still struggling to come to terms with the new world. Ultimately, in the midst of the community's searing pain of a senseless death, Colin's return reminds Dot that there is more humanity in her friendships than her abstract faith. She attends the wedding and once again millions of Britons were shown a world where love faces down homophobia and wins.

Lord Peter Pan

The least celebrated but most influential gay politician in Britain has an especially distinctive personal history, one bursting with firsts. Waheed Alli was the youngest life peer ever appointed to the House of Lords, and the first gay, Asian, and Muslim parliamentarian anywhere in the world. As of 2017 he remains the only out gay Muslim parliamentarian in the world. His own force of personality drove the most comprehensive overhaul of gay rights in the history of any established democracy.

Alli describes himself as "a reluctant politician." We talk in his company office on Aldwych, opposite iconic Bush House of BBC World Service fame. He looks so youthful it is hard to believe he has been a Lord for nearly two decades. We grew up in the same part of south London, Croydon, at the same time, although we went to different schools. While I came from the leafy middle-class lanes of Shirley in the south of the borough, Alli navigated the urban grit of Norbury in the north. His mother was a nurse, born and bred in Trinidad and brought up as Hindu; she became a single parent to three boys. His estranged father, a Guyanese Muslim, worked as a mechanic. Both were descendants of the half a million Indian indentured laborers brought to the West Indies to harvest sugar cane in the nineteenth century, replacing slaves from Africa who were free to leave their crushing labor after British Emancipation in 1833. Today there are a million Indo-Caribbeans in Trinidad and Guyana alone. The empire adapts, evolves, and matures. Waheed Alli's portrait is on show in the British National Portrait Gallery in Trafalgar Square as part of the Nations' Great Men and Women collection. Alli left school at sixteen and climbed ladders in the financial world before shifting to television production and establishing some of the most influential media companies of the last two decades. He was instrumental in the growth of reality TV in Britain, with shows like *Survivor* and *The Big Breakfast*. He then went on to acquire the rights to iconic British authors such as Agatha Christie and Enid Blyton before diversifying into comedy production, radio, and retail. He became very wealthy.

However, politics was not a world he felt he could ever be a part of. "If you were gay and black and grew up in the 1980s under Thatcher, there was very little choice about being political. You were essentially under threat because of your race, and your sexuality was something you were forced to hide," he told me. Alli has many strands, and that means many communities want to claim him. But do they want to claim all of him, including the gay part? "If they claim you they have to take that bit as well," he says. "They'd rather I'm straight and married. But I'm not, so they work their way round it." This means that he can be a role model to young gay Muslims and Hindus and black Britons.

Alli met his boyfriend and first business partner, Charlie Parsons, in the early 1980s when he was just a teenager; Parsons was six years older. Three decades later the discomfort of that time lingers in his memory. "From age seventeen to twenty-one I was forced to break the law. That feeling of having an entire legal system force you to not declare your sexuality never left me," Alli said. In the 1980s Waheed joined the Labour Party, when it was at its nadir. But an up-and-coming young MP, who talked of wrenching the party away from its staid postwar trade union roots, caught his eye. "In 1994 I liked the look of Tony Blair," he told me. "I wrote him a letter having never met him. He wrote back and I joined his campaign." Alli and Blair became close and, unlike many others, he remains loyal to the former premier to this day. Waheed Alli became an integral part of Blair's kitchen cabinet, giving him a reference point for a younger multiethnic generation born of age in the urban centers of Thatcher's Britain. When Tony Blair became the first Labour prime minister for nearly two decades in 1997, Alli felt a palpable change in values at the heart of Westminster. "It was an amazing time. Britain was on the brink of change." Soon after moving into the prime minister's office, Blair pulled Alli aside and said, "I'd like to put you in the House of Lords." Waheed was stunned, but said yes without pause. He was thirty-three and he was aware he would be the youngest Lord ever appointed. However, one week before the government was to publish its list of new Lords, the news was leaked to the press. The front page of the establishment *Sunday Times* blared the banner headline: "First Openly Gay Member of Lords."

Alli had not realized that he would be the first openly gay peer. "I had no comprehension that was the case," he told me. As he put down the paper he thought, "Oh my god. I'm going to be defined by my sexuality. I am going to be the *gay peer*—that's all I am." He made a decision to withdraw his name but waited to tell Blair personally. In the interim he spoke to a close friend who, Alli says, "slapped me." "Are you completely mad?" the friend asked him. "What a privilege." In that moment Alli had an epiphany: "I realized that you either run away from this, or you run towards it . . . I am going to be the first openly gay peer, I'm going to run towards it, and I'm going to put a ladder down for other people. And I am going to do this bloody well. And when I leave, I am going to leave behind a body of work for which I am proud. The payback," he says, for all the unwelcome and hostile attention to his sexual orientation, "is that I'm going to change the laws."

The first law up to bat for the new Lord Alli of Norbury dealt with the age of consent, which had criminalized him and countless others for a century. Homosexual acts had been decriminalized in Britain in 1967, but the age of consent for sexual relations was decreed to be sixteen for heterosexual couples and twenty-one for same-sex couples. In 1994 an attempt to equalize the age of consent was defeated 308 to 280 in the Commons (with thirty-eight MPs from Waheed Alli's own Labour Party voting against equality). As a compromise the same-sex age of consent was lowered to eighteen, but the law remained discriminatory. However, in 2000, the House of Commons, now with a large Labour majority, passed a bill to equalize the age of consent by 183, a huge majority. The legislation was sent to the House of Lords. It was Alli's first real test. This was the law that had made a criminal of him when he first met his boyfriend as a teenager. As the debate wore on late into the night Alli recalls that speakers described gay people as "wicked, sinful, disgusting, an aberration, and an abomination." Then it came time for his intervention. As he spoke he began to physically feel the impact of his presence on the air filling the spaces around the red leather benches. "Just by being there, just by standing up and speaking, something happened in the chamber. The tone slowly changed." Alli struggled to maintain his composure. "My Lords, many of your Lordships will know that I am openly gay. I am thirty-four. I was gay when I was twenty-four, when I was twenty-one, when I was eighteen, and even when I was sixteen. I have never been confused about my sexuality. I have been confused about the way I am treated as a result of it. The only confusion lies in the prejudice shown, some of it tonight, and much of it enshrined in the law."

Over a decade later Alli remembers this as a pivotal moment. "The fact that there was somebody there they were talking about, who they could visualize, a human being, changed the nature of the debate." After hours of debate the tellers announced the vote. Alli was shocked to hear that they had lost. He was devastated. "I remember sitting in my seat feeling physically sick. What is the point of this?" he thought. Then Margaret Jay, the government's leader in the House of Lords, walked to the dispatch box and said, "My right honorable friend the Prime Minister [Tony Blair] has instructed me to inform this house that he will use the Parliament Act to ensure safe passage of this bill." (The Act, introduced in 1911, allows a prime minister to overrule the power of the Lords.) Alli was stunned. I asked him why he thought Blair had spent so much capital on the issue. Alli fixed me with a stare and answered without pause: "He did it because of me, and Chris Smith and Peter Mandelson [another gay Labour politician who had been Blair's confidant and lieutenant]. He did it because of us, despite his deeply held religious beliefs." It was a turning point, Alli said. "I sat there and thought . . . now they know we're serious and we can do more. Over the decade or so that followed I built a political machine, in conjunction with Stonewall . . . who are extraordinary . . . to take stuff through the houses." Alli's machine took on a raft of hugely significant issues to the British gay and lesbian community. First came same-sex adoption rights in 2002, then abolition of the hated Section 28 and a prohibition of discrimination on the grounds of sexual orientation in the delivery of goods and services in 2003. In 2004 it was legislation for civil partnerships, and in 2006 immigration law equality. Finally, the greatest prize of all: marriage equality, in 2013. Alli believes each legislative milestone breed momentum to achieve ultimate and full equality. He tells me that the visibility achieved by gay couples after the introduction of civil partnerships was a driving force for marriage seven years later. "The public were ahead of the politicians," he tells me. "In 2013, 80 percent of people thought Britain already had gay marriage because we had passed civil partnerships. The country had got there in 2006. There cannot be many families in Britain who have not been to or are aware of civil partnership or same-sex marriage ceremonies in their extended family."

Alli is blunt about one of his most important assets: "I have money," he told me. "Which isn't everything, but it's a lot." On each of the legislative fights he helped bankroll the campaign for change. He hires staff, provides office space, and helps craft strategy. "Six people worked here on marriage legislation," he said as he pointed to the suite of terminals beyond his glass-walled office. "They ran the whip for both houses. I lobbied probably five hundred Lords in total—talked to them, texted them, called them on the phone, sent little notes." Alli argued that these entreaties coming from colleagues mattered hugely. "It's a much more powerful thing," he said. I asked Alli if he knew of specific Lords who had changed their vote because of the conversations they had with him. While not wishing to overplay his role, he told me that his team had recorded approximately one hundred Lords who were ambivalent about marriage who had changed their votes after Alli's lobbying. Many of them were surprising coverts, not all the low-hanging fruit and usual suspects—moderates who were on the edge to begin with. Presence and personalizing the issue defeats the argument that we can have "equal but different institutions argument. You cannot make that argument with sincerity when the person is standing before you."

While Britain is a far less religious country than the United States, the church still matters and sends signals that resonate. "I went to see the new Archbishop of Canterbury, Justin Welby," Alli says, "and asked him if he would let the bishops have a free vote on gay marriage in the Lords." There were twenty-six voting Lords in the House. Welby—whom Alli describes as an "amazing man"—told him that he couldn't control the House of Bishops, but if Waheed could find a bishop who would come out in favor of gay marriage Welby would make clear to them that they could do so publically with his blessing. "I found the Bishop of Salisbury," recalls Alli. Bishop Nick Holtham wrote a three-page letter that was featured on the front page of the establishment *Daily Telegraph*. "It changed the nature of the debate," Alli says.

In "A Letter from the Bishop of Salisbury to Lord Alli of Norbury," Bishop Holtham said in part:

> Dear Waheed,
> Thank you for asking me to set out why I am sympathetic to the possibility of equal marriage and have a different view from that stated in the Church of England's response to the Equal Civil Marriage consultation. You, as a gay Muslim, will not be surprised that there are a variety of views within the Church of England where we are experiencing rapid change similar to that in the wider society. Change and development are essential in the Church, as they are in life, and part of the genius of a missionary Church is its ability to root the good news of Jesus Christ in varied cultures in every time and place. One of the difficulties now is that globalisation and communication mean it is much more difficult for Christianity to develop in this culturally sensitive way. There has been a very uncomfortable polarisation of views even in our own country. Whilst marriage is robust and enduring, what is meant by marriage has developed and changed significantly. Christian morality comes from the mix of Bible, Christian tradition and our reasoned experience. Sometimes Christians have had to rethink the priorities of the Gospel in the light of experience. For example, before Wilberforce, Christians saw slavery as Biblical and part of the God-given ordering of creation. Similarly in South Africa the Dutch Reformed Church supported Apartheid because it was Biblical and part of the God-given order of creation. No one now supports either slavery or Apartheid. The Biblical texts have not changed; our interpretation has. The possibility of "gay marriage" does not detract from heterosexual marriage unless we think that homosexuality is a choice rather than the given identity of a minority of people. Indeed the development of marriage for same-sex couples is a very strong endorsement of the institution of marriage.
> The Rt. Revd. Nicholas Holtam
> The Bishop of Salisbury

"To have a bishop say that gay marriage was right and proper was an extraordinary thing," Alli tells me. He recalls that Archbishop Welby said that Holtham's letter was a "strong and welcome contribution," and argues that "without Archbishop Welby, the letter never would have happened."

At the end of the day the vote in the Lords was 390 in favor versus 148 against—an even larger majority for gay marriage than in the House of Commons. Remarkably, a majority of Conservative Party Lords voted in favor (80 to 66). In contrast, in the House of Commons, Conservative MPs voted 127 to 117 against the bill despite the pleas of their leader Prime Minister David Cameron. Waheed Alli believes that the Lords vote was "a testament to the change in the place and the visibility of people like Chris [Lord Smith], like Ray [Lord Collins], like myself." He acknowledges the role of others outside of Labour, notably Tory Press Baron Guy Black. Alli estimated "there were a hundred waverers in the Lords." Those on the fence who ultimately voted in favor of gay marriage "were surprised at what good company they were keeping. When they got home their wives, their children, their nephews, their nieces, congratulated them and they never went back to being against. They realized they were on the right side of history," Alli says. I asked him what the end-game is. What does success look like? Like Louisa Wall, Evan Wolfson, and many others, Alli is a normalizer. "Success looks like the depoliticization of gay rights. You can fall back into other political drives. When you've won the center ground you are free to do the other things in life." Gay issues may not be depoliticized—yet—in Britain, but the arc of history is clear. "I couldn't possibly imagine in 1998 when this journey started that we would be in this place. Not just the legislative change, but the attitude change." Alli sees LGBT rights in the developing world as the next frontier. "We are our brothers and sisters' keeper. Look at the Commonwealth, Africa, the Mid East: This battle is not won. We need to take the political capital we have built up in this country and start using it to help others outside of the UK." He also is exasperated with the complacency seemingly shown by some of the wealthiest in the gay community. When we spoke in November 2013 Alli was animated when discussing the LGBT donor community in America. "The United States kills me. Frustrates the hell out of me. I look at some of those rich American gay men and women and I think to myself: shocking. You are still turning up to premiers with women on your arms and you really are not funding a proper political movement? You let Proposition 8 [in California] get through? How could you do that?"

The Only Gay in the Village

On February 6, 2013, when the British House of Commons debated the Same-Sex Marriage Bill, one hundred MPs spoke in the debate and fourteen of them were openly gay or bisexual men or women. At the time there were twenty-three LGB MPs in the House. The legislative committee that drafted the bill had twenty-one members, of whom six were openly gay. In the debate all of the out lesbian, gay, and bisexual MPs, bar one, opened their remarks with the pronoun "I" and went on to tell a personal story about growing up gay in Britain, describing the danger, secrecy, and fear of a curtailed future. Politicians usually focus their remarks on what a law might mean to their constituents or the nation writ large, but for a few hours on a dreary February night by the Thames, a procession of members of the mother of all parliaments faced their straight colleagues and said *let me tell you what this means to me.* The gay and lesbian MPs made the debate very personal. The climate was set by the fact that the man in the speaker's chair for most of the six-hour debate was not Speaker John Bercow but his deputy, Nigel Evans. Indeed, Bercow has consistently demonstrated such passionate and substantive support for equality and inclusion that he can be almost considered an honorary LGBTQ member of the House.

Stephen Gilbert, a Liberal Democrat from Cornwall, said: "I am a gay man who grew up in a rural part of our country in Cornwall and am from a working-class background. I grew up in an environment that made it hugely difficult for me to be open, honest, and up-front with my family, friends, and workmates about the choices I wanted to take in life and the people I wanted to see. That was unacceptable twenty-odd years ago and it is unacceptable today, but it remains the case for many hundreds of thousands of people across our country. I welcome this historic bill, which I think will end a form of discrimination and, perhaps more crucially, send a signal that this House values everybody equally across our country. That signal will deeply affect people like me in the same way as I was affected twenty years ago, when I saw this House vote to equalize the age of consent. That was the first time I saw other gay people on a TV screen and it was the first time that I realized that I was not alone. It changed my life."

Stephen Williams, another Liberal MP from Bristol, echoed the sentiments. "I was born in 1966, when homosexuality was still against the law and a criminal offense. During my life we have seen much progress, but it has come in fits and starts and has not always been easy. Throughout my teenage years and my years at university being openly gay was virtually impossible, because occasionally it could be a terrifying identity for an individual to have. I am thinking of the abuse that I received myself, and the far worse that I saw meted out to other people at school and university. What I say to colleagues on both sides of the House who oppose what we are trying to achieve today is please have some empathy with what your fellow citizens have been through. Equality is not something that can be delivered partially—equality is absolute."

The Tory MP Stuart Andrew was particularly emotional. "For me, the points that have been raised reflect the many personal battles that I have faced and some of the most troubling and dark times in my life. From an early age I developed those beliefs, going to church without the support of my family. That faith grew over time, but in my adolescence, I began to realize that I was gay. Being gay in a small Welsh village really was like being the only gay in the village. It was the start of some very deep questioning about my faith and my sexuality that has taken me years to try to resolve, and I am still seeking answers. When the bill was announced it reignited that dilemma and raised many questions. I believe in personal freedom and equality, but I also hold dear the principle of religious freedom. But marriage changed from the moment civil marriage was enacted. The state created an act of union that was separate from religion and the Church, so as the state is involved in civil marriage, I cannot see how we can make it exclusive. I want to live in a society that does not discriminate. That is why I support the bill." Andrew's phrase "troubling and dark times" alluded to a horrific episode in his life. As a twenty-five-year-old he was visiting his family back home on the Isle of Anglesey. Walking back from the pub, he was attacked by three men who shouted "you Tory queer" at him. Andrew was beaten unconscious. When his father came to help one of the assailants hit him in the face with a brick, which fractured his skull.

At first the Conservative MP Mike Freer didn't want to speak in the debate. "I thought the tone would be foul," he tells me as china cups tinkle in the Commons tea room. In the months before Freer had received emails saying he was a spreader of AIDS, a pedophile, a danger to society. But the Tories were short on people speaking in favor so he thought if I don't speak, who will?" He wrote his speech on the evening before the debate and tells me that the speech he wrote was not the one that came out on the day. Freer was elected to represent Margaret Thatcher's old north London constituency of Finchley and Golders Green in 2010. In his widely quoted speech he said that his 2007 civil union with his partner of twenty-one years was the greatest day of his life. He made a very personal plea to his colleagues:

> Much of our time in this House is spent on technical legislation. Today, we have an opportunity to do what is right and to do some good. I am a Member of this Parliament and I say to my colleagues that I sit alongside them in Committee, in the bars and in the Tea Room, and I queue alongside them in the Division Lobby, but when it comes to marriage, they are asking me to stand apart and to join a separate queue. I ask my colleagues, if I am equal in this House, to give me every opportunity to be equal. Today, we have a chance to set that right and I hope that colleagues will join me in voting yes this evening.

It was the most important and emotional speech of Freer's career, but his Tory colleague Matthew Offord representing the neighboring constituency of Hendon North was seething. Offord tried to interrupt Freer as he spoke, but Freer held his ground—he knew what was coming. In the last debate Offord had wildly claimed that if you legalized gay marriage you'd have to allow incestuous marriage and polygamy. But the vast majority of colleagues were supportive. "One colleague who was against gay marriage put his hand on my shoulder as I sat down and said, 'That was a wonderful speech. I don't agree with you. But that was a wonderful speech.' Two colleagues who voted against, one who was gay themselves, sent me notes of support." Why did they vote no? I ask. "They were not against same-sex marriage," says Freer. "They took a libertarian view. Disapproved of the state having any role in marriage."

The challenge for Mike Freer in North London was not the legacy of Thatcher, but rather the idiosyncratic cultural diversity of the district. Within its borders was the largest black evangelical church in London; 7 percent of the voters are Muslim and 25 percent Jewish, and the largest proportion of the Jewish community are Hassidic. Nevertheless, Freer has built solid relationships with all groups, holding constituency surgeries in mosques and synagogues and defended by moderate Jews and Muslims from extremist attacks.

Iain Stewart, the Conservative MP for Milton Keynes, said: "I often recall the day a few years ago when I finally plucked up the courage to tell my parents that I was gay. I began the conversation with the line 'Mum, you know I'm never going to be able to marry' . . . I look at the marriage that my parents have—forty-five years and going strong—and I aspire to the same thing." In the tea room of the Palace of Westminster, Stewart told me of a senior Conservative politician who had come to him after the second vote on the marriage bill with tears in her eyes. She told him that she had just voted against the bill but felt awful about what that said about him. "You are my friend and I just cannot vote against you anymore." So, on the final vote this senior politician voted yes.

While the power of the second chamber in Britain has waned considerably over the past century, the unelected House of Lords still gets to review, amend, and delay legislation. As the bill made its way through the Palace of Westminster in 2013 the vitriol against gay marriage was much more jarring in the House of Lords than it was in the people's house. One important detractor of the bill was former cabinet minister Lord Nigel Tebbit, notorious as Thatcher's enforcer while in government between 1979 and 1987. On the hugely popular and influential 1980s satirical television show *Spitting Image,* Tebbit's puppet was clad in biker's leathers and the Doc Martin boots favored by thuggish skinheads. Tebbit's wife was disabled in the 1984 Provisional Irish Republican Army bombing of the Grand Hotel in Brighton, which took the lives of five Tory members and very nearly killed Margaret Thatcher.

A month before the June 2013 debate in the House of Lords, Tebbit had given a newspaper interview in which he said that gay marriage would allow him to marry his own son to avoid inheritance tax and that it would throw into chaos the lines of succession in the royal family. He asked: "When we have a Queen who is a lesbian and she marries another lady and then decides she would like to have a child and someone donates sperm and she gives birth to a child, is that child heir to the throne?" In the debate itself he argued that if you were going to let a man marry a man you had to allow polygamy between different sexes, repeated his worry about Royal succession, and topped it off with the accusation that the bill "seems to require that teachers promote marriage between homosexuals."

Another of the Lords most implacably opposed to marriage equality was Baroness Jill Knight, a former Tory MP from Birmingham. In her speech she opined, "marriage is not about just love. Of course, homosexuals are often very delightful, artistic, and loving people. No one doubts that for one single moment. However, marriage is not about just love. It is about a man and a woman, themselves created to produce children, producing children. A man can no more bear a child than a woman can produce sperm. No law on earth can change that. This is not a homophobic view. It may be sad, it may be une-qual, but it is true. This bill is either trying to pretend that it can change men into women, or vice versa, or telling us that children do not need a father and a mother and that a secure framework for children to be brought up in is not really important anymore."

In the face of Tebbit and Knights's derision, six openly gay men and women did speak in the Lords debate. Lord Chris Smith said, "My Lords, I happen to be gay. I was made this way. It is something I share with hundreds of thousands of our fellow citizens who are worthwhile, virtuous, hardworking, respon-sible, loving members of society. I am also a Christian and I believe in a loving, accepting, generous God who wants to include people, not reject them. I was in a civil partnership and I know that civil partnership confers nearly all the shared rights and responsibilities that marriage does, but it is not the same. It is not equality; it does not carry the same significance or symbolism and it still labels lesbian and gay relationships as somehow just a little second-class." The news-paper owner Baron Guy Black said, "I support it because I believe in the insti-tution of marriage, which is the bedrock of society and should be open to all. I support it because I believe in the values of the family, and the bill will, in my view, strengthen them. I support it because I am a Conservative. Respect for in-dividual liberty is at the core of my being and this is a Bill that will add to the sum of human freedom. I support it because I am a Christian and I believe we are all equal in the eyes of God, and should be so under man's laws. . . . I am in a civil partnership with somebody with whom I have been together for nearly a quarter of a century. I love him very much and nothing would give me greater pride than to marry him. I hope noble Lords will forgive that personal pronouncement, but it seems to me that my experience goes to the heart of this debate."

Baron Browne of Madingley, the former chief executive of BP, spoke of his own struggles as a gay man at the very highest levels of the corporate world. "In

2007, I resigned as CEO of BP because of the lengths I went to in order to hide my sexuality. I thought that coming out might threaten the company's commercial relationships and my career. I will never know if those fears were justified, but they are no way to do business. People are happier, more productive, and make more money for their company when they feel included and they can be themselves. As a business leader, I want people to focus all their energies on their job, not on hiding part of who they are. Inclusiveness makes good business sense and giving gay couples the freedom to marry will eliminate one more barrier to inclusion. If it helps them to be themselves in the workplace, it will represent another step toward the meritocracy to which we all aspire. Gay marriage is a matter of strategic importance for British business. The second reason comes from my personal experience. I grew up in a climate of fear, where homosexuality was illegal. My mother was an Auschwitz survivor and advised me never to trust anyone with my secrets. I avoided discrimination by simply keeping quiet. Young gay people today live in a different, more tolerant world, but they still worry about discrimination, marginalization, and how their families and friends will react. One of the most effective ways to dispel this stigma is through the provision of role models. If I had seen gay men in legally recognised public relationships of the sort my parents were in, I would have found it easier to come out and I would have been a much happier person."

The most stunning moment was when Liberal Democrat Baroness Barker came out as a lesbian during the debate. "My Lords, I declare an interest. Many years ago, I had the great good fortune to meet someone. She and I have loved each other ever since—that is, apart from the occasional spectacular argument, usually about driving or DIY." And in a delightful twist that could only happen in the United Kingdom, the Baroness' coming-out speech was immediately followed by remarks from the Archbishop of Canterbury on his view of the bill. Another openly gay peer who spoke in the debate, Lord Ray Collins, recounted the importance of being able to enter into a civil union with his husband, Raphael, when the legal union was introduced in 2004. He told me they had the ceremony on the very first day, proudly "beating out Elton John."

Figure 5.1 Robert F. Kennedy, "Ripples of Hope" Speech, University of Cape Town, June 6, 1966, with Margaret Marshall in the background. Credit: University of Cape Town archives.

5

From Mississippi to Marriage

Barney Frank, Mississippi, Summer of 1964

Barney Frank's first political battle was not over gay rights. It was about race, and over the soul of the American psyche. In the summer of 1964 the twenty-four-year-old Frank got on a bus to Mississippi to help register African Americans to vote. It was far from the comfort zone of the gay Jewish kid from urban New Jersey. "It was scary and I felt helpless," he recalls fifty years later, on a crisp winter morning at a friend's house behind the US Supreme Court in Washington. The seeds of the summer were sown five years earlier when faraway South Africa had made its first (of two) interventions into the life of Barney Frank. The teenaged Harvard student was deputized to drive Allard Lowenstein, the pied piper of young American intelligentsia, around in Cambridge, Massachusetts. Lowenstein was lecturing about his clandestine trip to Southwest Africa (later Namibia), at the time occupied by the apartheid South African regime. During the drives Lowenstein persuaded Frank to be part of the Mississippi Summer project, whose participants became known as the Freedom Riders.

Mickey Schwerner was from New York, also Jewish, and twenty-four. As a boy he protected a tiny kid in the neighborhood who had Fairbanks Disease, which retarded his bone growth. That little boy, Robert Reich, would go on to be Secretary of Labor under President Bill Clinton. As Congress for Racial Equality (CORE) volunteers, Schwerner and his wife Rita teamed up with James Chaney, a twenty-one-year-old black man from Meridian, Mississippi, to set up a community center in the center of Chaney's hometown. Chaney, the local, was the oldest of two boys and three girls. He joined the National Association for the Advancement of Colored People (NAACP) at fifteen and was promptly suspended from school. The town of Meridian had been taken from the Choctaw Indians in 1830. Civil War Union General William Tecumseh Sherman razed the town in 1864. By the 1960s, it was a stronghold of the Ku Klux Klan.

The town had history.

"The local FBI were collaborators with the racists and law enforcement were the criminals," Frank tells me of his time in Mississippi. "But it was enormously uplifting. Brave black people along with a handful of whites, who in some ways faced worse abuse, fighting so blacks could live like everyone else." But Frank also recalls how depressed he felt. "The worst thing about America you can think of . . . millions of people treated as badly as if they were in the Soviet Union, while the rest of the country was ambivalent." The young Barney Frank's belief that "most black Mississippians wanted to be like white Americans, though without the vicious racial prejudice" echoes his later efforts to encourage LGBT assimilation through legal equality: the normalization of sexual orientation differences, rather than seeing lesbians and gays as a distinct communal minority to be given distinct status.

On the evening of June 16, 1964, a meeting of local Klan members discussed reports that Schwerner and his team had been conducting civil rights work at the Mount Zion Methodist Church in Philadelphia, Mississippi, forty miles from Meridian. A group of armed Klansmen drove to the church and, failing to find Schwerner, beat a number of black parishioners and burned the church to the crowd. The Klansman who appeared to delight in the beatings most was a twenty-six-year-old window salesman from Meridian named Wayne Roberts. Roberts had been kicked out of the Marines and was pathologically bent on maintaining the supremacy of the white race. After the Mount Zion attacks, Roberts proudly posed with his bloody fists in the air.

On that day, Schwerner and James Chaney were at the CORE training center at the Western College for Women, in Oxford, Ohio, which is now part of Miami University. Between June 14 and 27, 1964, eight hundred volunteers went through training before heading to Mississippi. Upon hearing the news from Philadelphia, Mickey and James decided to drive back to Mississippi to investigate. A twenty-year-old college student named Andrew Goodman joined them. Goodman, like Schwerner—white, Jewish, and from New York—was a product of the progressive Walden School on Central Park West in Manhattan. Goodman ran with the arts crowd. He was something of an actor, and his best friend at Queens College, City University of New York, wanted to be a rock star.

On June 21, 1964, Barney Frank left the Ohio training center to drive the half-day down to Mississippi. At the same time, Schwerner, Chaney, and Goodman drove the hour from Meridian to Philadelphia to speak with the victims of the attack. As they left for the CORE office home in the middle of the afternoon, Nashoba County Deputy Cecil Ray Price recognized Schwerner's light blue station wagon and pulled the civil rights workers over. Deputy Price was a Klan member. He arrested the three men and took them to the Philadelphia jail. Then he called the local Klan leader, Edgar Ray Killen. Killen picked up two local Klan members and drove the forty miles to Meridian to enlist five other Klan members. The group returned to Philadelphia in two cars and reunited after dark to wait outside the jail.

At 10.30 p.m. Chaney was made to pay a $20 fine, and the three men were released. They headed straight out of town in their station wagon—followed by the Philadelphia Klansmen in a Chevrolet, the Meridian Klansmen in a Ford, and Price in his police car. After a short chase Schwerner, Chaney, and Goodman surrendered and were forced into Price's cruiser. They were driven to a remote patch of land off Rock Cut Road ten miles outside of the town of Philadelphia. Wayne Roberts put his gun to Schwerner's chest and asked, "Are you that nigger lover?" before shooting him in the heart. Roberts then shot Andrew Goodman. At this point James Jordan yelled, "Save one for me!" Chaney backed away to the clay bank and begged for his life. Jordan shot Chaney in the stomach and said, "You didn't leave me nothing but a nigger, but at least I killed me a nigger." Roberts then shot Chaney in his head. Their bodies were bundled back into Schwerner's station wagon and driven the few miles to a dam being built on Old Jolly Farm, owned by another Klan member, Olen Burrage.

Forty-four days later, acting on an informer's tip, the FBI found the bodies fifteen feet down in the dam. Goodman's arm was draped over Schwerner's body. Chaney was next to them, lying on his back. Reeling from his murder, Goodman's Queens College friend wrote him a song, "He Was My Brother." Paul Simon had been singing with his childhood friend, Art Garfunkel, since they were eleven. They put Simon's song for Goodman on their first album, *Wednesday Morning, 3a.m.*

For the three murders, Sheriff Deputy Cecil Ray Price and Klan leader Samuel Bowers served four years in jail. The lead triggerman, Wayne Roberts, served six years and the other, James Jordan, served four. Ringleader Edgar Ray Killen and other defendants were acquitted. Killen was retried forty years later in 2005 at the age of eighty and sentenced to sixty years in prison.

This was the scene Barney Frank drove into. He spent the rest of the summer sleeping on the floors of threatened offices, delivering leaflets and failing to make his Boston accent understandable to Mississippians. He had to navigate outsider status for the rest of his life. He was the most high-profile openly gay politician in the United States for a quarter century, perhaps even in the world. When he came out in 1987 he was the first US congressman to do so voluntarily. In 1989 a very public scandal threatened to derail his career. Nevertheless, he went on to be one of the most influential congressmen in modern history: a crusading regulator of the banking industry and chair of the House Financial Services Committee. He has been a polarizing figure, loved and admired for his unstinting and unvarnished ability to tell it the way he sees it, criticized for being too quick to sell out parts of the progressive movement in the interests of the whole. His lack of diplomatic filter comes off as rudeness; he is self-possessed, and his evangelical commitment to change things for the better can smell like arrogance—even to his allies.

I asked Frank if he saw a parallel with the progress of LGBT rights and specifically the way in which he had been accused of detaching transgender rights from the gay rights movement. "The first cases that the civil rights movement brought to the Supreme Court were to sit in the back of the bus but at least have it as clean as the front of the bus," he recalled. "The thing about LGBT activism is that they always push immediately for everything." Indeed, in 2007 Ken Sherrill found that the overwhelming majority of LGBT Americans thought it was better not to pass an Employment Non-Discrimination Act bill if it did not include transgender rights. "People say, 'well, Martin Luther King never held back,' but I say, 'of course he did, all the time,' " Frank says. "The July 1964 Civil Rights Act outlawed segregation, but the Mississippi freedom project focused on the right to vote. This was a conscious policy decision not to integrate the lunch counters. Transgender activists said, 'we want a total civil rights bill,' but blacks didn't get that. Voting rights came later, in '64 and '68. The key mistake is to think it's easier to get it all at once than incrementally."

Frank's revolution is a slow climb rather than a fast leap. "In every case of progress on civil rights the reality refutes the unknown. When Americans see the reality their fears dissipate—age, gender, sexual orientation, race, disability." Writing in his autobiography, Frank recognized that "setting aside important goals to pursue others more effectively is hard for emotionally committed advocates to accept."

He believes that the iconic issue that demonstrated the success of his view was marriage equality. He saw a state-by-state strategy as more effective than going for a constitutional amendment. "We needed to get a foothold, then defend it in Massachusetts, and be able to disprove all of the fears. That was the basis for moving forwards." In 2004 the mayor of San Francisco, Gavin Newsome, called Frank to ask for his blessing to marry same-sex couples in opposition to state and federal law. Frank told him it was a bad idea: "I was very angry," Barney tells me. "In a few months all the marriages were reversed. It was a cruel political trick to play on the people who had been married, who were naïve, and some of them were devastated. It is more important to do it piece by piece and build on that."

While the US civil rights movement struggled with the slow pace of incremental legal and social change, the South African anti-apartheid movement did not even have that luxury. For eighty years the white minority regime resisted all and every effort to liberalize their draconian racist laws, even in the face of huge pressure to do so. Theirs was an iron fist in a metal glove. The year after Barney Frank's summer in Mississippi, the National Union of South African Students (NUSAS) invited Martin Luther King Jr. and Robert Kennedy to South Africa. The apartheid government denied King a visa but said that Kennedy could visit, though without an entourage or reporters. In 1966 Kennedy traveled to South Africa to see for himself what apartheid looked like. On the way he stopped in London to stay with his close friend Anthony Lewis, at the time London bureau chief of the *New York Times* (he would go on to win two Pulitzer Prizes).

On June 6, 1966, Kennedy gave his "Ripple of Hope" speech at the University of Cape Town. A black-and-white photograph shows Kennedy flanked by the platform party. With 18,000 students crammed into Jameson Hall, it took Kennedy nearly half an hour to reach the stage. To his left is an empty chair for Ian Robertson, the president of the National Union of South African Students (NUSAS). Two weeks earlier Robertson had been banned by the state from participating in social and public life for five years—partly because of the invitations to Kennedy and King. Behind the empty chair is a blond woman who stares directly into the camera. Margaret Marshall was twenty-two. As vice president of NUSAS, she took over as Kennedy's host after Robertson had been banned from all public events.

In his speech Kennedy argued that futility was the greatest enemy of justice: "The belief there is nothing one man or one woman can do against the enormous array of the world's ills. Yet many of the world's great movements, of thought and action, have flowed from the work of a single man. A young man began the Protestant Reformation, a young general extended an empire from Macedonia to the borders of the earth, and a young woman reclaimed the territory of France. 'Give me a place to stand,' said Archimedes, 'and I will move the world.' These men moved the world, and so can we all. It is from numberless diverse acts of courage and belief that human history is shaped each time a man stands up for an ideal or acts to improve the lot of others or strikes out against injustice. He sends forth a tiny ripple of hope, and crossing each other from a million different centers of energy and daring, those ripples build a current that can sweep down the mightiest wall of oppression and resistance."

The liberal *Rand Daily News* wrote of Kennedy's visit, "it is as if a window has been flung open and a gust of fresh air has swept in." Years later, Margaret Marshall told the *Harvard Alumni Magazine* that Kennedy's five-day visit gave them hope. "We felt so alone at the time. So to have a United States senator, the brother of the president, come and speak to us in such plain, yet inspiring language was critical. He told us that any one person can make a difference; you don't have to be the leader of a gigantic political movement to make a difference. That was a very important message because we felt that what we were doing was so insignificant. It's a message I now try to pass on to younger generations: you can make a difference."

Margaret Marshall would go on to make a difference.

In 1958 the head of the African National Congress, Chief Albert Luthuli, was banished to within a fifteen-mile radius of his ancestral home in the tiny village of Groutville, on the shores of the Indian Ocean in KwaZulu-Natal. He was given a special dispensation to travel to Stockholm to receive the Nobel Peace Prize in 1961, but by 1964 the detention was strengthened to the immediate vicinity of his house. Groutville had been established as a mission station by a different sort of American missionary from Massachusetts, the Rev. Aldin Grout, over a century before. The village Grout had renamed after himself in 1844 was called Umvoti, or "voter" in Zulu. The American missionary had literally taken away a place of voters.

On July 21, 1967, Luthuli was hit by a freight train while walking on a trestle bridge over Umvoti river near his home. Margaret Marshall was one of the few whites to make it to the funeral. Things looked bleak: the state held an iron grip around the throat of the majority nonwhite population and the whites who opposed its racism. Marshall stood next to her friend in the student movement, Steven Biko. "He turned to me and he said, 'Margie, you see, the African National Congress is not dead.' " The movement was badly wounded, but still alive.

Apartheid became more and more insidious and violent, more invasive. Marshall had to be on the constant lookout for who was watching. She was hiding in plain sight. Her "kind" wasn't welcome: "When I traveled from town to town, I had an arrangement to call someone when I left and when I arrived at my destination," she told Lory Hough, "so that if I disappeared someone would know immediately. My telephones were tapped. My letters were read. My parents weren't opposed to my views, but they were opposed to my activities. It was so unusual for a woman to be involved in politics." Marshall was straight, but like gays of the time she was no longer welcome in the conservative society of her birth. She understood ostracism and bigotry. The year after Luthuli's funeral she fled to the United States. Biko would be murdered in police custody ten years later. Mandela would remain in jail for another twenty-three years. Marshall started a doctorate in art history at Harvard in 1969, but quickly found that "art was not what I'd been living" and switched to the education school. A visiting lecturer from Brazil, Paulo Freire, had just finished his classic book *The Pedagogy of the Oppressed*. According to Freire, majority oppression creates a "culture of silence that instills a negative suppressed self-image into the oppressed." To counter this the oppressed must make themselves visible: they "must be their own example in the struggle for their redemption." Sitting in class, Marshall was inspired—just as Ann-Louise Gilligan was by Freire a decade later. In 1973 Marshall enrolled at Yale Law School and met Bobby Kennedy's soul mate, Anthony Lewis, at a party. Tony and Margie fell for each other and would marry a decade later.

Marshall's life had become an American story rather than an African one: Yale law school, private practice as an intellectual property lawyer, Harvard's in-house lawyer. In 1996 she was appointed to the Massachusetts Supreme Court by a Republican governor—thirty years after the quintessential

Massachusettsan, Robert Kennedy, had inspired her in Africa. Three years later Margie was elevated to chief justice of the court. There had been no female chief justice when the Rev. Aldin Grout had left Massachusetts in 1834, no female chief justice when Kennedy spoke in Cape Town in 1966, and none until Marshall took the position in 1999—three hundred years of silence at the top. Six years later, Margaret Marshall cast the deciding vote and wrote judgment in *Goodridge v. Department of Public Health*, which brought gay marriage to America for the first time.

Barney Frank feels that Marshall's role in the history of marriage equality and gay rights is sadly undercelebrated. "Her leadership was extraordinary. We needed a breakthrough and importantly Massachusetts was a state where we could defend it. It wasn't just her vote, it was her leadership as the chief justice," he says. The vote was 4 to 3, and Frank told me that Marshall brought along at least one other associate judge. Early in 2012, Barney called Marshall and left her a message: "Will you marry me?" He wanted her to officiate at his wedding to his partner Jim. She said she would love to, but then Tony got ill and Barney and Jim were married by the governor, Deval Patrick.

Barney Frank has been at the epicenter of two great civil rights moments in American history. "Why has there been a dramatically faster pace of change in LGBT versus African American rights?" I ask. It is due to people coming out, he says: "We were making no progress on LGBT issues, until people started to come out. Most white people have LGBT relatives, but very few white people have black relatives. In the late 1980s when I came out, I said the American people were less homophobic than they thought they should be and more racist than they were prepared to admit." But it took a long time for Barney to fully come out. Like the rest of his generation, Frank did not believe he was allowed to hold a high-level responsible political job in the public eye as a gay man. In 1968 Kevin White, the newly elected mayor of Boston, asked Frank to be his chief of staff. Frank used the excuse that he had a PhD dissertation to finish and deliver at Harvard. White destroyed this excuse by getting his neighbor, the renowned Harvard professor and democracy scholar Samuel P. Huntington, to give Frank an open-ended extension. Barney became the mayor's chief of staff . . . and he never finished the dissertation.

But politics remained a fragile closet. "I started coming out in the late 1970s, but I put it on hold when I ran for Congress. I wouldn't have been elected if I was out." As a state legislator in the 1970s he got into a fight with the owner of a gay bar who then tried to out him. Once in Congress it was both easier and more difficult to hide. "I was half in, half out—that wasn't working. I had decided to come out properly, but then the Gerry Studds problem arose. And that delayed me." Studds, another Representative from Massachusetts, was outed after a relationship with a seventeen-year-old congressional page came to light.

"By 1986 everyone knew I was gay," Barney tells me. "Washington was like Switzerland during the war. But the press wouldn't out you unless you approved it, with the exception of a scandal. The perverse result was that the only people known to be gay were people who had done something wrong. I told the press, 'If you ask me, I'll tell you I'm gay.' But they said, 'We can't ask you.' But I didn't want to volunteer it because I wanted to minimize the fanfare." Mike Synar, a Democrat from Oklahoma, asked Frank whether he had a girlfriend. "No," Frank replied. "Are you gay?" Synar asked. "Well, yeah," Frank said. Conversation done. Representative Tom Carper from Delaware and Frank were at a New Year's party in Egypt. At the stroke of midnight Barney did not kiss his (female) date. He told Carper why. Carper was quoted years later as saying, "Barney told me that it was one of the conversations that gave him the courage for him to tell others. It was a funny moment, but it was an important moment for him, and maybe for the rest of us." In 1987 Bob Bauman was about to publish a book implying Frank was gay. Barney felt he now had to tell his mentor, House Speaker Tip O'Neill. O'Neill sighed with resignation and said, "I thought you might be the first Jewish speaker."

"Do you regret not coming out earlier?" I ask on that cold Washington morning thirty years later. Barney clears his throat and looks down. "Yes. It distorted my personal life. One needs to meet the emotional and physical needs . . . that's why I got involved with a hustler . . . that was stupid and unworthy of me. I was a mid-forties member of Congress." I ask him whether there was there a danger of becoming known as "the gay rep." "Yes and no," says Frank. "If the first thing they knew about you is that you were gay or lesbian there is the danger that it would narrow the range of my effectiveness, but if you already know then you were no longer the stereotype." Did you feel psychologically lighter when you came out, I ask? "It felt like a great weight had been lifted off of my shoulders . . . but I got on the scale and still weighed 320lbs!"

Frank found friendship in unlikely places after he came out. Two Republicans went out of their way to be supportive. Alan Simpson, who had been an ally of Frank's on some legislation, wanted to apologize: "I must have told you some anti-gay jokes, I just feel awful," he told Frank. But Frank couldn't remember any such jokes. One night soon after he came out Frank was grocery shopping at Roland's, a late-night convenient store on Capitol Hill. Republican Senator Warren Rudman nodded greetings. He waited until Frank was at the back of the store and Rudman was at the checkout, and said very loudly: "Barney, I'm proud of you."

The value of being out to Frank was about changing the conversation. "Legislating is a very personal business," he says. "I could force issues that they did not want to deal with." In 1990 Frank was able to remove sexual orientation as a reason for being denied entrance to the United States; a few years later, he had sexual orientation and gender identity included as reasons to allow refugee status. Along with a myriad of other LGBT civil rights issues, he worked on repealing the 1953 Eisenhower Executive Order 10450, which banned gay men and lesbians from working for any agency of the federal government. He was also able to shift the dial within the Democratic Party, reaching down to pull up a new generation of lesbian and gay Democrats. And in 1998, Frank intervened as the Democratic Congressional Committee was leaning toward opposing Tammy Baldwin's House race because they were worried she couldn't win her race as an open lesbian.

I Do

In May 1974, American public television aired a debate titled "Should Marriage Between Homosexuals Be Permitted?" on *The Advocates*. Astronomer and gay rights icon Frank Kameny led for the pro side, and opened with an eloquent argument for the benefits of marriage equality that would accrue to both homosexuals and heterosexuals if enacted. (This was exactly the same argument that the Freedom to Marry campaign made successfully forty years later.) On the show Kameny called Elaine Nobel as his first witness. Nobel was then an instructor at Emerson College, and six months later destined to be the first-ever out person elected to a state legislature in Massachusetts. She confirmed that she was happy, stable, in love, and had no desire to be reincarnated as straight. She just wanted to be given equal rights as her straight neighbors.

Leading the against side was Tobias Simon, a onetime lawyer for the Rev. Martin Luther King Jr. He argued that "the male-female marriage is now, and always has been, the place where babies are born, reared, and conditioned. That is the first and the only reason why the state recognizes marriage and rewards it with special privileges and financial help. Without babies there would be no society. And since homosexual unions do not produce babies, there is no justification for them to be specially recognized or equally rewarded. This is not discrimination. There are essential differences between hetero- and homosexual couples that warrant differences in treatment. For homosexual couples to insist upon the same recognition as married couples is a falsification of basic biological realities. Same-sex marriages constitute civil silliness, not civil rights."

His key witness was Professor Charles Socarides, a psychiatrist at the Albert Einstein Medical School, described by Freedom to Marry founder Evan Wolfson as the "leading psychiatrist enemy of gay people." (For his senior thesis at Harvard Law School in 1983, Evan Wolfson wrote a seventy-seven-page thesis titled *Samesex Marriage and Morality: The Human Rights Vision of the Constitution*.)

In his book *Homosexuality: A Freedom Too Far,* Socarides summed up his view of the gay rights movement: "First, it takes deadly aim on the primary unit in society, the family. Second, it is eliminating one of the very obvious, but very key factors in the making of a civilization: the fact that one generation succeeds another generation. Third, the very fact of AIDS is the same-sex movement's terrifying contribution to this terrific century." For his entire career Socarides maintained that gay people were sick and dangerous. In the PBS debate he led with this statement: "The homosexual—that is, an exclusive homosexual, and there are various types of homosexual; there is homosexual behavior which is not true homosexuality—is a person who out of inner necessity must engage in homosexual relations. Otherwise, he experiences a great deal of anxiety. As a matter of fact, the homosexual act itself we now conceive of analytically as an exquisitely designed symptom which helps keep him in equilibrium, and that's why homosexual counseling centers should not tamper with this very, very delicate balance. Those people were not trained to do so."

He went on to say, "I've seen very few homosexuals who ever really wanted marriage. It occurs sometimes in older males who have younger male lovers and sometimes in older women with other young lesbian women . . . Most homosexuals must seek, and strive, and look for numerous partners in order to try and find themselves, the replicas of themselves. I believe that this is a social recklessness to raise homosexual marriage to the status of heterosexual marriage, an extreme form of social recklessness, and also psychiatric disaster which has already happened recently in trying to normalize homosexuality." Socarides argued the homosexual is "a product really of a process of very, very bad child rearing practices, which have caused certain difficulties in his own sense of identity, certain types of anxieties, and certain other inner conflicts, which make him on many occasions have an equilibrium which is quite unstable." With delicious irony, Socarides's gay son Richard became President Bill Clinton's adviser on LGBT issues and was the founding president of Equality Matters. Clearly Charles's bad parenting was to blame for our good fortune.

On June 26, 2015, the Supreme Court of the United States issued a landmark opinion in *Obergefell v. Hodges,* expanding same-sex marriage nationwide. The case was the capstone to the most rapid than social transformation in US history. A decade earlier no person could choose a same-sex legal spouse; it was illegal to be openly gay and serve in the military; there were scant employment protections for gay people; and the 1996 Defense of Marriage Act denied not just spousal recognition, but a whole host of benefits and protections. Only a handful of LGB politicians were elected statewide, and only Representatives Barney Frank and Tammy Baldwin held national office. Yet by the close of 2015 the Defense of Marriage Act was rendered unconstitutional; Don't Ask, Don't

Tell was repealed; federal and state benefits to same-sex couples were being extended; and same-sex marriage had become legal throughout the United States.

If anything, the transformation in the values of the American public has been even more earth-shattering. Gallup and the Pew Research Center have been gauging support for gay marriage among the US population for nearly twenty years. Gallup found a doubling in support from 27 percent in 1996 to 55 percent in 2014. In 2017 Pew found 62 percent of Americans in support, while in 2001 they only found 35 percent in support. Democrats, independents, liberals, and moderates lead the change, but Republicans and conservatives have also increased in their support for gay marriage by large amounts. In 2001 only 20 percent of Republicans supported marriage equality; as of 2016 it was 40 percent. Eighteen percent support among conservatives has grown to 41 percent in 2017. At first, there was some resignation reflected in these numbers. Pew found that 72 percent of Americans saw the recognition of same-sex marriage as inevitable in 2014, and 59 percent of those opposed to gay marriage thought its introduction was inevitable. But now there is greater embrace. Once the data is broken down by age groups, the trajectory becomes even more startling. Sixty-seven percent of millennials supported gay marriage in 2014, and as of 2017 that figure is 74 percent. In 2014 support among baby boomers was 46 percent—a doubling since 1996—and in the last three years it has shot up to 56 percent. Gallup also found that the issue Americans had become more satisfied with than any other economic or social policy question was "the acceptance of gays and lesbians in the nation." Fifty-three percent of voters were either very or somewhat satisfied on the issue in 2014, an increase of 18 percent over satisfaction in 2001.

Writing on the eve of the Supreme Court rulings, the pollster and commentator Nate Silver noted in the *New York Times* that support for same-sex marriage in the United States had been rising at a reasonably steady rate since Massachusetts had initiated gay marriage in 2004, with about half the increase attributable to generational turnover and half to changing opinions of Americans who remain in the electorate. Using state-by-state demographic data and the trajectory of evolving public opinion, Silver estimated that voters in thirty-two states would be willing to support same-sex marriage in 2016, and in forty-four states by 2020. According to a 2013 report from the Williams Institute, support for marriage equality increased in every US state between 2004 and 2012, with an average increase of 13.6 percentage points. The most dramatic growth in support during this period occurred in South Dakota (+21%), Connecticut (+18%), Hawaii, Oregon, Montana, and North Dakota (all +17%). When President Barack Obama came out in support of gay marriage in May 2012, it did not hurt his popular support or favorability rating.

Between same-sex marriages beginning in Massachusetts in 2004 and the *Obergefell* Supreme Court decision in 2015, 390,000 gay couples were married across the United States. In the first two years after *Obergefell* 157,000 new couples married, boosting local economies by over $4 billion. As of 2017, 10 percent of LGBT Americans are married to same-sex spouses (although roughly half of all LGBTQ Americans identify as bisexual). Thirteen percent were married to an opposite-sex spouse, a fall of 1 percent since *Obergefell*. In 2017, Gallup found that married same-sex couples were more likely to be male and older.

The front line of legal equality in the United States remains not at the national level, but at the state level. Equality advocates saw a combination of popular pressure and litigation as a way to cause more dominoes to fall as more states considered gay marriage. Their argument that momentum would create a climate in which it would be inevitable for the Supreme Court to rule for same-sex marriage was correct. Equal access to the institution of marriage has become the focus of the social, political, and legal battle over equality rights for lesbian, gay, bisexual, and transgender Americans. It was a practical recognition of legal equality with commensurate state and federal benefits, but also a symbolic talisman. If there is equality in state-sanctioned marriage, went the theory, then a plethora of other legal provisions were likely to be equalized in short order.

While the historic battle for marriage equality was ultimately won with this national-level decision, the war was waged over a decade prior in state-level courts and legislatures. There is considerable evidence to show that LGB state legislators were instrumental to the introduction of marriage equality. The phenomenon was a virtuous circle. Electorates that are more accepting of electing out LGBT candidates are also more likely to support marriage equality, but once the LGBT candidate is in office they increase the chances of legislative success and, by their presence and action, further increase tolerance and support in the electorate at large. In almost two-thirds of the states the bill legalizing same-sex marriage was sponsored or cosponsored by an out lesbian or gay legislator. In many cases very visible individual advocacy by these legislators was crucial to the passage of the bill. There was an explicit message to state house members from the lesbian and gay legislators that if you are going to vote against this equality measure, then you are going to have to vote against me as a person standing in front of you. In many cases individual advocacy was crucial to the passage of the bill.

Along with Alissandra Stoyan of Kansas State, I wanted to explore the relationship between lesbians, gays, and bisexuals in US statewide legislative office and the passage of marriage equality laws. Did the presence of out state legislators really improve the chances of a state passing gay marriage? We looked at nineteen states and the District of Columbia, which by September 2014 had introduced marriage equality, and one state (Colorado) which was in the midst of legislative action. We looked at the votes and the debates, and interviewed out state legislators. We also surveyed the more than two thousand state legislators who had voted on marriage equality since 2005. All the evidence we found strongly suggested that the presence of out LGB legislators had a significant and positive effect on the initiation of legislation and its ultimate passage into law. The state legislators themselves told us that their out gay and lesbian colleagues influenced them significantly in deciding how to vote on the pre-eminent gay rights issue of their time.

The Washington State senator Jamie Pedersen is convinced that the personal interactions that he, his husband Eric, and their kids had with his colleagues made the difference. State house debates also provided a unique platform for very personal narratives to be presented. Karen Clark had been in the Minnesota House since 1980. In their 2013 debate on marriage equality she said, "My family knew firsthand that same-sex couples pay our taxes, we vote, we serve in the military, we take care of our kids and our elders and we run businesses in Minnesota . . . same-sex couples should be treated fairly under the law, including the freedom to marry the person we love." David Pierce's speech on the floor of the New Hampshire House in 2009 was cited by many as swaying a number of undecided legislators to support the legislation. Three legislators—Delaware State Senator Karen Peterson, Maryland Delegate Peter Murphy, and Nevada State Senator Kelvin Atkinson—actually came out during the same-sex marriage floor debates. Peterson became the state's first-ever openly LGB legislator and Atkinson the first gay male African American representative in Nevada (and only the fourth in the country). When the statute took effect on July 1, 2013, in Delaware, Peterson and her partner were the first same-sex couple to marry in the state. Atkinson proposed to his partner on the stage as they celebrated on the very day marriage equality became law in Nevada on October 7, 2014. Likewise, Senator Beth Bye of Connecticut was the first person to marry under their new legislation in 2008, and Ed Murray of the Washington State Senate, the man credited as being the architect of Washington's gay marriage law, married shortly before he was elected mayor of Seattle. There were countless other examples of speeches and interventions by out LGB legislators that moved values and votes. In Colorado, State Senator Pat Steadman and State Representative Mark Ferrandino introduced the Colorado Civil Union Act (which was superseded by the legal mandate of marriage equality in October 2014). Ferrandino argues that the presence of out state house legislators changes the dynamic of the chamber itself: "Words become more respectful." He noted that his husband Greg had come to testify twice and their daughter was a constant presence in the hallways of the state house. "It is hard to look at us and see something different from other families."

Others used influential leadership or committee chair positions to push the issue. In Vermont, Bill Lippert, as the vice chair of the House Judiciary

Committee and as the chamber's only openly gay member, was central to the work of drafting and passing into law the landmark civil union law that granted legal recognition to same-gender couples in 2000. Following the 2004 election, the Democrats regained their majority and Lippert was appointed to chair the Judiciary Committee. This enabled him to play a central role in facilitating the passage of marriage equality in Vermont in 2009. In Washington, Ed Murray's successor in the state house, Jamie Pedersen, chaired the House Judiciary Committee that initially prepared and processed the marriage equality law. The out gay House speakers John Perez of California and Gordon Fox of Rhode Island were both crucial to the passage of marriage equality.

The presence of LGB legislators was felt in every chamber that voted on the issue. Indeed, the phenomenon is encapsulated in a story about the Massachusetts legislative effort to rescind marriage equality told by Marc Solomon in his book *Winning Marriage*. Sean Kelly was a "conservative Republican from the Berkshire Mountains," Solomon writes. His legislative colleague was the Democrat Liz Malia, a lesbian representing gritty parts of Boston. In breaking ranks and voting for marriage equality Ryan said on the convention floor: "Liz, this is for you . . . is she eight-tenths of a citizen? Nine-tenths? Anything less demeans the spirit of Massachusetts, it seems to me. If you believe that the love Liz has for her partner is less than the love that you have for your spouse, I would suggest that you are wrong." Solomon writes:

> The whole chamber was dead silent, and the only sounds were Kelly's voice and the singing [from supporters] outside. Malia was shocked and overcome with emotion. Tears streamed down her face . . . Liz Malia knew that the debate had been transformed. Her colleagues had talked about gay people in their lives, but no one had made it personal to someone they all knew. Liz gave Kelly a giant hug while others wept at the poignancy of Kelly's remarks.

Carl Sciortino was also crucial in securing the votes of his wavering colleagues in Boston. In New York, Democratic Senator Jim Alesi voted yes to marriage equality in 2011, after having joined Republicans to vote the motion down two years before. In an act of contrition in front of Governor Cuomo he apologized to Tom Duane, the leading gay member of the New York Senate. "I feel terrible about the 2009 vote," he told Duane. "It was a political vote. And I apologize to you, Tom, for that vote."

While there is considerable evidence that out gay legislators affected the voting behavior of their colleagues, there are also manifest effects of gay relatives and friends on the voting behavior of straight legislators. Presence has positive effects reinforced by visibility across a number of realms of life. For example, in their debates, Senator Elizabeth Schneider of Maine and Washington State Senator Kevin Ranker both emotionally spoke of their parents who were gay. In floor speeches a slew of Republicans cited personal connections as the foundation for their yes votes. Delaware's Mike Ramone, New York's Theresa Sayward, and Washington Representative Maureen Walsh spoke of their gay sons and lesbian daughter. Another Washington Republican, Glen Anderson, spoke of his gay brother. Representative Janet Duprey of New York described her friendship with the lesbian couple on her street.

Alissandra Stoyan and I decided that to learn more, we needed to talk to the straight legislators. We asked them if their openly gay state house colleagues influenced their votes on marriage equality legislation. Throughout 2014, a couple of thousand state legislators voted on marriage equality legislation. In our online survey, the response pool was close to the overall split of party, gender, and place; crucially, we had a close relationship between the sample and population when it comes to voting behavior on marriage equality. Sixty-five percent of our respondents voted yes (versus 58% for the population as a whole), and 35 percent voted no or abstained (versus 42% overall).

We asked a series of questions surrounding voting behavior on three issues: (1) marriage equality legislation, (2) legislation based on another identity issue (women or race), and (3) nonidentity-based legislation. For each piece of legislation we asked two very basic questions. First we asked, "How did you vote on [name of bill]?," where responses were simply yes, no, or abstained. Secondly, we asked, "How important were each of the following factors as you decided how to vote on [name of bill]?" Legislators were presented with six factors: (1) party leaders, (2) constituents, (3) lobbyists, (4) openly LGBT/female/black colleagues, (5) family or friends, and (6) personal beliefs. For each factor, responses included "not important at all," "minimally important," "moderately important," and "very important."

We expected that the out gay legislators would have a stronger effect on vote choice for identity legislation than for nonidentity legislation, but we also wanted to see how the effect of openly LGB colleagues on marriage equality votes compared to that of other identities, such as the effect of female colleagues on votes over women's issues. In each state, we selected a bill where voting yes would imply support of the given identity. The results of our survey of state legislators dramatically highlighted the positive effect that openly gay legislators have on the voting behavior of straight colleagues when it comes to marriage equality. As in the broader population of state legislators, the majority of respondents to our survey self-identified as heterosexual (97.4%). Overall, straight legislators' responses indicate that their openly gay colleagues influenced them significantly when it came to deciding how to vote on the greatest gay rights issue of their time.

The vast majority of legislators assessed their lesbian and gay colleagues as important to the way in which they voted on legalizing same-sex marriage. The effect of LGB state house members was greater than the comparative effect of other identities, such as female colleagues on gender-oriented bills and African American colleagues on bills of special relevance to African American communities. At the same time, both of these presence effects were, as expected, more significant than the influence of colleagues on nonidentity related legislation. The results were even more striking when one separated the yes voters from the nos. Of those voting for marriage equality, over 68 percent of respondents described their LGB colleagues as important in affecting the way in which they voted. Over one-third of respondents voting yes chose the highest level, and said their gay colleagues were *very* important. In contrast, less than one in five stated that legislators who voted against marriage equality assigned any import to the influence of their gay colleagues, and when import was assigned, it was only moderate. A full 82 percent of the legislators voting no on marriage equality ascribed little or no importance to the presence of LGB state house members around them. In essence, when the presence of an LGB elected official has an effect on voting behavior, it is a positive effect: familiarity breeds respect rather than contempt.

A complex and varied set of influences weigh in to voting decisions, and we did not expect that openly gay colleagues were the only thing driving marriage equality. Among those who voted for marriage equality legislation, personal beliefs and constituents were assigned a very important rating as well. However, LGB colleagues were rated as very important more often than either friends, family, party leaders, or lobbyists. If the separate friends and family categories are combined, then these personal connections represent an even larger influence on legislators' vote choice. This lends further support to the importance of personal interaction: whether conversations take place in the halls of state houses or around the dinner table, these connections are likely to affect legislators' voting patterns. The power of personal beliefs is striking, if not surprising. Still, there is a multitude of evidence that out LGB legislators are key agents in transforming personal beliefs from homophobia to acceptance.

As one might expect, as the number of openly LGB legislators increases, these individuals have a greater impact on the voting behavior of their straight colleagues. Our survey found that where only one lesbian or gay legislator held office at the time of the marriage equality vote, only 15 percent of respondents noted a moderate or very important impact of LGB colleagues. However, in states where there were four or more LGB legislators, 59 percent of respondents noted a moderate or very important influence of LGB colleagues. Thus, the importance of LGB colleagues tends to increase with the number of them holding state office. LGB legislators are more likely to meaningfully impact the voting behavior of their straight colleagues in states where at least three LGB legislators are serving in office.

We were also interested to see if our survey results varied according to the gender or race of the respondent. However, we found this not to be the case. Men and women assigned high importance to their colleagues in almost equal proportions, if they voted yes on marriage equality. If they voted no, men were slightly more likely to assign moderate importance to their colleagues than women. Whites were slightly more likely to assign import to LGB legislators than those who identified as another race, but our nonwhite pool was small. If they voted no, both whites and those of another race told us that their gay colleagues had little influence on the way they voted.

In essence, when it comes to the introduction of same-sex marriage in US states, we found multiple push factors, all moving equality forward and reinforcing each other. No element was responsible alone, but at any given time certain variables—such as judicial action or legislative initiatives—may be more prominent, while at other moments elements such as advocacy campaigns or national political dynamics may be more salient. At its heart, the story of how marriage equality and gay rights advanced in the United States is one of individual agency. Judges, elected officials, and civic leaders move in overlapping social circles. As LGB individuals become more present in these realms, there is assimilation and a diffusion of support. Liberal Democrats can influence conservative Democrats on gay rights questions, who then can influence Republicans. Sometimes the narrative is of the gay son or best friend prompting a change of view, while at other times the story revolves around colleagues serving together, but every story is predominantly one of personal relationships. As Evan Wolfson says, the adage that "knowing someone who is gay increases your support for gay rights" is not exactly correct. It is more about having "meaningful conversations with someone who is gay." Someone you trust. It is more than a passive knowing; according to Wolfson, "what is necessary is the 'close the deal' conversation." The space for those conversations to happen is as ripe within the backrooms of state legislatures as much as it is around the family dinner table. Openly gay elected officials change politics and society on a number of levels: legislative, emotional, and psychological. They put gay rights issues on the agenda, build alliances to create majorities for action, and assume positions of influence to shepherd legislation. But perhaps above all, their simple presence alters the discursive dynamic of a legislative body. After meeting a lesbian couple advocating against the repeal of marriage equality in Massachusetts, Steve Brewer, a state senator from the rural, conservative upstate, advised them, "one of the best things I can tell you to do is to become more visible in your community. Be part of your community and become involved in your community."

Some say that marriage equality was more a function of Democratic lawmakers being a majority in certain states instead of other factors. While not all Democrat-controlled states had same-sex marriage before 2013, marriage equality legislation was overwhelmingly led by the party. In the sixteen cases of states holding legislative votes, 86 percent of Democrats voted for same-sex marriage while only 10 percent of Republicans did. Only in Rhode Island was there a majority of Republicans in favor of marriage equality. This elite behavior reflected the mass views of the time. In September 2014, Pew found that 57 percent of Republican voters opposed same-sex marriage while only 34 percent favored it. In contrast, 62 percent of Democratic voters were in favor while only 30 percent opposed it. But in the senates of New York, Rhode Island, and Washington State, Republican votes *were* needed to pass their respective marriage equality bills. By definition, a "defector" in a marriage equality legislative vote was a Democrat who voted no or a Republican who voted yes. By this measure, there were more Democratic than Republican defectors. Men were also more likely to defect. There were forty-two (6%) female defectors out of 744 women who voted, and 159 (10%) male defectors out of 1,598 men who voted.

In the United States, female legislators are much more likely to support gay rights than their male colleagues. Indeed, one might give the lion's share of credit to women for the laws that allowed same-sex couples to marry. The gender differences in propensity to vote for marriage equality were striking: just over 1,650 male legislators voted on the issue, and 53 percent were in favor. However, a full 74 percent of the 713 women voted in favor. In twelve votes in nine of the US states, women made the difference between success and defeat. A majority of women voted yes (and tipped the balance), while men voted majority no in the Maryland House and Senate, the Delaware House and Senate, the California House and Senate, the New Hampshire House, the New Jersey Senate, the Washington State Senate, and the Illinois House. Women made the difference when the male vote was tied in the Minnesotan and New York senates.

Marriage is one issue on which gay legislators have a particularly strong impact, as the issue often impacts them directly. When the issue is debated, the openly gay elected official ceases to be an elite spokesperson of a marginalized community; they become an individual denied a basic right that the person sitting next to them enjoys. The power of their presence is heightened. When a gay legislator advocates for more funding for HIV research, attention to be paid to the disproportionate numbers of LGBT youth who are homeless, homophobic bullying in school, or workplace discrimination, they are taking up the cause of a community they come from, but not necessarily for an issue that affects them directly. With the issue of marriage, the representative can—and usually does—say, "Look at me." In two of the states where same-sex marriage was made legal before *Obergefell,* the very first person to be married under the new law was the state legislator who sponsored the legislation: Beth Bye in Connecticut and Karen Peterson in Delaware.

Beth Bye's expertise was in preschool education, so it made perfect sense for her to run for the West Hartford Connecticut Board of Education in 2001. She was out to close family and friends, and partnered with two young children, but not out beyond that trusted circle. She won her race and a year later the West Hartford Board vice chair and chair, Bye and Jack Darcey, were both gay and in the closet. Six years later Bye decided to run for the Connecticut State House, but she was nervous. No Democrat had been elected to the 19th District for twenty-six years; she wasn't out, she was running against a well-liked kinder-garten teacher, and she had kids entering their teens when the likelihood of pa-rental embarrassment was inevitable. But she needed campaign money, and the LGBT candidate Victory Fund would help with that if she came out. She tells me that the lesbian part of her campaign was a "whisper," but it was there. Bye won by a fifteen-point margin.

Beth and her partner Tracey began to venture out further—most of her colleagues had no idea she was gay. Freshman state house members were supposed to be seen and not heard, but a few months after taking office a same-sex marriage bill was tabled for discussion in the judiciary committee. "I felt like I should say something, but what should I do?" Bye recalls a decade on. Her colleagues said, "Stand up and tell your story," so she did. She outlined how her father had refused to go to his own brother's wedding because he'd been divorced, but came to terms with his daughter's love for another woman. In her speech Bye showed a photo of a grandmother, who had appeared before the committing begging that her grandchild be allowed to marry. "I cried through most of the testimony. It was emotional, but it was who I am," she tells me. The estimated count going into the April 2007 vote was tied. Only Massachusetts had even allowed such a legislative vote on gay marriage, with a 27–15 vote in favor. The governor threatened a veto and the bill went nowhere, but a line had been crossed. Bye's testimony changed a lot of votes. She recalls she had no idea her presence would matter so much. Over time she learned the Barney Frank lesson: "The legislature is a club. You support each other, your currency is relationships with other members and treating them well." Having me, a colleague and friend, say, "I don't want to be the *other*, I want to be married," was crucial. There were five or six people on that committee who said, "I can't vote against Beth." "My favorite story," she goes on, "was when I was speaking. A guy in a suit at the back of the room was welling up, tears in his eyes. I hadn't been there long enough to know who he was, but it turned out to be Chris Powell, who was a very conservative journalist in the state. I just saw him as a guy in a suit. As I left the room he pulled out a mass card from his mother's funeral and gave it to me. He said, 'My brother is gay and hasn't been able to live his life. My mother's hope before she died was that he would be able to. What you did today was so courageous.'"

The election and the judiciary vote had outed Bye more dramatically, quickly, and extensively than she had ever intended. After the committee vote the *Hartford Courant* had a front-page picture of her wiping tearful eyes, head down, with her wedding ring in focus. She was "mortified" to be out to the whole state in an instant. "I wasn't ready," she says. But she acknowledges that her being on the inside made a big difference: "Momentum just built after that, and I was comfortable being out." Bye stresses that the advances in gay rights were driven not by her alone, but by the cohort of out state house members who had been plowing much less fertile land for many years. Two other gay men, Michael Lawlor and Andrew McDonald, would chair hearings and endure "hateful shit and say thank you very much, with grace. They were two of the most respected members of the general assembly." When Bye was first elected there was a comparatively large LGBT cohort of six. But even so, she says, "there were three or four guys who couldn't come out and they felt like cowards. It was so sad."

Bye regrets the fact that Lawlor (elected in 1987) and McDonald (elected in 2003) never got the credit they were due. Their skill was to incrementally move forward and take a wide span of views with them. She notes that not all in the gay community accepted the civil union compromise in 2005, but argues "that's exactly how we got marriage" two years later. The cohort was incredibly tight. The credo was "never break rule number one." "What's rule number one?" I ask. "Don't fuck with one of us," she replies. The normalization of out lesbian and gay members has been swift. Every year Beth and her wife Tracey are asked to help train incoming freshmen on what it's like to have a family with kids while in the assembly. In 2013 she became the chair of the powerful appropriations committee. "In not one article was it mentioned I was gay," she says.

Bye stresses that presence and friendship are not merely about votes. Over the years she befriended a conservative Republican from Waterbury, Selim Noujaim, a Catholic who fled war-torn Lebanon in 1974. One day they were chatting in his office and she saw a huge framed picture of the front page of the local *Republican-American* showing him speaking under the headline "Selim Defends Marriage in Hartford." Bye did not mention it. "Three days later he comes down to my office and says, 'Beth. I have taken that picture down. I will never put it up again and I feel horrible that it was up and if it offended you in any way I'm so sorry.'" Beth Bye and her wife Tracey were the first couple to be married in Connecticut on November 12, 2008. They stood around a computer at the West Hartford Town Hall waiting for the email to say "go." After years of being together "you think it won't mean much," says Beth, "but it means everything."

Figure 6.1 Coos Huijsen in Parliament (front row, center), 1976. Credit: The collection of Coos Huijsen.

6

Being First

Coos Huijsen: The Unknown Soldier

History books love the firsts: Neil Armstrong, Barack Obama, the Wright Brothers, Roger Bannister, Edmund Hillary, and Sherpa Tenzing. But we rarely remember the second. It doesn't matter how few steps behind the runner-up you are—the glare of the spotlight is dimmed. Unless you happen to be the first out gay man to be elected to a national parliament. While the iconography suggests Harvey Milk was first, he was not even the first out gay person in public office in the United States. That moment of ceiling-breaking is co-owned by Jerry DeGrieck and Nancy Wechsler, who came out together when serving on the Ann Arbor, Michigan, city council in 1973. Kathy Kozachenko was the first person to be elected while out when she won a seat on the same council in 1974. Likewise, the first publicly out gay man or lesbian to be elected a member of Parliament has not been feted—perhaps because he was not from the United States or Britain. In the mid 1970s envelopes were being gently pushed around the world. Marilyn Waring was elected as an MP in New Zealand in 1975 and was outed by a newspaper in 1976, but on the advice of her party leader, refused to confirm. Maureen Colquhoun was a Labour MP in Britain between 1974 and 1979 and came out to a select group of journalists in 1977, but not to the public. But the first prize goes to James "Coos" Huijsen, who spent six months in the Dutch Parliament in 1972 and came out publicly as a gay man before being re-elected on March 30, 1976.

Today, Coos is trim, spritely, and approaching eighty. He and his husband Lank have been together for over forty years. In Lank you can see the tall, broad-shouldered student that the young politico Coos fell for in the early 1970s. Lank cooks for us in their elegant Amsterdam apartment while Coos tells me the story of their life.

James Huijsen was born in the Dutch capital, The Hague, on March 20, 1939, as the winds of war began to gather in Europe. He got the nickname "Coos" later. When he was fourteen months old a Nazi parachute regiment began its assault on The Hague, but were repelled by Dutch soldiers. But the moment of joy was short-lived. The ill-equipped and understaffed Dutch military was quickly overrun by the invading Germans and General Henri Winkelman, the Dutch commander in chief, surrendered the country four days later. During those four days 4,800 soldiers and civilians died. Many more were to die under occupation. Coos's parents divorced when he was two, and during the war he flitted around the countryside with his mother and grandparents. Coos's mother was unstable and every few months tried to renew her life in another town. The longest time was on the island of Goeree-Overflakkee—the Dutch equivalent of the American Bible Belt, the heartland of the fundamentalist Calvinist Reform Political Party (RPP). Only in 2006 did the RPP finally bend to pressure to allow women to become members, and they still cling to a deeply socially conservative view of gender relations and homosexuality. At last, when Coos was thirteen, his mother married a conceptual artist and settled in Amsterdam. But like her, the new husband also suffered from mental illness. Coos, the only child, was often responsible for his mother. He describes being "in camouflage" at school. He was politically ambitious, and that meant hiding his homosexuality. "In the 1950s I was a haze of sadness," he tells me. "It was theater. No one knew I was homosexual."

Fifty years ago the Netherlands, while progressive compared to countries, was not yet the beacon of tolerance it has become today. Huijsen navigated a fragile borderland between old traditional religious values and a new generation who were more willing to gave him the space to be the man he was. He joined the Christian Democrats. "Why them?" I ask. The center-right seemed to be a strange choice. "There were three parties," he tells me. "Two Calvinistic and one Roman Catholic. The Christian Democrats were in the center for people who were not really socialist and not real conservative." But Coos quickly gravitated to the left wing of the party. He became president of the youth group that was all about equality for women, family planning, and against discrimination of homosexuals "of course, not for yourself, but for others," he tells me.

From June 20 to the end of the term on December 7, 1972, Huijsen was an MP for the Christian Democrats. He was on the left of a broad party. By 1976 Coos was being groomed for greater things. The leaders wanted to elevate him to number four on the national list and position him for the party leadership a few years hence. As the crown prince of the party, he attracted more and more hostile attention. The right-wingers started a whispering campaign: "Why is he not married?" He brought women to events, but his enemies whispered they were call girls. The party leader asked if the rumors of his homosexuality were true. Coos denied it, but he was becoming more and more uncomfortable. "I decided someone needs to come out. Confront people with real homosexuality, tell the truth. That's why I came out." But first he had to tell his mother. "She had two marriages that were a catastrophe. I didn't want her to read in the press that I was homosexual. I prepared her before I told the papers." Coos vowed that the next time a journalist asked him if he was gay he would say yes. Over 1976 he discussed Lank and his homosexuality in several newspapers. Upon taking office in April 1976, he wrote an article about his politics and sexuality for the liberal newspaper *NRC Handelsblad.*

The Christian Democrats were unhappy, but unable to remove him from their candidate lists. Upon election in 1976 he became an independent. A year later he joined the Labour Party. In 1976 the Dutch Parliament was reviewing and renewing the constitution. Article 1 stated that it was forbidden to discriminate on the basis of five identities—but not homosexuality. Coos notes that this gave explicit permission to discriminate against gays. He engaged as an openly gay man with conservatives, liberals, communists, and socialists. He proposed that the constitution say that you could not discriminate "on any ground." Ultimately he won, and the government accepted his position. Coos also took on same-sex partnerships. Men were beginning to enter into contracts around financial partner benefits. A judge ruled that the practice was immoral, so Coos took the question to the minister of justice. The minister told Parliament that such contracts were valid. A very conservative Catholic MP was sitting next to Coos in the chamber. He blurted out "Oh no! How disgusting." Coos recalls that there was silence in Parliament. "You could feel the silence." The MP quickly tried to make amends by saying it was "not the person, it is the sin," while the chamber stayed silent with embarrassment.

There was power in Coos being in the room. But more than that, Lank represented something even more powerful: family, love, partnership. Coos describes how MPs would leave their offices early in the morning and be picked up by their wives. Lank would wait with the wives. One day Lank took a seat in the family boxes in Parliament to watch Coos speak. An usher tried to remove him, but the chairman of the assembly told Lank he could stay. He told Coos and Lank, "It is the beginning of a long way, but I support you." Views about what a family is were shifting. The MPs and diplomats and their wives used to congregate on the platform of The Hague train station to travel home. There were a flurry of kisses and hugs. Could Lank and Coos kiss goodbye? Lank tells me their hearts were thumping, but they said, "If we don't do it, how is anyone else going to have the courage?"

Coos Huijsen very explicitly chose the inside route. He was the gay man in the establishment. He felt that you needed activists inside and out. In 1979 he helped convene a group of international celebrities, including Jean-Paul Sartre and Simone de Beauvoir, to place an advert in *Time* magazine to attack the laws being pushed for by the anti-gay rabble-rouser of 1970s America, Anita Bryant. Coos went on to become a writer, headmaster, and the leading historian of the

Dutch Royal House of Orange. In 2005 he was commissioned to write a book on the anniversary of the Queen Beatrix's silver jubilee. The Queen invited the celebrated gay writer behind the scenes to gain an insight to her life. When the president of Switzerland came to visit, Lank took his place next to Coos at the state dinner. There was no fear on the railway platform now.

Today the Netherlands has the most progressive equality laws on the books—gay people are able to marry, adopt children, and serve in the military, and national law prohibits discrimination in the workplace and treats homophobia as a defined class of hate crime. Twenty-five more out lesbian and gay politicians have been elected to the Dutch National Assembly since Huijsen. Indeed, the Labor Party finance spokesperson, Henk Nijboer, did not even know how many other gay MPs there were when interviewed in 2013 and stressed how little his sexual orientation defined him as a political animal. Coos started it all. I ask him if he has been surprised by the pace of change. "There are moments when Lank and I say 'it went so fast, so quick,'" he says, but he also bemoans the fact that the climate can still be so difficult for young gay kids in the Netherlands, especially those from new migrant and Muslim communities.

They're Here, They're There, They're (Almost) Everywhere

As of January 1, 2018, 326 openly lesbian, gay, bisexual, or transgender representatives have been elected to national parliaments in forty-five countries, since Coos Huijsen in 1976. There were 302 of them elected to lower or people's houses, while twenty-four were elected to upper houses (Senates). There were an additional thirty-five appointed LGBT senators. At the start of 2018 there were 196 Members of Parliament holding office in thirty-eight countries. The largest cohort was forty-five in the British House of Commons (alongside twenty-one out British Lords). Though the number of out LGBT MPs has increased substantially over the last forty years, the total numbers remain small—a tiny fraction of the 46,000 current parliamentarians in the world. The balance in the numbers of gay men versus lesbians in elective office has remained constant over time, with approximately four gay male MPs for every lesbian MP.

LGBT MPs may be rare birds, but they are overwhelmingly of the majority ethnic group in their country. There have only been a few ethnic minority gay MPs: Jani Petteri Toivola (Finland) is of Kenyan and Finnish descent; Charles Chauvel (New Zealand) is of Tahitian ancestry; Louisa Wall, Georgina Bayer, Meka Whaitiri, Claudette Hauiti, Kiri Allen, and Tamati Coffey (New Zealand) are Māori, while ten of the South African MPs have been white South Africans of European ancestry and one colored. The vast majority of LGBT MPs have been elected in the established democracies of the West (Europe, North America, and Australasia). However, there have been twenty-three Latin American LGBT parliamentarians, eight Central-Eastern Europeans, thirteen Africans (all in South Africa), and four in Israel. No out Muslim has ever been elected.

There have been sixty-three senators or lords elected or appointed to the upper parliamentary chambers of twenty-one countries—forty-four gay men, two bisexual men, fifteen lesbians, and two trans women. Most nations had LGBT representatives in their lower houses before they had senators or lords, but David Norris was an Irish senator for twenty-five years before two out gay men were elected to the Irish Dail. Kanato Otsuji was briefly in the Japanese Senate in 2013, and was elected to the Japanese lower house in 2017. There have been fifty-three LGB cabinet ministers in the governments of twenty-seven countries since 1995 (thirty-seven men and sixteen women). An additional two ministers came out after leaving office. Two countries had out cabinet ministers without ever having had LGBT members of Parliament (Ecuador and the Czech Republic), while Serbia still has not. Outside of the seven prime ministers, there have been two Foreign Ministers (Germany and Latvia) and five economics or finance ministers (Australia, Luxembourg, Netherlands, New Zealand, and Norway). The top legal job has only been occupied by a gay man in New Zealand. When appointed to cabinet posts, LGBT politicians are more likely to oversee environmental or culture portfolios. Outside of Ecuador and the Czech Republic, it took an average of sixteen years after the first LGBT politician was elected to Parliament before an LGBT leader was appointed to a cabinet-level position.

At the highest level of government, gay men have made a big impact in the low countries of Europe. Elio di Rupo took over as prime minster of Belgium in 2011, leaving office in 2014. In neighboring Luxembourg, Xavier Bettel became prime minister in 2013, presiding over a coalition government including a deputy prime minster, Etienne Schneider, who also happened to be gay. A decade before, in 2002, the conservative finance minister of Norway, Per-Kristian Foss, filled in briefly as acting prime minister. One of the most popular Icelandic politicians was the Social Democrat Jóhanna Sigurðardóttir, who after a long parliamentary career became social affairs minister in 2007 and then the world's first out lesbian prime minister between 2009 and her retirement in 2013. In 2015 Allan Bell, the chief minister (prime minister) of the small autonomous crown dependency in the Irish Sea, the Isle of Man, came out as gay. Bell told *The Guardian* that homophobia in the Parliament was rife in the 1980s and 1990s: "It was disgusting. I felt dirty at the end of it. I felt for a period ashamed to be Manx because of the debate that was going around." Ten months after Bell came out the first same-sex wedding was celebrated on the island after marriage equality had been passed into law. In June 2017 Ana Brnabić was appointed prime minister of Serbia. Soon after another significant out gay prime minister took office in Europe—more of which later.

The increase in out LGBT representation is dramatic, but has not kept pace with the increase in people who say they are LGBT. The US Victory Fund said that there were 448 out elected officials in America in December 2017, which constituted 0.1 percent of the positions available. They estimated that over 21,000 new LGBTQ Americans would need to take office to reach parity with the estimated 4 percent national population that identifies as LGBTQ.

Nor does the LGBT representation mirror the internal diversity of the population. Gary Gates and the Gallup polls found that the proportion of American adults identifying as lesbian, gay, bisexual, or transgender in 2012 was 3.5 percent, but by 2016 it had hit the 10 million mark and 4.1 percent of the population, a 1.75 million increase in identification over two years. The highest concentrations were in Washington, DC (8.6%), and the states of Vermont (5.3%), Massachusetts (4.9%), California (4.9%), Oregon (4.9%), and Nevada (4.8%). The lowest were South Dakota (2.0%) and North Dakota (2.7%). Vermont, Massachusetts, California, and Nevada do have the highest level of LGBT state house representation, and conversely South and North Dakota are two of the ten states as of 2017 with zero out LGBT state house representatives.

The increase in LGBT identification in the United States is driven by millennials (born between 1980 and 1998). At 7.3 percent they were more than twice as likely as any other generation to identify as LGBT. They account for nearly 60 percent of all LGBT Americans (58%). The increase is more among women than men, and as of 2016 women constitute 55 percent of the community. A Harris/GLAAD poll in 2017 found even higher rates—partly due to the more open-ended questions they posed. In their survey 12 percent of Americans identified as LGBTQ in some way. This was driven by 20 percent of millennials identifying as something other than strictly heterosexual. The relatively larger increases in LGBT identification among racial and ethnic groups other than white non-Hispanics mean that these racial and ethnic minorities now account for 40 percent of all LGBT-identified adults compared with 33 percent in 2012 (Gallup). Out elected officials are whiter, gayer, and more male than the LGBT population as a whole. While close to 4 percent of the US LGBTQ population identify as bisexual, there is only one bisexual congressperson, one governor, and only four of the 109 sitting state house members. Only one of the seven LGBTQ congresspersons is a minority (Asian American) and only twenty-three (21%) state house members: ten black, ten LatinX, two Asian-Pacific Islander, and one Native American. The Victory Fund found that 80 percent of the overall 448 elected officials in the United States were white (356), compared to fifty-one Hispanics (11%) and twenty-three blacks (5%).

The Palm Springs, California, city council became a curiosity in November 2017 when its three incumbent gay councilors were joined by two new members: Lisa Middleton, a prominent local activist and trans woman, and Christy Holstege, a lawyer who identifies as bisexual. This made the five-member council 100 percent LGBTQ. One of the incumbents, J. R. Roberts, told Frank Bruni: "I really don't want us to be known as the Queer Council. I want this to be about the things we accomplish . . . I feel a lot of pressure. We are known as a gay community, and we need to project the cleanest, best government." Mayor Robert Moon told Bruni, "The city manager: gay. The assistant city manager: gay. The newly hired city clerk: gay . . . You see why having an all-gay City Council is no big deal? Nobody cares anymore."

The March of Women

The male closet was lonely, but the female one even more so. When Angela Eagle became the first out lesbian in the British Parliament she was only the seventh ever in the world. She remained alone for thirteen years. In 2010 she was joined by Margot James of the Conservatives, and in 2015 by three more from the Scottish Nationalists. In the interim she had been the first out woman in the British government, appointed by Gordon Brown in 2009. Five years after being elected to the House, Angela's identical twin sister Maria was elected Labour MP for the neighboring Liverpool Garston. Angela's sexual orientation was not the only thing that made a career in politics seem unlikely. The Eagle sisters' parents were not rich or connected. Mother Shirley was very smart but too poor to go to university; she worked in a biscuit factory much of her life and died at fifty-one. Andre Eagle wanted to be David Hockney, but he had to be a printer rather than a painter. The Eagle parents were determined to give their children the education they had been denied. "While Dad was working shifts he taught himself to play chess," recalls Angela. "He taught us when we were eight." As a fifteen-year-old she won the British Girls Chess Championship.

Angela was elected for the Liverpudlian seat of Wallasey in 1992, just after Thatcher's downfall but long before homophobia became unacceptable in polite British society. "I was never secret about sexuality, but I did not parade family things on leaflets, didn't have a partner at the time," she tells me. In 1992 a large wedge of British voters was susceptible to the charge that the Labour Party was suspect: the dying embers of colonial thought, "Labour's for the blacks and the queers" was the refrain. The unions were slowly coming around to supporting gay rights, but Thatcher's dog-whistle politics still turned heads. While the Labour government's decriminalization of homosexuality in 1967 was a great leap forward, "section 28 took us backwards," Eagle says. Her sexual orientation was not the issue when she was selected in Wallasey only a month before the election. The real issue, she claims, was a "big Trotskyite infiltration into local party. I knew I would come out at some stage but I wanted people to know me for me rather than just see that about me as opposed to anything else." Five years on, in another election, Britain was turning a collective corner on gay rights. "I wanted to come out, wanted to move in with my girlfriend," Eagle says. "I told John Prescott, my boss at the time, [and] he replied, 'Tell me something that I didn't know already, love.'" At the time she was a junior minister in the department of environment, transport, and the regions. Prime Minister Tony Blair said he would back her 100 percent. Angela successfully media-managed her coming out. She approached Suzanne Moore of the *Independent*, who wrote a front-page story in 1997 headlined: "I Need to Get Things Sorted." "How did people react?" I ask. "There was the odd comment in the constituency, but people were very supportive. By 2001 there was no backlash: "People's attitudes change so dramatically," she muses. But Eagle believes the nastiness of the Thatcher era created an unanticipated backlash, and public attitudes on gay rights moved way ahead of the politicians. In 2002 Eagle was "let go by Tony" from the front bench, which actually gave her more freedom to speak in the civil partnership debates. She confides that when same-sex adoption was being discussed, "quite a lot of Tories came to talk about things on the quiet. You are there as a witness."

As of January 2018 there were forty out lesbian, bisexual, or trans women MPs in eighteen countries, but that remains a tiny sliver of the 46,000 parliamentarians in the world today, a mere drop in the ocean. Jóhanna Sigurðardóttir of Iceland became the first out lesbian elected as prime minister in 2009. Ana Brnabic became the second in Serbia eight years later. Eagle also made a run for the top spot. In July 2016 she challenged Jeremy Corbyn for the leadership of the British Labour Party. She was in the race for a week. An online campaign of homophobia flourished, she was called a dyke at party meetings, a brick was thrown through the window of the building housing her constituency office, and a man was arrested in Scotland for sending death threats. On the eighth day she stepped aside to give another Labour MP, Owen Smith, a free run at Corbyn. In the leadership election two months later, Smith was crushed. It was clear that Eagle's withdrawal was driven by practicalities rather than the abuse, but it stung nevertheless. Eagle told Anushka Asthana of *The Guardian* "that her time in politics has taught her that however intensely personal it feels when you lose, it often isn't." She says, "I'm inured to it now. If men get death threats, they stand up and are seen as brave. When women get death threats, they are portrayed as if they are victims. I am not a victim." But it had taken two decades for Eagle to feel the full force of unvarnished homophobia. She confirmed to *The Guardian* in 2016 that "the most trouble I've had with it is in the last month."

I interviewed Eagle just four months after the euphoria of marriage equality being legalized in the United Kingdom. There was much buzz about how much the Tories had seen the light and led the charge, but Eagle could not hide her irritation. "The Conservatives are not leading. They have taken advantage of the change. Yes, they adapted but they did not have the guts to lead the change. *We* had to live through Section 28. When *we* were used as a political football, having our lives trashed. I'm not going to sit here and listen to Conservatives pretending that it all happened naturally." She went on to say that "it happened because progressive people took the risk and made it happen despite an over-whelmingly hostile press. I've had my family door-stepped by the media. My primary teacher and his wife were tricked into talking about whether I was gay when I was eleven years old! It was awful and disgusting. I'm glad the Tories feel they ought to be modern now but they haven't brought this change about." I mentioned that I interviewed the gay Tory MP Conor Burns that morning— Thatcher's progeny—and Eagle had no time for it. "Thatcher might have been personally very nice to the people she knew were gay but she was actively hostile in the legislation that she passed."

Annise Parker grew up and was educated in Houston, Texas, with brief stints living in Mississippi, South Carolina, and on a US Army base in Germany when she was a teenager. As a kid Parker was painfully shy, with paralyzing anxiety. But she forced herself into places where she had to learn how to talk to people. She scripted her interactions. She still doesn't like the small talk that defines political schmoozing, but has learned how to do it. Her family's nickname for her was "the turtle," shy and slow. Today she has a large turtle collection that was started when she was a kid.

In 2010 Madeline Appel of the Houston Oral History Project asked Parker about her shyness and her coming out as a teen. "Just as I could see if I did not tackle how painfully shy I was, I was not going to be able to do any of the things I really wanted to do in life. I could see that if I could not get more comfortable with who I was in terms of my sexual orientation and if the world was not going to be more comfortable with me, then I could not do what I wanted to do in life either," she told Appel. But the road was far from smooth, echoing the fright-ening journey of so many queer teens. Parker opened up to filmmaker Cindy Abel for the documentary *Breaking Through*, telling Abel, "I became a cutter. And I have a whole series of scars."

Crucially, Parker found a mentor: an older lesbian woman named Joe, who was a leader in this new out gay community. "I was like a mascot," Parker says. She founded a lesbian student group in her second year in college in 1977 and then "spent the first ten years being an officer and board member in every gay organization you could think of. Got a little burnt out." One of Parker's chief attributes is persistence. She ran unsuccessfully for the city council in 1991. "I did not think I would ever run again but knew what I would need to do. I came back in 1995." There was a special election, and after a grueling campaign, Parker finished third behind the Democratic and Republican party establishment candidates. She was "devastated, because I knew I was the best candidate in that race. Curled into a fetal position for a couple of days." At the time she said, "I am never going to do this again, ever, I swear." But three years later she did do it again, and won. In 2003 she was elected as Houston's chief financial officer. In 2009 she became the first openly LGBT mayor of a large metropolitan city. Her victory was a comfortable one, and she was re-elected in 2011 and 2013 before being term-limited out of office. In all she was elected nine times by the voters of Houston—a lesbian woman in a very straight man's world.

She had all the attributes that made her relevant and relatable to the Texas old-boy network: fifteen years working in the oil business, respected by the police and chamber of commerce leaders, a married mom with four kids. She met Kathy Hubbard in 1990. They moved in together soon after, looked after grandparents and raised kids, and married in 2014. Hubbard seems to be the perfect complement to the mayor. "She loves being First Lady," Parker told Appel. "She is much more social than I am. She enjoys the attention. And I will say that the former first ladies of Houston have been very gracious with her because she is creating a new role. I have had to correct a couple of people, 'No, no, I'm the mayor. I'm not the First Lady.'"

While never shying away from being open about her sexual orientation, Parker has never let it define her, nor does she play on it for gain. Appel asked Parker how being gay had shaped her life. After a single sentence about coming out, Parker spent the next five minutes discussing her father's career and her transitory teenaged life, never returning to the issue of her being a lesbian. She refers to her breakthroughs as communal achievements rather than individual ones: "I believe that by the time I leave office, I will have, in some way, changed the way Houstonians think about themselves. We seem to have an inferiority complex here. I will take credit for having raised Houston's coolness factor. When I was first elected, the responses fell into two categories. One was 'Houston elected a lesbian?' The other was, 'Houston? This happened in Houston?' Well, yes. People don't understand Houston. Houston is about what you can do more than who you are. And the rest of the world is looking at Houston in a different way because of my election and Houston has, in some ways, looked at itself in a different way."

Making a Difference, Not Making History

Both Angela Eagle and Annise Parker reflect a very human desire to be seen in more than one dimension. Every out elected official struggles to liberate themselves from the "gay politician" label. It is a label rooted in society's usually salacious curiosity, as much about a public figure's sex as their sexual orientation.

Building a reputation which renders irrelevant the "gay" prefix at the start of every news story is often the first challenge a newly elected, or newly out, legislator faces. Before coming out Eagle had enjoyed something of a profile in the British press; after, she says, "I completely disappeared from the papers." They were only interested in her voice if she would say more about her sexual orientation and reveal who else was gay. Even when the interview purported to be about some policy matter, "halfway through they would ask who else was gay," she says. Eagle was exasperated. "I wouldn't play their game. I just wanted to get on."

Jared Polis, the congressman from Boulder, Colorado, and candidate for governor in 2018, insists he is "a Coloradoan, a Jew, a father, son, and entrepreneur." He does not hide his sexual orientation, but he does not trumpet it either. Tammy Baldwin rarely mentioned her sexual orientation when campaigning for the Wisconsin Senate seat in 2012. She had entered into a domestic partnership with her long-term partner, Lauren Azar, when they were made available to same-sex couples in Wisconsin in 2009, but the couple broke up the following year. In twenty years of public service in the Wisconsin House, US House of Representatives, and now US Senate, she has never hidden who she was but at the same time sought to avoid being seen as the lesbian representative and the representative of lesbians. After her election as the first out senator in US history, she repeatedly used the line "I didn't run to make history; I ran to make a difference." Some, like Mark Pocan (who inherited Baldwin's Madison, Wisconsin, seat in the United States House of Representatives) operate in a proximate climate largely sympathetic to gay politicians. Baldwin held the US House of Representatives seat from 1999, during which time Pocan represented the state capital in the Wisconsin State Assembly. He was politicized as a young adult. Just after graduating from the University of Wisconsin at Madison in the mid-1980s, Pocan was followed by two men after leaving a gay bar and beaten with a baseball bat as they screamed "faggot." This event, he says, convinced him to run for office as an out gay man.

It is tempting to believe that the Netherlands became a post-homophobic society long ago, but while their social maturity has led the world—decriminalization of homosexuality in 1811, equal rights act in 1993, domestic partnerships in 1998, the first to institute same-sex marriage in 2001—the reality of life for LGBTQ people in the Netherlands is more nuanced. The Dutch have climbed more of the mountain than anyone else, but they are still not quite at the summit. Boris van der Ham was in Parliament representing the center-left D66 party for a decade between 2002 and 2012; today he remains in the public eye as president of the Dutch Humanist Society. We chat over coffee and cake in the old-world café of the Hotel Kapinski in Amsterdam's Dam Square, with large plate-glass windows framing the Royal Palace over his shoulder.

As a teenager, van der Ham was fueled by his contrariness. He realized early on that he was different, but he despised the conventions of 1970s and 1980s gay activism. Van der Ham describes Nieuwkoop in the South of Holland as "countryside surrounded by cities." His parents were liberal, but his grandparents were orthodox Dutch reform and voted for the religious Christian Union party. Above his bed was a poster of the writer Gerard Kornelis van het Reve, the teenaged Boris's hero. In it, Reve stares intently at the camera, writing with a quill, wearing a black leather jacket, surrounded by curiosities—a garden gnome, open wine bottles, a white piano, an animal in a cage, children's toys. Gerard Reve was raised as a communist in the immediate postwar years but moved rightward and converted to Roman Catholicism in the 1960s. In 1966 he was the last person in the Netherlands prosecuted for blasphemy for his masterpiece *Nader tot U* (*Nearer to Thee*), in which the central character makes love to God, who is incarnated as a year-old donkey. After a two-year trial, he was acquitted. Boris says he loved Reve because he was a gay man who "was strong, not soft." He hated the stereotypical feminine gays he saw on TV. If anything, being gay was an annoyance to Boris. "At fifteen I would have preferred to lose a leg than to be gay," he tells me— not because he believed it would close windows, but rather because it would unfairly open them and because he hated to be pigeonholed about who he was and what he believed. At nineteen he was against gay marriage: "I didn't like the people who were promoting it. I didn't want to belong to that group—the 'gay community' is an anathema to me—it doesn't exist."

When he was first elected to Parliament in 2002 for D66 he avoided taking the lead on gay rights issues and would bridle when a journalist brought the subject up. He did not object to equality; he just didn't like the gay activists, the pride marches, and gay newspapers. "I didn't want to be the token gay. I did not go into politics because I was gay." He says that when it comes to being identified as a single-issue politician, "if you give one finger to that direction then they've got the whole hand." As a former actor, van der Ham says he evolved something of a performance character: to journalists he played the truculent, bullish man irritated with the assumption that he was the gay mouthpiece. Ironically, the political space is the most tolerant place in the Netherlands, more tolerant than society and the media. He had cover to shy away from being a gay MP—D66 had been one of the first to push for marriage equality in the Netherlands, and their success opened the door worldwide. Boris Dittrich was already in Parliament for D66, and he had enthusiastically embraced the gay MP label. Indeed, by the time van der Ham was elected in 2002 gay MPs were old hat; there had been twelve in office over the previous quarter century. Van der Ham liked the line used by Wim van de Camp, who was a Catholic, conservative, and gay Christian Democrat MP. When the Labour and D66 parties would have their gay MPs ride on floats in the annual gay pride parade van de Camp would say, "They put them on a boat, we put them in the cabinet."

However, over time, Boris mellowed and began to be more vocal around issues that affected gay people. By 2006 he had taken on the D66 LGBT portfolio, and after he left Parliament he fully stepped ahead of the new frontline of gay rights in Europe. In 2011 he became the father of a boy, conceived in concert with a lesbian couple, with whom he shares parental responsibilities. For the first time he felt compelled to be a public role model. He went public with the details of his fatherhood to demonstrate that gay men could aspire to parenthood.

Figure 7.1 Lord Christopher Smith, Master of Pembroke College, Cambridge. Credit: Pembroke College, Cambridge.

7

St. Christopher

I'm Chris Smith

It is perhaps easy to forget how recently life in Britain was so frightening for LGBTQ people. From the famous to the unknown, the wealthy to the poor, homosexuality in Britain in the twentieth century was still a "love that dare not speak its name," a phrase coined by Oscar Wilde's lover, Lord Alfred Douglas. Alan Turing, W. H. Auden, John Gielgud, Dusty Springfield—so many famous people lived lives in the shadows. Between 1885 and 1967, 75,000 British men were arrested for the gross indecency of being gay. The Thatcher years (1979–1990) were characterized by institutionalized homophobia and a spiraling HIV/AIDS epidemic. Upon Thatcher's death, Matthew Todd of *The Guardian* said, "the reality is that Thatcher presided over and took advantage of the most devastatingly homophobic time in recent British history." In 1987 the Conservatives sought to portray the Labour opposition as being in league with perverts and pedophiles. One of their billboards showed young men wearing badges such as "gay pride" and "gay sports day" with the slogan, "This is Labour's camp. Do you want to live in it?" After attacking schools for teaching children that, in her words, "they have an inalienable right to be gay," Thatcher introduced Section 28 of the 1988 Local Government Bill, which mandated local authorities not to "intentionally promote homosexuality or publish material with the intention of promoting homosexuality" nor to "promote the teaching in any maintained school of the acceptability of homosexuality as a pretended family relationship." Remarkably, Section 28 remained law until Tony Blair's Labour government repealed it in 2003. When Thatcher was being memorialized by many, Peter Tatchell said "she was extraordinary for mostly the wrong reasons . . . At the 1987 Conservative party conference she mocked people who defended the right to be gay, insinuating that there was no such right. During her rule, arrests and convictions for consenting same-sex behavior rocketed, as did queer bashing violence and murder. Gay men were widely demonised and scapegoated for the AIDS pandemic and Thatcher did nothing to challenge this vilification."

The Thatcher government's homophobia actually contributed to the growing AIDS epidemic. In 1986 Health Secretary Norman Fowler proposed a "Don't Die of Ignorance" media campaign, pointing out that unprotected anal sex carried a disproportionately high risk of transmission. But Thatcher blocked them. As she wrote in internal memos, "Do we have to have the section on risky sex? I should have thought it could do immense harm if young teenagers were to read it?" and "I think the anxiety on the part of parents and many teenagers who would never be in danger from AIDS exceeds the good it may do . . . adverts where every young person will read and hear of practices they never knew about will do harm." Approximately 3,500 Britons died from AIDS during Thatcher's tenure, with the peak in deaths in 1995, five years after she was ousted. In her defense, the man who inherited her parliamentary constituency, Mike Freer, says the Conservative party couldn't run without gay men. He argues that Thatcher's true disposition when it came to homosexuality and sex was a libertarian "I don't care." Indeed, he notes that she was one of the thirty Tory rebels in 1967 who voted to decriminalize homosexuality, and says in the 1980s she was "badly advised" on gay issues.

Nowadays, coming out seems like a walk in the park for a British MP. After the 2015 general election they were dropping like ripe plums. Seven MPs came out in an eighteen-month period, three of them cabinet ministers. There is little doubt that the climate for politicians in Britain to come out has dramatically improved. Today, the challenge is telling friends and family rather than the anonymous public. The stigma remains, but in public life a space has opened up allowing gay people to be visible and authentic. But in the 1980s, saying you were gay was an act of courage, and telling the world you were gay while being in the gaze of high office was unthinkably brave. On November 24, 1984, amid the swirling vitriol against homosexuals of the time, Chris Smith, the Labour Member of Parliament for the London constituency of Islington South, took his seat on the morning train to the midlands town of Rugby. The local city council had been taken over by the Conservatives, who had removed sexual orientation from the list of things that it was illegal to discriminate against in employment. The change was accompanied by a litany of homophobic remarks about not wanting to be around men wearing dresses and earrings. A rally was to be held in town that Saturday at which Smith would be the keynote speaker. He was known as an ally of gay folk.

As Smith sat by himself for the ninety-minute ride from London's Euston station, he was still wrestling with what to say at the meeting. He had come to the conclusion that at some stage he needed to come out publically. He watched other closeted gay MPs being hounded day and night by the tenacious and salacious British tabloids on the suspicion of being gay, and he was tired. As his political career evolved, Chris Smith could not live with a blanket of fear surrounding him. He worried that one day he would be found out, vilified and ridiculed. He told me about his Labour Party colleague, Alan Roberts, a closeted gay man with a penchant for living life to the fullest, who also lived in mortal fear of being exposed. Smith did not want to be that man.

But the actual moment of the coming out was more theoretical than real. He found it hard to imagine saying the words. What happened that day in Rugby was unscripted, spur of the moment. Sitting in his office next to the Tate gallery, overlooking the river Thames, Smith looked upward as he recalled the moment thirty years before. "On the train I prepared a speech which was all rather boring," he told me. But as he arrived at the rally, a switch in his brain flipped. "When I came into the hall, there were about a thousand people. I walked up through the audience to take my seat on the platform as the meeting had already started. I can remember thinking at that point . . . well, if I'm going to do it, then now is as good a time as ever. The argument was about the ability of someone who happens to be gay to do as good a job at anything as anyone else. That applied to MPs as much as it applied to people working for Rugby council." Smith scanned the crowd as he waited to be introduced. "Having made this decision in my head, I was absolutely scared stiff. I have never been as terrified on a public platform before or since," he said. "I was introduced, I stood up, and I began my speech by saying, 'My name is Chris Smith. I'm the Labour MP for Islington South and Finsbury . . . and I'm gay.' At which point the entire audience got to its feet and gave me a standing ovation." I asked him if he felt that the spontaneity of the moment had helped. "Oh yes," he nodded. "If I'd had two weeks to think about it I probably would have scared myself out of dong it. No one had ever done this before." No one on his staff or in his office knew what he was going to do.

Smith gathered himself for the onslaught of vitriol that would come. He waited, and waited, and waited. But nothing came. His colleagues were supportive; his party leader, Neil Kinnock, "took a range of opportunities to say well done." At the first Islington Labour meeting after his announcement the chair of the local party stood up and said, "I want it recorded how proud we are of what our Member of Parliament has done." Even the tabloid press reaction was muted. By coming out voluntarily, Smith had stolen the wind from their sails. But would Smith's London constituents turn against him? Everyone in the district read the *Islington Gazette*. A week after Rugby there was a huge picture of Smith on its front page: "I'm Gay, Says MP." "After that there was no way that anyone in Islington would not have known," says Chris. "On one occasion someone shouted abuse across a street at me but there was not another word."

Chris Smith's majority when first elected in 1983 was tiny: 363 votes, or less than 1 percent. He had won the seat from the defecting incumbent Labour MP George Cunningham, who had joined the Social Democratic Party (SDP) the year before. In 1987 Cunningham stood again, and it was the SDP's top target

seat in the country. Hundreds of SDP volunteers came down: "they threw absolutely everything at it," recalls Smith. But the "happy thing for me, was that
lots of lesbians and gay men came in to help me counter." Nationally the Tory
government was running on homophobia, but locally it was the SDP. They
played the queer fear card on the doorsteps. Labour primed its canvassers on
how to respond if the gay issue came up: "One, 'Isn't it good to have an MP
who is honest for a change?' Two, 'But you know that Chris Smith works for
everyone?' If neither of those worked," Smith says, "we told them to say 'You're
not telling me that you're prejudiced are you?'" Chris smiles: "No one ever had
to get to number three." In June 1987 Margaret Thatcher became the first prime
minister in 160 years to win three general elections in a row. But Smith doubled
his majority in Islington South and Finsbury to 805 votes—"going in the right
direction," he says, smiling. By 1992 the majority was over 10,000, and Smith
was safe.

Smith went on to be the first out gay man in the British government as the
minister for culture, media, and sport in the government of Tony Blair. He was
the man who made British museums free to the public. He became Lord Smith
of Finsbury after leaving the House of Commons in 2005. Thirty years after that
morning train ride, we spoke in his office as he was completing his second term
as chair of the UK Environmental Agency—a stellar career in the public eye. But
he will always be remembered, above all else, for that moment in Rugby.

That singular act of courage allowed thousands of other flowers to bloom.
Almost every openly gay British politician I have spoken to over the past few
years cites the "Chris Smith moment" as one which shattered their notion that
politics was not a realm an openly gay man or woman could exist within. When
I ask Michael Cashman about Chris Smith he sighs: "Ah . . . *Saint* Chris," he says.
"During the dark days he was an amazing symbol. His coming out in a completely hostile environment showed greater bravery and was a test for the rest of
us. It was truly heroic. People found it hard to attack him for his honesty. His is
a life that is well lived and therefore he is well loved." The man who might have
been the first out MP, Peter Tatchell, reflects on Chris Smith's moment. "His
coming out did not at the time make a huge impact apart from in [the] LGBT
community—but in [the] following year or two as he kept on it had [an] effect
on confidence and public consciousness. When he came out and suffered limited backlash it gave others the hope and sense that coming out need not be a
disaster. When other MPs started coming out a decade later it was something
of an anti-climax." The Labour Party leader (and Islington seat-mate) Jeremy
Corbyn said in 2017, "Nobody symbolizes the solidarity, bravery, and courage
of the LGBT+ community more than my old friend Chris Smith."

Like Harvey Milk, he touched not only those in his homeland. Smith relates
a story that still gives him pause. "Svend Robinson [the Canadian MP] came to

see me in London because he was thinking about coming out. I have it on my conscience to this day. I said, 'Oh just do it, it'll all be very positive, yes they will be a few brickbats from the right-wing press but it'll all be worth doing.'" But Robinson's experience was the opposite of Smith's. In 1988 "he came out on prime time television, and all hell broke loose. His constituency office was firebombed, he received bucket loads of hate mail," Smith says. Despite his modesty, he acknowledges that he did make it easier for others to come out, and it also created a perceptible change in the atmosphere in the corridors of British power. No longer could British debates be about the invisible other. They had one of *them* in the room—sitting next to them, looking at them.

In a debate on Section 28 in the 1980s the Conservative MP Nicolas Winterton—whom Smith describes as a "Neanderthal Tory"—was speaking about the need to shield children from homosexuality. Smith stood to intervene. The speaker recognized him and he made a short counterpoint. "As I sat down, he looked at me and said 'I thank the honorable member for his intervention. The House has learned to listen with respect when he speaks on these matters, but I'm afraid I disagree.' He felt he had to say that because the tone had changed."

Smith's voice and presence undoubtedly were key in shifting votes and mindsets, but nothing can match the symbolism of being the out MP in the United Kingdom, the first cabinet minister. He thought his groundbreaking days were long behind him, but then, in 2003, he received a call from a journalist of the *Sunday Times* who said, "We have heard from doctors at Middlesex hospital. We'd like to talk to you about your health." Chris knew his other secret was seeping out. Smith asked to speak to the paper's editor. John Wintherow was a Johannesburg-born journalist not known for his LGBT sympathies. Indeed, in 2010 he defended one of his writers' comments about the prominent TV personality Clare Balding being "a dyke on a bike" by saying: "In my view some members of the gay community need to stop regarding themselves as having a special victim status and behave like any other sensible group that is accepted by society. Not having a privileged status means, of course, one must accept occasionally being the butt of jokes. A person's sexuality should not give them a protected status."

Chris Smith told Wintherow that the Press Complaints Code was very clear that personal health information was not of public interest, and could not be reported without consent. But he told Wintherow that when he was ready to announce his status he would do it through the *Sunday Times*. Two years later Chris Smith decided that it was time. "I realized it was possible to make a difference for people with HIV, and I ought to say something." He had fallen out with Tony Blair over the Iraq war, had left the cabinet, and announced he was not going to fight the next election. Wintherow kept his side of the bargain, and two years later, in January 2005, the paper led with "Why This is the Time to Break My HIV Silence." Smith was comforted to see that their story was "entirely responsible," and the rest of the press "more or less took the same line." He wanted to communicate two things: "First, it is perfectly possible for someone to have HIV and live a full and contributing life. Second, in a peculiar kind of way, I am lucky. I have access to a National Health Service, a full range of treatment that has kept me alive. There are millions around the world of people who don't have that chance." Support came from unlikely quarters. The *Evening Standard* said, "Well Done Chris Smith." The only exemption was the right-wing *Daily Mail*, which published a "particularly virulent" opinion piece, Smith says.

I asked him to compare what it felt like to come out as gay to coming out as HIV positive. "I was much more nervous about it," he tells me. "Health is a much more personal thing. While there is a moral imperative in relation to coming out as being gay, I don't think that the same imperative applies to any health condition."

The Last Taboo

Smith's experience is emblematic of the space within which HIV-positive/AIDS men and women are forced to exist the world over, even in 2018. While visible gay men and lesbians are slowly moving into the political sphere in many parts of the world, the HIV-positive/AIDS community remains deeply marginalized, feared, and misunderstood. Despite the great strides forward in the understanding and treatment of HIV and despite the near-normal life spans and experiences HIV-positive folks are able to have today with access to the right medicines, being open about your status is perceived to be the death knell for a public life, especially a run for political office. The number of national parliamentarians who have been elected while being out and positive is precisely zero. There have been a handful of men who were elected while their status was known at the local level, and they seem to come in pairs: Tom Duane and Corey Johnson in New York, Larry McKeon and Greg Harris in Chicago, and John D'Amico and John Duran in West Hollywood, along with Larry Forrester in Signal Hill, California; Nelson Roman in Holyoke, Massachusetts; and Sean Strub in Milford, Pennsylvania. While there have been some high-profile unsuccessful candidates in America and Britain—such as Michael Petrelis in San Francisco, Todd Heywood in Michigan, and Adrian Hyyrylainen-Trett in London—I can find no evidence of any out HIV-positive women, people of color, or transgender candidates running for office, anywhere in the world.

Corey Johnson occupies the "gay seat" on the New York City council—including Manhattan's Hell's Kitchen, Chelsea, the West Village, and parts of the Flatiron and SoHo. He was diagnosed HIV positive at the age of twenty-two, in 2004, only four years after being featured on the front page of the *New York Times* after coming out to his Masconomet High School football teammates. As he told Robert Lipsyte, "Someday I want to get beyond being that gay football captain, but for now I need to get out there and show these machismo athletes who run high schools that you don't have to do drama or be a drum major to be gay. It could be someone who looks just like them." He more than went beyond being the gay football captain by becoming the speaker of the New York City Council in 2018—by far the most significant position ever taken by an out HIV-positive elected official in the world.

HIV/AIDS delimited being gay for the best part of three decades: the virus was there, even when it wasn't. But the understanding and response to the epidemic was excruciatingly slow. On June 5, 1981, the Center for Disease Control's (CDC) *Morbidity & Mortality Weekly Report* reported five unusual cases of pneumonia among previously healthy "active homosexuals" in Los Angeles over the previous seven months. It was the second of six bulletin items and was five lines long. Few people even noticed it. Twenty-eight days later the *New York Times* published its first story on the new disease, titled "Rare Cancer Seen in 41 Homosexuals." The article noted that men were presenting with *Kaposi's sarcoma* cancerous spots, which previously had been extremely rare (two out of every 3 million people) and this new outbreak was much more quickly fatal than the previous *Kaposi sarcoma* cases on record.

The phenomenon was described as something of a medical opportunity more than a crisis. "The cause of the outbreak is unknown, and there is as yet no evidence of contagion. The experts say it could have as much scientific as public health importance because of what it may teach about determining the causes of more common types of cancer," said the *Times*. However, there were clues about the diseases spread: "Nine of the 41 cases were diagnosed in California, and several of those victims reported that they had been in New York in the period preceding the diagnosis." A CDC spokesman said there was no apparent danger to nonhomosexuals. "The best evidence against contagion," he said, "is that no cases have been reported to date outside the homosexual community or in women."

Soon, a generation of gay men would be decimated. Two years after the first reports, 3,000 AIDS cases had been reported in the United States, and half of those infected were already dead. Fifteen years later more than 300,000 Americans had been lost to AIDS. Thirty-five years later, the magnitude of the figures are horrific in their simple starkness: round numbers devoid of faces and hearts. According to the World Health Organization, just under 40 million people around the world have HIV/AIDS. Less than half of those people have access to anti-viral treatments. Some 78 million have been infected since the start of the epidemic; 38 million of those died from AIDS-related illnesses, and over one million continue to do so each year. Some 1.8 million of those are in the United States, and 50,000 Americans still contract HIV each year. There have been dramatic successes in the fight, but while the trajectory is in the right direction, the human catastrophe rumbles on.

Very early on it became clear that being the face—any face—of HIV/AIDS was tantamount to becoming the world's pariah. In 1982 one of the virus's first investigators, William Darrow, was told by three men from different towns that they had all had sex with a French Canadian flight attendant named Gaétan Dugas. In the map of the epidemic that Darrow's team produced they labeled cases as C1 (California 1), and so on, and Dugas as O1 (other 1), but this was misread as 01—"patient zero," the man responsible for AIDS. Gaétan Dugas died in 1984 and was vilified for years; in Randy Shilts's book *And the Band Played On* he was depicted deliberately spreading the disease. But in 2016 researchers found strains of HIV beginning in the United States around 1970 that were different from Dugas's.

Carl Sciortino Jr.'s television ad when running for the Massachusetts 5th Congressional District in 2013 was, to put it in nontechnical terms, adorable. Carl, blond and baby-faced, sat in his chic, modern, pine-scented New England study while his father, Carl Sr., was grouchy in a recliner in his man cave. They traded loving barbs about how the liberal son had successfully passed laws to irritate his conservative Tea Party–supporting dad. But at the close they express their love for each other. Carl Jr.'s gayness was never mentioned out loud; it was the knowing joke and heartwarming backdrop.

Sciortino first ran for office in November 2004, when he was only twenty-five. A few months earlier he had gone with a group of activists to lobby his state house representative, Vincent Ciampa, to oppose the homophobic Defense of Marriage Act. "When I first met with him, he was so rude and so offensive. That was what inspired me to run," Sciortino told *HIVEqual* magazine in 2015. "He avoided answering how he would vote for forty-five minutes. When he realized we wouldn't go away without some answer, he got really belligerent, calling us 'you people' and pounding the table with his fist. He told a woman from the district who wanted to get married to provide a better life for her children, 'I don't understand why you don't just move to Vermont and get a civil union.'" Carl had no political experience, while Ciampa had been in the state house for sixteen years. A lot of people told him that Ciampa was unbeatable and that he shouldn't waste his time. But Carl says, "I'm stubborn. I don't like being told no. Even if you get in the ring and lose, sometimes it is still worth fighting."

Sciortino won the primary by ninety-three votes. Ciampa was so incensed that he ran a write-in campaign in the general election to try and hold on to his seat. The campaign got ugly fast. Carl began to worry that with gay bashing at its height, the controversy was pushing people back into the closet. Ciampa painted him as the radical militant extremist homosexual, all about gay marriage and nothing else. Carl recalls that it still felt new being out as a gay man, and the aggressive homophobic targeting he had to endure was overwhelming. But when he beat Ciampa in the general election he felt like the voters had said "You may be a radical militant extremist homosexual, but we are okay with that." "It gave me space," Sciortino says.

Nevertheless, the Democratic establishment—even in liberal Massachusetts—were not sure what to make of the freshman. "I was the new guy . . . very young. They stared at me and you could tell they were wondering, was I a bomb thrower? I'd just beaten one of their friends." There was no mentoring, and Carl felt alone. He bounced most of his ideas and heartaches off his good friend Marc Solomon, who, with Evan Wolfson, would be instrumental in winning marriage in the United States in 2015. Four years later, in 2008, another establishment Democrat, Bob Trane, challenged Sciortino in the primary. Both collected the necessary signatures to qualify, but Carl's papers were stolen from his desk just before the deadline. "I am 98 percent confident [I] know who stole them," Carl tells me. "But we couldn't prove it, so I moved on." As a result, Sciortino's name did not appear on the ballot, leaving Trane as the only candidate. Carl began his own write-in campaign, and remarkably won by 10 percent.

Where Carl sat in the state house literally shaped his influence. The bomb-throwing Democrats, Liz Malia and Cheryl Coakley-Rivera, sat behind him in the chamber. "Whatever the debate, I joke that the lesbians always had my back," says Carl. But as fate would have it he also sat next to Republicans, as the Democrats were too numerous to be contained on just their side of the aisle. He became water-cooler friends with conservatives. "As I'd been seen as the gay rep who got elected on the marriage issue, I was something of a symbol. Thus my tactic was to build meaningful relationships with those predisposed to be against equality." Sciortino says that the Republican he had the most profound impact on was someone who never changed her vote, but her psychological shift was profound. In his first term Carl was mesmerized by a "lunatic fringe right-wing Democrat from Milford, Massachusetts. She was so wacky and vitriolic that I couldn't take my eyes off her." Marie Parente was seventy-six. Sciortino sat beside her. Despite being a Democrat, Parente built her career on maligning homosexuals and immigrants. But Sciortino developed a relationship with her, and "the gays" went from dehumanized to humanized in her eyes. After his freshman year the *Bay Windows* news site reported that "The Gays Love the Freshman Rep and So Does Marie Parente."

A belief in visibility was at the core of Sciortino's life in the public eye. When he was in high school, an LGBT youth group was established by a gay couple in their thirties in nearby New Haven. Carl went religiously every week, despite the fact that he was usually the only kid who showed up. "One other kid showed up once, and of course I immediately had a crush on him. But at least I had a place to talk about being gay." When he was elected in 2004 a number of younger politicos asked him for advice on running for office, "but many still wanted to run from the closet." Carl was appalled. "Never run closeted. If you do you are no Harvey Milk, you're just another closeted politician. Win or lose, why would you start your political career in the closet?"

In 2013 Sciortino had a chance of making history when he ran in a special election for the US Congress 5th District in Massachusetts. He was diagnosed as HIV positive in 2010 while he was in the state house. After the initial shock, he realized at some point he needed to go public. But as he prepared for the 2013 congressional race he was concerned that announcing it in the midst of the campaign might be seen as a play for sympathy. He would do it after the race—win or lose. Carl did lose, coming third in the primary behind Katherine Clark, with 16 percent of the vote. He resigned from the state house and became the chief executive of the AIDS Action Committee of Massachusetts. He went public with his status. Carl called his friend Marc Solomon and said, "Between us we know every high-profile gay person in his city—tell me, who is public about their HIV status? We could think of no one," recalls Carl. Visibility applied even more strongly to HIV/AIDS. "Harvey Milk said 'Hope is never silent,' and when it comes to HIV silence equals death. I knew too many people with HIV who were out as gay but had built a total closet of shame around HIV. But when it comes to HIV visibility we are going backwards, because people live healthier and longer with HIV it's easier to go back into the closet." Carl hears white gay men say "it's not about us any more," but that's not true. "Yes, the disparities between black and white are high, but the bulk of new infections are still white gay men." Considering the power of his visibility, I ask Sciortino if he would stand again for elective office. "I have the itch. I have the bug," he told me in 2015. "I love politics but I'm happy to walk away from it for a while. I was so young in office. I never wanted to be trapped." But it is clear that he wants to re-enter the fray one day.

On the other side of the Atlantic, Adrian Trett grew up in the epitome of an English country market town. Norwich is more a collection of villages than a city. A nine-hundred-year-old Norman castle sits at the center, and cobblestone lanes flow down to rivers, leafy suburbs, and working-class terraces. But in Cringleford, on the outskirts of the city, the teenaged Trett endured years of physical and verbal bullying for his otherness. There was anxiety, depression, isolation, and suicide attempts. To cope, Adrian obsessively studied to the point where fibromyalgia (an inflammation of the central nervous system) consumed him, and he was bedbound for a year. He recovered from that and began to feel at peace at university in Kent, but once he had graduated and begun working in London, the isolation and anxiety returned. Shy and lacking confidence, like many men he took comfort first in online brokered hook-ups and then drug-fueled sexual escapades. Thoughts of suicide returned, but Adrian began to see deliberately contracting HIV as a method of self-harm. The self-destructive behavior led to the almost inevitable HIV-positive diagnosis, and he was quickly abandoned by those he thought of as friends.

Adrian righted his own ship, despite the fact that his strain of HIV was and is particularly resistant to some of the HIV drugs that have been successful (he relies on AZT). His political activism led him to be selected by the Liberal Democrats for the inner London Labour Party safe seat of Vauxhall, a neighborhood of spies and queers and the looming modernist riverside headquarters of the British intelligence services—MI5 and MI6 sits directly opposite celebrated gay bathhouses under the train tracks. Vauxhall had become such a hub for the gay community that in the 2015 election, the only major party candidate in the seat who was not gay was the incumbent Labour MP.

But as the election of May 2015 approached, Trett discovered that a jealous rival within his own party was about to out him as a former drug user and as HIV positive. He had no choice but to get ahead of the story and bare his soul to the media. Sitting in the café atrium in the British Parliament eighteen months later, Trett is still astonished at the whirlwind of attention that the story generated. He recalls that a small proportion of the thousands of messages he received were negative— but those were vicious attacks blaming him for being the architect of not only his virus, but of bringing Sodom and Gormorrah to Britain. Richard Littlejohn, the infamous columnist in the largest-selling British newspaper, the *Daily Mail,* wrote in the paper, "Would you want an ex-porn star who has tried to commit suicide by HIV, while under the influence of recreational drugs, representing you at Westminster?" He ridiculed everything from Trett's name to behavior, and dubbed him the "monster raving loony candidate." It was exhausting, but for every nasty attack there were a dozen emotional thank-you's for breaking the taboo of being HIV positive in public. The Liberal Democrats were never going to win Vauxhall, but Adrian Trett did creditably in a very tough year for his party.

Back in America, when Carl Sciortino was leaving the Massachusetts legislature, Bob Poe was considering his future. By Labor Day of September 2015, he had decided to run for the newly created 10th US Congressional District in Florida. Poe had long been a fixture of the Florida Democratic party. A successful former state party chair, he made his money in broadcasting and communications and helped bring the Orlando Magic basketball team to central Florida. Later in life he discovered a talent for photographic art. He had money, friends, confidence, and backing. The Florida 10th takes in much of central and south Orlando and the swampy forest to the west, and it borders the Villages, one of the largest retirement communities in America, and includes the iconic Disney World. The district had been redrawn to be so solidly Democratic that the only race that mattered was the primary in late August 2016.

Poe was up against some heavyweight opponents. Val Demings, the Orlando police chief between 2007 and 2011, was one of the very few African American women to hold such a high-level position in law enforcement. Demings was also the darling of the Democratic establishment and had run the Republican incumbent close in 2012, when it was a much safer Republican seat. Poe also had to contend with former state senator Geraldine Thompson, another powerful black woman, and the "Bernie" candidate, Fatima Fahmy, backed by Sanders luminaries such as Cornell West. The new Florida 10th is "majority-minority"— 27 percent black and 23 percent Hispanic—with the Democratic primary skewed even more toward minority voters. The displaced Republican incumbent, Daniel Webster, argued that the district was "designed for one thing: to elect a minority." Poe's husband happens to be black, but it was still going to be tough for him to present himself as the authentic voice of the marginalized black community of the district with Demings and Thompson in the race.

Poe was perceived to be a strong candidate, but his life story was colorful. In elementary school his family moved from Long Island, New York, to Sarasota, Florida. The Democratic Party headquarters were opposite his father's store, and the local politicos let him hang out. A move to Orlando in high school placed him next to Disney World, and as a seventeen-year-old his summer job was playing Winnie the Pooh's bouncy friend Tigger in the amusement park. As he later told the journalist Tom Dyer, in the 1970s the "character department at Walt Disney World was one of the few places in the world where it was safe to be gay . . . I'd been told that being gay was wrong—on all sorts of levels—and here were these great people."

Poe's sexuality was in flux. He had only dated girls as a teen, and indeed he had been unfazed in dating one of the four black girls in his school, at the time as taboo as dating a boy. He was also repressing the experience of being molested as a child in Sarasota. "There was a lot of shame," Poe told Dyer. "It wasn't until years later in therapy that I realized the imprint of that experience, and how it conflicted and confused my sexuality." At the 1972 Democratic National Convention in Miami, Poe fell in love with an older man. To the older man it was a fling, but was more to Bob; it was heartbreaking. After a stint in California as a tour manager, Bob was back in Florida married to a stunning woman, a baby girl on the way, and slipping off for same-sex encounters in the shadowy corners of central Florida. It was "unclear where I was in the spectrum," Poe says. "I was never a denier, but I'd avoid pride parades. I was careful about getting a little too close." He was living on an edge, but politics still drew him in. In 1980 Poe ran for the Florida state senate seat to the southwest of Orlando, receiving less than a third of the vote in a head-to-head Democratic primary.

The guilt and confusion around his sexuality fueled his alcoholism and put understandable strain on his family life. In 1994 he got sober, but by his own account he continued to spiral out of control, seeking out experiences and adventure but with a self-destructive streak. When he met Ken Brown in 2008, he knew that he couldn't carry the secrets any longer. Brown had been a millworker in Ohio for almost thirty years, had raised a daughter, and was also putting his life back together. They were a matched couple. Bob and Ken moved back to Orlando together and came out by osmosis, dinner party by dinner party. In 2012 he told Dyer, "Hiding was destructive for me, and for the people around me. Now I know I can be totally out, totally authentic."

That turned out not to be fully true.

On June 9, Bob Poe announced to the world that he was HIV positive and had been for the past eighteen years. He returned to Tom Dyer, the journalist to whom he had bared his soul four years previously, to tell the story. Poe noted that he was healthy and had been lucky enough to benefit from the early wave of AZT anti-viral drugs. His immunologist, Edwin DeJesus, said, "Bob takes one pill a day that prevents the HIV virus from replicating in his system. And because there's no detectable virus, transmission to others is also unlikely." But the emotional strain had been high. Poe told his friend Dyer of how it felt receiving the news in 1998: "It hits you and you forget to breathe, then your mind goes blank and then you wish it would stay blank because you project the worst, particularly back in those days. And I had to go home and tell my wife—she's the first person I told."

Two weeks before the primary election, I asked Poe about coming out as HIV positive in the midst of the campaign. "It was a very difficult decision— a decision some of the people closest to me disagreed with," he said. Indeed, throughout our conversation he repeated that acknowledging his HIV status had caused ruptures in his personal relationships. Poe described a momentum inside of him that ultimately pushed him into going public. There were a myriad of factors. First, there was the fear that as he entered the political fray someone else would tell the secret: "The fear of being outed was always on the back of my mind. The pathology of hiding can be a very dark place." He likened it to his experience as being a survivor of child sexual abuse. "It is our secrets that make us sick." He laughs in the memory of how much the secret controlled him. "I would go so far as to peel the labels off my medication bottles—not just the name, the whole thing. I'd then wrap them in a separate bag and drive to a dumpster far away from home." He looks at me. "That's not normal behavior," he says with understatement.

As the primary campaign began to gear up, Poe started to dread going into his immunology doctor's office. "There are only a couple of reasons why you are there," he stresses. "I would imagine sitting in the waiting room and one of my TV commercials would come on, or I'd be recognized by someone. Politics can be a mean sport. I knew I could be outed at any time." The fear never left him.

"Every time I got a phone call from a reporter I would think, is this it?" It became important to control his own fate. "When they are running you out of town, get to the front of the line and make it look like it's a parade." But there were also moments in the campaign that pricked his conscience.

He visited a wellness center that primarily helped Haitian and Caribbean immigrants. The head of the clinic told him that HIV infections were on the rise in central Florida, and probably half as many known infections were unknown. The stigma and fear that surround HIV stopped people being tested and treated. Someone like Bob could stand proud and say, "Look at me, I have HIV and I'm healthy and successful." Then, two weeks later at a rally, a distraught woman asked him for help. She had just been diagnosed as HIV positive and thought it was her death sentence. "I gave her the usual platitudes," Bob says, "but I really wanted to just comfort her and let her know she wasn't alone. But I wasn't at the point in my journey to be able to reveal to her." He walked away deeply upset, conflicted and unfulfilled.

Like Chris Smith and Carl Sciortino, Bob Poe's coming out as HIV positive was more painful than his coming out as gay, but after there was great relief. The importance of HIV-positive elected officials was demonstrated by Poe's experience. "There was no template to follow," he says. "The needle is moving much slower because there aren't as many visible leaders who are HIV positive. People in the campaign were saying it would end my political career."

When Poe joined the primary race in early 2016 polls put him at 7 percent, Thompson at 22 percent, and Demings at 44 percent. It looked like a lost cause. Then the Pulse nightclub attack happened. Situated in the south Orlando part of the district, Pulse was the preeminent LGBT dance club in the city. At 2 a.m. on June 12, Omar Mateen used a submachine gun, semiautomatic rifle, and Glock pistol to murder forty-nine men and women and severely injure fifty-three more. They were mostly young gay men. The attack was immediately framed as an attack on the LGBT community, and the horrific scenes and heartrending narratives went around the world. It was Latin Night at the club, and 90 percent of the patrons that night were Hispanic. Orlando became the byword for murderous homophobia. Despite the Pulse attack, Poe says he felt surprisingly little homophobia or HIV phobia in the primary campaign. What about being a gay politician in America today? I ask him. Poe says he has seen so much change in the last few years when it comes to gay identity: "You used to run on it, or run from it, but now it's neither, it's not an issue." By early August, after plowing considerable money into TV advertising, Poe had made it up to 18 percent, tied with Thompson, but Dennings was still at 48 percent. Could he make up the difference in the last few weeks?

He could not, and the world would remain without an out HIV-positive parliamentarian. The final result was Deming 57 percent, Thompson 20 percent, and Poe 17 percent. In the purported Year of the Woman, the African American ceiling breaker would be the new Florida 10th representative in the US House of Representatives. If there is one part of the LGBTQ community that needs voice it is those who are HIV positive, and especially those of color and gender nonconforming. While medical advances have transformed the nature of the epidemic, the consequences are huge. HIV-positive men are still twice as likely to commit suicide, and infection rates vary widely by access to information, resources, and peer groups. In 2017 the Centers for Disease Control found that the lifetime risk for HIV infection in the United States was one in 524 for straight men, one in eleven for white gay men, one in five for Latino gay men, and one in two for black gay men.

Rory O'Neill—a.k.a. Panti Bliss or the Queen of Ireland—is not surprised by the enduring taboo of HIV: "People still don't understand and fear is still part of the ether. We have a fabulous history of blaming people for their sexual behavior in Ireland. The stigma against HIV even endures in the gay community itself." While he was open about his status very early on, Rory recalls how tough it was emotionally and psychologically. "It was harder to tell my parents about the HIV thing than the gay thing: the gay thing is part of who I am and it's not my fault. But I have taken on some of that stigma and shaming ickiness internally. I felt in a way it was my fault. I could intellectualize that I wasn't to blame, but when telling my parents it felt like my fault. You should never have to tell your parents that you are going to die before them."

Figure 8.1 Zakhele Mbhele. Credit: Zakhele Mbhele.

8

More Like Hell Than Heaven

The Dangerous Places In Between

There have been great cinematic moments of euphoric triumph in Dublin, London, Washington, and Wellington, but there remains an unsettling polarity in the state of LGBTQ rights around the world today. The march toward equality in much of the developed world has sped up to a dizzying pace. At the beginning of 2018, 1.1 billion people live in the two dozen countries where gay marriage is legal; 41 percent are in majority Catholic countries. New laws reflect the reality that views of homosexuality in the West have become wildly more positive. There are lesbian and gay weddings from New Zealand to New England, and same-sex couples can adopt children from Belgium to Brazil. There are growing numbers of out LGBT elected officials, and social values have improved in many countries. The march to equality is not merely a phenomenon of Europe and North America; as a continent, Latin America has dramatically evolved on gay and transgender rights over the last decade. *Time* magazine named Uruguay its country of the year in 2013 based in large part on its introduction of marriage equality. Every Spanish/Portuguese-speaking country in South America (outside of Paraguay) now has openly gay or lesbian or transgender parliamentarians. Even in Asia there are signals of progress. Sunil Babu Pant was elected in the Nepal constitutional assembly elections of 2008, becoming the first gay MP in Asia. He went on to single-handedly persuade the Nepali Supreme Court to recognize the "third gender" community as a specially protected minority group.

But gay and transgender people in most of the world still face extreme violence, social ostracism, and legal repression. Homosexuality remains illegal in seventy-six countries, and in five of those conviction can bring the death penalty: Iran, Mauritania, Saudi Arabia, Sudan, and Yemen. In 2014, Brunei passed a law in which conviction for same-sex acts would bring death by stoning. In 2013 India, the largest democracy in the world, reinstated a 153-year-old law passed under British colonialism branding sex between consenting adults of the same sex "unnatural" and punishable by up to ten years in jail. In South Asia, laws against homosexuality are strictly enforced in Bangladesh, Malaysia, and Pakistan. In 2013 only 2 percent of Pakistanis said that society should accept homosexuals. On the African continent, Uganda, Nigeria, Ethiopia, and Zimbabwe have led the way in state-promoted homophobia.

Despite the great legal progress in Latin America, homophobic attacks continue to devastate lives. In 2013, 292 LGBT individuals were murdered in Brazil, while 2012 saw a 21 percent increase in murders over 2011. According to the advocacy group Grupo Gay da Bahia, 44 percent of all the world's anti-LGBT violence occurs in Brazil. Human Rights Watch has data showing that nearly 100 lesbian, gay, or transgender Hondurans were murdered between 2009 and 2012. In 2012, twenty-four-year-old Chilean Daniel Zamudio was beaten in a Santiago park and had swastikas carved into his skin. He died of his injuries three weeks later. Capitalizing on the public outcry, the conservative President Sebastián Piñera forced through an anti-discrimination bill. In January 2014, eighteen-year-old Joseph Sanchez, who wore women's clothes, was stabbed to death in Belize City.

While Russia and Uganda capture headlines for their anti-gay crusades, the Caribbean is one of the most dangerous regions to be queer. Eleven islands have anti-sodomy laws where men face up to life imprisonment for having sex with other men. In December 2017 the Bermudan parliament actually voted to rescind marriage equality, which had been brought to the island by judicial ruling six months before. Indeed, the Caribbean has begun to rival Africa as the most perilous place to be gay. Emblematic of the extreme homophobia in Jamaica were the deaths of two sixteen-year-olds in Montego Bay in 2011 and 2013. Oshane Gordon was hacked to death by three men in August 2011 for "questionable relations with another man." Two years later Dwayne Jones, a biological boy who identified as a girl, was stabbed, shot, and run over by a car at the hands of a mob at a street dance party for daring to dress as a girl in public. Such murders dovetail with broader social attitudes on the island. Bucking the trend of increasing social tolerance toward homosexuality globally, a 2012 study found 46 percent of Jamaican respondents felt "repulsion" toward homosexuality, while under 6 percent felt "acceptance." Over 80 percent of Jamaicans felt homosexuality was "morally wrong." Those who chose "repulsion" as an option in the survey increased in number between 2011 and 2012. Three-quarters of LGBT Jamaicans have seriously thought about migrating. The majority of LGBT people on the island have experienced some form of harassment or discrimination, but most did not report the incidents to the police.

With Vladimir Putin at the helm, Russia has become the poster child for homophobia. A law against making "propaganda of nontraditional sexual relations" available to minors passed in 2013, making it illegal to suggest that gay relationships were equal to heterosexual relationships or to distribute material on gay rights. It has to be noted, however, that as Russia was being criticized for introducing the gay propaganda law, eight US states effectively did the same thing: Alabama, Arizona, Mississippi, Louisiana, Oklahoma, South Carolina, Texas, and Utah ban the promotion of homosexuality in schools; Alabama and Texas actually compel teachers to describe homosexuality as abhorrent to the general public and as a criminal behavior, even though it is not. In Russia the Moscow pride parade is banned, hate crimes against gays have escalated, and LGBT advocacy groups are driven underground. Gay clubs in Moscow and Saint Petersburg are closed for business. Reacting to international condemnation of the homophobic laws, Putin said that gay people were welcome at the Sochi Olympics, although this was followed by "just leave kids alone, please." In early 2017 the pernicious violence spread to Chechnya. First, gay men were rounded up, detained, beaten, and returned home bloodied. By July the regional *Novaya Gazeta* newspaper was reporting the secret executions of fifty-six gay men. Russia's pivot to repress gay rights spurred copycats in neighboring states. Post-2013, anti-gay propaganda laws were introduced in Lithuania and Ukraine, and proposed in Georgia, Armenia, and Kazakhstan.

The difference between public acceptance of homosexuals in Western and Eastern Europe is stark. In 2010 the Pew Research Center found that support for the statement that "gay men and lesbians should be free to live their own lives as they wish" ranged from 59 percent support in Finland to 92 percent in the Netherlands and Scandinavia, while in the Eastern and Central European countries the high was 65 percent in the Czech Republic, but all other states were below 50 percent with a low of 25 percent support for the statement in Russia. By 2014 Pew found that only 16 percent of Russians said that society should accept homosexuals, but the Czech Republic had gone up to 80 percent.

Homophobic politicians rant that homosexuality is a pernicious white disease imported to Africa, Asia, and Latin America by white European colonists, but history shows otherwise. The anthropologist Margaret Mead found that 60 percent of "primitive" societies not only accepted homosexuality, but institutionalized it. Clellan Ford and Frank Beach found that same-sex relations were considered normal in two-thirds of the seventy-six tribal societies they surveyed from the 1920s to the 1950s. As David Norris notes, "It is extraordinary how the prejudices of a small nomadic tribe in the Middle East spread first to the Roman Empire, then throughout Christendom and Islam, ending up finally in the British Empire, which spread it through the entire globe." Indigenous peoples in New Zealand have long accepted and respected gay people. In his book *Hokakatanga: Māori Sexualities*, Clive Aspin of Auckland University notes that those with same-sex attraction often held positions of importance within their *whanau* (extended family) and *hapu* (clan). They were not rejected nor marginalized, and were considered to be valued members of the community. Indeed, as Christopher Penczak notes, "the creation myths of many traditions involve sexual, bisexual or androgynous motifs, with the world being created by genderless or hermaphrodite beings or through sexual congress between beings of the opposite or same apparent gender." In Filipino creation myths, gods manifest as different genders. *Maguayan* (deity of the sea) can be a man or a woman. *Sidapa* is generally known as the masculine deity of death, but can also be female. In the Indian areas the moon deity is a man; in Visayas, a young androgynous boy. Duane Brayboy wrote in *Indian Country Today* that European settlers—Christian missionaries and Spanish Catholic monks—extinguished the Native American two-spirit tradition before it could be recorded. He notes that when Christopher Columbus encountered two-spirit people, he and his crew threw them into pits with their war dogs and had them torn limb from limb. The American Indian Movement founder, Russell Means, said, "In my culture we have people who dress half-man, half-woman. *Winkte*, we call them in our language. If you are *Winkte*, that is an honorable term and you are a special human being and among my nation and all Plains people, we consider you a teacher of our children and are proud of what and who you are."

> "The Native American belief is that some people are born with the spirits of both genders and express them so perfectly. It is as if they have two spirits in one body" [according to Means]. Native Americans traditionally assign no moral gradient to love or sexuality; a person was judged for their contributions to their tribe and for their character. It was also a custom for parents to not interfere with nature and so among some tribes, children wore gender-neutral clothes until they reached an age where they decided for themselves which path they would walk and the appropriate ceremonies followed. The Two Spirit people in pre-contact Native America were highly revered and families that included them were considered lucky. Indians believed that a person who was able to see the world through the eyes of both genders at the same time was a gift from The Creator. Traditionally, Two Spirit people held positions within their tribes that earned them great respect, such as Medicine Men/Women, shamans, visionaries, mystics, conjurers, keepers of the tribe's oral traditions, conferrers of lucky names for children and adults (it has been said that Crazy Horse received his name from a *Winkte*), nurses during war expeditions, cooks, matchmakers and marriage counselors, jewelry/feather regalia makers, potters, weavers, singers/artists in addition to adopting orphaned children and tending to the elderly. Female-bodied Two Spirits were hunters, warriors, engaged in what was typically men's work and, by all accounts, were always fearless.

One of the most troubling developments cited by LGBT advocates around the world has been the spread of evangelicals from America traveling overseas to promote anti-homosexual agendas. The Southern Poverty Law Center issued a report in July 2013 identifying six American religious groups, including Pat Robertson's American Center for Law and Justice, the Alliance for Defending Freedom, and United Family International as anti-gay Christian groups that brought anti-gay messages to foreign countries. In February 2014, American evangelist Scott Lively and Peter LaBarbera of Americans for Truth about Homosexuality launched a global anti-gay coalition called the Coalition for Family Values at the National Press Club in Washington, DC. Lively outlined the goals of the organization "to promote and protect the natural family as the essential foundation of civilization, and family values as the sources and guide to mainstream culture in every society, while advocating reasonable tolerance to those who choose to live discreetly outside the mainstream." Lively noted he had been to Russia three times. Caleb Orozco, a gay rights advocate in Belize, bemoans how American intervention revolved around exporting homophobia rather than exporting homosexuality. "Before the arrival of the anti-gay groups, most people had a live-and-let-live attitude toward gays," he said, adding that the "controversy really gave people permission to express their hate in a way they didn't see they had permission to do before."

The Spear of the Nation: The First African

There are millions of LGBTQ Africans, but almost all are forced to hide from the light. Until a few years ago not a single out black African had been elected anywhere on the continent. On May 7, 2014, Zakhele Mbhele changed that when he was elected as a member of South Africa's parliament. Three years later he remains unique. Mbhele is young, poised, and urbane, sporting trendy glasses on a boyish face. When elected he was only twenty-nine years old. Born in Durban on the Indian ocean to a Zulu family, Mbhele moved to Johannesburg when he was eleven. He plunged into gay rights activism at the University of Witwatersrand, reactivating a dormant student organization and organizing Jo'burg pride. I ask whether growing up gay in his Africa was a constant battle. "Not really," he says. "Our experience is strongly mediated by class, access to services, amenities, spaces. If you have those you have a pretty easy life, very little fear of violence and discrimination." While Mbhele's family is Zulu, he notes that he is from the city and not the countryside. "Ethnic labels in urban South Africa are nominal, there is more of a generic black urban culture," he says. But as Mbhele stresses, his story is not the story told by the vast majority of gay men and women in South Africa, let alone the continent as a whole.

Even when national law recognizes gay rights, the distance between legal niceties and the reality of daily life can be a chasm. South Africa's constitution is by far the most gay-friendly in Africa, entrenching marriage, adoption, and anti-discrimination rights, but the fate of gays and lesbians on the ground can be horrific. Nelson Mandela evolved dramatically in his thinking on gay rights and the way to approach the HIV/AIDS epidemic, the latter motivated in part by the death of his son Makgatho. But day-to-day gay, lesbian, and transgender South Africans do not live in the constitution. Violence is used as a punishment for breaking gender rules; the "corrective rape" of lesbians is driven by the view that victims can be violently converted away from same-sex attraction. In a 2012 *New Yorker* article titled "Violated Hopes," Charlene Hunter-Gault noted that since the end of apartheid at least thirty-one lesbians had been killed in attacks motivated by their sexual orientation. In a nation where a woman is raped every seventeen seconds and lesbians face assault twice as often as heterosexual women, Hunter-Gault told the story of the murder of Eudy Simelane, once a player on the national soccer team and one of the few out lesbians in the township of Kwa Thema, who was stabbed to death in 2008. Gay men are equally vulnerable. Beginning in 2010, a well-organized gang lured at least eight men from Johannesburg, along with an unspecified number from Cape Town, to apartments and then beat and strangled them to death and doused their bodies in acid.

While homophobic hate crimes may be on the rise in Eastern Europe and the Caribbean, Africa remains a very dangerous place to be gay. The Pew organization asked adults whether society should accept homosexuals in six sub-Saharan African nations in 2013, and the levels of tolerance ranged from 8 percent in Kenya to 1 percent in Nigeria. Even in South Africa the figure was only 32 percent. In Uganda, where gay men live in daily fear of their well-being, a law to make homosexuality a capital offense percolated for years—promoted by ruling party MP David Bahati, in cahoots with the US evangelist Scott Lively. The "anti-homosexuality" bill legislated Bahati's publically expressed desire to "kill every last gay person." Attacks on gay Ugandans reached a crescendo in October 2010 when the Kampala-based *Rolling Stone* newspaper, under the headline "Hang Them," published the names, photos, and addresses of a hundred Ugandans they identified as gay. One of the named, David Kato, sued the newspaper to stop them publishing the names of men and women with claims that they were gay. On January 26, 2011, Kato was beaten to death with a hammer inside his house. Before the murder, the Ugandan Minister of State for Ethics and Integrity, James Nsaba Buturo, declared that "homosexuals can forget about human rights."

The bill was ultimately passed by the Ugandan legislature in December 2013 with the death penalty clauses removed. President Museveni said that before he would sign it into law he wanted to see "scientific evidence" as to whether homosexuality was genetic or a lifestyle choice. After receiving evidence from government-appointed scientists that there was no evidence to suggest that individuals were born homosexual, he signed the bill. Museveni's statement was a shocking jumble of attacks on gays and Western aid agencies. He accused the West of recruiting children for homosexual prostitution, and called gays abnormal and disgusting. Desmond Tutu responded by saying there is "no scientific basis or genetic rationale for love . . . There is no scientific justification for prejudice and discrimination, ever." The day after Museveni signed the bill, the Kampala *Red Pepper* newspaper's front page featured the banner headline "Exposed!" Underneath it said "Uganda's 200 Top Homos Named," and under that, "M7 (Museveni) Signs Anti-Gay Bill."

David Kato's death was not an isolated incident. Prominent gay rights activists have been murdered across the continent over the last decade, sending a devastating message to others about revealing their homosexuality. In 2004 Fannyann Viola Eddy, founder of the first gay rights organization in Sierra Leone, was gang-raped, stabbed, and had her neck broken in the Freetown offices of her organization. In April 2011 the South African lesbian activist Noxolo Nogwaza was gang-raped, stoned, then stabbed to death east of Johannesburg. In July 2013 Eric Ohena Lembembe was tortured and killed in Cameroon after issuing a public warning about the threat posed by "anti-gay thugs." In February Gambia's president, Yahya Jammeh, said that gay people were "vermin" and that homosexuals should be fought as if they were malaria-carrying mosquitoes. "As far as I am concerned, LGBT can only stand for Leprosy, Gonorrhea, Bacteria, and Tuberculosis, all of which are detrimental to human existence," Jammeh concluded.

President Goodluck Jonathan of Nigeria, Africa's second most powerful country, signed into law in January 2014 a bill that banned gay marriage and imposed penalties of up to fourteen years for homosexual activity. The language was terrifying to Nigerians who happened to be gay: "Any person who registers, operates, or participates in gay clubs, societies or organisations or directly or indirectly makes a public show of a same-sex amorous relationship in Nigeria commits an offence and shall be liable on conviction to a term of ten years in prison." In the weeks following the implementation of the law, gay men were arrested in four northern Nigerian states. In Bauchi, police tortured four gay men into naming another 168, and then began tracking down and arresting them. In February, an armed mob invaded the homes of fourteen "suspected homosexuals" in the capital Abuja and beat them severely.

The climate in Africa is not entirely without glimmers of sunlight; in the face of shadowy violence and legal darkness, a few prominent Africans have raised their voices. The prize-winning Kenyan novelist Binyavanga Wainaina came out in an online essay in 2014 at the age of forty-three, in large part to protest the gathering storm of repression against gay Africans. "I can't sleep at night because there are people who I may know or who I don't even know... who may be dying or being beaten or being tortured right now in a Nigerian cell or three weeks ago in a Ugandan one," he told the Associated Press. In an open letter to African leaders the former president of Mozambique, Joaquim Chissano, said that "we can no longer afford to discriminate on the basis of sex, ethnicity, migrant status, sexual orientation and gender identity, or any other basis—we need to unleash the potential of everyone." In response to those who considered homosexuality to be "unAfrican" Chissano quoted Nelson Mandela: "To be free is not merely to cast off one's chains but to live in a way that respects and enhances the freedom of others." Former archbishop Desmond Tutu has long been an advocate for gay rights and says that he would refuse to go to a homophobic heaven. "No, I would say sorry, I mean I would much rather go to the other place," he says.

Indeed, the African leaders who fan the flames of homophobia may be playing into something much deeper within a psyche built on secrets, closets, and fear. *Mother Jones* analyzed the global distribution of Google searches of gay porn sites in 2013. The top three countries where searches for "man fucking man" on those specific porn sites were not America, the Netherlands, or Britain but Kenya, Pakistan, and Uganda.

Despite the fact that Presidents Mugabe, Museveni, and Jammeh have railed against homosexuality as "un-African," *Boy Wives and Female Husbands*, edited by Stephen O. Murray and Will Roscoe, and *Heterosexual Africa* by Marc Epprecht give lie to the notion. Gay Africans were going about their lives with little fuss before Europeans began colonizing the continent in the sixteenth century. The sixteenth-century English adventurer Andrew Battel wrote in the 1590s of the Imbangala of Angola: "They are beastly in their living, for they have men in women's apparel, whom they keep among their wives." Gay sex was recorded as commonplace across the continent, most notably in what are today the countries of Benin, Cameroon, Gabon Ghana, Sudan, South Africa, and Egypt, with marriages codified in some tribes. Lesbianism was also common.

Even before Zakhele Mbhele came out at eighteen, politics was a passion for him. "It took root in high school," he tells me. "Reading newspapers, talking, the role of politics became more and more relevant and interesting as I grew." When the Democratic Alliance (DA) asked him to run for the Student's Representative Council at Wits University, he was "ripe for the picking to be drafted." I ask him whether his identity ever gave him pause about running for office. "I was aware of it and thinking," he answers, "but in a generally conservative and prejudiced environment my concerns were assuaged by my openly gay colleagues and staff in the provincial parliament." Indeed, Zakhele had more ambivalence about his party loyalty at the start. He tells me he split his first vote in 2004 between the DA and African National Congress (ANC). There were no LGBT role models growing up, so Zakhele gravitated to the intellect and vision of President Thabo Mbeki—setting aside Mbeki's catastrophic blinkers on the causes of HIV/AIDS.

When I first talk with Zakhele it is the day after his swearing-in ceremony, and the symbolism of his election has not sunk in fully. "I'm still discerning the personal meaning of this milestone is because it caught me unaware," he muses. I'm surprised that he didn't know that he was to be the first. "It never once crossed my mind that it was the case," he continues, "but it is an historic milestone. In this country we revel in narratives of first black man to do this or that—as soon as somebody opens a doorway, it makes it easier for others to come through afterwards. We have a huge shortage of LGBT role models. I know what that can mean for younger LGBT people's sense of affirmation, hope. Even if they are in difficult situations, it does, and can, get better."

Like the hundreds of others who have gone before in other countries, at other times Zakhele is nervous of being identified as the gay MP: "I know what it means as a historical milestone, but I'm not walking around thinking of myself as the first openly gay black MP in Africa or singularly defining myself by it." "But what's the impact of presence?" I ask. He describes the different orbits of his life. There is the very open Democratic Alliance family and caucus, and then the outside world. When he was the spokesperson for the premier of the Western Cape, Helen Zille, "everyone assumed I was straight. I told one person and the next day everyone had changed their pronouns." Did it come up at all in the election campaign?" I push. "No. Not at all," he replies. But then again, Zakhele was running on a list of candidates—number five of 56—without the magnifying focus of a constituency. There is little doubt it would have been tougher to be elected from a single-member district in South Africa, but Mbhele does not think it would have been insurmountable. "There are ways to mitigate against it," he says. He actually believes that challenges of youth and class may have been more difficult to overcome than his sexual orientation.

Mbhele is surprisingly relaxed about the historical marker he represents, but the symbolism of that moment, in a continent where for millions being gay equals a life of fearful secrets and risk of imprisonment or death, cannot be underestimated. In 2015 Mbhele told an LGBT-friendly life insurance company web magazine that "the first tool of LGBTI activism is visibility. My first Pride at the age of nineteen was very significant for me. I went all alone. I didn't have any gay friends. But I knew that I wanted to be at Pride so I went by myself and I walked in the parade by myself. I enjoyed it so much that it didn't matter that I was there by myself. Homophobia and prejudice shame and coerce gay people into being invisible and to hide. Therefore the primary counter against that is to stand up and say no I will not be silenced and invisible. You will know that I am here and you will know that I am gay." In July 2016, Mbhele became the shadow minister of police. The once illegal man was now watching over the police.

There have been gay black MPs in Africa, but the dangers of coming out are terrifying. Themba Bwalya (a pseudonym) was a national member of Parliament representing a very poor district in a central African country—one of the nations where homosexuality is illegal. Many of his friends and a small circle of supporters knew he was gay when he ran for office, but he had not come out to his family. Indeed, he denied being gay in the media. When I asked whether he had been nervous that his sexual orientation might be revealed in his first run for office, he said that he was afraid that it was going to be an issue but decided to take a risk. "My opponent did bring it up during campaign, but he was too unpopular for people to listen to him." Once in Parliament he achieved some prominence but believes he was never considered for a ministerial position because of his sexuality. "There is hypocrisy around here, everybody would smile at you as if everything is in order. Most of them know but if I dared to come out then that would be another story," he says. Nevertheless, on a day-to-day basis his work is not focused on gay rights, rather on seeking to lift his constituents from their poverty. "Socially, economically, it is the poorest constituency," he notes. "No potable water, no health facilities, no secondary schools, delinquency among the youth, early marriages, no infrastructure. The list is endless." Bwalya tells me that he has "built about seven small bridges, a health center (lacking equipment), drilled about twenty boreholes, built fifteen school blocks, and one community secondary school."

Would he come out at some point in the future? Bwalya says the climate in his country has become even more pernicious over the last few years. "The religious institutions and media have really poisoned the environment so much that the politicians are blowing up the issue beyond proportion. If I came out everybody will be in arms to chop off my head and I suspect during this campaign period most of my enemies will take advantage of this to bring me down," he told me. "For me it is an open secret to everyone. What is remaining is for people to hear it from my mouth. Two people tried to come out, but it led to a backlash. Unless I am assured of my security and well-being after coming out then it is a risky business. Nobody would be willing to employ me."

But ultimately Bwalya believes that visibility is the way forward, by demonstrating that politicians who happen to be gay are just as capable of representing their district. "If I give scholarships to poor kids to finish secondary school, if I provide potable water and a health center to a community, if I build a nursery school, if I build a bridge across a river, people will see my good work and support me. Even if my opponent stands on hill tops and declares me gay, no one will care. In some communities people worry what they will eat today and tomorrow, before they care whether their member of Parliament is gay." Bwalya hopes to pursue a postgraduate degree in human rights or work in an international NGO. "If my government was not homophobic, I would ask for a position as an ambassador," he laments.

Shira and Itzak, 2015

Shira Banki was a golden girl. She was from Jerusalem. She had long curly black hair. She was sixteen. She liked boys. She was Jewish. She was opinionated. She loved playing the piano. She wasn't gay. Itzak Shmuli was a golden boy. He was from Tel Aviv. He was grown. He was the leader of the student movement. He was Jewish. He liked boys. He was a member of the Israel Parliament. He was private.

Shira went to the Jerusalem gay pride parade because her parents had taught her to love. There was a deranged man with a knife, crazy eyes brimming with anger and hate. He was an ultra-orthodox Jew. He had served ten years in prison for stabbing three people at the 2005 pride parade. He had been released three weeks before.

Itzak's closet was large but walled in. Many colleagues, and some enemies, knew that he was gay but he was not out. On the day of his swearing-in to the Knesset a number of MPs from religious parties walked out. Some LGBT activists accused Shmuli of cowardice for not saying who he was, though they stopped short of outing him.

Shira died at that parade. Itzak came out. Shira's parents Uri and Mika said, "this innocence, beauty, happiness, and goodness fell on the altar of hatred." Itzak thought of Shira and said, "The knife is being wielded at my community . . . we've kept silent. I've kept silent. No more." Shira Banki had Gilbert Baker's rainbow flag pinned to her black shorts when she died.

If religion and gay rights were in a relationship, their Facebook status would be "it's complicated." David Wolpe, *Newsweek*'s Most influential rabbi of 2012 and a leading conservative thinker, says that "same-sex marriage is simple, sacred, and very Jewish indeed." He notes that "Jews support gay marriage at even greater rates than comparably liberal non-Jews," speculating that this has something to do with Jewish values of justice, compassion, and what it means to be the "other" in a dangerous world. It was once thought that Catholic societies would be among the most resistant to gay rights, but today over a half million people live in Catholic majority countries where gay marriage exists. The Argentine priest Jorge Mario Bergoglio, today known as Pope Francis, raised eyebrows when four months after ascending to the papacy he mused, "If someone is gay and he searches for the Lord and has good will, who am I to judge?" In response Archbishop Desmond Tutu gushed, "He's taken a selfie! He's a tremendous breath of fresh air," and the LGBT magazine *The Advocate* named Pope Francis their 2013 Person of the Year. They overlooked the fact that just a few years earlier, in 2010, the then-Archbishop of Buenos Aires fundamentally opposed the introduction of gay marriage in his native Argentina, calling it a "real and dire anthropological throwback." But he supported the idea of civil unions for gay couples in Argentina, and in March 2014 he repeated that view as Pope when he said that one should "regulate diverse situations of cohabitation, driven by the need to regulate economic aspects among persons, as for instance to assure medical care." But Francis has managed to stir the pot in more negative ways. In 2016 he seemingly referred to transgender people as the "annihilation of man as image of god."

If anything the Anglicans are even more riven by questions of LGBT rights. At the time when marriage equality was introduced in the United Kingdom in 2013, 38 percent of Anglicans were in support while 47 percent were opposed, but by 2016 the balance had switched with 45 percent in support and only 37 percent against. In 2016 Nicholas Chamberlain was consecrated Bishop of Grantham, in the face of some objections. In July 2016, the Anglican Church of Canada voted to authorize same-sex marriage and 54 percent of Australian Christians were in favor of same-sex marriage as the issue came to a head in 2017. But the Anglicans of Africa and the Caribbean remain adamantly opposed to equality, and a schism in the church of 85 million worldwide is all but inevitable.

Mormon scriptures predispose members of the faith to be deeply suspicious of homosexuality, but they also have a libertarian streak that creates a space for some visible LGBT leaders and allies in Utah. Indeed, the out lesbian Jackie Biskupski was elected mayor of Salt Lake City in 2015 and soon after married her partner, Betty Iverson, creating a blended family of two mothers and two children. In 2017 the Salt Lake City council became equally balanced between straight and lesbian or gay board members. Biskupski and incumbent Derek Kitchen were joined by newly elected out officials Amy Fowler and Chris Wharton, balancing the city council four to four. *Kitchen v. Herbert* was the case that brought marriage equality to Utah.

The Middle East has the most pernicious and repressive homophobic laws, but the Islamic faith's relationship to gay rights is also complex. In 2009 a survey of five hundred British Muslims found not one who would say that homosexuality was morally acceptable. In France the figure was 35 percent, and in Germany 19 percent. But when the German Bundestag voted for marriage equality in 2017, all six Muslim MPs voted in favor of the measure and Lebanese, Turkish, and Indonesian LGBT groups exist on the fringes of society.

Black, Brown, and Gay

Conventional wisdom would have it that there is a heightened pressure when a person is both black and gay. Africa and the Caribbean are two of the places on earth where it is most dangerous to be gay. In the United States, African American legislators, drawn from urban areas and often with strong connections to historically black churches, are expected to be less inclined to support gay rights measures. Indeed, in 2014 Pew found that 53 percent of whites supported gay marriage but only 42 percent of blacks did. By 2017 those numbers had increased to 64 percent and 51 percent, respectively. Forty-four percent of black Protestants support gay marriage (although this is higher than the support among white Evangelicals, at 35%). Similarly, Latino legislators rooted in Catholic communities might also be expected to be less inclined than the average Democrat to vote for marriage equality. However, the reality is quite different. The support for same-sex marriage among African American and Latino legislators between 2005 and 2013 was much higher than among their white, Asian, and Pacific Islander colleagues. A full 78 percent of all African American legislators voted for marriage equality, and 82 percent of Latinos. Only 56 percent of whites did. It is true that African Americans and Latinos are much more likely to be Democrats, but Democrats voting against gay marriage are no more likely to be black or Latino.

Nowhere was this more manifest than the battle over gay marriage in Maryland in 2011. As a state Maryland is one-third black, but Baltimore, its major urban center, is two-thirds black. State house member Mary Washington's entire life has centered on building coalitions. Her story is emblematic of how presence matters. Washington is a black woman from a middle-class suburb of Philadelphia, educated in a Catholic school. She came out at thirteen. Her life has revolved around navigating alliances. She is a professor of sociology, an elder of her Presbyterian Church, and a radical feminist. Growing up, Mary had a sense of relative privilege rather than oppression. As the oldest of six children, there was a sense of entitlement. "I was raised in the house my father was raised in," she says. "He was raised in a middle-class Jewish neighborhood—there were just a couple of African Americans. When folks moved to the suburbs he stayed put." That meant Washington saw decline and inequality from her porch. Mary tells me that she grew up thinking that "if I am in a position to use my relative privilege, I should." Discrimination was more of a puzzle to be solved than a direct threat. As she navigated college she threw herself into organizations and felt competing tugs: "I had to be a woman, I had to be gay, I had to be African American." She believes that identity division still plagues the movement. Washington calls herself a coalition-builder by nature: "I was always the head of the thing that could bring people together."

Elected to the Maryland House of Delegates from Baltimore in 2006, she went about making friends and allies. When marriage equality finally passed the Maryland state house in February 2012, it passed by three votes in the Senate and nine in the House of Delegates. "Did your presence matter?" I ask. Washington's response is unequivocal. "I am the only out African American [legislator] in the entire state of Maryland." I push further: "How about in the Senate?" "I personally secured three votes," she says. "Just because of my relationships. That was the margin." The three were a fellow church-going African American, a conservative Democrat, and a nervous Republican. Mary Washington had a pulpit—a legitimacy—unlike any other. She could speak to "black folks" and the "black church." During the campaign she was on Fox TV arguing with a homophobic pastor. "The audience was going with him," she recalls, "but I said the great legacy for black people is that our movement inspires people around the world, something we should be proud of." Mary is clear. "I could say that, a white legislator couldn't say that. On the floor of the House I was the antidote to the religious pastors that spoke." Maryland also benefitted from having a comparatively large cohort of out LGBTQ legislators. There were seven, and then Peter Murphy came out on the floor of the House in 2011 just before the big vote. The out lesbian and gay state house caucus met regularly for two years, and when it came to the final vote Washington says there was considerable pressure applied to black Democrats and white Catholic women to vote for gay marriage, but Mary is still irritated that the straight male white Democrats were given a pass to vote against equality.

Even once the legislative vote was won, there were still two hurdles to surmount. First, Governor O'Malley had to sign the bill. Washington notes that O'Malley, despite being known as a progressive Democrat, is at his core a conservative Catholic and many of his major donors were "very uncomfortable" with gay rights. "But toward the end he hit his stride. His wife was very influential in driving him forward on the issue." Then the law had to be adopted by the voters of Maryland as a whole. Question 6 was put on the November 2012 ballot. Now Mary Washington's voice carried far beyond the state house. She recalls that "the polling told us that our only chance was to win African American women ages thirty-five to fifty-three." That 7 percent was the swing vote. "If we could get them we would win the referendum." In public speeches Mary stressed fairness and equality, and avoided framing the question in civil rights terms because that was "such a flash point for older African Americans." She had to battle for support even within her own family. Her sister has a "big church ideology and almost didn't vote for Kerry because of abortion," Washington tells me. But she argues that the black community's progress on gay rights is not as shocking as some may think. "African Americans and working-class whites are used to espousing a certain view, and then doing something else in the privacy of the voting booth. At the end of the day we were able to remind them about their brothers and sisters, nieces and nephews." Plus, the gay and lesbian state legislators had built solid resumes with the constituencies they needed to persuade. "Alliances with labor didn't happen because of marriage equality. I was already a strong progressive and union loyalty was there. I was bringing money and jobs into the district." Even if working-class and religious voters struggled to cross over completely, Mary Washington explicitly asked them to abstain. "I never ask you for anything; if you can't support me, can you not vote against me?" she pleaded. Ultimately the results showed that the strategy worked: some people did pass on the referendum and just voted on the election races.

Figure 9.1 Sarah McBride. Credit: Human Rights Campaign.

9

Cinders Goes to the Ball

Sarah McBride and the Future of Transgender Politics

Sarah McBride is unable to read books of fiction.

"What. At all?" I am incredulous.

"No," she answers.

"The classics? Literary novels?"

"No."

"Detective novels?"

Also no.

"Chick-lit?"

"No, just can't do it."

"Pulp fiction?"

We stare at each other. She is waiting for the next question that she will reply to with a "no." My eyes narrow as I looked at her.

"You know why, don't you?" I tell her.

"Tell me," she says with an air of good-humored resignation.

"Because your life up until three years ago was a fiction. You weren't the author of your own story. Life imposed fictions upon you—told you that you were a boy and you should do boy-ish things. You were afraid of coming out, of breaking the fiction, of letting down all the friends and family who had invested in you as a man."

"Hmmm . . ." Sarah hums without commitment while stealing a French fry off my plate.

At just twenty-five years of age, Sarah McBride has a lot on her shoulders. She has been anointed as the future of transgender politics. When she was mentioned as the most likely first out transgender person elected to high office in America in the *New Statesman* in November 2015, a flood of well-connected supporters urged her to run on social media with the hashtags #draftmcbride and #runsarahrun. Roddy Flynn, the executive director of the US Congressional LGBT caucus, commented: "This article makes the case for what I've said for years: Delaware *needs* Sarah McBride to run for office! It would not only be a step forward in LGBT equality, but Sarah has the passion, brilliance, and experience to lead Delaware into the future. Congratulations to Sarah for getting well-deserved recognition in this article, but I see it as a call to action! I want Sarah to run soon . . . when she does I'll be the first one knocking on doors for her!" In July 2016 her star was catapulted even higher. First, she was listed on the Internet as one of the "people under thirty-five who inspire us to reconsider the age requirement for President." Then she became the first openly transgender person to address a major party convention.

McBride took the platform at 5:30 p.m. on Thursday, the last night of the Democratic Party convention, just before the prime-time lineup of Chelsea Clinton and Hillary Clinton herself. She began by saying, "My name is Sarah McBride and I am a proud transgender American." Then she told her stories— her very personal stories. Flynn told me that when the LGBT Caucus was offered, for the first time ever, a speaking spot at the convention, they really wanted to put a real face and story behind who they were. "We had a list of over fifty possibilities of folks to invite on stage with us, but Sarah had the right combination of a compelling narrative, rhetorical confidence and unending genuineness," he said. That night she told Don Lemon of CNN about what lay behind her openness: that she is compelled to demonstrate that "behind the debate on rights are real people. Who hurt when they are mocked, who hurt when they are discriminated against, and just want to be treated with dignity and fairness."

Up until recently the T was largely silent in LGBT. Transgender individuals found it tough to get a seat at the table with lesbian and gay activists, let alone mainstream society. Barney Frank justified decoupling trans rights from gay rights in Congress in the 1990s on the basis of the art of the possible. The head of the Human Rights Campaign, Chad Griffin, publically apologized for the HRC's history of trans phobia in September 2014. When Carl Sciortino led efforts for a trans equality bill in Massachusetts in 2012, established gay leaders warned him off: "Whoa! too soon, too early. It doesn't raise money and it's going to hurt you politically." Sciortino noted a generational divide with older gay men, saying, "They [trans people] are not part of my community." A small fringe element of the feminist movement attacked with vitriol the very legitimacy of trans women. But being trans is now in vogue, and in *Vogue*. The visibility of transgender people in American television and media has grown noticeably. *Orange is the New Black* star Laverne Cox became the first transgender woman featured on the cover of *Time* magazine, and starred in the remake of the *Rocky Horror Picture Show*. Similarly, the Amazon show *Transparent* was widely lauded by critics and audiences for its portrayal of a transgender woman coming out to her adult children and transitioning later in life. The show won multiple Golden Globes and Emmys for its first season, including for best television series. Beyond fictional portrayals, Janet Mock, a transgender woman of color, is a writer and media star. Her memoir *Redefining Realness* was a bestseller in 2014, and she now hosts her own show on MSNBC. In January 2017 *National Geographic* featured nine-year-old Avery Jackson on its cover, illustrating its "Gender Revolution" feature story and forthcoming TV documentary. And, of course, there is Caitlyn Jenner.

Sarah McBride's short life is already the stuff of epic narrative—too well-scripted to sully with fictions. In August 1990 Sally McBride gave birth to her third child, in Wilmington, Delaware. Her husband Dave recalls, "We brought her home at five days old—she had a big grin on her face and that grin has been there ever since." Their growing "boy" was politically precocious. (Sally and Dave refer to Sarah by her name of choice and gender identity when talking about her pre-transition history.) When Sarah was in elementary school, Dave was asked to teach a class at their church. As he recalls, "Sarah comes into the room, sits on the floor at my feet and throughout stares up at me with this bright eyed gaze. I thought she must be so impressed with me—how nice. After the class was over she walked up to me with that wide-eyed look and said, 'Dad, Dad.' I said, 'What?' thinking she was going to say 'You're so interesting,' but instead she said, 'Where did you get that podium?'" She pleaded with Sally and Dave to buy her a podium, and eventually Sally gave in. Dave continues: "I came home from work one day and went up to her room to say hi. There was an American flag draped over her curtains, a presidential seal she designed for herself and the podium. She's standing in her underwear reciting FDR's first inaugural address. We knew we were in trouble at that point." Sally McBride told me that by middle school Sarah loved to design and construct buildings. She was fascinated with the White House, building a series of models. After a while she said, "Gee, it might be fun to live here."

After a run for student body president in middle school, the politics got serious. In 2004 Dave McBride's law partner, Matt Denn, ran for Delaware State Insurance Commissioner. Fourteen-year-old Sarah lugged around a huge video camera, taking over one hundred hours of film. "Big camera, little kid," Sarah says. McBride was spotted by then–Delaware State Treasurer Jack Markell. The infectiously enthusiastic teen in a tie became something of a talisman for the local Democratic elite. When Markell ran for governor in 2008, Sally and her "son" were at the heart of the bruising primary. Markell was running against the Democratic Party's chosen successor, but he won by 1,700 votes, which Dave McBride notes was close to the number of new voters that Sarah and Sally registered. In 2010, Vice President Joe Biden's son Beau ran for state attorney general. Sarah was his "body man," driving him around the state. They spent a lot of time together, which Sarah cherishes today. She loved Beau. Governor Markell told me that even as a seventh-grader, McBride was so compelling that he had her introduce him at meetings. "I wasn't just the child who wanted to be president; by eighteen I was spending nights at the governor's mansion and dreaming about it someday being my house," Sarah tells me in a buzzing DC restaurant. Markell validated the dream. "He'd frequently say to me with a smile, 'when this is your home' or 'when you're governor.'" Roddy Flynn has been friends with McBride his entire life. Their fathers worked in the same law firm, and they lived a few blocks from each other. "She's always been a little larger than life," he tells me. "Even in high school she had a presence that made you assume she was in charge, even though she was just door-knocking or making calls."

In 2011 McBride was elected student body president at American University, a stone's throw from the White House, after the most elaborate campaign the campus had ever witnessed. McBride was building a resume for a serious career in politics. At that point presenting as a "straight, cisgender guy" with all the talents and connections to climb the ladder fast, Sarah recalls, "I wasn't even out as gay. The first time I dated a guy was four months before I came out as transgender." Previously McBride had only dated women. "I'm taking an ex-girlfriend to the White House for the holiday reception," she told me. "Five years after we first dreamed about it. She told me she's not surprised on the timing, but a little surprised we are both wearing dresses."

Then, in her last week in office as AU president, McBride published a jolting editorial in the campus newspaper:

> Yesterday, I ended my term as AU's student body president. I have learned and grown so much over the last year, both personally and professionally. As proud as I am of all of the issues we tackled together, the biggest take-away, for me, has been the resolution of an internal struggle. For my entire life, I've wrestled with my gender identity. It was only after the experiences of this year that I was able to come to terms with what had been my deepest secret: I'm transgender.
>
> For me, it has been present my whole life, but, for the longest time, I couldn't accept it. At an early age, I also developed my love of politics. I wrestled with the idea that my dream and my identity seemed mutually exclusive; I had to pick. So I picked what I thought was easier and wouldn't disappoint people. To avoid letting myself and others down, I rationalized my decision: if I can make life a little fairer for other people, then that work would be so fulfilling that it would make me feel complete and somehow mitigate my own, internal struggles.
>
> As SG President, I realized that as great as it is to work on issues of fairness, it only highlighted my own struggles. It didn't bring the

completeness that I sought. By mid-fall, it had gotten to the point where I was living in my own head. With everything I did, from the mundane to the exciting, the only way I was able to enjoy it was if I reimagined doing it as a girl. My life was passing me by, and I was done wasting it as someone I wasn't.

I told my family and some of my closest friends over winter break. My brothers and parents greeted me with immediate support and unconditional love. This was the first time that my parents have had to worry about my safety, my job prospects, and my acceptance. This story is my experience and my experience alone. There is no one-size-fits-all narrative; everyone's path winds in different ways.

The experience highlights my own privilege. I grew up in an upper-income household, in an accepting environment and with incredible educational opportunities. I never worried about my family's reaction.

But those worries are all too common for most. For far too many trans individuals, the reality is far bleaker; coming out oftentimes means getting kicked out of your home. I say this not to diminish my own experience, but to acknowledge the privilege and opportunities which have been afforded to me.

Today is the next day of the life I've already had, but at the same time, the first day of the life I always knew I wanted to lead. Starting on Saturday, I will present as my true self. Going forward, I ask that you use female pronouns (she/her) and my chosen name, Sarah.

With every birthday candle extinguished, with every penny thrown, my wish was always the same. I am now blessed with the opportunity to live my dream and fulfill a truth I have known since childhood. My gratitude is great to my family, friends and this university for accepting me as the person who they now know me to be, and for letting me show them the possibilities of a life well lived.

I now know that my dreams and my identity are only mutually exclusive if I don't try.

A few months later McBride interned at the Obama White House, becoming the first openly transgender woman to work there in any capacity. At the age of twenty-three she was the face of the campaign for legislation to protect Delawareans from discrimination on the basis of gender identity and expression. The bill passed the state senate by one vote and the state house by a 24–17 vote. It was immediately signed into law by her friend and mentor, Governor Markell, in June 2013.

The moment McBride first dated a guy was the moment she realized "that I could deviate from the 'norm' . . . there is no question that the largest personal issue for me in not coming out was the fear of disappointing my family, friends, and mentors. I thought my parents' dreams for me would be crushed. I was so in my head that I believed the moment I even confided in a friend it would make it real." Sarah twisted her long hair in her fingers as she thought. "The main theme in my life has been fear of letting people down. When I started to date a guy I worried that friends would be disappointed because my future was dashed. I thought any deviation from the norm would lead to questions of whether I would succeed and whether they would associate with me." She was unsure whether her friends saw value in her outside of the success. The brief moment of acceptance as a gay man—or at least being perceived as one—gave Sarah the confidence to be completely authentic. "It was my license to totally come out as trans." It is tough to comprehend, but the yearning for a life in politics stopped Sarah from being Sarah.

When Sarah became Sarah she didn't lose her friends, her family, her mentors, or her future. She found her center. "My first twenty-one years were defined by a secret I held; now I feel like I have no secrets," she says. "The best I can describe it is as a constant feeling of homesickness. Everything I did I had to reimagine in my head. It was exhausting. There was this secret shame, embarrassment, and fear. Coming out was the first time my mind was at rest. A weight off my shoulders . . . just a simple feeling of well-being swept over me. I felt liberated having it out there. Not validated per se, but loved, supported, embraced. Validation takes much longer."

Many transgender people prefer that their pre-transition name not be used. Despite the fact that Sarah's male name was so prominent before her transition, she shares the unease about being "treated as two different people."

"Why did you choose the name Sarah Elizabeth?" I ask.

"It was like picking a name for a child," she replies. "I didn't know any bad Sarahs—every Sarah I knew encompassed femininity, intelligence, and wit—it is a timeless name."

Like all parents of transgender children, Sally and Dave McBride stumbled and groped for answers in the off-kilter fog that descends after such a monumental secret has been shared. But because of their inherent openness and decency, they stumbled into a demonstration of how to be the very best parents of a transgender child—they did all the right things, inventing for themselves a playbook for how to navigate the experience of having your child come out. Sarah came out to her family on Christmas Day 2011. Sally recalls being "devastated. I saw her whole future shatter, all our dreams for her destroyed. My whole world collapsed. That first night I lay in bed crying, asking Dave, 'Am I ever going to be happy again?' "

Sally and Dave had experienced something like this before, but they were still unprepared. Their oldest son Sean came out as gay in 2003 while in medical school. "We knew what it meant to be gay," says Dave. "Our big fear that he would be defined by being gay, when there is so much more to him." Indeed, with Sean they had already worked out that he was gay and were just waiting for him to tell them. When Sarah came out as transgender the impact was so much bigger. "With Sarah I didn't quite understand it, there was so much fear," says Sally. Dave asked himself, "Why am I so much more upset about this? I understood sexual orientation, but gender identity was a whole new concept to me. What did we do to make him want to be her? I knew many very happy and successful gays—but I didn't know any transgender people." Sally adds, "Sarah was our golden child. Her being transgender never entered our minds. She was a happy kid. She was able to live for twenty-one years not as her true authentic self, but never seeming depressed, rarely sad. She was able to compartmentalize it somehow."

Realizing their ignorance, the McBrides did the best thing they could do: they educated themselves. First, they asked their pastor if the church could put them in touch with parents in a similar situation. A family living across the Connecticut border was found and the four parents met and talked, and talked. Their son Sean McBride, the doctor, put them in touch with a leading medical expert on transgender adolescents. Five days after Sarah came out they all went to Washington, DC, to meet with him. "That was monumentally important to us," notes Sally. "We felt so much better, so much more confident about her future. He said, 'She's going to be fine. There are no other issues than the gender dysphoria. She is authentic and real. She will be happy, successful, fulfilled. Your daughter is going to be okay.'" Sally and Dave were also comforted the more they spoke with Sarah. "In the first week the three of us were in constant dialogue, with Dave and I asking questions. I began to understand what it meant to be trans. She was so confident, and so sure, and so courageous, that she comforted me." Dave adds, "Sarah was so patient with us, she never got flustered with all the questions."

The unconditional support of Sarah's erstwhile mentors, Markell and Biden, and the rest of the Delaware political establishment, was also transformative for the McBrides. "They embraced her before and after. Their support for our family when she transitioned was huge," says Sally. "We have been embraced as a family by church, by the Democratic party, and friends and neighbors. Even though it was hard it felt like the whole state rooting for our daughter. It was accepting and respecting. They said 'You are loved.'" Dave recalls he was very afraid that all the people who had been so supportive before would now step back—not negatively per se, but just back away. When Sarah decided to apply to the White House intern program as Sarah, she had to call Governor Markell about his reference letter. He had to be told about the transition. After speaking to Sarah, Markell called Sally, who was at the mall. After hanging up Sally collapsed on the floor in relief. She recalls his words in detail: "Sally, I will do whatever Sarah asks me to do. We support you, what can we do for you?" Dave notes that both Republicans and Democrats—people he had not expected to be supportive—were on their side: "friendship trumps ideology." Sally agrees. "Our journey has been such a positive journey but we know our experience is often not replicated—so many trans people don't have that experience. We are so lucky." Sally McBride has become friendly to two young transgender men whose families have not been supportive. "I've seen the heartbreak of those who don't have supportive families. Sarah and many others are helping this people. She has a gift to speak for these people."

In 1962 a teenager left Newcastle, KwaZulu-Natal, in South Africa to spend a year at the Tatnall School in Wilmington. She watched television for the first time, read books that were banned in her homeland, and watched the unfolding civil rights movement. Her eyes were opened. The school, founded by Francis Dorr Swift Tatnall as a school for girls in 1930, has a mission to nurture a "community founded on the values of altruism, honesty, and respect that will enable students to discover what is true, pure, lovely, and of good report." We met that African teenager earlier: Margaret Marshall went on to be the first to sign marriage equality into law as chief justice of the Massachusetts Supreme Court. A few years after Marshall saw the world anew from Barley Mill Road, Sally McBride enrolled at Tatnall. She would go on to give birth to the brightest political star of the transgender movement of the twenty-first century. When Joe Biden cast a vote for himself as vice president of the United States in 2008 he did so in the Tatnall School, which is a short walk from his house. *Slate* writer Mark Joseph Stern says the vice president will be remembered as President Barack Obama's conscience on LGBTQ rights. In 2012 Biden made public his support for marriage equality, opening the floodgates for senior politicians to come out and say what they had felt all along. The Tatnall School's moto is *Omnia in Caritate*—"all things in love." They have clearly fulfilled their mission well.

Roddy Flynn describes Sarah as a combination of her parents. "Both have a lot of personality, but they socialize in different ways. Sally is the life of every party. Dave is quieter, but in the corner with a smaller group making everyone double over laughing. Sarah pulls people together for small group salons, in-depth exchanges of views. She uses her sparkling personality to pull people out of their shells, not just draw more attention to herself." Flynn thinks that it's her desire to pull people in that makes McBride such a powerful force. He tapped Sarah to lead "Introduction to Transgender Identity" sessions for Capitol Hill staff. "They were off the record, so attendees were comfortable asking any question. Some were worried that the questions may be ignorant or inadvertently offensive, but Sarah wanted people to be willing to ask her anything. I've never seen her thrive more than in these Trans-101 sessions . . . communicating on something she's passionate about, and working incredibly hard to make personal connections with each of the staffers in the room."

Being transgender became Sarah's full-time job, first as the LGBTQ campaigns manager for the Center for American Progress and then a national press secretary for the Human Rights Campaign. Both utilized her as the face of their transgender advocacy—she became the trans storyteller-in-chief of America for a new generation. Her face is on billboards in the DC subway, magazines feature her large smile and flowing dresses, and no LGBTQ pride awards show is complete without a Sarah McBride speech. This led to a tension: being a minority role model versus being a woman. "Do you tire of being *TransSarah* rather just being Sarah?" I asked. "I am a transgender person and a woman, not a 'trans woman'— all in one word. It worries me that it boxes me in long term. The tension is being seen as myself without the asterisk. Ultimately I want to broaden my advocacy beyond LGBTQ issues. But at the same time I feel a sense of personal responsibility that I should be open with my identity to demonstrate to people that they have met a transgender person." She paused. "I feel compelled to bare my soul. To be seen as the multidimensional humans that we are." She argues that she came out in such a vulnerable way in order to "bring people on the journey with me." As the North Carolina bathroom bill dominated headlines, McBride traveled down to Charlotte to film for the Center for American Progress. She posted online an "illegal" selfie taken in the bathroom of the county government office. With some hyperbole, *Teen Vogue* called it "what may well be the most powerful selfie ever." Promoted by Yahoo, *Buzzfeed, Huffington Post, Cosmopolitan,* and on multiple television shows, the photo was seen and shared by millions. Flynn noted that Sarah's selfie helped her get the Democratic Convention speaking slot. "For a lot of America it put a human face on an absurd, bigoted policy," he says.

The Williams Institute at UCLA estimates that 1.4 million or 0.6 percent of Americans identify as transgender—a doubling of the estimates from a decade before, and including 150,000 transgender youth aged thirteen to seventeen. Where are all these people? Transgender people seek invisibility. Over two-thirds say they hide their gender or gender transition to avoid discrimination. This is understandable when you realize that the consequences of being openly transgender can be awful. Over 78 percent of transgender people say they were verbally harassed during K–12th grade and 12 percent had been sexually assaulted in school, with rates substantially higher for transgender people of color. Nine percent of transgender adults who do not have a high school diploma left school due to harassment. Transgender students are between two and four times as likely as all other LGB youth to experience verbal harassment, physical harassment, and physical assault due to their gender and gender expression. The demonization continues into adulthood. The vast majority of transgender people say they've been bullied at work; nearly half say they were not hired because of their gender identity, and one-quarter say they were fired because of who they were. Trans women are two to three times as likely than other LGBT people to experience physical violence, discrimination, sexual violence, threats, intimidation, and harassment, and the treatment of trans women of color is even worse. By the middle of December 2017, twenty-eight transgender people had been murdered in America—an epidemic on the increase, as there were twenty-one fatalities in 2015 and twenty-three in 2016. In Britain the attempted suicide rate among young people is 45 percent, and one in nine trans kids have received death threats. Eighty percent admit to self-harming.

The epidemic of abuse is not merely an Anglo-American phenomenon. A survey of over 2,000 Chinese trans and gender nonconforming people in 2017 found that 46 percent had considered self-harm or suicide, with 13 percent making attempts. There were extraordinarily high levels of neglect, as well as verbal and physical abuse at home, school, work, and in public spaces. This resulted in 73 percent of respondents with anxiety and 60 percent with depression. Trans Chinese individuals were twice as likely as other LGB people to encounter violence.

Trans Americans were always lagging behind, but in 2017 it appears as though transgender Americans have slipped so far behind that they can no longer be seen from the rearview mirror of gay men and lesbians. They may still be heading in the direction of equality, but they are losing touch with the leaders and falling further behind. A Movement Advancement Project (MAP) report in February 2017 found that twenty-three states still had hostile laws regarding gender identity—meaning that transgender people were not protected from bullying and discrimination in schools, could not access medically necessary health care, and could be fired, evicted, or kicked out of public places. Sixty-eight percent of transgender people still were without an ID that matched their gender identity. Twenty-seven percent of transgender workers say they had been fired, denied a promotion, or not been hired because of their gender identity and 31 percent denied service, verbally harassed, or physically assaulted in a public place. After the election of Donald Trump, a HRC survey of 50,000 youth between thirteen and eighteen found that over 70 percent had witnessed bullying, hate messages, or harassment. Seventy-nine percent said they thought it had taken place more often since the start of the campaign. The vast majority of incidents were based on homophobia and transphobia. The massive 2015 US Transgender Survey found that 82 percent of transgender people had seriously considered killing themselves at some point in their lives, nearly half in the year previous. Among respondents who had attempted suicide, more than a third made their first attempt at age thirteen or younger; three-quarters did so before age eighteen. This deliberate invisibility gave rise to the remarkable statistic in 2015 that 18 percent of Americans claimed to have seen a ghost, while only 16 percent of say they had met a transgender person. After a year of attention the number who said they had met a trans person rose to 30 percent. We know that the more straight Americans know and interact with gay and lesbians the more they accept and embrace them, but transgender Americans remain cloaked in the invisibility of fear.

Promoting pernicious laws that demonize transgender people compounds the catastrophic health outcomes among an already vulnerable population. The largest study found that 41 percent of transgender Americans attempt suicide at some point in their lives, compared to 1.6 percent of the general population. Young transgender Americans were even more likely to attempt to kill themselves, with some estimates putting the suicide attempt rate among transgender youth at 57 percent. William Buffie notes that in 2009 the *American Journal of Public Health* presented data on the effects on the LGBT population in states that had banned marriage equality—effectively saying to their gay and transgender citizens "you are not valid, nor equal." After the legislation generalized anxiety increased by 248 percent. In 2010 the National Center for Transgender Equality found that after increased bullying, harassment, assault, and rejection, suicide attempts rose to 51 percent from 41 percent overall. To some which bathroom you use may seem trivial, but for transgender Americans it speaks to your place in the world. The Gay, Lesbian and Straight Education Network's 2013 National School Climate Survey of middle and high school students found that over 63 percent of transgender youth avoided bathrooms at school because they felt unsafe, and 52 percent avoided locker rooms. Research published by Kristie Seelman of Georgia State University found that 60 percent of transgender individuals who had been denied access to school bathrooms had attempted suicide, compared to 43 percent who had not been denied. The epidemic of abuse was just as disturbing in the United Kingdom. A Stonewall report on schools in 2017 found that 80 percent of British transgender schoolchildren had self-harmed, and half had attempted suicide.

The strongest weapon in the public health arsenal to counter the epidemic proves to be simple acceptance. Stephen Russell and Jessica Fish found that transgender youth who are accepted by their communities did not experience disproportionately high rates of mental health issues. If accepted, transgender kids averaged an anxiety score of 50.1 on a National Institutes of Health scale— almost the same as the national norm of fifty. Transgender youth whose parents reject their gender identity are thirteen times more likely to attempt suicide than transgender youth who are supported by their parents. In inclusive schools, or schools where youth may choose their bathrooms, between 19 percent and 43 percent of LGBT youth or adults attempt suicide. When schools are not inclusive, or when transgender adults are denied access to bathrooms, between 31 percent and 67 percent of LGBT youth or adults attempt suicide.

Progress in transgender visibility and rights is more apparent in parts of the developing world other than in the United States. In much of Asia, "third gender" or *hijra* communities are visible, albeit if often relegated to lower-class status. One *hijra*, Shabnam Mausi, was elected to the Indian state house of Madhya Pradesh almost twenty years ago, while transgender advocacy groups are growing in strength in Thailand and Burma. The *hijra*/third gender community has special legal recognition in Bangladesh and Nepal. The leader of the Ladlad political party in the Philippines, Bemz Benedito, is a transgender woman. The party won 113,000 votes in the general elections of 2013. In Tagalog, *ladlad* means the unfurling of a cape and is a poetic way to describe coming out. Their campaign strategy did not shy away from courting the gay vote. *The Guardian* described them as "hitting every beauty parlor and Miss Gay pageant" in the vast archipelago. For Benedito, standing up for LGBT rights was as much a class issue as an identity question. Many third-gender Filipinos are beauty or sex workers, discriminated against as much because of what they do as who they are. Surprisingly, Benedito was not the first trans woman to be elected to the Filipino Parliament. Geraldine Roman was elected to the National Assembly in 2016. But in Roman's case the scales were heavily tipped in her favor. Despite being a charismatic and capable candidate, she would have never been elected if her father had not been the congressman for Batan from 1998 to 2007 and then her mother from 2007 until handing the position over to Geraldine in 2016. Family dynasties trump gender dysphoria in the eyes of the voters.

Offering an uncensored personal narrative has become the main form of defense for transgender people, and it is Sarah McBride's calling card. The anti-transgender discrimination campaign in Delaware in 2013 was headlined by Sarah and her family. "We were baring our souls to the state, asking legislators to feel what it feels like to be me." The day after the successful vote the *Delaware News Journal* ran a photo of Sarah in tears on its front page. However, McBride's most famous act of soul-baring had nothing to do with politics. A month after coming out she met Andrew Cray at a White House reception. Sarah and Andy, who happened to be a trans man, were quickly inseparable, even to the point of Sarah joining Cray as a colleague at the Center for American Progress. However, a few months later, in September 2013, Cray was diagnosed with oral cancer and had an operation to remove part of his tongue followed by grueling chemotherapy. In April 2014 he was given the all-clear, but the cancer was back by July and had spread to his lungs. McBride says that after the diagnosis he turned to her and said, " 'If it turns out that this is terminal, would you marry me?' Of course the answer was yes. He was only twenty-eight and I was just out of college. We were told that with treatment, he would probably have about a year left."

McBride wrote about their love story for the Huffington Post—"Forever and Ever: Losing My Husband at 24"—in February 2016. It became a sensation, shared and read by millions of people around the world. As Cray's health declined, family and friends gathered to arrange a wedding in less than a week. Gene Robinson, the first openly gay bishop, would conduct the ceremony on the roof of McBride and Cray's DC apartment building. By the wedding day, Andy was only awake for brief periods of time and taking in just a few mouthfuls of ice cream. Sarah wrote out the three lines Andy would be required to say: "I do," "That is my solemn vow," and "Please accept this ring as a symbol of my abiding love." "Til Death Do Us Part" was replaced by "Forever and Ever."

They got through the ceremony, but five days later Cray was barely conscious in a hospital room. A nurse told Andy's wife and family that sometimes you have to tell your loved one it is okay to go because they are afraid of disappointing people. Sarah whispered in her husband's ear: "I love you, Beanie, I'm going to miss you every day, but it's okay for you to go. No one is going to be mad at you." Then she slipped a handwritten note into his clenched fist that said, "You are loved." He passed away that afternoon.

"Why so honest about such an open wound?" I asked. Sarah paused to find the right words. "We are defined and diminished by the singularity of our trans identity," she replies, "but once you've read a story about a trans person who has felt love and loss, you will never feel the same. And if my story can help open even a few more hearts, then that means Andy continues to live on."

McBride's authenticity stems from an early life of inauthenticity. Her gathering momentum toward a political life hit a roadblock of internal conflict, but that block has now been swept away. She recalls the first moments when becoming Sarah no longer felt like the end of her dreams. "When I came out publically at American University I thought if AU is reflective of where we are going as a country . . . if I can be celebrated here, then in five, ten years it's possible to make it in politics." While interning at the White House in 2012 she thought, "If our country is capable of electing an African American president only forty years after DC burned in riots, signaling a radical change in the most deeply held and vicious prejudice, then anything is possible." In Delaware in 2013, lobbying for the equality bill, she said, "It felt like a referendum on me and I presented the law as 'let me come home.' If I can convince [these men] to risk their careers to allow me to go into bathroom then we can probably convince a majority of people to trust us to be elected officials."

Will Sarah listen to those urging her to run for office now? "Yes, someone needs to be the first but I need to run for office when the time is right." She argues that symbolic visibility is, in itself, a major agent of change. Her experience in Delaware was that the anti-trans discrimination law sent a very personal message to transgender people in the state: "It was the first time that the state that they loved, loved them back. It gave a place to people who worried there was no place for them. That's what it's about for me. I didn't realize what was missing until that moment." She also wants to demonstrate that trans people are reliable, intelligent, competent people who can get things done. She needs to gauge when enough social change has occurred to maximize the chance of success. "If I run, I'd run to win because I wouldn't want to let down those expectations," she says. The obvious starting point would be a run for the Delaware State Legislature, where Sarah has high recognition and support. While she continues in her job at HRC traveling the nation, Sarah's home base is now back in Delaware. If a seat opened up in the House or Senate, especially in her hometown of Wilmington, she would be a strong contender likely able to draw significant volunteer and financial support both in and out of the state. Should she choose to pursue higher office, the likeliest track would be statewide office or perhaps even one of Delaware's three seats in the US Congress. No out transgender person has ever been elected to Congress.

Transgender politicians are the Cinderellas of the LGBT family: they are invisible in public office. Only seven transgender people in the world have ever been elected to a national parliament. Georgina Beyer was the first, in New Zealand, in 1999. Vladimir Luxuria was in the Italian Parliament between 2006 and 2008. Anna Grodzka was elected in Poland in 2011, but after being defeated in her re-election bid in 2015 there were exactly zero out transgender MPs in the world for two months. Then Tamara Adrian was elected in Venezuela in January 2015, Geraldine Roman in the Philippines June 2016, Diane Rodríguez Zambrano in Ecuador in February 2017, and then Michelle Suarez stepped up from substitute to full in the Uruguayan Senate in October 2017.

In 2014 Dr. Petra de Sutter was appointed to the Belgian Senate. A handful of others have won local office, most notably Jenny Bailey, the former mayor of Cambridge, England. But transgender people find it dramatically more difficult, even more so than lesbian and gays, to win. The numbers tell a dispiriting story. Around 150 transgender candidates ran in thirty countries between 1977 and 2016. They were elected just seventy-five times (including re-elections). Every year, millions of people offer themselves for election to office around the globe, from small-town school board positions to national president. As of January 2018, there were 10,750 female members of Parliament in office, out of approximately 46,000. There were 196 lesbian, gay, or bisexual MPs but only five transgender MPs in office (in Belgium, Ecuador, Philippines, Uruguay, and Venezuela). There were fewer than thirty transgender elected officials in office at any level across the globe. The vast majority of elected trans officials the world over, as well as the majority of unsuccessful candidates, are trans women.

Individual stories illustrate how tough it is for a transgender person to be a political actor. Jennifer Gale was an ex-marine living in Austin, Texas. She ran thirteen times for public office, never winning. She became homeless. On a cold December night in 2008 she froze to death as she slept on a concrete ramp, covered by newspapers. At nineteen years of age Jowelle de Souza was the first person to undergo sex-reassignment surgery in Trinidad and Tobago. In September 2015 she ran as an independent in the San Fernando West constituency in Parliament. When I asked a local pollster whether she stood a chance, he answered, "I imagine that Ms. De Souza is polling less than the margin of error right now." The disdain of a transphobe, I thought. But on election day she got 108 votes—0.6 percent—far less than the margin of error.

In the summer of 2016 two trans women made serious runs to be American state legislators. When Brady Piñero Walkinshaw resigned from his Seattle seat in the Washington state house, the field running to replace him reflected the deeply progressive district, with the longest representation by a procession of gay incumbents anywhere in the world. Local activist Danni Askini was up against seven other candidates, three of whom were openly gay or lesbian. Askini garnered considerable attention as the first trans woman with a serious shot at office in Washington, and early on she did relatively well in fundraising (although lagging far behind the front-runner, a gay lawyer named Daniel Shih). But in May, Askini upended the race by pulling out and backing the housing advocate, Nicole Macri, who happened to be a lesbian. Askini initially said she was withdrawing to focus on battling the proposed North Carolina-like initiative that would have banned local governments in Washington from protecting transgender people from discrimination in public places, including in public restrooms. But in June, Askini revealed another, more personal and sadly emblematic reason for her exit. It turned out that in late 2015 she had fled an abusive relationship—an experience disturbingly common to women who are transgender. Her ex had started to disrupt her campaign events. A judge issued a temporary restraining order, but a few days before the King County Young Democrats debate Askini became fearful of what he might do. "I couldn't predict or guarantee my safety in that place," she told the Capitol Hill Seattle blog. Sarah McBride will often use the line in her speeches, "If you've met one transgender person [pause] you've met one transgender person," reinforcing the notion that shared experiences can be very different and trans individuals are very individualized. McBride and Askini represent two wings of the front lines of the embryonic transgender political movement.

Even farther west, in 2016 Kim Coco Iwamoto ran a strong campaign for the Hawaii State Senate in an overwhelmingly Democratic district. Coco-Iwamoto has long been one of the few visible transgender politicians in the United States. When elected to the Hawaii Board of Education in 2006, she was the first transgender American to win statewide office. She served a second term and then was appointed to the Hawaii Civil Rights Commission. Iwamoto, a fourth-generation

Japanese American born on Kauai, started as a fashion designer and then became a lawyer before going into politics. She battled incumbent state house
member Democratic Representative Karl Rhoads for the District 13 Senate
seat. But Rhoads got the backing of the party elite, progressives, and the unions.
Even the LGBT Democratic Party caucus of Hawaii endorsed both Iwamoto
and Rhoads—which, considering that Iwamoto was seeking to be the first out
transgender state legislator in America, was something of a snub. In the August
primary she received 32 percent of the vote.

On the other side of the country, almost as far away as one could be from
Hawaii, Bob Marshall was first elected to the Virginia House of Delegates in
1992. He based his career on extreme right-wing demagoguery, opposed to all
forms of abortion and birth control and relishing homophobic and transphobic
rants. He anointed himself Virginia's "chief homophobe." David Sherfinski in
the *Washington Times* noted that Marshall believed that disabled children were
God's vengeance against women who have had abortions. He has described incest as sometimes voluntary, and he questioned the Justice Anthony Kennedy's
sexuality because he ruled for marriage equality. His legislation mirrored his
obsessions. He cosponsored the Marshall-Newman Amendment that voters
approved, banning same-sex marriage in Virginia in 2006. He scrambled at the
end of the 2015 legislative session to try and pass legislation to allow business,
state agencies, and the Virginia government to legally discriminate against LGBT
people. In 2017 he introduced bathroom-bill legislation copied from North
Carolina to target transgender Virginians. While extreme, even for a Republican,
he held the Virginia 13th House of Delegates seat comfortably for twenty-five
years over thirteen elections, often winning with huge majorities.

Danica Roem grew up in Prince William County, Virginia, and was the lead
reporter for local newspapers for nine years covering education policy and local
politics. She also played guitar for the thrash metal band called Cab Ride Home.
She came out as a trans woman in 2013, but as she told Diana Tourjée of the
news site Broadly, "By the time I was in fifth grade for sure I knew I was trans. By
seventh grade there was zero question about it. But I had no one to talk to. All
the trans people I had ever seen were caricatures on Jerry Springer. I had a lot of
sorrow."

In January 2017 Danica Roem announced she would run against Marshall for
the Virginia House of Delegate's seat 13, thirty-five miles west of Washington,
DC. Straight out of the gate Roem signaled that she was going to run as a local.
Her platform was focused on fixing Route 28, the main artery through Northern
Virginia, which during rush hour resembled a parking lot. She told the local
MetroWeekly paper, "I'm not going to run away from my identity whatsoever, not
even in the least bit. But at the same time, I'm going to be campaigning strongly
on the issues of the district: taking care of Route 28 finally—it was a mess

twenty-five years ago when Del. Marshall got into office, and it's still a mess. I know how to get it done *without* raising taxes—economic development, and education."

At the beginning Roem's campaign appeared quixotic: she was taking on a highly visible conservative in a solid Republican seat. Plus, no trans person had ever taken office as a state legislator in America (Stacie Laughton had been elected to the New Hampshire House in 2012, but resigned in scandal before taking office). Despite the odds, Roem's election race caught fire in the imaginations of Democrats both locally and nationally who, after Trump, began to view her run as emblematic of the battle for the soul of the country. Early on Roem outraised Marshall five to one, and even after Republican donors started to worry Roem still managed to raise twice as much as the incumbent. Chris Abele, a millionaire councilman from Milwaukee, sent close to $200,000 alone, despite never having met her. By election day Roem's campaign had spent nearly one million dollars—for a state house race. By the summer Marshall was running scared. He refused to debate Roem in public. He claimed she was "lying about *his* sexual identity." "You can change appearances, but your DNA fixes your bodily structures for your entire life," Marshall said. "Danica will never get cervical cancer. Danica can't get ovarian cancer because those body parts are not part of a male structure." Marshall ridiculed Roem's gender identity in his leaflets and allowed an outside group, the American Principles Project, to run particularly transphobic robocalls focused on demonizing gender variant children.

Diana Tourjée of Broadly followed Danica Roem on the campaign trail in the week of the election. She asked Roem about the transphobic nature of her opponent's campaign: "Does it surprise you?" Roem sighed. "When people talk smack on you based on your gender it's not about you . . . there are dangers . . . great dangers. I know the risks associated with it, but at the same time just by running this race I'm making it more possible for other people like us to run races like this." Her go-to slogan was "Discrimination is a disqualifier—Inclusion is a victory lap." That victory lap did not look particularly likely.

Delaware's Governor Jack Markell thinks Sarah McBride's time will come. "She is not only smart and a terrific communicator, but she understands politics," he tells me. "I hope she goes for it." As to her chances as a transgender politician in a transphobic world? "Ten years ago I would have said no. Now I think anything is possible," the governor says. Roddy Flynn says, "I would like nothing more than to chair a McBride for Senate campaign back in Delaware, but if that happens it'll be a longer process to get there than I think many people expect. Sarah is a smart, strategic thinker, and has her finger on the state's political pulse. She has plenty of time to figure out her next move, the move after that, and the move after that, all before she's thirty. Regardless of what she decides to do with her career, it'll be fantastic."

The stakes are high. If she runs she has to win and be the best legislator in town: the curse of the glass ceiling breaker. And there are other misgivings. The run would not be just under local microscope; it would be national, too. The abuse of the last few years would be magnified dramatically. Markell counseled Sarah: "I don't think many people could do it, but you could, but you have to have a tough skin."

"Do you have a tough skin?" I ask her.

"I do on some things and don't on others. I'm fine with people calling me a freak or the t-word. But when people attack how I look or how I sound, those things get to me," she says.

When I first met her, in public places McBride could resemble a nervous deer, scanning the room for threat, watchful of being watched: Who is out there? Who is noticing her? Friend or foe? In December 2015 the *Washington Post* published a video in which McBride discussed her experience of interning at the White House. The comment sections can feel like a shooting gallery. "There were some comments that really got to me. I cried at work. Called my parents and cried. There may be a thousand positive comments, but I only hear the one negative. It is exhausting. With Trump as president it is much more difficult to rationalize that the mean comments are just a small minority," she says. It is inevitable that such attention would be amplified in any election campaign Sarah entered.

"I also worry about my safety," she continues. "Being an openly trans woman means that you are open to an even higher level of discrimination and violence." McBride is troubled by the "unbelievably visceral and negative way some men respond to trans women." "Why do you think there is such strong hostility?" I ask. Sarah looks at me. "Many people who are genuinely straight at some point have worried that they might not be straight, and that fear lives with them for the rest of their lives. There are few things more dangerous for a trans woman than a straight man who finds out he's attracted to a trans woman—the visceral response can be strong." Sarah's parents worry that her work can place her in the middle of the hate, imperiling not just her physical but emotional safety. "We talk every day," Sally says. Dave admits, "If I had a choice I might rather see her have a career unrelated to the movement. But if she doesn't lose herself she'll be fine, whatever she wants to do."

McBride's simple but hugely consequential skill is that she makes people care about her—and by extension, other transgender people. McBride's former colleague at the Center for American Progress, Sharita Gruberg, believes that McBride is driven by a compassion surplus. "She cares deeply. She's not just advocating for herself, she's advocating for the people in her life and even those she's never met. She empathizes with the shared aspects of their experience." She communicates what it is like to be transgender in a way that resonates with people across the spectrum. In 2015 McBride posted a note on Facebook that went viral. One section pointed out the well-meaning mistake that allies make when they tell her they just "want her to be happy."

> I didn't transition to be happy, I transitioned to be me. It wasn't to create a positive, but to remove a negative. It was to alleviate a nearly constant pain and incompleteness. Transitioning didn't bring me happiness; it allowed me to be free to pursue *every* emotion and opportunity; to live more fully; to survive. But being me didn't make me happy. It made me free. It made me "me."

One lesson Dave McBride has learned on their journey is to never underestimate how meaningful a small gesture can be. He says something that could apply to any interaction with any transgender person. "If all of us evidenced just a little bit of courage, then nobody has to be a hero. That is our story. Sarah had incredible courage. All the rest of us just had a little bit of courage to do the decent thing and it made such a huge difference. I hope the same thing can happen for other people."

In December 2016 McBride was leaving Vice President Joe Biden's holiday party at the ornate mansion on Observatory Circle in Washington. Biden saw McBride leaving and broke away from his conversation. As he enveloped her in his arms she said, "Thank you for eight years of exceptional leadership." Biden stepped back, looked her in the eye, and said, "Thank you for being so loyal to my son." "I nearly broke down," Sarah tells me, when she responded to the vice president: "Thank you for raising someone who didn't hesitate one second to stand by me and fight with me." Seven years after the coming out, the transition, and the start of the glare, McBride has grown into her role as the future of a movement. She was always poised beyond her years, but now she has embraced the role of diplomat in chief—the deer-in-the-headlights look has been replaced by growing self-confidence. As humans we are conditioned to hear the critics more than supporters, but McBride receives so much love from strangers that the weight of it must have helped dampen the sound of the few haters.

Figure 10.1 Farrell and Mel Wymore Tucson, Arizona, 1974. Credit: From the collection of Mel Wymore.

10

Mel and the Bees

Round One

Mel Wymore roamed the Arizona desert in ripped shorts and dirty t-shirt, the sidekick to an older brother, Farrell: the Scout Finch of the West. Mel's mother, Muriel, had designed a house on the borderlands between suburban Tucson and the great desert. Farrell and Mel were the free-range explorers of a child's frontier of the 1970s. Insects, lizards, birds and bees, cacti and fire cracker bushes. Mel loved the bees best of all. Mel would chase and capture, photograph and study. "It wasn't the science that grabbed me but the social life that interested me most," Mel recalls. The hive works in unison, a high-functioning community where "everyone has a sense of purpose and higher identity." When under threat, the bees work together to protect the hive. They communicate impending danger with a wild dance and high flapping of wings. When the hive temperature drops too low, worker bees generate heat by pulsating their thoracic muscles, a mass shivering. When it is too hot they fan their wings and press themselves against the walls of the hive—a heat shield of bee bodies. When the hive gets too overcrowded, a subgroup will swarm to start a new hive. The community picks a new queen when the time for accession comes.

When Mel was twelve, a swarm came to a tree in their garden. A beekeeper was called, "scooping up bees with his hands, it was so cool," Mel tells me, smiling. Mel was given a kit to build a hive and was put on a list to receive the next swarm found in the neighborhood. But before bees came Mel's family moved to Costa Rica for her father's sabbatical at the Agricultural farm laboratory at Turrialba, enveloped by thick volcanic jungle. Mel got to ride along with a German scientist who was studying the genetics of killer bees: a little kid bouncing around the back of a jungle truck inseminating aggressive bees with docile, watching the queens build their empires. Finally, back in Tucson, "I finally got my own hive. I didn't care about stings. I'd be out there in my bathing suit, four or five stings, watching, photographing, studying. I became adept at handling the bees." As a teen Mel started a honey company. By college Mel was working on pollination at the USDA Bee Research Lab.

The legacy of the bee obsession on Mel's political philosophy is obvious. When the community is under threat, they unite as one. When the hive is threatened the bees swarm together for protection. Their enemies—the evil beewolves, bee-killer wasps—are solitary and predatory. They shun other bees and live alone. If they catch a bee away from the hive they will paralyze it with their sting—not kill it—and then carry it back to their lair, alive but incapacitated, to be slowly fed on by their larva. The other lesson that Mel takes from the bees is that humanity will fail if selfishness overwhelms selflessness. "We fail to look at our communal identity. As humans we increasingly need to develop higher levels of collaboration." The challenges are about the survival of the species and our dysfunction is at a mass systems level. Gender has great purpose in bees, but unlike humans they embrace variety—their roles are far from binary. Male drone bees come from the DNA of the queen bee that laid the eggs; they only have a mother, no father, in a form of natural, asexual reproduction. Workers and queens are both female, and have both a mother and a father. The DNA is chemically adapted in the larva.

Mel's father Wayne Wymore was one of the fathers of systems engineering theory: an Iowa farm boy who hated the cold. Part of his military service in World War II was spent as a weather watcher on San Andres Island in the Caribbean Sea, five hundred miles north of the South American mainland. A couple of centuries earlier San Andres had been pirate Sir Henry Morgan's base of operations. Wayne was a brilliant mathematician, and after the war he got a PhD in math from Iowa State on the GI bill. In the 1950s he was one of the first Americans to have an inkling of the potential of computers, and he established the inaugural computer department for Standard Oil. But he hated Chicago winters, and so in the mid-1950s wrote letters to colleges in warm places to ask if they wanted him to start departments of systems engineering for them. By Mel's accounting her father wrote thirty letters and received thirty-one job offers. So in 1956, Wayne and Muriel began a new life at the University of Arizona.

Six years later Mel was born, and would parlay a fascination with the secret life of bees into the family business of systems engineering: learning how large human social structures work and can be improved. As well as being the father of a discipline, Wayne Wymore fathered four children, and Mel took a bunch of college classes with her father. When Mel was five, Wayne was paralyzed from the neck down in a terrible bodysurfing accident. It was not clear that he would walk again, but with steely determination he recovered and ran every day for the next thirty years.

Mel's mother Muriel was a cook, artist, investor, homemaker, and real estate mogul. While Wayne studied systems, Muriel designed them. "When I was nine," Mel tells me, "I had to submit a budget for my allowance—how many coats, over how long, etc. We negotiated and we settled on a price. And that's exactly how much I got—nothing more, nothing less. I managed my own funds." At first Muriel was stalwart in supporting Mel as a tomboy—short hair, dirty knees, boy's clothes. "She negotiated with the school principal so that I didn't have to wear a dress." She made Mel custom pants when she could not find them in stores. She argued with the karate teacher to "let the girl play!" "She was my biggest advocate," Mel recalls. But after puberty expectations changed. Mel merged back into the understood social norms and followed the expected path. She married the prince, had two beautiful children, and moved to Manhattan. But there was something not quite right. Some cogs on the wheel were misshapen; the machine worked, but it was slightly off. Mel wrestled with internal tension and ambiguity. She struggled to work out what exactly was wrong. In her midthirties, she came out as a lesbian. This proved very difficult for her parents. "They were paralyzed for years," Mel says. But the hole inside Mel remained. "I was trying to figure out why my coming out didn't solve my sense of internal angst," Mel muses, sitting at the dining room table where his children grew up.

She got involved with the parent–teachers association at her daughter's middle school on the Upper West Side. As part of the school's anti-bullying campaign they brought in trainers from the Miami-based Yes Institute to educate on sexual orientation and gender identity. "I was the parent sitting in on my daughter's class," says Mel. "They showed a clip of this little kid on *Oprah* who had been born a girl but wanted to live as a boy. Could have been exactly me at the age of six. It was the scariest moment of my life, but I knew I had to explore what it meant to me." Oprah Winfrey was one of the first celebrities to discuss trans issues on national television. The TV icon welcomed Jennifer Boylan to talk about being transgender in 2003, and continued to highlight positive trans role models all the way through her reign over daytime TV. Mel flew to Florida and took the Yes Institute's courses to try and understand whether he was that boy.

Mel says the progression of his activism in the Upper West Side was predictable, but the instigating event was the exact opposite. As Mel and husband were carrying boxes into their new apartment on 70th Street on the Upper West Side of Manhattan, a man jumped from an upper floor of the building opposite. His lifeless body was surrounded by horrified passersby, who were quickly replaced by police cars and ambulances swarming the street. But after forty-five minutes the body was taken away, the blood was cleaned up, and the street returned to as if nothing had happened.

Mel was shaken and sought to understand what had happened. It turned out it was a single-occupancy building where social services placed poor people with mental health needs. The Reagan administration had withdrawn funds for social services, and people were falling through the cracks into lives of homelessness and despair. Some of Mel's neighbors recommended avoiding the building: "That's over there, stay away," they said.

Mel thought, "that's not okay," and enlisted a friend to help to understand the needs of the residents. They knocked on five hundred doors and brought in services where they could. This led to an appointment to the local community board (Manhattan CB7) in the mid-1990s. After fifteen years on the board a local Democratic activist, Helen Rosenthal, had become board chair. But under her leadership Mel felt the CB7 had lost its drive and imagination. It had become moribund. When Helen stepped down in 2009, Mel ran for chair and won.

The personal was about to intersect dramatically with the political. Mel leans back. "In the first meeting as chair of the community board in the fall I knew changes would be coming," he says. "I didn't know what they were going to look like, but I knew they were coming. I first outlined my plans for leading the board, then said, 'I have to tell you guys something.' I have discovered that my gender expression is not consistent with who I am inside and I'm going to start to masculinize myself." Mel recalls shaking like a leaf and feeling more vulnerable than ever before. "I said I was committed to us all being educated around this. I'm as new to this as you are and they should ask any questions they wanted. But ultimately we all should have the opportunity to be the most authentic selves and I wanted us to be brave enough to go through this together."

"What was the reaction?" I asked.

"The room exploded with a tidal wave of empathy and support. It felt poignant . . . an acknowledgment that someone had shared something *that* deep. But immediately thereafter there was awkwardness. None of us knew where to go next." The *Columbia Daily Spectator* led with the headline "CB7 Chair Welcomes New Transition." Wymore said she would be transitioning. "She is also very open to sharing the experience of her transformations. She said her willingness to publicly discuss her personal life—for example, immediately announcing her gender transition her first full board meeting—makes a difference. 'By being open and vulnerable, there is a lot of freedom and power, even if it is scary,'" the article said.

Mel deliberately undertook a slow transition—as much for others as himself. Initially retaining birth name and gender pronoun, having top surgery in the summer of 2010, then shortening name to Mel, and finally, two years later, beginning to use the male pronoun. As of 2017 Mel still feel like he is navigating uncharted waters, finding it difficult to put labels on experiences. "The binary model is what we are all born with, but it's not valid," he says, "and we are exploring what gender is. I was always searching for a more androgynous experience—reclaiming that six-year-old kid. I never thought 'I'm going to be a man.' I still don't feel like that. I'm read as a man, but that's not exactly who I am. Perhaps I'm more comfortable with a two-spirit experience of masculinity but also a powerful maternal experience."

After being chair of CB7 for two years, Mel realized he loved the cut and thrust of local politics and the art of the possible: bike lanes, affordable housing, parks, and childcare. The next step on the ladder was the local city council seat. District Six of New York City Council stretches over the Upper West Side of Manhattan, bordering Central Park to the east and the Hudson River to the west. It is one of the most liberal, Democratic, and wealthy districts in the United States. It is over 90 percent white, and Democratic voters skew close to 50 percent Jewish. Indeed, NYCC6 is known as the "Jewish woman's seat" on the council. The whole game is the Democratic primary—win that and the seat is yours. The incumbent council member Gale Brewer was term-limited and seven Democrats were in the mix to replace her, one of which was Mel's former board colleague Helen Rosenthal.

Wymore's 2013 campaign struggled to find its center—should they downplay Mel's transgender status, or celebrate it at every turn? There were two camps inside the campaign, those who wanted to downplay identity and those who wanted to embrace it. Abraham Axler notes that "there was a clear effort made by the Wymore campaign to ensure that Wymore wasn't considered 'the transgender candidate'"—a novelty, a curiosity. Indeed, "Wymore frequently commented on his trans identity [but] only to emphasize that it wasn't really relevant." The campaign put out a variety of fliers, brochures, and posters, and had an extensive website, but never mentioned the candidate's transgender identity.

In his study of the 2013 race Axler notes that no one in Wymore's campaign had experience with a trans candidate, and "Mel's LGBTQ consultants sought to run him like a gay candidate. That is to say, act as if the issue is entirely irrelevant. This strategy had been employed by many successful clients of the Campaign Workshop, including Senator Tammy Baldwin, the first out gay senator ever elected." Wymore was encouraged "to have his campaign materials emphasize the normalcy of his life . . . nearly all of Wymore's campaign materials showed him with his dog, or with his children in idyllic scenes." The tension was magnified by the fact that the camp seeking to highlight the value of identity was led by the candidate himself. In multiple media interviews Wymore sought to make a connection between his identity, living experience, and political skills. A story in *The Nation* quoted Mel as saying, "It's very important to me to highlight that the fact of being transgender is an expression of a lot of different skills and qualities that are consistent with being a good leader, like being courageous, being inclusive, being able to manage change and balance, and seeing people for who they are—all these things are assets to leadership."

The media coverage of the 2013 city council campaign was equal parts curious, celebratory, and salacious. The *New York Observer*'s December 20, 2011, article was titled "Madame Chairperson Now Mister Candidate: Transgender Wymore Runs for UWS Council Seat." The *Wall Street Journal* was more subtle: "Hopeful

Makes Historic Run." In a surprising coup, Wymore received the endorsement of the *New York Times*—but that endorsement made no mention of Wymore's trans identity or the momentous nature of the campaign:

> **MANHATTAN'S DISTRICT 6** (Upper West Side): There are plenty of good candidates in this race to replace Gale Brewer, now running for Manhattan borough president. They include Helen Rosenthal, a former official in the city budget office; Marc Landis, a lawyer and Democratic Party leader; the education activist Noah Gotbaum; Debra Cooper, an advocate for women's issues; and Ken Biberaj, a businessman. But the leader in this field is Mel Wymore, who in recent years has headed the local community board and the West Side Y. Mr. Wymore, a systems engineer and entrepreneur, was instrumental in persuading a developer to build a large school as part of a housing project, and he helped develop new zoning regulations that limited the ground-floor width of stores to help small shops survive. We prefer Mr. Wymore in this race.

Mel says there was pushback from local voters: not transphobia per se but an uneasiness, a sense of avoidance. "There was an awkward silence around my journey when it came to face-to-face conversations. The gender two-box system is so ingrained—it's the first thing we ask before we are already born, before we breathe air." Mel describes a neighborhood that prides itself on being liberal and progressive: "*So* post-gender they don't have to deal with you as a trans person. *So* liberal that gender identity is irrelevant." But that means the issue is not engaged or embraced. Every conversation is made more difficult—an "extraordinary sense of otherness." Mel describes a typical event. "You can feel the awkwardness when you meet people for the first time: 'Is that a man or a woman?' Flashed in front of you is a huge challenge to your sense of identity and belonging. An androgynous person elicits discomfort. I understand it because that was *my* experience as a young woman—'Is that a boy or a girl.'" Mel laughs. "A hundred people thinking 'What's wrong with that dude?'" He brings up Pat, the *Saturday Night Live* character from the 1990s played by Julia Sweeney. The joke was the inability of others to determine the character's gender. "I was Pat," says Mel. "A soft demeanor, but masculine clothing and haircut."

Looking back on his 2013 run for office, Mel recalls, "I wanted to take that unease out of the room by addressing it. 'I'm a transgender person, I'm a mom of two kids.' But that was not our strategy. It sat in the air as something left unsaid. Because of that what I said wasn't landing. My words were going through this filter—'Who is this person?' I now start speeches by saying, 'I want to tell you something about me. I was born female, I present as a white guy but I was born female. I tell you that not because I want you to be thinking about it but because I don't want you to be thinking about it. And now let's talk.' This take a few minutes to for folks to process. You have to create space to allow the person to have their reaction."

The New York Democratic primary was held on September 10, 2013. Twenty-seven thousand votes were cast. With 6,149 (22.2%), Mel Wymore beat all candidates bar one. He was 1,400 votes behind the winner, Helen Rosenthal. If Wymore had won in 2013 it would have been the most significant electoral victory by a trans man in history; even within the rarefied ranks of transgender and gender variant candidates, transmen are a rare and exotic breed. In 2013 only one trans man had ever been elected to any office, anywhere in the world, and one had come out while in office.

Round Two

On a bright day in October 2016, Mel and I sat on a bench in Central Park. Would you ever run again, I asked? "Perhaps . . . maybe back in Arizona," Mel said. He was toying with the thought of returning and establishing a base for a future run for state legislative office. Then, early in the spring of 2017, I was on my porch having a staring contest with an owl perched on a tree twenty feet away when I received a phone call from Mel. He had been approached by movers and shakers in District Six to consider a rematch against Helen Rosenthal. There was unease about some of Rosenthal's positions and lack of vibrancy in office. Well-connected Democrats wanted Mel to run again. What did I think?

"Two questions," I said. "First, do you really want to run? Second, can you win?" There was a pause. "I think so," came the reply. Over the next few weeks Mel took soundings. The more he spoke to people the more he wanted to run, and a narrow path to victory began to appear through the haze.

For the previous couple of years Mel had been the executive director of TRANSPAC. He told me that the work had "put me in touch with trans people who were really suffering . . . especially trans kids. The children move me. Trans kids have a glow if they are allowed to thrive. They are amazing beautiful kids, and the fact they can't find a safe environment breaks my heart. They really need a voice. Gender norms have us all so shackled." Mel also was driven by a sense of shock about the November 2016 presidential election. "We have been asleep at the wheel," he says. "Trump, of all people, was the one connecting with people. We have fallen so short of what we need to be doing at a community level."

The world struggles to make sense of nonbinary gender. The challenge for transgender politicians is less about combating outright transphobia and more about navigating society's desire to put people and things into clear discrete boxes. Our brains like binary, and we have millennia of being schooled that gender is binary. Anything and anybody that challenges that reality is treated with confusion and distrust. Liberal voters may desperately want to make sense of the ambiguity, but even they have a bridge to cross. When you are not familiar with the reality of a trans—when you do not have a child, lover, colleague, or friend who happens to be trans—your learning curve is steep and daunting.

In the first major study of US voters' attitudes to potential transgender candidates, Andrew Flores, Donald Haider-Markel, Daniel Lewis, Patrick Miller, Barry Tadlock, and Jami Taylor found that opposition in 2015 was at around 35 to 40 percent. Unsurprisingly, highly educated, Democrat, liberal, affluent, female, gender nonconforming, and less religious Americans were most likely to vote for a hypothetical trans candidate; Republicans, conservatives, heterosexuals, those who were more religious, and those with higher disgust sensitivity were far less likely to do so. Danica Roem managed to win a four-cornered race for the Democratic nomination in the Virginia 13th House of Delegates seat in 2017. It was an impressive victory for the thirty-three-year-old local journalist and trans woman. But the general election race against the incumbent Republican, Bob Marshall, was always going to be tough. Marshall had been a notoriously homophobic and transphobic legislator, but the money and attention that Roem garnered also drew Republicans to rally around Marshall to try to preclude any symbolic victory for progress over the past.

The proportion of trans Americans who are people of color is significantly higher than the overall population. That is why it is so crucial that trans men and women of color are visible leaders, and why Andrea Jenkins's and Phillipe Cunningham's races were so important in 2017. Jenkins, a black trans woman, and Cunningham, a black trans man, ran for seats on the Minneapolis City Council. Jenkins won after having to face a Green Party candidate in a heavily Democratic district, while Cunningham beat a well-connected white Democrat who was president of the city council and had held her seat since 1998, one her family had held for more than forty years.

Attitudes toward transgender people are changing. In the first global study Andrew Flores, Taylor Brown, and Andrew Park found that 70 percent of respondents in the twenty-three countries they surveyed agreed that transgender people should be allowed to have gender-affirming surgery and should be protected from discrimination by the government. Being allowed to use the restroom associated with your gender identity was supported by 77 percent of Spaniards, 72 percent of Argentinians, and 72 percent of Indians. The United States was ranked only ninth out of twenty-three in the trans-positive table.

Society needs to learn a new paradigm, but how do we learn? The British philosopher Gilbert Ryle gave us the concept of "the ghost in the machine" in his 1949 book *The Concept of Mind,* outlining two types of knowledge: the factual, propositional kind, *knowing that,* and the learning, experiential kind, *knowing how.* Modern society has expended huge effort in ensuring that we *know that* gender is binary—boys are boys and girls are girls. But this is unfortunately incorrect on both a physiological and psychological level. So in this case *knowing how* becomes a corrective mechanism, and we will only *know how* when we learn the stories of real trans people. We need to make sense of this new world.

The organizational theorist Karl Weick studied how people make sense of organizations and how organizations make sense of their environment. For Weick, sense-making is a question of wrestling with ambiguity and uncertainty—or making *equivocality* work. Weick outlined seven properties of sense-making, all of which apply to gender nonconformity:

1. We start by saying, "Who do we *think* we are?" Owned identity shapes how we interpret events.
2. *Retrospection* provides the opportunity for sense-making; we look back, we notice, we interrupt the flow.
3. We perform. As individuals build narratives and tell stories, we better understand experiences and are able to comprehend events.
4. Sense-making is also very strongly a *communal* task: stories are "both individual and shared . . . an evolving product of conversations with ourselves and with others."
5. Sense-making is never-ending—*we* continuously shape and react to new contexts. There is looping feedback: we deduce our identity from the way others treat us and then try and influence the way we are seen.
6. We constantly look for cues which provide "reference points of meaning."
7. Finally, Weick noted that we are more attracted to *plausibility* than *accuracy*: "In an equivocal, postmodern world, infused with the politics of interpretation and conflicting interests and inhabited by people with multiple shifting identities, an obsession with accuracy seems fruitless, and not of much practical help, either." That means proving the scientific, medical, and human reality of transgenderism is not enough—it must also be plausible to be valid.

As the results came in from the Upper West Side on the night of September 12, 2017, it looked bad for Mel Wymore; Rosenthal's lead was considerably greater than it had been four years earlier. In the end Mel won 6,280 votes, just 31 percent. Rosenthal held her seat with 65 percent of the vote.

Two months later in Northern Virginia, the Democrat challenger Danica Roem shocked America by defeating incumbent Republican Delegate Bob Marshall by nearly 2,000 votes—a healthy 8 percent margin. Just after noon on January 12, 2018, she became the first transgender American to be sworn in as a state legislator, the highest US office ever occupied by an out transgender person. Marshall remained true to form by refusing to concede or congratulate Roem. Rather than gloat, Danica took the high road, saying, "I don't attack my constituents. Bob is my constituent now." Marshall's own sister, the actor Paula Marshall Nucci, posted on Twitter the day after: "That was my brother who lost his seat in the House of Delegates race in VA. He wouldn't debate her. He wouldn't call her 'her' or 'she.' Maybe if he weren't so judgmental and homophobic, he could have lost with dignity. I'm not happy my brother lost his job, but all I can say is, karma, brother.'"

The irony is that it was the Republican Marshall who ran on identity issues; Roem ran on bread-and-butter local issues and won. Frank Bruni of the *New York Times* summed it up well in a column titled "Danica Roem Is a Really, Really Boring." Of course, that could not be further from the truth. Roem's victory was thrilling, her story tantalizing, she herself ebullient and dynamic, but Bruni's point was that she won by focusing on traffic and not the global zeitgeist. Bruni wrote of Roem, "Being transgender isn't the whole of her identity, the extent of her purpose or the crux of her mission. The obstacles in her life are particular, but the hell of rush hour is universal. And her job as a lawmaker is to attend to the nitty-gritty that has an immediate, measurable impact on all of her constituents. When circumstances warrant it, she can be every bit as boring as the next politician." But Roem never shied away from talking about her identity when needed. In her victory speech she began by directly addressing "every person who's ever been singled out, who's ever been stigmatized, who's ever been the misfit, who's ever been the kid in the corner, who's ever never had someone to stand up for them because they didn't have a voice of their own, this one's for you." Danica Roem's, Andrea Jenkins's, and Phillipe Cunningham's victories were in no small part testament to the Trans United Front political action committee that had been established the year before. With just two staff members, Hayden Mora and Daye Pope, the organization was the little engine that could, raising significant resources for trans candidates in 2017 and generating extensive media attention.

I have a Google alert set to send me any new story that includes the words "transgender candidate." In 2017 I received over 150 articles about Danica Roem with the words "transgender candidate" in the story, and less than ten referring to Mel Wymore. Roem's opponent Bob Marshall made the race about Danica's gender identity and lost; she skillfully turned every transphobic attack into an opportunity to rise above him. Wymore's opponent Helen Rosenthal, however, never once brought up his gender identity and thus Mel was not able to play that card for gain. Nevertheless, at the same time Wymore also steered away from making his identity a reason to vote for him—a vote of resistance against Trump and the Republicans, despite taking the same strategy unsuccessfully in 2013. Thus Upper West Side voters were left with a choice between a very liberal Democratic incumbent and a very liberal Democratic challenger. If Wymore had campaigned on "send a message to Trump" by electing a trans council member from Trump Tower, he probably would have done better.

Mel's father Wayne passed away in 2008 and his mother, Muriel, two years later. They did not live to see Mel's role in the transformation of American

politics, but they saw—and were at peace with—his own very personal transformation. "By the time I was transitioning my mother was in decline. I was flying
out to take care of her. On her deathbed I said, 'I think I'm going to transition.'"
Mel tried to explain that the internal struggle had not been over sexual orientation. "I said, 'You remember me as a kid as a tomboy'; it was all so clear. That
explanation made sense to her." Just before she died Muriel said to Mel, "I always
wanted two boys and two girls." That was the closure Mel needed. "It was really
lovely. We had struggled over the years," he says.

Mel wishes humans were more like his beloved bees: "An exuberant community . . . full of purpose. Working together, communicating, for the greater
good. It is a compelling vision for humanity—where we all individually fulfill
our sense of purpose and work together to protect and uplift the whole. Every
time I have seen someone marginalized and downtrodden because of who they
are it has driven me crazy." At a campaign event, Wymore bemoaned the fact that
the community was not coalescing to defend the hive. "No longer is it enough
just to vote. Our residents are poorly served and our most vulnerable neighbors
are completely un-served . . . we must be strong together and have each others'
backs." Mel is focused on the local. "We often focus on federal and state," he said,
"but nothing matters if we don't organize in our buildings and up-and-down our
avenues. That's where it starts." But Wymore notes that this worker bee doesn't
look exactly like all the others. Any transgender candidate has to run from the
outside. In his first speech Wymore rallied the troops by saying, "This is an insurgency race . . . not being afraid of bullying, [the] power of incumbency is strong."

My life rule is "be comfortable in your own skin 90 percent of the time," Mel
tells me as he makes coffee. "Did you have role models growing up?" I ask. "I was
one of those kids who adored their parents. They cared about people. They were
real citizens."

"What about identity role models?" I probe further.

Mel laughs. "Most of my friends came out by eighteen—I was the only
straight person!"

Then I see something in Mel's eyes drift back in time. He pauses.

"When I was a kid we would bike to a local ranch and hang out before
going to play in the desert. The ranch was owned by two women, Tuffet and
Laura . . . perhaps it was *tough-it* . . . not sure . . . it was just what we called her.
Tuffet was the neighborhood star—a cowboy, rough and tumble—we called her
the 'man-woman' but we adored her. They had a giant pig that went in and out
of the house. It would lay on their couch. Tuffet was so real, comfortable in her
own skin. She probably would have transitioned if that had been available to her
back then."

Mel looks at me.

"Now I look back and realize—I'm Tuffet."

Figure 11.1 Pauli Murray. Credit: Schlesinger Library, Radcliffe Institute, Harvard University— All rights to the photograph are with the Pauli Murray Foundation.

11

Southern Queers

Whatthefuck Mountain, North Carolina

The Southern Bible Belt of America remains fallow ground for LGBTs. The gays are there—in many places visible—but acceptance is much more grudging. Pernicious anti-gay laws flourish in the places where LGBT elected officials are few and far between (Texas, North Carolina, and Alabama) or entirely absent (Mississippi and Louisiana). A Williams Institute analysis (based on data from the 2012 US census) estimated that there were 650,000 LGBT Americans in the Deep South states of Alabama (130,000, 2.8%); Georgia (260,000, 3.5%); Louisiana (111,000, 3.2%); Mississippi (50,000, 2.6%); and South Carolina (105,000, 2.9%). But outside of the six state house members elected in Atlanta, only two have come from these Deep South states: Patricia Todd in Alabama and Jason Elliott in South Carolina. Over 250 out LGBT state house members have been elected in other states.

Mississippi tells one the story of the South. The state has never had an out LGBT person elected at any level of government. When a whole community is forced to hide, private and personal tragedies become the currency of life. Jon Hinson was only thirty-seven when elected to represent the Mississippi 4th Gulf Coast district in the US Congress in 1978. Two years later, during his re-election campaign, it was revealed that the married Republican had been arrested for exposing himself to a police officer at the Iwo Jima memorial in Washington in 1976. Hinson blamed alcohol and insisted he was not gay. In his game of hide-and-seek, Hinson played Russian roulette. Years later he revealed that he had been at the Cinema Follies gay porn theater in October 1977 when a fire ripped through the darkened theater and side rooms. Nine men died; only four survived. Hinson was pulled out from under a pile of bodies but never identified himself. As the police noted, "homosexuals do not carry identification when they visit homosexual gathering places." Being gay meant you lived and died anonymously. Just weeks after his second term began Hinson was discovered having oral sex with a congressional librarian in the House of Representatives restroom. He was charged with sodomy and resigned from Congress. Ultimately he came out and transformed himself into a gay rights activist. He never returned to Mississippi. He died of AIDS in 1995.

Little has changed in the state. In 2011 Mississippi gained its first openly gay office holder—Greg Davis, the mayor of Southaven. Davis had been elected in 1997, but his career careened off a cliff when it was revealed he had sought to be reimbursed for items purchased from a gay sex shop. He was forced to come out and promptly lost his bid for re-election in 2013. He was charged with embezzlement, convicted and jailed, but was then released awaiting a new trial. Just to enrich the telenova that had become his life, Davis's ex-wife sued his ex-boyfriend for damages.

As much as gay men in the South are unknown qualities, Clay Aiken was known by all of America. In 2003 he won over 12 million votes on the second season of the hugely popular *American Idol* singing competition, and despite coming in second in the final vote, established himself as a national celebrity. He had a legion of fans who referred to themselves as "Claymates," and a high profile on television and magazines. In 2012 he came in second on Donald Trump's *Celebrity Apprentice* show, watched by another five million Americans. Aiken told CNN during the presidential campaign that he had affection for Trump. "I'm a friend of his. I like him as a person. He's always been very kind to me except for when he made me lose on *The Apprentice* . . . but he's a good guy and I certainly think people are mistaken if they don't take him seriously and we see that in the poll numbers. He's like that uncle who embarrasses the hell out of you sometimes and you still love them, but damn, you wish they'd shut up." The affection seemed mutual. While being interviewed about the show in 2012 Trump stood next to Clay and gushed, "He's tough, he's smart, he's cunning . . . I'm very proud of him." Two years later, in 2014, the openly gay man from North Carolina decided to take on the incumbent Republican congresswoman in his deeply conservative home district.

Aiken is open and engaging. A decade on you can still recognize the geeky kid who stole the hearts of America on television. He is taller, more solid, and more profane than you expect. He is a big gregarious man, but in my mind I expected the sensitive feather who sang "Bridge Over Troubled Water" like an angel on TV. He says his political views were molded by his sexual orientation. "One of the reasons I am a Democrat is because I am gay. Recognizing in school that something was different about me, and I was left out for reasons that I did not understand, made me empathize with the people who were being left out on the fringes of society," he says. As a teen he was very liberal, "thinking socialism was a dandy idea." He made his own fantasy campaign posters, but there was something setting him apart from the crowd and deep inside he knew that he would not be allowed to be part of the club. As he's aged, Clay says he has become less liberal: "not socially, but less fiscally liberal."

Aiken did not come out early or with a bang. He leaked out over many years. Indeed, he says that one of the worst things you can say to him is "I always knew you were gay." He hears that all the time. He came across as gay on TV but had not come to terms with it himself. "I was out to millions of strangers before I came out to myself," he tells me. It was not until the taping of *American Idol* that he dated his first boyfriend. Even while in a TV closet, the media was rabid for salacious details. The first question Clay received at the post-finale press conference was "Clay, are you gay?" "It was offensive," he says. By the time the show aired in 2003 he had come out to a small circle of friends, then his mother, and by 2007 the people he worked with. In the entertainment industry, none of this was earth-shattering. But "when I decided to have a kid in 2008 it was a turning point, I knew I had to come out in public," he says. And so he did—on the front cover of *People* magazine, with the headline "Yes I'm Gay."

By 2013 he had become angry and frustrated by the erosion of democracy in his home state of North Carolina: elections were bought and sold and rigged out of all competitiveness. He began to toy with the idea of going home to run and sought the counsel of Elaine Marshall, the former Democratic North Carolina secretary of state. "I had ambitions, but as a gay man thought I could never win," he recalls. But Aiken was persuaded that he could serve a purpose by just running and losing: "loosening the jar," as he puts it, for someone else to win in 2016. "If I could bring attention to her [the unpopular Republican incumbent Renee Ellmers] and make it competitive, then when Hilary is on the ticket in 2016 maybe her coattails would win the seat for the Democrat."

That was the plan, but the 2nd Congressional district of North Carolina had been redrawn by the GOP state house to be a safe Republican seat: a mish mash of high-tech workers, suburbanites, the Old South, and soldiers on military bases. It stretches from the western suburbs of Raleigh—the most progressive part of district—through a southern corridor down to the huge Fort Bragg US Army base, then skips over liberal Chapel Hill to the famed golf courses of Pinehurst, and into hamlets of the rural Deep South where Confederate flags replace rainbow ones. After the Civil War the district was known as the "black 2nd" for its African American majority and history of electing four black Republican congressmen. But those days were long gone, and the gerrymandered NC 2nd of 2014 was now two-thirds white.

Aiken's first battle was to win the May 2014 Democratic Party primary against two local established figures. His main threat was the former North Carolina commerce secretary Keith Crisco, who owned an elastics company in the Republican stronghold of Asheboro. The primary was more bruising than expected. Aiken started twenty points ahead, but the lead had slipped away to nothing by election day. Crisco threw $700,000 of his own money at the race. Aiken was taken aback at how personal and negative the primary was: when there is little to tell candidates apart on policy, personal attacks seem to be the only way to differentiate. The count began the evening of May 6, but six days later it was too close to call—Aiken was ahead by only 390 votes out of 28,000 cast. Then he got a call. Crisco had died after a fall at his home. He was seventy-one years old. Aiken says that he "accidentally won the primary," but not because his opponent died; he did win the most votes, but he laments the fact that there was "lots of 35,000-foot advice from outside but little on the ground organization." Polling showed that voters liked and trusted Aiken, but very few thought he had the qualifications to be in office or felt that he knew what he was talking about. Only 28 percent of voters felt he had the expertise to do the job. Aiken's opinion was that his likability was not enough to get voters to vote for him, so they had to change the perception that he was an intellectual lightweight. He wanted to publish policy papers once a month and reposition himself as a policy wonk, but his primary campaign advisors didn't agree. They wanted to focus on his likability and fame and ignore the negatives.

Once he was in the general election running against the unpopular Ellmers, Aiken talked himself into believing. "My role is not to loosen the jar any more, now we have a path to victory," he told me two weeks after being anointed as the Democratic congressional candidate. But could a Democrat win the gerrymandered NC 2nd—could an openly gay man? Early internal polling found Aiken far behind Ellmers, doing no better than the previous Democratic candidate, who had lost by 15 percent. But by September, Civitas, a conservative group, found Ellmers only up by 8 percent with many undecideds.

"How difficult was it running in North Carolina while being famously gay?" I ask. Aiken thinks that it was a bigger factor in the primary because his Democratic opponents tried to make it an issue: "Clay can't win because he's gay" was the whispered campaign. When it came to the essential Democratic core vote base, Aiken notes that the black religious leaders were more supportive than their congregants. "But Clay, shouldn't you have had a secret weapon?" I suggest. "Don't you sing for them in church?" "I have a hard time bringing politics into church. I grew up in white Baptist churches," he replies, where politics was supposed to be separate. Plus, he is gun-shy of being pigeonholed as *just* the singer. If anything, the real hyphen he battles against is not the gay one; it's the celebrity. "The gay hyphen has not yet been the big issue," he stresses, because the celebrity hyphen is so big and bold underlined and italicized. He likes to call it "Whatthefuck Mountain"—the knee-jerk reaction of voters bewildered as to why a celebrity singer would be running for office. Aiken describes his whole campaign as a mission to climb Whatthefuck Mountain. "They know me as the guy from *Idol*," he says. But it's not all bad. "The benefit is that it gets me in the door, they are excited to meet me. There is an ownership of me in this state which others don't have. When I go to Brownie Lu's diner in rural Siler City, middle-aged women come up to me and say 'I voted for you on *Idol*!' 'Well, you get another chance,' " Clay tells them. " 'I know,' they reply. 'I'm going to vote for you again, but don't tell my husband.' "

In 2014 Clay had years of experience as one of the most visible gay men in America—all the disdain and plaudits. "I came out in the uncanny valley of 2008 when it was too late to be considered a trailblazer but before the big wave where it became commonplace," he reflects. "I and Lance Bass are the ones who you can still crack a joke about." Sometimes it does seem like Clay has become as much a punch line as a person. But if late-night comedians mock Aiken, there are hundreds of thousands of middle-aged women who adore him like a son. He notes that his fan club is heavily drawn from Pennsylvania, Michigan, Ohio, and Florida—all states that voted for Trump in 2016.

In 2008 many of these women were conservative Republicans, and after he came out many were disappointed they couldn't be fans anymore, but "within a year they were back. Now they are practically P-Flag members," he says (activist parents of gay and lesbian kids).

This may explain, in part, Aiken's public persona as the boy you'd take home to mother. "In every great cause there are normalizers and marginalizers," he tells me. He may be a normalizer—"you catch a lot more flies with honey than with vinegar"—but he knows you need the marginalizers as well. "The current normalizers are like Ellen Degeneres, Neil Patrick Harris, and myself. There was a time when Ellen was actually distancing herself from gay issues—although now she has embraced them again. Way before my grandmother knew I was gay she was normalized by Ellen—because she liked Ellen—and 'didn't shove it in my face.' " Clay continues, "I'm not in a relationship—I'm in dry dock. But if I were I wouldn't parade it around during campaign. It is important that gay is not always a sex thing. If you ask ignorant people they think gay is about sex—when Adam Lambert grabs some guy and kisses him at the American Music Awards on live TV [it] doesn't help with folks in Sanford and Siler City." It was no secret that Aiken was gay, but he did not stress that part of his identity on the doorsteps. He argues he was so well known he did not need to. "I didn't run away from the gay folks," he says. "I ran to the voters. Raeford, North Carolina, is not San Francisco."

A month before election day, Aiken's run for office was punctuated by the shock of gay marriage being brought by the Supreme Court to North Carolina. While he didn't feel an immediate backlash, the only rough conversation with a voter he had on gay rights was on the day marriage equality happened. But the ruling certainly wasn't good timing for a man trying to not make his sexual orientation the dominant narrative of his run for office.

Aiken woke up on November 5, the day after the election, thinking it was the "weirdest day of my life. I had nothing to do at all." So he went to see the Welsh feel-good movie *Pride*. "Did you expect to win?" I ask him over burgers two months after the election in a generic roadside restaurant near his home. "There are moments when you do," he says. "I wouldn't have run if I didn't think I could win. But you end up in a bubble. You start to think that it is more possible than even your polls are telling you. People are so friendly on the doorsteps." Clay tells me that he was in Republican towns like Southern Pines and Pinehurst, when dozens of folks would come up to him and whisper, "I love you. I'm a Republican, but I'm voting for you."

"Shit, we just might win this," he thought.

But by the last week of the campaign reality had set in. "I didn't have to disappear to pick myself up off the ground—I knew it was coming."

Clay did not win. He was not even close. The incumbent Republican Renee Ellmers won by 17 percent—an even larger majority than the last race in 2012.

The reality disconnect was helped by the fact that the Aiken campaign spent its money on advertising, not polls. The plan was (1) win the debate; (2) flood TV with ads, and "maybe we can do it." "Why did you lose?" I ask. Yes, the district was heavily rigged against him and turnout was not great for Democrats in 2016, but Aiken believes that Whatthefuck Mountain was a lot higher than he realized. "I'm not sure that even if I'd planted my flag at the top I would have won," he says. The national media was positive. "The *Esquire* magazine feature made me look great," he says, and there were heavyweight profiles in the *Washington Post* and other big outlets. But on the ground, "we couldn't change the story with thirty-second TV ads alone—it was not enough—people don't like to take people out of boxes." Because of his celebrity, Aiken had to be so much more substantive than a normal candidate would be. The sad fact was that he was. The *Raleigh News and Observer* found that 65 percent of those polled said Aiken won the single debate between him and Ellmers. The leading North Carolina Democrat, Representative David Price, "sat in a room with me for forty-five minutes before he understood that I had the chops," Aiken tells me.

Would he run again? He says he is open to opportunities but only in North Carolina, and it will take much longer to build a reputation that counters the celebrity lightweight. Ellmers came to a much more inglorious end. After politically alienating much of the GOP establishment (despite reports of an affair with House Majority Leader Kevin McCarthy), she was crushed by over 30 percent in the Republican primary of 2016 by George Holding. In the autumn of 2016 Clay walked back his affection for Donald Trump, calling him "delusional."

North Carolina has long been on the fault line of the battle for the soul of America: civil rights are the currency of social change. North Carolina was the last state to succeed from the union, last to return to it, and the next to last to sign the Constitution. In 1898 white supremacists overthrew the elected black/white local government of Wilmington, North Carolina, in what became seen as the moment white power began to reassert itself across the American South. Scores of African Americans were murdered and thousands forced out of their homes and the city—transforming Wilmington from a majority black city to majority white. Rioters destroyed the only black newspaper in the state, the *Daily Record*. But farther west, Durham had become emblematic of black progress in the South. After Emancipation former slaves established the vibrant Hayti neighborhood lauded by W. E. B. du Bois and Booker T. Washington. At the beginning of the twentieth century Durham was known as the "black Wall Street." The North Carolina Mutual Life Insurance Company, the nation's largest black-owned insurance company, was there, alongside the Mechanics and Farmers Bank and other black-owned businesses.

After World War II, North Carolina became a focal point for the burgeoning civil rights movement. On February 1, 1960, at 4:30 p.m., four students from North Carolina A&T State University sat down at the whites-only Woolworth lunch counter on South Elm Street in Greensboro and asked for coffee. They were denied service but refused to leave. Next morning they were joined by twenty new students, then sixty more, and on day four by three hundred. The movement caught fire. Nearly 100,000 activists ended up taking part in segregated lunch counter sit-ins around the country. When asked to comment, President Eisenhower said he was "deeply sympathetic with the efforts of any group to enjoy the rights of equality that they are guaranteed by the Constitution."

In the late 1970s a small communist-allied group began organizing African American textile workers in Greensboro. On November 3, 1979, they gathered outside the Morningside Projects on the corner of Carver and Everitt roads, a couple of miles east of the Woolworth lunch counter, to rally against the local Klan. The rally was not couched in terms of nonviolence; flyers said the Klan "should be physically beaten and chased out of town. This is the only language they understand." If the Klan took the bait, fistfights were expected. As the protesters sang on the sidewalk, roughly forty members of the KKK and American Nazi Party cruised slowly in their cars and trucks alongside the protesters. Sticks were wielded, rocks were thrown, and the Klansmen got out of their cars. Guns were retrieved from open trunks. Chaos ensued and dirt flew; the communists had fists and sticks. The Duke alum Cesar Cauce, originally from Cuba, was shot dead, along with Dr. James Waller, who specialized in treating brown lung in textile workers. At close quarters the Klansmen killed the Harvard Divinity School graduate Bill Sampson. When Sandi Smith, a nurse and former student body president at Bennett's College in Greensboro, peeked out from behind a car, she was shot between the eyes. Dr. Michael Nathan, the chief of pediatrics at the local health center, died of his gunshot wounds two days later. Five others were critically wounded, two of them shot in the head. One was a church minister and two others were medical doctors. All-white juries twice acquitted the Klansmen who were on film carrying out the murders, and it emerged that the police had aided the Klan in both preparing for the attack and the aftermath.

Carolina had its gays long before Clay Aiken, but they navigated a back-lane world of shadows and whispers. In the early 1960s Armistead Maupin Jr. traveled the twenty-five miles from Raleigh to the state's flagship university in Chapel Hill. He became an acolyte of the conservative firebrand Jesse Helms, who made a career of being vehemently against integration, communism, and gays. But Maupin *was* gay, and ultimately came out in 1974. He went on to become the chronicle laureate of gay America with his hugely popular *Tales of the City* books. Jesse Helms went on to become America's bigot in chief. The longest-serving senator from the state of North Carolina in history (1973–2003), he railed against queer perverts and racial integration. But there have always been two faces to the Tar Heel state. In the midst of the Helms hate crusade, a historian named Joe Herzenberg ran three times for election to the Chapel Hill town council until he was finally successful in 1987—thus becoming the first openly gay man to be elected in the state. He was followed by Mike Nelson in neighboring Carrboro, the dormitory town of Chapel Hill, where workers were being replaced by students and hipsters. Nelson became the first out gay man elected as a mayor in North Carolina. Then the homophobes pushed back. In 2012 a shadowy group named the NC Values Coalition, funded by the religious right and led by a troubled woman named Tami Fitzgerald, pushed for Amendment 1, which would introduce a constitutional ban on gay marriage in the state. Despite considerable mobilization against the plebiscite, the amendment was passed with a vote of 61 percent to 39 percent. The college counties of Buncombe, Orange, Durham, Wake, Mecklenberg, and Watagua voted heavily against the measure.

If you look up the definition of "likable" you could imagine seeing a photo of Billy Maddalon of North Carolina, but he has a penchant for taking the hard road. He is an openly gay businessman in Charlotte, and a therapeutic foster parent for abused and maltreated children. In 1997, three-year-old Jed was found in rural North Carolina chained to a bed eating out of a dog bowl. He went through twenty-nine families in the next decade before the authorities gave up and just sent him to a mental institution when he turned fourteen. Maddalon and his partner, Brooks Shelley, volunteered at the treatment center where Jed was sent. Despite owning a major hotel and hospitality business, with no time to take on a challenge like Jed, Billy and Brooks could not resign themselves to his fate. Despite all evidence to the contrary, they were naïvely optimistic that with them, Jed could be different. In *People* magazine Maddalon recalled their first night at home. "That first night we made spaghetti," he says. "He sat underneath the table and ate with his fingers. He didn't know how to bathe, couldn't write his name." For the next few years Jed would fight and run. Once he stowed away on a train; they tracked him through his phone. But Jed always came back—it was the only family he'd known.

Billy and Brooks fostered fifteen kids and adopted three of them. Their lives were the hotels and the boys. But Billy always felt the pull of politics, which had entranced him since childhood. In 2015 he decided to run for the safe Democratic inner Charlotte seat in the North Carolina legislature, the NC100. Running against the incumbent city council member for the area, he knew he was facing an uphill battle. He came close to victory—but no prize.

The day after his defeat Maddalon posted a letter to his supporters:

> Obviously we're disappointed that we didn't prevail. I was running a race as a proud, confident gay man, which in District 100, like so many others, is a blessing and a curse. So we knew we had to out-campaign, out-fundraise, out-mobilize, and out-everything our opponent to even have a chance. And yet, it still wasn't enough to get us over the hump. We came up 539 votes short out of more than 8,400 cast. Before we move on and get back into our normal routine, it's important to point out the obvious: because of our loss, North Carolina is still not likely to have an LGBT voice in our legislature in the coming years. That's the sobering, brutal fact.
>
> As I campaigned I was frequently reminded how important this race was to people in our community. I'd like to share a few stories. While canvassing several weeks back in Windsor Park, an older gentleman answered the door. I stuck my hand out to introduce myself; he smiled and said, "I know who you are." Then he called for someone inside to join him at the door. Another older gentleman joined him. They explained that they had been a couple for almost thirty years. We immediately had common ground. We talked about our children and our pets. We agreed about how hard it is to run a small business. But what was meaningful about the meeting was that when I said goodbye, they hugged me and one quietly said, "Thank you for being so brave for all of us." I dismissively said, "Oh, you're welcome." I wish I hadn't been so quick to move past that moment. Because in a process that's all too often very superficial, it was real. Then, back in January, I received a letter from a senior at Northwest School of the Arts. Among other things, he shared with me that he had recently come out to his parents. He said that he had first become aware of me during the City Council race last year. He said, "I attended an LGBT forum and heard you say, 'We are all wonderfully, fearfully made, in the image of a loving God,' and for the first time in my life it all made sense to me." He went on to say, "When I told my mom I'm gay she cried, because she was

worried about how limited my life would be. So I showed her an article I had saved about you. And I told her it's not like that anymore . . . see, Billy did it."

So when the Republican majority comes after Charlotte's nondiscrimination ordinance in the coming months and the only pronoun heard during deliberations is "they" instead of "we," listen closely and take note. Listen as our straight allies struggle with "they" and "them" as there's an attempt to separate fiction from fact, myth from reality, propaganda from truth. Listen for the notable absence of "we" in the debate, except when it is on the side of those who oppose equality and equal protection of law. Note how astoundingly most heterosexual people misunderstand LGBT people on every level. They misunderstand it as a psychological phenomenon, as a moral issue, as a social construct. When they look at it they see things that aren't there and don't see things that are. They magnify its inconsequential aspects and pay little attention to its vital features. Once again, note how inadequate a substitute "they" is for "we." And note how the LGBT community will, once again, not only be unable to use our presence to change laws, we'll be unable to use our humanity to change hearts and minds.

Billy's words were more than prescient. The Republicans did come after Charlotte's nondiscrimination ordinance—and added in transgender North Carolinians for good measure. The GOP saw Charlotte's action as an opportunity to lob some grenades in the culture wars, signaling to their core Christian conservatives that the old order of bigotry was clinging to power. The Public Facilities Privacy & Security Act (otherwise known as HB2 or the "bathroom bill") was an explicit call to arms to the cultural right. The Republicans felt that it might marshal a few more votes in the upcoming elections of November 2017. It was a law in search of a nonexisting crime. No transgender person or person masquerading as a transgender person has ever been charged with assaulting anyone in a bathroom in the United States. The law was simply a dogwhistle to the fearful and ill-informed. HB2 proved to be a disaster. The state went from conjuring up images of beauty and basketball to bathrooms and bigotry. The economy lost thousands of jobs and a projected $3.76 billion over the next dozen years. Six states and over twenty-five major cities banned their employees from using public money to travel to Carolina. The maneuver did not even help the GOP. Governor Pat McCrory, who had thrown his lot in with the bigots after initially being lukewarm on the law, was punished by the voters and lost his re-election battle to the Democrat Roy Cooper by less than 5,000 votes out of 4.5 million cast.

The battles between 2012 and 2017 over Amendment 1 and HB2 were conducted under dark clouds, but the gloom did reveal beacons in the dark. One of the brightest is Jasmine Beach Ferrara, who is both an agitator and normalizer. Married with a young child, she is a minister in United Church of Christ with a master's degree from Harvard Divinity School—a lesbian your parents would approve of. As director of the Campaign for Southern Equality, she is articulate, beautiful, and nonthreatening but also uncompromisingly radical. In 2016 she was elected to the Buncombe County Commission, which includes the town of Asheville. Many expect Beach-Ferrara to become a more prominent leader in the future. Another beacon is Mark Kleinschmidt, who was mayor of Chapel Hill between 2009 and 2016 and hit his stride as the voice of progressives in the period between Amendment 1 and HB2. Kleinschmidt grew up in the Army town of Fayetteville, where over 50,000 soldiers are stationed at Fort Bragg—the largest military installation in the world. After law school in Chapel Hill, he was elected as a thirty-one-year-old to the town council and then became only the second openly gay mayor in North Carolina. Two years after leaving the mayor's office Mark beat the incumbent to be elected Clerk of the Superior Court of Orange County, NC. If the chips fall his way, Kleinschmidt could well become the first openly gay man to be elected to the US Congress from the South of America.

The Mother's Name Is Harriet

A few miles to the north of Kleinschmidt's home in Orange County is a white clapboard house perched on bricks where Pauli Murray grew up. Murray is perhaps the most consequential American woman you've never heard of. The house on Carroll Road in Durham was built in 1898 by Murray's grandfather, Robert Fitzgerald, who had fought for the Union in the Civil War in the 5th Massachusetts Colored Regiment. Her biography suggests statues in town squares, named highways, and the honor of countless buildings and schools bearing her name. But North Carolina honors straight white male slave owners, not black, female, queer great-granddaughters of slaves.

As her biographer Rosalind Rosenberg relates, Murray "grew up to be an activist, lawyer, poet, professor, and priest, who challenged well-settled conventions, mostly in obscurity, but with transformative effect." It seems as if there was no boundary she did not transgress. As a smart, young black woman, Murray quickly exhausted education opportunities in the "Jane Crow" segregation of prewar North Carolina and fled to New York as a sixteen-year-old. Denied entrance to Columbia University because of her gender, she enrolled at the all-female Hunter College of the City University of New York a mile away (one of only four black women out of a class of 232). Later, denied entrance to the University of North Carolina to do a graduate degree in sociology be-cause of her race, and Harvard College, again because of her gender, she enrolled at UC Berkeley law school. She transferred to Howard University's law school and was the first in the graduating class of 1944 and the only woman. Ten years later Thurgood Marshall used her senior seminar paper, "Should the Civil Rights Cases and *Plessy v. Ferguson* Be Overturned?" as the cornerstone of his arguments in *Brown v. Board of Education.*

Being denied a place at the University of North Carolina was particularly galling for Murray. Her ancestors had built the university—some with their hands, others with their money. Her grandmother Cornelia was the daughter of a white slaveholder, Sydney Smith, and his sister's slave Harriet, whom he had "brutally and repeatedly raped." In records Harriet is identified as mulatto, and there is ev-idence she was of Cherokee descent, with long flowing black hair and olive skin. Harriet had been purchased for $450 in 1834, when she was fifteen years old. She had a son, Julius, with her husband Reuben Day, a freeman, but the jealous Smith drove him off the plantation. Smith's elder brother Frank also had designs on Harriet and took over de facto ownership of her body. Harriett gave birth to three more Smith children by Frank: Emma, Annette, and Laura. Sydney's sister (and Harriet's owner) Mary Ruffin Smith took pity on little Cornelia and her half sisters and raised them in the house rather than the slave quarters.

It was an unusual arrangement, even for the times. Some said that the family's move to the Oakland mansion in the woods of the southern part of the county—on Smith Level Road just south of the UNC campus—was a way to avoid wagging tongues. The children received an education and on Sundays Mary, her friend Maria Spear, and the girls would ride in horse and carriage to the Chapel of the Cross abutting the university buildings in Chapel Hill. The mixed-race children were baptized into god's family but sat in the upstairs balcony for slaves. Their aunt and governess sat in the Smith family pew down below. Kim Smith writes (in Harriet's voice) that Cornelia's household transgressed conventions and blurred lines: "To be clear, we were slaves and they were slave-owners, a fact that applied to everyone save my daughters. It was their contradictory roles as slaves, as daughters, as nieces, as children, that emphasized the grayness in between the blackness and whiteness. The rigid racial designations they were publically assigned, by law makers and census takers, were tempered at home by daily circumstance—and further distorted by the conflicting roles of fa-therhood and fathering, motherhood and mothering. The particulars of my children's paternity and maternity were not strictly governed by genetics or the law but, rather, by the daily interactions of all of us muddling through life's events; sickness, harvest, drought, war, a trip into town." Even Mary Ruffin and Maria Spear's relationship was mysterious and unconventional. After Spear was employed as Mary's tutor, they lived together as intimates for close to fifty years.

Closeted lesbians? Who knows, but an intimate partnership at the very least. Mary wrote to a friend that Maria's death was devastating: "I am alone in this world. I miss her too much." In August 1872, during one of those tumultuous foreboding Carolina storms, Harriet was struck by lightning while in the cabin she lived in by the main house. She was terribly injured and died a year later.

In the late 1930s, Pauli Murray applied to study toward a graduate degree in sociology when the University of North Carolina was pushing liberal boundaries. Howard Odum, Guy Johnson, and Guy's wife Guion were investigating race relations and actually teaching classes about the black experience even while blacks were still denied entrance as students. The playwright Paul Green and historian Howard Beale argued strongly for Murray's admission. There was even a fellowship for poor students funded by the will of Pauli's great-grand-aunt Mary Ruffin Smith that Murray applied to. UNC president Frank Porter Graham was considered a liberal lion of the South, inviting President Franklin D. Roosevelt to deliver a passionate endorsement of the university's liberalism on campus in December 1938. But even with the greatest of resumes and a family who had provided the foundation of the university, Pauli Murray was denied admission because of her dark skin. Echoing the university's current uneasy relationship with the state house, President Graham was fearful that a unilateral attempt to break segregation would prompt an unholy backlash. Even Howard Odum found he could not support Murray's admission, saying, "It is asking too much of a region to change over night the powerful folkways of long generations."

Pauli's maternal great-grand-aunt Mary Ruffin and great-grandfather Sydney Smith were themselves the grandchildren of the preeminent North Carolina landowner of the eighteenth and nineteenth centuries. Francis Jones (1760–1844) wanted the university to be built on his Jones Grove Plantation, but the powers that be decided to locate it at the hamlet of Chapel Hill a few miles to the north. Sydney's father and Cornelia's grandfather, Strudwick Smith, was a poor white boy from Hillsborough who made rich, if not good. He was elected to the US Congress in 1817 and became a member of the Board of Trustees of the University of North Carolina in 1821.

Murray's rejection from the university of her ancestors became something of a cause celebre and initiated a long friendship between her and the first lady, Eleanor Roosevelt. The relationship endured fights and disagreements along with mutual admiration and respect. Indeed, when Murray was hired at Cornell University her referees were Eleanor Roosevelt, Thurgood Marshall, and A. Philip Randolph. (Remarkably, shortly after, she was fired because her three referees were deemed to be too radical.)

In 1940 Murray took a bus with her friend Adelene McBean to visits her aunts in Durham. In Petersburg, Virginia, the place where her grandfather had fought for the Union, McBean and Murray moved out of broken seats in the back of the bus a few rows forward to seats in no-man's-land between black and white. Maintaining their dignity in the face of a truculent white bus driver, the situation escalated to the point of the police being called, and the women were arrested and jailed. This was fifteen years before Rosa Parks's celebrated act of defiance in Montgomery. Murray never stopped generating transformative electricity. Thurgood Marshall called her 1951 book, *States' Laws on Race and Color*, the "bible of civil rights law." She was one of the highly educated African Americans who lived in newly independent Ghana in the early 1960s, and on her return she cofounded the National Organization for Women alongside Betty Friedan. Murray's concept of Jane Crow was the foundation of Ruth Bader Ginsburg's Supreme Court victory in *Reed v. Reed*, which provided a woman's right to equal protection.

There was one last boundary to be transgressed. In 1974 Murray entered the Episcopal seminary at a time when women were not even allowed to be ordained. A few months before the end of her studies the church voted to allow women priests, and she was ordained—the first black female to take the cloth. In 1977, at the age of sixty-six, Murray celebrated Eucharist at the Chapel of the Cross in Chapel Hill, where her enslaved grandmother had been baptized 123 years before. Kim Smith found that the Chapel of the Cross baptism records of 1854 contain all five of Harriet's children's first names and their ages under the heading "December 20. Five Servant Children belonging to Miss Mary Ruffin Smith." In parentheses, underneath the children's names, penned in the same cursive handwriting, are the words "The Mother's name is Harriet."

Pauli Murray leaped over the walls built around her but struggled with her own internal walls. In childhood she was known as "the little girl-boy." She had both tumultuous and deep and stable relationships with women. She was romantically partnered with Irene Barlow for a quarter-century. Rather than calling herself homosexual, she said she had an "inverted sex instinct." She lived as a gender nonconformist, blurring lines and pushing boundaries in her dress, look, and presentation. While young she was sure that she had been born into the wrong body, the wrong gender. She sought out hormonal treatments and surgery to align her body and soul, but medicine and society had not evolved to a point of understanding gender dysphoria. In the years since her death in 1985 she has begun to be embraced as a transgender icon and pioneer, as well as a saint: in 2012 she was raised to the pantheon of "Holy Women, Holy Men" by the Episcopal Church.

Murray wrote in the preface to her book *Dark Testament and Other Poems*, "I speak for my race and my people—The human race and just people." Her poem "Prophecy" could be the hymn of the modern intersectionality movement.

On one of those hot steamy Maydays when Carolina forgets it is not yet summer, I took my regular run on the wooded trails north of town. As I plodded through the pristine forest that once had seen wagons travel from Pauli Murray's home to her grandparents' farm, I felt it was time to seek out the ghosts of the characters of the passion play that is North Carolina. I drove past the enlarged Chapel of the Cross, over the James Taylor bridge, "half a mile down to Morgan Creek," past the eponymous Smith Level and Jones Ferry Roads—named for Pauli's ancestors—and through the rich green forests that used to be the Jones Grove plantation. When I arrived at the university in 2001 most of the land I passed between Chapel Hill and the town of Pittsboro looked much as it would have in Harriet's time: woods and fields, barns and white wood farmhouses. But sixteen years on there are mini malls and burgeoning neighborhoods—as Taylor sang in "Copperline," "all tract house and plywood."

The Smith-Jones cemetery was discovered "out yonder in the woods" by John Row, who was living in the luxury assisted-living facility constructed on the old Jones plantation land in 2005. Row told his fellow resident, the eighty-three-year-old, H. G. Jones, about the graves. This was serendipity, as before his retirement Jones had been one of the leading historians of North Carolina. The old professor spent the next eight years writing the book that would become *Miss Mary's Money: Fortune and Misfortune in a North Carolina Plantation Family, 1760–1924.* Galloway Ridge is a sprawling network of bright white buildings—more country club retreat than end-of-life holding zone. Before the buildings expanded the cemetery was overgrown and forgotten in deep woods. For years Row maintained the dry-stone walls himself, the crumbling headstones and creeping poison ivy.

The cemetery is still and quiet. You can faintly hear the rumbling of cars down the road, which once played host to horses and wagons. There are nine graves inside the square walls nestling up to a creek bed and woods beyond. The patriarch Francis Jones (1760–1844) lies with his back to the brick-strewn entrance. Just in front of his headstone is that of Pauli's great-grandfather, Sydney Smith. Long ago his marker crumbled into two parts: the top now lies on the dirt pointing up to the dominant grave in the burial ground, that of Mary Ruffin Smith, "Who Died Nov. 18 1887. Aged 71 years." Mary, the (probably gay) woman who owned the mulatto Harriet and raised her brothers' children; Mary, Pauli Murray's great-grand-aunt. I sit at the base of the towering cross in the pulsing heat, brush away mosquitoes, and read Pauli's description of her ancestors who lay beneath me in her book *Proud Shoes: The Story of an American Family.* The dragonflies swoop and the hawks glide overhead, just as they did when the General Smith B. Atkins rode down this trail at the head of four thousand Yankee troops in April 1865 and told the slaves that they were free.

When Mary died without heirs in 1885 she left the Jones Grove Plantation—1,400 acres—to the university, which they sold a few years later. The proceeds brought electricity, heat, and plumbing to campus. One hundred and thirty years later the "good old white boys" of North Carolina enacted a deeply transphobic bathroom bill that applied to not only state facilities but the university as well. Oh the irony: the family of the queer, black, transgender groundbreaker had brought bathrooms to the university in the first place. A century after Mary's gift the university sold its utility systems for $32 million and invested the money into their libraries. Today the lifeblood of the woman the university said was of the wrong color to attend is built into DNA of every fiber of the campus—including its "sex-appropriate" bathrooms.

Ken Sherrill and the Expression of Affection

In the late 1920s Pauli Murray drove five hundred miles north from North Carolina to the City University of New York. Four decades later the political scientist Kenneth Sherrill traveled the same path home, making the journey in the other direction to do what Murray could not do, in obtaining a doctorate at the University of North Carolina. Forty years further on Sherrill is the dean, if not the father, of LGBTQ scholarship in America. What sets a life course? It is often the world that surrounds you as you grow. Sherrill was raised in his grandparents' house in Brooklyn in the postwar years; they were turn-of-the-century Romanian refugees who were avid consumers of news. Sherrill grew up with newspapers and radio around him all day. His family was not political per se, but they were eager to know what was happening in the world. He was engaged by his classmates at James Madison High School—one being future presidential candidate Bernie Sanders, with whom Sherrill overlapped at both school and college but did not know.

By his freshman year at Brooklyn College in 1960 he was president of the Students for Kennedy Club. At that time New York was not a state that the Democrats could take for granted. This spurred the Kennedy campaign to seek to energize the large Puerto Rican community in Spanish Harlem to register to vote. At the time, however, New York still had a literacy test for registration. The test was simple—seven questions, five correct to pass, and a paragraph to read. But the Puerto Ricans were nervous. Sherrill and his classmates went door-to-door in East Harlem showing Spanish speakers the test and reassuring them of its simplicity. A few weeks later the Committee for Racial Equality (CORE) rented buses to take locals to register. No one showed up. Spanish Harlem was in control of old Italian Democratic party machine of Carmine DeSapio. They were afraid that enfranchised Puerto Ricans would throw the Italians out of power. The established machine went around after the students scaring the Puerto Ricans. They said they could fail the test, that public benefits could be cut off, or that they might be deported. The Kennedy campaign was incensed. "There was one hell of a shouting match between Bobby Kennedy and DeSapio," recalls Sherrill. "'We going to get you!' Bobby was screaming in the street, "and when we are president—you're out of office. You are nothing!'"

This was Ken's initiation into the colorful world of ethnic politics, polling, and the right to vote. He was hooked. At the time the cutting-edge work on race and politics was being conducted by Howard Odum, Don Matthews, and Jim Prothro at the University of North Carolina at Chapel Hill. Their research into race and political participation was the first significant social science investigation of how blacks were engaging in postwar American politics. Matthews and Prothro published "Negroes and the New Southern Politics" in 1966.

North Carolina in the 1960s was a long way from Brooklyn. "I had known about segregation but it was only when I got off the train in Raleigh that I saw what it was," Ken recalls. "Was there a connection in your mind between being gay and your interest in ethnic minorities?" I ask. "In my mind, yes. Was it articulated, no. I was sexually active from fourteen . . . out to myself, but not to others," he answers. In his mind Sherrill made a decision that the new start— leaving New York and family, starting grad school—would allow him space to blossom. "I'm not going to hide this anymore," he thought. "But Chapel Hill was a terrible place to be gay," he goes on. "I had the hardest time distinguishing between southern gentlemen and screaming queens. Some were both. It was a different world from New York. Even the gays were segregationist. One graduate student used the term 'picaninnies.'" For Ken going to UNC was "like entering a monastery with nothing to do but study." Study was what he did. Entering school in the fall of 1963, by the spring of 1965 he had completed all requirements save for the final dissertation, and returned to New York. "I had to get out of town," he says.

He was back in his comfort zone, pushing the envelope. In 1972 he was teaching statistics, and briefed his students to set up an experiment, more to learn the methods than the substantive question. A Chinese American student in his class discovered that the city had just given a decommissioned fire station on Worcester Street in Chinatown to the fledgling Gay Activist Alliance (GAA). They held Saturday night dances and biweekly business meetings. Was there crossover in ideology and activism between the two groups? The student wanted to conduct interviews. Sherrill said, "I can't let you do it alone," and he offered to help. He met the GAA leadership in the firehouse—coming straight from an event, dressed in a suit and tie. After making his request to interview patrons one guy said, "You are heterosexual, why would we let you?" "I'm not!" Ken replied. They let him do the survey. Sherrill has always married his activism to his scholarship. There is a clipping on my noticeboard from the October 25,

1977, *New York Times* that reads: "In the Democratic primary, Kenneth Sherrill, a candidate of the Gay Independent Democrats, and other clubs, won the post of District leader in the 69th Assembly District on Manhattan's Upper West Side, becoming the first openly gay man to be elected to any party or public office in New York State."

When Sherrill began his career, scholars who were out and gay were as rare as out elected officials, and scholarship into LGBT politics was not deemed a legitimate field of inquiry. It took twenty-five years before his article on gay mobilization, based on the firehouse surveys, was published. Reviewers said that his work was not political science, but it was the subject matter that was at issue, not the methodology. If he had applied the Negro participation study methods to ethnic politics, reviewers would have applauded the construct. Using exactly the same approach to gay politics, he was summarily rejected as not conducting proper research. There were few templates and even fewer role models. If you were gay and making a career in academia, you kept it on the down-low.

In the late 1960s his college mentor invited the handsome young professor to dinner parties twice a month. "I met extraordinary people at his dinners," recalls Ken. "Paul Lazarsfeld, iconic scholars, famous artists." A regular dinner companion was the man who introduced Freud to Einstein. "He was a student and traveled around Europe getting the greatest scholars to sign a letter warning against the oncoming World War I. He met Einstein in Switzerland Einstein saw Freud's name on it and said that he would sign on the condition that the student introduce him to Freud," Sherrill recalls. Another regular at these parties was a senior administrator at one of the CUNY campuses. "We became fast friends, and it was very clear to each of us that the other was gay although, being of a certain age, at the time, it was left unstated. He said to me, 'You really have to meet my friend Harold Lasswell. We get together for martinis most Friday nights and I want to introduce you to him.' So, for about two years, I spent many Friday nights fixing martinis for Harold and his friend. We talked about politics, political science, universities, Harold's extraordinary visions for a peaceful, rational world of the future."

If you were compelled to speak from the mainstream in favor of gay rights or sexual orientation equality you had to tiptoe around the point, never explicitly stating your case but signaling elliptically to those in the know what you were trying to say. In 1948 Howard Lasswell, the father of the field of political psychology, published his hugely influential book *Power and Personality*. Three years later in a follow-up, *The Political Writings of Harold D. Lasswell*, he wrote that in the characterization of democratic personality there must be "equality of opportunity for the expression of affection" and "the scope of affection must be as wide as humanity itself." Sherrill says, "I knew what he was talking about." He has been using those quotes for fifty years, not only because he believes that they are true but also as an homage to his mentor and friend.

Over half a century Sherrill built a field of study: an intellectual home for scholars in America and beyond. Because his research has remained considered and principled, it has been used as the foundation of many judicial challenges to the unequal status quo, not least in the major cases on marriage equality, military service, and same-sex benefits.

"It was thrilling to sit at Supreme Court oral arguments and to see my academic work help make history. It's wonderful to be able to look at it and know that you had a hand. How many political scientists ever have—or take—the opportunity to use their professional skills to do something good? I credit Don [Matthews] and Jim [Prothro] for teaching me that I could. When I first started doing this, I merely thought I was extending their work to another movement." In 2015, Sherrill addressed a panel at the American Political Science Association meetings in San Francisco titled "Marriage Equality in the US: How Did We Get Here." He ironically thanked the enemies who had attacked gay people, thus instigating and energizing a movement. As he came to thank "the Reagan administration for its murderous evil failure to respond to AIDS," he choked up. "Had it not been for them and my dead friends . . . there wouldn't have been Larry Kramer . . . there wouldn't have been Gay Men's Health Crisis . . . there wouldn't have been ACT UP . . . there would never have been the development of the organizational capacity which enabled the extraordinary political activity that Marc [Solomon from Freedom to Marry] and others did. The whole marriage movement stands on the shoulders of the AIDS movement."

It was a moment that no one in the audience will forget.

Figure 12.1 Mayor Ed Murray in front of his portrait of Cal Anderson, Seattle City Hall, 2014. Credit: Andrew Reynolds.

12

The Washington 43rd

Forget the Roaring Twenties; when it comes to the gold standard for elective office it's the Gay Forties, or to be more exact, the 43rd district of the Washington State legislature. The district encompasses downtown Seattle and the well-to-do neighborhoods of Capitol Hill, Lake Union, Green Lake, Freemont, Eastlake, and the University of Washington. Wealthy and bohemian, it has been represented consecutively by an out gay state senator or House member since 1987—the longest representation by a procession of out LGBT incumbents anywhere in the world.

Fifty years ago the 43rd was a bailiwick of moderate Republicans—indeed, for eighty years the 43rd had always been represented by a Republican. But by the beginning of the 1970s the Republican grip had been broken, and the House seat was occupied by newly minted Navy psychiatrist and Democrat Jim McDermott, who had just returned from a tour of Vietnam. Over the next forty years the district would become one of the most progressive and safest Democratic seats in the nation. McDermott moved to the Washington State senate in 1975, and when he resigned to become a foreign service doctor in Zaire in 1987 the incumbent house member, Janice Niemi, moved up to his senate seat. This opened up an appointment to the now-vacant house seat.

Cal Anderson checked all the boxes for an aspiring politician apart from one—his sexuality. He was born in Tukwila, a suburb of Seattle, in 1948, and as a teenager threw himself into school politics. When his father decided to stand for election to the city council, the sixteen-year-old personally wrote a letter to every voter in the district. The elder Anderson won by four votes. After graduating from high school, Cal took a job with Seattle City Councilor Jeanette Williams. The war in Vietnam was reaching a crescendo and the draft was in full swing. Anderson could have played the "homosexual tendencies" card to stay home but was worried that the papers would say "Cal Anderson, Jeanette Williams's secretary, is a fairy." In Vietnam he was assigned to be a court reporter, but remained in areas where the bullets were flying. He was the lead reporter for the investigation of the My Lai massacre and the subsequent trial of the officer in command, Ernest Medina.

On his return to Seattle he went back to work at the council, eventually becoming the mayor's secretary. Gay men could be behind the scenes but not out front; like children, seen but not heard. Despite the presumption that it would destroy any political career, Anderson never second-guessed his decision to come out in the early 1970s, telling a reporter: "It was a good decision absolutely. I don't believe I've been hurt by it. If I was concentrating my energy on hiding who I am and hiding my relationship with my partner, I wouldn't have energy to do anything else. I'd be a basket case." Anderson was the Pacific Northwest's Harvey Milk. "Hopefully, what I'll be able to show other people is, 'Hey, it ain't a big whoop. Come on in, the water's fine.'"

But it was a big whoop. In the early 1970s a gay community had coalesced around downtown Seattle, Capitol Hill, and the University District, but they were far from mainstream political actors. The Gay Liberation Front opened its first community center in Pioneer Square in 1971, and a plethora of support and advocacy groups sprung up in the district. Seattle was becoming a beacon for queers, with many new arrivals meeting other out lesbians or gay men for the first time in their lives. The Seattle City Council was comparably progressive: the 1973 Fair Employment Practice Ordinance protected gays and lesbians from discrimination at work. In 1976 the sodomy law was repealed and sexual orientation was added to housing discrimination regulations. Though some pride parades had been organized in earlier years to commemorate Stonewall, Mayor Charles Royer declared an official Gay Pride Week in 1977. But these were all actions taken by straight allies on behalf of LGBTs. Politics remained a no-go area. Gays and lesbians were getting juicy morsels thrown from the table, but were not sitting around it.

For many straight Democrats and the gay community, Anderson's candidacy was emblematic of change. The Seattle Democrats saw a personable, measured man, perhaps even unthreatening, whom they could present to the outside world as a symbol of their progressive bona fides. Some gays saw Anderson as their glass ceiling-breaker, but not all. Gary Atkins notes that even Cal's mentor, Harvey Muggy, said that "he's not as radical as some of us wanted" and, early on, what upset Anderson most was not being accepted by other gays and lesbians. His appointment to the legislature in 1987 was far from guaranteed—indeed, over the following quarter century, every transfer from gay representative to the next in the 43rd has been a knock-down battle royale. In the idiosyncratic fishbowl of Seattle politics, the race to succeed McDermott in the 1980s was a titanic struggle between the representatives of the dispossessed. Fifty-one of the 116 Democratic precinct captains in the 43rd nominated Anderson. The gay machine was purring, but a fair slice of the local establishment was behind Pat

Thibaudeau, a former party district chair and longtime lobbyist for the women's political caucus. A third aspirant was Gene Peterson, a senior party official who happened to be African American. It was race versus gender versus sexual orientation.

The ultimate decision on who to appoint to the vacant seat rested not with the party but with the King County Council—five Democrats and four Republicans. They were not obliged to go with the local district vote. Despite coming in last in the precinct vote, Thibaudeau began to maneuver to have her name come out of the hat rather than Anderson's. She had powerful allies. Audrey Gruger, one of the Democratic King County Councilors, was determined that it would be Thibaudeau and not Anderson; she was working on the four GOP members to vote with her. Nevertheless, Dave McDonald, the young Democratic King County chair, was adamant that Anderson would take the seat. Recalling the events of nearly thirty years ago McDonald, who is now a lawyer in private practice, told me that he was "fully aware of the symbolism [of the first gay man in office] but truthfully my primary focus was making sure that the local district got the representative it had chosen and that the choice was made and implemented fairly and transparently. I was (and am) proud of the fact that the district selected Cal, who I knew well from having worked with him for years in party politics and who was eminently qualified for the job. But I did not want either the history or his appointment to be cheapened by nonfrivolous claims of back-room deals or unfairness. It was important to me that he go to the legislature because of who he was, not who he knew."

But McDonald was pessimistic about Anderson prevailing in the King Council vote when Gruger was so well positioned to engineer Thibaudeau's appointment. "In addition, at least one of the other Democrats was pretty conservative (though I never spoke to him about gay issues) and another was Catholic, so you could not be sure of a solid Democratic vote," McDonald noted. "When I looked at the situation in advance of the legislative district meeting I figured I had at most three of the five Democratic votes for Cal. Audrey had made it very clear that she would do whatever it took to get Pat to the legislature." McDonald came up with an audacious end-run plan. He would get a two-thirds vote from the more sympathetic King County Democratic Central Committee to remove Thibaudeau's name from the list of three that had been sent by the 43rd district. He argued that because Thibaudeau sought to persuade the county council to ignore the local district party's first choice, she deserved to be removed. It was a desperate attempt by McDonald to stop the county council selecting Thibaudeau over Anderson. However, Audrey Gruger wasn't done. McDonald recalled, "I remember running into Audrey on the street and her telling me that she had figured out how to do it [get Pat Thibaudeau selected]—that she would block the county council from acting and then the list would go to the governor."

But McDonald had anticipated the strategy and had already written to then-Governor Booth Gardner to urge him to leave the appointed as a local above-board, rather than a back-room, decision.

Did McDonald believe there was a significant likelihood that Thibadeau would have succeeded in overturning the nonbinding vote and getting appointed over Anderson if he had not engineered her removal as a candidate? "Yes, absolutely," he recalled. "The temper of the times was much different and bias, both latent and overt, against gays much stronger. AIDS was just sweeping the country and terrifying many folks, whether gay or straight." Plus, there was a buzz around pushing strong female candidates. "Geraldine Ferraro had just made history as the first female member of a presidential ticket." The memory of the fight it took to appoint Washington's first openly gay man to public office is burned in McDonald's mind. "It was a politically bruising event. I had many calls, not all friendly, from women donors, black donors, and gay donors, and various party officials during that period. As I recall I lost something like fifteen pounds during the process." But Washington State had its first openly gay man in office. The Seattle Democrats licked their wounds and moved on.

In the 1980s and 1990s homophobia, even in such a progressive district, was par for the course. When he first stood for election in the 1988 Democratic primary Anderson's opponent made sure she was always referred to as *Mrs.* Debra Wilson Mobley. One of her ads asked, "Which one of these candidates for state representative in Position 1 in the 43rd District could I honestly look my kids in the eye and say, 'This is a good role model to follow?'" When elected, some representatives refused to sit next to Anderson, and a state senator from his own party suggested that he wouldn't receive so many death threats if he wasn't so out: "If you wouldn't go around bragging that you're a homosexual, maybe it wouldn't happen. Don't you think that's true? Don't you think it's better to keep quiet?"

Nevertheless, over seven years in the House seat Anderson was re-elected with overwhelming majorities three times and then won the open Senate seat in 1994 with 81 percent of the vote. Early on he fought against the "gay legislator" label. He was known for interests in housing, gun control, drug issues, and voting rights. But in the summer of 1988 his friend Ed Murray gave him a copy of Randy Shilts's *Mayor of Castro Street*. In an interview with Gary Atkins, Murray recalled, "He came back and totally embraced everyone. The leather community, the drag community. Cal the private gay man became the public gay man . . . as time went on and his legislative skills became apparent, then the gay and lesbian community really adopted him. They grew to love him for what he was able to do."

Through demonstrating legislative savvy, Anderson had gone from being "the gay politician" to being a state representative who happened to be gay. He was funny and he was well-liked. Civil rights began to rise to the top of his daily to-do list. Every year, like clockwork, he reintroduced the gay and lesbian civil rights bill, which had first been offered to a recalcitrant legislature in 1977. Every year it died. It would take until 2006 to see the bill finally passed in the Washington State Legislature. The fact that Anderson was the gay rep didn't stop the more radical of the LGBT community from charging him with selling out. In 1993, his house was daubed with "Budget Cuts Kills" and "AIDS Money Now."

Little did the anonymous activists know that Cal had been diagnosed as HIV positive in 1985. By 1995, he was undergoing chemotherapy for AIDS-related non-Hodgkins lymphoma. As Anderson moved into his Senate seat he became sicker, but his presence put a very human face on being gay. He told a *Seattle Times* reporter, "I think my being down here has shown that gays are not monsters. We're just like everybody else except that we like to have sex with people of the same gender. We care about education and transportation and agriculture. We eat food grown east of the mountains." On August 4, 1995, Cal's lover and partner Eric Ishino found him dead at their home. He was forty-seven years old.

The appointment of Cal Anderson was a moment that altered the paths of many lives and laws. The passing of the torch from gay man to gay man in the 43rd was personal, intimate, never predetermined but cloaked in an aura of historicism larger than the stakes of which Democrat represented a few hundred square miles in a state house. Anderson's anointed successor was his friend who had grown up in the suburbs of Olympia, Ed Murray. But again, it was far from a foregone conclusion.

The Protégée: Ed Murray

Ed Murray took his mentor Cal Anderson's seat in the Washington State House in 1995 and went on to be elected mayor of Seattle in 2014—the highest executive position in America occupied by an openly gay man. Murray told me that the only reason he is in politics was because of Anderson. Murray's interest in politics began in high school and evolved at college in Portland, Oregon, but Ed never imagined he could be an elected official. In fact, he was sure he *couldn't* be elected. In the mayor's office on the top floor of Seattle City Hall, with the summer sun streaming in, a photo of Anderson over one shoulder and a view of the Seattle docks over the other, Murray mused, "I knew of only one gay man who had been elected and he had been shot. I couldn't imagine living anything but a secret and painful life." "When did you first feel that there was a space in politics for you?" I asked. "Is Cal part of that story?" "Cal *is* the story," Murray responded. "He was a trailblazer . . . by blazing that trail, he made it a hell of a lot easier for anyone else who came after him." Although Murray lost a special election to fill Anderson's Senate seat, he was appointed to the fill the 43rd's seat in the Washington State House of Representatives two months after Anderson's death.

"I was five when John Kennedy was elected, but I was very aware of the significance his election meant to my Irish Catholic family," Murray says. "It really was a sense that we belonged. When Cal Anderson, who I knew as a friend, ended up in the legislature it was at that moment that I believed . . . oh, I can be this too. I didn't believe that before. It was a revelation for me." Murray was the anointed son. "Cal, as he was dying, had decided I should get the appointment. He was busy from his hospital bed helping to recruit precinct committee officers to make sure I got it. He was a master politician. It was the darkest days of AIDS. There had been so much loss." Murray paused, swallowing hard. "Cal's loss on top of that. I felt like there needed to be somebody gay there." The anger on the streets of downtown Seattle was palpable. AIDS was decimating a generation. Ed Murray's inheritance of the 43rd House seat must be seen in that context. That anger did not dissipate. When Murray ran for Anderson's Senate seat, Dan Savage wrote a piece in *The Stranger* that Murray recalled as "just over the top vicious, but it reflected how people felt at that time." Savage and Murray have been (and had been) by-and-large allies. The woman Murray ran against was Pat Thibadeau.

Two thousand people attended Anderson's funeral at St. James's Catholic Cathedral on First Hill in Seattle. Murray had not only persuaded the presiding priest, Father Michael Ryan, to use the cathedral, but also to officiate. The ceremony included chanting Native Americans, the sitting governor, the city's senior clergy, and the drag collective—the Sisters of Perpetual Indulgence—dressed in their nun's habits. It was televised statewide.

Early on, Murray began to forge a career in the state house with the same strength of purpose that Anderson had shown. He very deliberately set a course to destroy the notion that he was an undeserving pretender and one-trick (read: gay–liberal) pony. The presence of Cal Anderson in the state house hadn't destroyed the homophobia; "some Republicans would not speak to me, shake my hand, or acknowledge me," Murray recalls. He focused on transportation and began to connect with legislative colleagues over bread-and-butter issues.

Demonstrating legislative chops and building personal relationships gave Murray the chips to play on—and for—gay rights issues, which at the start was very clearly *not* about gay marriage. "The big battle in Washington State was not marriage equality but the twenty-nine-year effort to pass the LGBT civil rights bill," Murray says, which was signed into law in 2006. "It started in 1977—I worked on it for eleven years. Before that, Cal lived and died trying to pass it over eight years in the legislature." In the early days Murray's playbook was not universally popular. "My strategy was one of incremental change—building alliances with business leaders, Republicans, moderates," Murray said. "Make it about what the bill would do for the community rather than the old model of presenting the LGBT community as victims. When I first proposed an incremental approach almost every leader in the gay and lesbian community and my colleagues in the legislature opposed it. We fought with each other for several months behind the scenes before I got them to agree. Move forward incrementally . . . test the waters . . . start changing minds. Dan Savage at *The Stranger* and Governor Christine Gregoire were the two biggest supporters I had in a very tough time when my own community leaders said we should just go for marriage." When it passed in 2006 the strategy was vindicated and, as Murray says, "it broke the dam." Despite being at the center of the whirlwind, the mayor has been shocked by the pace of change in America. "I believed we could get the civil rights bill—I never believed I would see marriage while I was in elected office."

In 2013, after eighteen years in the Washington state house, Murray set his sights higher. He fought a very tough race against the incumbent mayor of Seattle, Michael McGinn. It was his first time running citywide and the first time he'd really felt the sting of homophobia. McGinn's campaign targeted the large East African and African American communities, not-so-subtly raising Murray's sexual orientation to frighten minorities away from his camp. As the mayor puts it, these groups were "pushed around on gay issue"—which was doubly infuriating to him when he sees gays and lesbians in those communities who are "trapped in a city where [homosexuality] is accepted, but a culture where it's not."

As a kid Murray knew of only one gay man in office and he'd been shot dead. I asked if when he first decided to run for office he'd been afraid it could happen to him. Was it a dangerous time to be out and visible in public and put your head above the parapet? Murray sighed and shifted in his chair. "I usually don't talk about security but there has been a consistent level of concern . . . the bad days of AIDS, when marriage took off, and certainly now [as mayor]. Letters, phone calls." But isn't it much better now? I asked. "No. Actually it has never gone away."

Murray's experience sheds light on the challenges of being a curiosity and the importance of electing a cohort of LGBT politicians. One is the loneliest number; two or three can make all the difference. "When you are alone it's very isolating and, while not all gay elected officials get along with each other, there is a comfort level of mutual understanding which is very helpful," Murray says. For seven years he sat alone as the only openly gay legislator in Olympia. In 2001 he was joined by Joe McDermott, in 2002 Jim Moeller and David Upthegrove were elected, then Jamie Pedersen in 2006, and Marko Liias in 2008. In 2010 the first woman, Laurie Jinkins, made seven. This not only provided camaraderie, but allowed the caucus to spread the workload. "Marco Liias took on bullying issues," Murray says. "Jim Moeller focused on HIV, Jamie Pedersen allowed me a partner in the House on marriage issues." In 2014 two more lesbians, Christine Kilduff and Joan McBride, were elected to the Washington House.

Ironically, reaching the pinnacle of the office of mayor of one of America's greatest cities returned Murray to isolation he felt as the only gay in the state house. "There are tough days, but when I was in the Senate or the House I could turn to somebody else who was a peer," he says. "Go for a drink, have dinner. But as mayor I don't have that. Even nation-wide there is only Annise Parker [mayor of Houston]. It's re-created the sense of isolation I had twenty years ago."

So It Continues

In the rearview of history the continuity of out gay representation in the Washington State 43rd state house district appears to be the deliberate passing of the baton. Indeed, Murray proudly notes, "I came in at the end and endorsed Jamie [Pedersen]. Jamie and I actively recruited and worked to get Brady [Piñero Walkinshaw] put in there." But when Ed Murray moved up to the State Senate seat in 2006, Jamie Pedersen was far from an inevitable successor. Pedersen, a lawyer who grew up in the Puyallup valley—the farmland home of the Washington State Fair—faced six candidates in a highly competitive Democratic primary. Half a million dollars was spent in what turned out to be the most costly house race in the state's history. Pedersen won 23 percent of the vote, with the former city council president Jim Street just 229 votes behind. While Pedersen describes a "clean and civil campaign, with almost no issue disagreements," he notes in retrospect the fragility of his entrance into elective politics. "If you had taken any of the other five candidates out you can argue that I might not have come in first." Indeed, Murray had a number of allies and friends in the race and only endorsed Jamie a couple of weeks before the primary was held.

Pedersen's experience illustrates the dichotomies that are navigated by a gay man in modern American politics. Before his election Pedersen's political reputation was built on the struggle for gay rights. He had been a highly visible proponent of marriage equality ever since 1995, and cochaired the Lambda Legal Defense Fund board in Seattle. As LAMDA's staff lawyer he was lead counsel in the momentous *Anderson v. King* case, in which eight couples sued the state of Washington for denying them marriage licenses. Even so, Pedersen didn't feel the pressure of needing to shed the gay politician label. "That was really a big deal for Cal," he told me as we sat in an expansive staff canteen of McKinstry, the large Seattle-based company he now works for. "It was a pretty big deal for Ed. It's not something I spent a lot of time worrying about." In fact, his legislative colleagues in Olympia think of him as "the lawyer," not the gay politician. Indeed, Ed Murray would often urge Jamie to try and avoid being pigeonholed as the lawyer. But Pedersen argues that with the rest of his profile, "politically moderate . . . downtown corporate lawyer, I would have not been competitive for the seat if I were not gay. That's the only thing that made me a viable candidate in this district."

Once in office, Pedersen and Murray teamed up to build momentum to move marriage equality forward step by step. Pederson, the legal strategist, was the perfect foil to Murray, the emotional advocate. The Democratic majority placed Pedersen in the chair of the judiciary committee to get the marriage bill over that hurdle. It passed by a 7 to 6 vote. The vote was along party lines, but some Democrats were as difficult to persuade as Republicans. For years Pedersen sat behind Tami Green on the legislature floor. Green was a conservative Democrat from a district south of Tacoma. An active Mormon, she faced huge pressure from her family and her congregation to vote against gay rights measures. In 2007 she voted against the first domestic partner bill. Over time, "we cried and hugged and talked," says Jamie. Slowly she came around. In 2012, "even though it caused a pretty significant rift with her husband and her congregation, she voted for marriage," Jamie recalls. Frank Chopp, the speaker of the house, told me, "Tami Green had a fundamental sense of what's right," but her friendship with Jamie gave her the courage to go out on a limb.

Pedersen is emblematic of Milk's adage that being an authentic gay man in elective office shatters innermost-held negative preconceptions and beliefs. He has the all-too-familiar backstory of growing up gay in a place that did not know what to do with that. He was the Eagle Scout, the Sunday school teacher, and the senior-year class president. When he came out in high school in the mid-1980s the girl he'd been dating "freaked out," he says, and wrote out three pages of Bible verses for him. In his words, gay people were "invisible"—in his town, school, and Lutheran church—so when the bible was thrown at him he was taken aback. "Her mother told her not to talk to me anymore because she'd get AIDS . . . It was a journey for my parents—mum cried, because they thought that it would mean I'd never realize my career potential or have a family." Yale was a much more welcoming environment, and Pedersen became a Russophile and sang with the Yale Russian Chorus. Although the passion has waned, "homophobia has chilled my interest in Russia," he says. "I lived there for two years. It's scary now thinking of trying to go there with husband and kids."

But his journey touched his straight colleagues. In 2007 Jamie and his husband Eric had their first son through a surrogate mother in San Diego. The next pregnancy resulted in triplets. He chuckles when describing how at Children's Day in the state house there were more than enough babies to pass around. In 2012 the marriage equality proponents knew they needed twenty-five votes for the bill to pass in the Washington Senate. They identified twenty-one solid votes and seven possibilities; they needed to swing four of those seven. Mary Margaret Haugen was a Democratic state senator from a swing district covering part of the rural coast and wealthy islands. She sidled up to Pedersen during a debate and whispered, "I never really understood these issues until I met your family—now meeting you and the kids I get it." She was the twenty-fifth vote. Later that year she lost her seat to the Republicans.

After fighting for so long for marriage equality, Pedersen says that the *Obergefell* US Supreme Court decision in June 2015 was somewhat anticlimatic for him. The real celebration was winning the referendum in Washington State in November 2012. In his first Seattle Men's Chorus performance in the 1990s the chorus had sung "Finally Here," a song of coming out. It began;

> Its alright,
> hold him tight,
> brush your hands through his hair.
> You no longer need to fight,
> for he's always been there.

In 2012 the opening stanza was rewritten for their holiday concert, with the last two lines becoming "You no longer need to fight / for the love that you share." Pedersen says at that moment on stage he was hit by the notion that the battle was won and is grateful that he was part of that battle. "Very few people get the chance to make so many people's lives better off. A lot of issues there is no clear right answer—everybody is right to some degree—and it's never actually . . . done. This is an issue where there is a right answer—and we've gotten it."

Brady Piñero Walkinshaw was the fourth man of the Washington 43rd and the new golden boy: a bundle of dark good looks and youthful energy, a degree from Princeton, former employee of the emperor of the Pacific Northwest, Bill Gates. His ancestry presses the right buttons for new and old Seattleites alike—second-generation Cuban American on his mother's side, Washington state homesteader on his father's—a family so wrapped up in the topography of Washington that two of his great-grandfathers have peaks named for them in the Olympic Mountain range. Walkinshaw was a shiny new Latino and rooted Anglo patrician wrapped into one. The July sun beats down on the shore of the 43rd's Lake Union when we meet, so we sit in the cool marble lobby of the new Museum of History and Industry as school kids file in and out. The museum is a stone's throw from the headquarters of the Bill and Melinda Gates Foundation, where Walkinshaw spent his years after graduation as a policy analyst.

Just like Cal Anderson in 1987, Ed Murray in 1995, and Jamie Pedersen in 2006, Walkinshaw faced an uphill struggle to be selected by the local party as their candidate for the 43rd to keep the streak alive. He was running against the head of the local party, Scott Forbes, and another local activist, Christina Gonzalez. The race was not about policy differences. It was a choice between three equally progressive candidates." The 210 party precinct captains would vote to choose the new member. But in the spring of 2013 only ninety-six of those positions were filled and Forbes, as the district leader, was going to win. Pedersen told Walkinshaw, "If you want this you have to change the composition of the electorate." Brady recruited close to seventy new captains, many from the LGBTQ activist community. By the end there were 180 precinct captains in place and the vote was extremely close. "I worked pretty hard to make sure that Brady got the appointment," Pedersen tells me. Walkinshaw concurs. "Jamie and Ed endorsed me, but not until I'd proven myself." *The Stranger* led with the tongue-in-cheek headline "Another Gay Man Appointed," which Walkinshaw says implied there was more of a gay machine at work than there actually was. It is true that the LGBT network is strong in Seattle, but Walkinshaw also drew from other activist and professional networks. Indeed, the hunger and cohesiveness of the LGBT community is waning over time with each big victory.

Recalling how Cal and Ed had grown up knowing they had no place in political life without anyone needing to make it explicit, I asked Brady if, by the time he came of age in the 2000s, all that had gone away. Had the groundbreaking of his predecessors removed all obstacles to public office, both internal and external? "Not at all," Brady said. "I grew up in a rural conservative place—near the town of Everson in the Nooksack valley. I don't remember meeting anyone who was openly gay until I was in college. I grew up feeling I couldn't get into politics." This was a problem, because Brady loved politics. As a kid he named his dog George Washington, dressed up as Washington for Halloween, and made his Playmobile into a functioning United Nations with various nation states to visit. It wasn't until arriving at Princeton for college that he came out. Today Walkinshaw embraces his ethnicity and identity, but regrets never "officially" coming out to his Cuban-born grandparents. "I wished I had," he says. "My grandfather passed away earlier this year and grandmother has Alzheimer's."

Walkinshaw's mentor in college, Mark Burstein, opened up the political world for him by connecting him to the Victory Institute. Burstein, now the president of Lawrence University in Wisconsin, told me that Walkinshaw was an extraordinary presence as the senior-class representative on the Princeton Board of Trustees. "It was remarkable how he could sit alongside long-term board members with a wealth of international experience, CEOs of Fortune 500 companies, and hold his own immediately. He was thoughtful, carefully chose his battles, and fought them in a measured way. I was just struck by his presence and felt the resonance of his personal story. He had all the ingredients. Not just to be a good 'gay candidate' but a great candidate—period."

To Walkinshaw, the Victory Fund was a revelation. "I was involved with Victory before I came out to my parents," he says. It made him realize he *could* be both things: a politician and a gay man. After graduation he returned to Seattle, and Ed Murray took him under his wing. The "patriarch of the LGBT caucus" (as Brady refers to Ed) had once been a legislative aid to former Seattle City Councilor Martha Choe, and now Choe was Walkinshaw's boss at the Gates Foundation. Mayor Murray is a big fan of Walkinshaw: "He's extremely ambitious and I expect him to move quickly to something beyond the state house," he told me.

I ask if it still matters in the legislature that a gay man is present, or whether it isn't old hat by now. "I feel it matters so strongly now," Walkinshaw responded. "We are the source of a political influence and power, so we need to be represented." He believes the presence of six openly gay and lesbian legislators in Olympia still changes the dynamic of the conversation, and that new tone spreads across the state. Recently he returned to Nooksack Valley High to accept a distinguished alumni award—the town where he'd never met someone else who was gay. He told the teenagers about being gay and being in politics. Kids took him aside after to share their private stories. His mother, who is a teacher at the school, has people stop her in the hallways to talk about her son. For Brady, this illustrates the "power of representation as someone who is gay, someone who is Latino." In a decade or so a new political leader who grew up in conservative Nooksack Valley will tell a reporter about how Brady made him feel he could stand up, just as Brady looked up to Ed, and Cal inspired by Ed a generation before.

In August 2015 Brady Walkinshaw married his husband, Micah, in a ceremony on Capitol Hill. They were married by Mayor Ed Murray with State Senator Jamie Pedersen in attendance (and no doubt Cal Anderson looking down from on high). Brady describes Micah, a marine biologist, as "my moral and ethical compass." Ed Murray says his husband Michael is his "best political advisor," a man who excels in his role as "political spouse." "On the day I was going to declare for mayor," Ed recalls, "I woke up and said, 'I don't think I want to do this.' Michael talked him round in short order, saying, "I can't live with you for the rest of your life with you asking whether you should have done that." Four months after his wedding, Walkinshaw shocked the Seattle politicos by declaring to run against the long-term incumbent Seattle city US Congressman Jim McDermott in the Washington 7th. McDermott had held the seat for twenty-eight years and was by all accounts invulnerable to challenge, never winning by less than 70 percent of the vote. Was this a stroke of genius or an idiotic move? At first McDermott squared up to fight—"you wouldn't give a Maserati to a fifteen-year-old," he told the *Seattle Times*, "this is the government that runs the world." But the seventy-eight-year-old had second thoughts over the holidays and decided it was time to do other things. If elected, Walkinshaw would be the first out US congressman from Washington, only the fourth from the West, and only the eighth ever to be elected into office while out. And perhaps more important, the first out gay Latino to be elected to the US house, giving voice to the 1.4 million LGBTQ LatinX community.

Time for a Woman in the 43rd?

With Brady Walkinshaw exiting the 43rd, would the three-decade streak continue? At the beginning of 2016 there were nine candidates in the race (one later dropped out): two gay men, one lesbian, one trans woman, and four straight men. The environmental activist Sameer Ranade wrote to me apologetically, saying he wasn't gay. "But please know that I am a strong ally and supporter of LGBTQ rights. One critical theme of my campaign is to create a more emphatic, compassionate society in which people recognize the common bonds of humanity that they share with each other." There are few places in the world where one has to apologize for not being gay when running for office. When the transgender activist Danni Askini dropped out, her endorsement was enthusiastically sought. When it went to Nicole Macri, the advocate for the homeless, it gave Macri's campaign a significant boost. It confirmed her status as the gold standard progressive candidate: the lesbian, radical, leftist progressive backed by the transgender voice. It was noted repeatedly that a woman hadn't been elected in the 43rd since Pat Thibadeux was ousted from the Senate seat in 2006.

Macri was born in Bernie Sanders's old stomping ground of Brooklyn into an Italian American family. She met her partner Deb at Rutgers University when they were undergraduates. A resident of Seattle for nearly two decades, she helps direct the Downtown Emergency Services Center ,which provides housing and care for the thousands of homeless people, most laboring under the multiple challenges of addiction, mental and physical disabilities, and extreme poverty. There is some controversy around their programs, which offer accommodation and counseling services without a commitment to abstain from alcohol. She swept the endorsements of the 43rd district Democrats, student organizations, the unions, the city council members, and over sixty of the city's leading progressive activists.

There is something compelling about Macri—she is earnest and vulnerable, but at the same time self-possessed and warm. She has a big smile. She acknowledges how it has been a steep learning curve to feel comfortable in the spotlight, take on leadership roles, and navigate the archaic maze of big-city politics. She believes her reticence to be at the forefront stemmed more from internalized sexism rather than being a lesbian. Like many women, she was comfortable in doing the behind-the-scenes work; not being the front person felt ingrained. Even though the timing was right in 2016, and her credentials were impeccable, she says she had to be "pushed" into throwing her hat into ring.

Fittingly, we talk in an Italian café in the heart of Seattle's downtown. She is visibly nervous about the results, which are due in a few hours. She tells me that she had to be encouraged to be more open about being a lesbian in a long-term relationship and how that colors the world in which she dwells. She was never in the closet, but her sexual orientation was never her opening line in conversation. Indeed, Ed Murray told her, "I didn't realize you were a lesbian. You really should be more out there with your identity." "Some of it [is] maybe the cultural difference between gay men and lesbians," says Macri. Indeed, while the 43rd has had LGBT representatives since 1987, they were all white gay men. "One of the questions when I entered the race was: is the 43rd ready to open up beyond just a gay man?" Throughout her career Macri has often been the only woman and lesbian in the room. Despite the paucity of out lesbians in visible political office, early on in the election the focus on a "history-making opportunity" was centered on Danni Askini. Macri's aura and uniqueness was somehow diluted. But once Askini dropped out and endorsed Macri, she was minted. Nicole described her strategy as "pushing to the left. Being more inclusive. Being less hetero-normative."

As we chat an apparition appears as if from nowhere next to our table. Filling out a cream shirt and wearing a Native American bolo necktie, the phantom was instantly recognizable as the long-term congressman and former 43rd state house representative Jim McDermott, the man who had helped kick-start the streak by taking the 43rd from the Republicans in 1970. Macri jumps up and introduces herself as a candidate in that day's election for the 43rd house seat.

"Did the *Times* endorse you?" he asks her.

"They didn't, the *Stranger* did," she replies.

"Ah," McDermott smiles. "Who did the *Times* endorse," he asks.

"Dan Shih," Nicole tells him.

"He's a lawyer," I interject. "Chinese American. Also openly gay."

McDermott laughs. "Hey. It's the 43rd!"

I smile back.

"It's not the way it was," he says, becoming more serious. "I had about ten gay precinct captains in my district—all in the closet. None of them came out until the AIDS epidemic."

"How would you feel if your seat in the US House was filled by an openly gay representative? Would that make you happy?" I ask McDermott.

"If they do a good job I don't give a damn who they are." He belly-laughs.

"Seriously," he continues. "It's about trying to add something to Washington, DC, that they need."

We shook hands and I sat back down, looked up, and McDermott had disappeared as fast and mysteriously as he had appeared. Had he been just a figment of our imaginations . . . the ghost of elections past?

Macri touches my shoulder as we leave the table. "I'm amazingly nervous. What comes out today isn't necessarily where things are going to land."

There is no doubt that Dan Shih is the chief threat to Macri's success. Later I describe Shih to Brady Walkinshaw as "the Chinese Jamie Pedersen." Walkinshaw winces, but I'm not sure if in agreement or objection. On the surface Shih and Pedersen are mirror images: they both went to East Coast Ivy League schools (Shih to Princeton, Pedersen to Yale), and they both went to Ivy League law schools (Shih to Stanford, Pedersen to Yale); they became very successful public interest lawyers and had prestigious clerkships; both became wealthy, worked for LAMDA legal, do socially responsible pro-bono work, and now are married with a mess of small children (Dan three, Jamie four). Both are the breadwinners whose husbands take primary responsibility for childcare. The *Seattle Times* endorsed Shih by saying, "With a superb résumé, a nuanced grasp of policy and a steady temperament, Shih has the potential to be an excellent lawmaker from a legislative district with a history of producing leaders in Olympia." Another potential candidate who chose not to throw his hat in the ring, Michael Maddux, told a widely read blog, "Dan is raising a boatload of money. He's trying to go the Jamie Pedersen route of what he did in 2006, which is trying to get through the primary by raising more than anyone else." Nicole Macri sees the race as being between the center and left—in Seattle terms. She characterizes Shih's message as "I'm not the radical, I'm the one you can trust." Indeed, Shih dismisses *The Stranger* as "geared to the irreverent, self-consciously radical." "Dan is nonthreatening to the wealthy movers and shakers of the district, but can he get enough of the Left vote to get him over the line?" Macri muses. A number of activists tell me that Shih's biggest challenge is being too much like Pedersen. "Ultimately Jamie is great, we count on him, but we have the Frank Chopp–Jamie Pedersen team, [so] do we need another Jamie?" Macri asks.

Shih acknowledges that he wrestles with identity issues. Being both Chinese American and gay, he grew up "a bit on the outside." He describes it generously as giving him "overtones and flavor" in the Chinese community, which was socially and religiously ambivalent at best in reacting to his sexual orientation. "Being gay was something white people did," he notes. No one else was out in his extended family: "I didn't have the support of that bachelor uncle." Shih says his family were ultimately supportive, even if they were not at the start. "Was I still the kid they knew me to be?" they wondered. In his twenties he endured the second-guessing which comes with minority status. "When you are an outsider and you experience a slight you never quite know whether it's bigotry or something else," he says. On the campaign trail, being gay has come up in positive ways. With Ted and the kids on the campaign trail, voters have said "it's great to see what your family looks like. I met a mother of a gay son, who told me she was thrilled to support me."

Shih describes his backstory as the classic immigrant story. As a small boy in postwar China, his father fled with his family from Mao's takeover to the relative safety of Shanghai and then Taiwan. In 1969 his parents came to America with "two suitcases and nothing else to their name." Speaking little English, his mother got her nursing credential and his father started a leather import shop on 2nd and Pike in downtown Seattle. They did not install in little Dan a yearning for the public sphere. "Their conception of a good life is having privacy, whereas mine is one of being very connected," he tells me. Shih was smart and majored in computer science at Princeton. But that was too introverted for his tastes, and so he did an MA in economics at Stanford. That led to a stint in business with the Boston Consulting Group, and then he returned to Stanford for law school. He quickly worked his way up to partner at Susman Godfrey, "the No. 1 litigation boutique firm in the nation," as proclaimed on the firm's website. He specialized in being on the right side of white-collar fraud cases: he took on Google for overcharging advertisers, biotech firms for insider trading, and represented a number of tech companies against larger tech companies. The corporate work allowed him to do pro-bono work for LAMDA legal and volunteer for API Chaya, supporting survivors of domestic violence, sexual assault, and trafficking in the Asian American community. But unlike many others, for Shih politics was not a burning passion from childhood. It wasn't until 2015 that he gave it serious thought. He went to a Victory Fund training in Indianapolis and was bitten by the bug.

In the race for the 43rd he has tried to downplay identity. "We hear 'it's time for a woman,'" he says. "I don't want to get into that fight of who is more underrepresented. I don't want to be the candidate who argues that they check more boxes than the others." Perhaps in a veiled slight against Macri, he says: "There are candidates in the race who are more readily susceptible to be pigeonholed than me." He acknowledges that he has been characterized as the centrist option. "The media always wants some sort of shorthand," he notes. "'Seattle Attorney' is a fair description of what I do to make my money, but it doesn't capture what else I do. People seem to be pleased that I've done well professionally—partner in a law firm. It gives them comfort that I'm not some joker. But when they ask about the issues they ask about the nonprofit work I do." Shih proudly tells me he lives with his family in the Eastlake neighborhood in a house on the water. "A house boat! That must be lovely!" I say. "Well, it is a floating home," Dan corrects me. "There's a distinction. It's a house that floats." He goes on to explain the difference and how his home is a regular house built on a concrete float.

It's not enough *just* to be gay in the 43rd now. That statement has been made by the voters of Seattle and will continue to be made. As Macri notes, "LGBT has become a baseline qualification that many voters like to see," but today you need something more. The residents of one of the most wealthy and most liberal districts in the nation want to make a new statement; there are competing identity issues to choose from. In 2016 it was race versus gender: the immigrant experience versus the female experience. In 2016 there were only forty out lesbian state legislators in all of the US, although three of those were in Olympia. But there were also no Chinese Americans in the state house and no out gay Chinese Americans at all in the United States. Indeed the only Chinese gay man in office in the world was Raymond Chan Chi-Chuen in Hong Kong. Shih says that initially he wasn't aware of groundbreaking potential of being the first out Chinese American in elected office. It's something "for reflection, not playing up," he says. "Would fundraising have been easier if I wasn't gay? Probably," he concludes, answering his own question.

But Macri versus Shih was also about style and lived experience. Fairly or not, the race became characterized as an insider (Shih) versus outsider (Macri) contest—Hilary Clinton versus Bernie Sanders, centrist versus radical. Looking at their policy platforms from the outside, one might be forgiven for seeing them both as radical progressives who would look like extreme liberals in any other place in America, but in the 43rd somebody has to play the part of the Right, and unfortunately for him, this time that was Dan Shih. In the primary race Shih raised significantly more money than his opponents. In August, Shih had $140,000 while Macri had closer to $90,000. But that was double the total of the next candidate in the race. While behind in money, Macri had the bulk of the endorsements, and the ones that mattered in the progressive Disneyland that is the Washington 43rd. During our conversations Shih had struck me as the more confident of the two about the outcome of the primary. He knew he would be in the top two, and I got the impression he expected to be in the top position going into the general election.

Just after 8 p.m. on Election Day, a couple of hundred people gathered at a trendy new warehouse brewery in Capitol Hill. Fifteen minutes later the first election results came in: a count of ballots postmarked up until a few days before the deadline, approximately 40 percent of the total; while not the final totals, it was a significant indicator of the final outcome. Would Macri make it into the runoff? Cheers went up and someone rushed over to Macri with iPhone in outstretched hand—49 percent. Her face lit up. "What did Dan get?" Twenty-six percent, she was told—a shocking blowout. Over the next few days Nicole's lead was embellished further, and when all votes were counted Macri was at 52 percent and Shih at 25 percent. The three openly gay candidates had garnered

79 percent of the vote between them. But Shih would have a mountain to climb in the head-to-head general election in November.

Similarly, the primary candidates for the US House 7th district of Washington State became proxies for schisms and battles beyond the borders of Seattle. Pramila Jayapal harnessed the angst of Bernie Sanders supporters who were so disappointed in Hilary Clinton's nomination. With strong Sanders backing she had raised a few hundred dollars more than Walkinshaw—1.3 million versus 1 million. Something of a wunderkind, Jayapal was born in Tamil Nadu, South India, but came to the United States as a sixteen-year-old to attend Georgetown University. She became an American citizen in 2000. After a stint in investment banking, she founded an immigrants' civil rights group, OneAmerica after 9/11.

When I chatted with Brady Walkinshaw in Pioneer Square in the late afternoon on primary day in August 2016, he was nervous. Their internal polling had suggested Jayapal was out ahead, and it was a very tight race between Walkinshaw and Joe McDermott for second. His team thought that if he could make it into the top two, with not too big a lead to surmount, he could pull off a head-to-head victory in November. "What are the differences between you and Pramila?" I ask him. "Ours is run from the outside in, ours is much more local," he argues. If Jayapal and Walkinshaw made the top two, "the 7th becomes a marquee race about what type of progressive moment you want." Teams would line up—it will be national Latino and LGBTQ money versus women and Indian American money. In the primary Walkinshaw consciously led with being gay, Latino, and progressive. Indeed, Macri sees one of his great strengths as "being a progressive who has garnered the support of the establishment. Brady has that quality that many great politicians have, he is an optimist."

As supporters swarmed around Macri, I checked the results of Walkinshaw's race. Jayapal had taken 39 percent and McDermott 21.6 percent, 536 votes ahead of Walkinshaw at 21.1 percent. Brady's election-night party was a couple of blocks away in a dive bar. The candidate stood with glass in hand under a large screen projecting the results web page, showing him frozen in third place. There would be no more updates tonight. But he seemed ebullient. "Don't worry, it's fine," he assured me. "I'll make that up." Indeed, it proved to be the case. The next day McDermott's 500-vote lead became a 500-vote lead for Walkinshaw. By Wednesday Brady was up by 1,200, and once the final results came in he had taken second place by over 3,000 votes. But Jayapal had 42 percent to Walkinshaw's 21 percent—a hefty advantage to take into the November election. Could Brady make that up? The immediate aftermath gave succor to both finalists. McDermott threw his support to Walkinshaw, giving him—in theory—a total close to Jayapal's votes, but Pramila received the endorsement of Danni Askini, cementing her image as the standard bearer for the zeitgeist of the times.

What do the "five from the 43rd" teach us? First, that even in the most progressive places, and after thirty years, gay legislators feel the constant burden of needing to prove themselves worthy. Murray notes that for him it was both a practical issue of trying to be taken seriously by his colleagues and a personal issue: "I had to keep proving to myself that I was more than just gay. Each of the four [of us] has been very competent and well respected." But there were always doubters, Murray notes. "Could I really perform at the level Cal did? When Jamie, the very bright academic, came in, did he have the political sense that Cal and Ed had? Brady went through much the same thing." Indeed, elected a quarter of a century after Cal Anderson, Brady Walkinshaw noted that being a gay elected official means you still have to "try harder and be better." Nicole Macri felt the extra burden of expectations being a woman and lesbian, and referenced the way in which Hilary Clinton was constantly striving to prove her credentials when many believed her to be one of the most experienced presidential candidates ever.

Second, the history of the 43rd shows us that you cannot over-estimate a seat at the table. The first four men became intently focused on being visible — and three decades on Macri was encouraged to make her identity more visible. Murray's credo has been handed down: "Get to know somebody, walk in their shoes. When you are sitting at the table with somebody you get to know that person."

What is it about the Washington State 43rd? Yes, the district is very liberal, very Democratic-leaning, encompassing wealth and the "young people and hipsters on Capitol Hill," as Murray describes it. At the heart of the 43rd are two large universities with their progressive heartbeats. But there are many places in America, and the world, that fit this profile, and none have been quite as friendly to gay politicians. The place that comes closest is the 78th district of the Wisconsin State legislature, which was represented by now-US Senator Tammy Baldwin between 1993 and 1999 and then by Mark Pocan until 2013. When Baldwin moved up the US Senate in 2014 Pocan took her US house seat, but his successor in the 78th house seat was not an LGBT Democrat. The run had ended at twenty years. Jamie Pedersen describes representing the 43rd as a luxury. "Most legislators worry about their districts, but here 90 percent of my constituents agree with me 95 percent of the time . . . In a swing district every vote you take makes half the people mad . . . If I were going to have an opponent it would be from the Left." Macri turned out to be that opponent, but she was running against Dan Shih.

Two state representatives are elected from each House district in Washington, and, as the other member from the 43rd, Frank Chopp, first elected alongside Murray in 1995, has had the best seat to observe the Anderson–Murray–Pedersen–Walkinshaw–Macri phenomenon. Chopp has been Speaker of the washington state house since 1999, and when told his district held the "gay legislator record" he laughed and said, "That makes me feel proud." Chopp argues that the thread connecting Anderson to Walkinshaw, through Murray and Pedersen, was not sexual orientation but skill and warmth. He was appointed to fill Anderson's house seat and then worked closely with the next three men. "Each of them are very different personalities and each had a major effect on me . . . Cal was beloved by everybody. Ed was crucial as budget chair. With his legal skills Jamie was just so competent. Everyone loves Brady, and he knows everyone." Chopp watched them all shatter the stereotypes expected of them. Quality people, with talent, experience, and the ability to bring in a broader network and coalition, combine to make them highly effective legislators. When it did come to issues of gay rights, "all exemplify perseverance, and made direct appeals to people," Chopp told me. Other legislators "got to know them as colleagues . . . personal presence really helped." He mentioned Lynn Kessler, the Democratic majority leader who represented a conservative part of the state. Through day-to-day interactions Ed Murray impressed on Kessler the moral and personal imperative of marriage equality. Chopp had faith in Kessler's inherent values and thinks she would have come to supporting equality at some point, but with Murray's presence she "got there more quickly."

From a very different partisan perspective, Dan Evans, now in his nineties, remains an active player in Washingtonian life. He started his political career as one of the last Republicans representing the 43rd in the state house (1957–1964). Evans was a Rockefeller Republican, advocating environmental protections, tax reform, public education, and investing in infrastructure projects. He went on to become one of the most lauded governors of Washington, serving three terms from 1965 to 1977, and as a US Senator from 1983 to 1989. He was considered by both Nixon and Ford as a vice presidential running mate. He created Evergreen State College, which is renowned as one of the most liberal colleges in America—a competitive title. Evans's brand of conservatism was far removed from the Republican Party of today: he encouraged Vietnamese refugees to come to Washington, appointed African Americans to positions of responsibility, and was an early cheerleader for women's rights.

He recalled Cal Anderson's appointment in 1987 as momentous. "The gay community was underground—politically, being gay was a death blow for almost anyone. When I first came into politics Seattle viewed itself as a liberal and open community but was still a community that had a significant amount of racial discrimination . . . for example many communities had provisos against selling homes to minorities. When Cal Anderson was appointed it was a significant breakthrough because it opened up what had been hidden for a long time." I asked whether Evans had observed Anderson and his successor Ed Murray affecting the conversation. "Certainly . . . Cal and Ed's presence affected people.

They got to know them as colleagues and as friends. People began to realize they were like themselves. It made a huge difference—both in Republican and Democratic caucuses."

The former governor was unequivocal about his support for gay marriage in 2012. "As a Republican, I believe strongly in individual liberty and freedom. So, for me, approving Referendum 74, supporting our bipartisan marriage law, and giving everyone the freedom to marry the person they love, just seems right and reflects the fundamental value of fairness that we treasure here in Washington," he said at the time. I asked the governor if he had evolved on the question. His answer surprised me: "I was settled much earlier," he said. Then he continued, "I just couldn't . . ." but he trailed off without finishing the thought. After a long pause Evans went on. "To me marriage is a very personal thing. After declaring the rights that go with marriage, government should stay out of the way." Evans has little doubt that history won't be kind to those who stood blocking the door. "We have a long way to go but I have great hope because the young people are way more in favor of these changes than their parents or their grandparents were. Twenty years from now we will look at gay marriage and ask what in the world was the problem? Just as we look back and say how could people have *ever* thought that slavery was good?"

Figure 13.1 Portraits of Crispin Blunt and Winston Churchill, Reigate Conservative Party Headquarters. Credit: Andrew Reynolds.

13

The Right Gays

Crispin Blunt: The Chameleon

When you first meet Crispin Blunt you get the impression he has just motored down from Downton Abbey in his 1911 Renault Landaulette. Dispensing with the chauffer, Blunt drives a tad too fast, with his niece Emily Blunt in the back seat—all chiffon scarves and straw hat. Crispin Blunt is the classic patrician Conservative, born to rule, but an inherently decent chap with an overactive conscience that makes him uneasy about his birthright. The former Conservative cabinet minister William Waldegrave wrote that "among successful politicians, there are two recurring types: Peelites and Disraelians. Peelites are driven, anxious, sometimes boring, often irritating, with their high moral tone and overwhelming sense of duty. They make bad party politicians but can be great prime ministers. Disraelians, on the other hand, are fun. To them, politics is a game; the summit of the greasy pole the goal; wit the weapon; heads for standing on; principles for mugs. They are the ones to sit beside at dinner." Blunt is definitely a Disraelian, and would not have been out of place in the enlightened wing of Benjamin Disraeli's cabinet in the 1870s. One could picture Sir Crispin negotiating the purchase of the Suez Canal and fretting over the plight of the natives.

There is great power in *not* conforming to the stereotype. The son of a major general, he was educated at the prep school for little generals, Wellington College, and the Royal Military Academy at Sandhurst, which led to a commission in the Queen Mary's Own Royal Hussars Regiment. After military service and an MBA, he was a special advisor on security issues to Conservative doyen Sir Malcolm Rifkind for four years, first when Rifkind was defense minister and later when he became foreign Mmnister. In 1997 Blunt became the MP for the so-called stockbroker seat of Reigate, Surrey, from which well-heeled business types commute in to central London. Many high-profile politicians are brutally honest in private, but Blunt is one of the few who are just as forthright in public. At the selection meeting for the constituency in 1997, he told the assembled local

Tory grandees that Reigate could be won by a "donkey in a blue rosette." They weren't amused.

For thirteen years Blunt played the role of the good Tory back-bencher, voting against almost every gay rights measure that came to Parliament. He was Tory security spokesperson in the run-up to the 2010 general election that would bring David Cameron to power and catapult Blunt into office as the minister for prisons. He also played the role of the good middle-England husband: wife, two kids, two dogs, a place in the country, cricket on Sunday.

Three months after the 2010 general election he announced that he was leaving his wife to "come to terms with his homosexuality." He told the *Advocate* magazine that during a postelection break in Barcelona he met a honeymooning gay couple from Massachusetts. "I needed to come out to my wife," Blunt told them, and "it's going to be on the front page of every newspaper. They thought it was the drink talking. But they told me to be honest. And I was. Of course, a few weeks later they fell off their chairs when they realized I was serious." When the story broke Blunt went to hide in the countryside with his cousin to avoid the tabloids. He worried that the army would be the "bit of my hinterland that I would lose completely." But that didn't happen. He recalls a regimental reunion in 2009, just before he came out. When the subject of homosexuality came up he characterizes the comments generously as "pretty old-fashioned." But after coming out, all was fine. He received a raft of positive letters from old army buddies and others. His Tory colleagues were also supportive—almost: "I can only recall one incident where a friend was reticent after I came out."

But back in Reigate, the fallout was more serious. In 2013, in a highly unusual event, he had to beat back an effort by his local constituency party to deselect him as their candidate. One executive member, Roger Newstead, wrote: "There is no doubt in my mind that his very public and totally unnecessary announcement that he was 'gay' was the final straw for some members. A number of lady members were very offended by the manner in which his marriage broke up." The prime minister personally intervened, and, by a postal ballot of the four hundred local members, he was reselected by a margin of five to one. This was an echo of the old Tory Party. Blunt recalls leaving college. "I wanted to be a soldier and a politi-cian, and I certainly wasn't going to be a conservative politician if I were out," he says. "Was the Reigate incident the last hurrah of the ugly old Tory party?" I ask. "Yes. I think so," he says, smiling. He believes there would now be no block to a lesbian or gay Tory being leader of the party and prime minister.

Blunt doesn't think the rights of lesbians and gays will ever be seriously challenged in the Tory party again: "We are the establishment party and it [being pro-LGBT] is now an establishment issue." In contrast, he worries that gay people will become less successful because they no longer have to be so driven. He asserts that some of the most remarkable people in public life struggled in the closet, and it gave them enormous drive to succeed. The Tory party has always had a large number of gay men in the backrooms—the old joke was that the Conservative research department was in Old Queen's Street for a reason—but now some of those gay men are coming out of the backrooms to sit on the front benches. In 2015, the first election in which he had offered himself as an openly gay man, he massively increased his parliamentary majority. Blunt now holds one of the safest seats in the country. Crispin is no donkey.

After leaving the Ministry it was time to "chillax . . . reappraise where I should take my career." After a period of reflection he became one of the go-to politicians for LGBT causes, chairing the Kaleidoscope Trust, a campaign focused on global LGBT rights, speaking out on all the major issues. Before meeting Blunt, I am told by Harry Prance, his researcher, that "he won't tell you this, but he's told me that he's taking on all these LGBT causes to do penance for how he behaved before." I ask my first question in the noisy atrium cafe of Parliament, and Blunt leans in to me and whispers: "It's payback. Penance for how I behaved before." He says if he had been an advocate on LGBT issues when not out people would have just looked at him askance and said, "Why's he doing that, then?" But coming out gave him freedom, he says, to support "people in other countries fighting the fights I was noticeably absent from in the UK." He notes that his path was different to many. "I didn't understand myself . . . or the challenges that gay people, now my age, were facing who had come out at eighteen . . . going through those fights in other countries who need our support."

Does he regret any of his votes on gay rights in those years when he was Crispin Blunt, the traditional Tory? When the age of consent was equalized to sixteen by the Blair government in 2000, Blunt proposed an amendment prohibiting adults over twenty-one from having same-sex relationships with sixteen-year-olds. He said in the debate, "It is also clear that there is a much greater strand of homosexuality than of heterosexuality which depends for its gratification on the exploitation of youth." On reflection, "it was outrageous to say that," Crispin confesses. "I'm embarrassed that I lost the flame in those debates. I thought I had some special insight. I knew what I was inside but I genuinely thought I had made a choice about how I lived my life. My speech was (rightly) howled at with derision by the Labour side." The out gay Labour MP Ben Bradshaw replied, "You can't choose your sexuality." From that moment the façade Blunt had constructed began to crumble. He acknowledges the debt he owes to those who paid with their careers to be true to themselves. "One is conscious one has come rather late to the party . . . [the] Labour Party were there a long time before we were. I didn't understand myself. Didn't recognize the truth."

Some might say that Crispin is a political contradiction, but his mix of socially liberal and economically conservative policies is increasingly the norm in the parties of the right in developed democracies. The former army officer was elected chair of the Foreign Affairs Select Committee in June 2015, beating four other Conservatives. He is also keen to be a player in British defense policy, and perhaps, if the chips fall the right way, in the cabinet. He believes there would today be no issue with an openly gay man heading Her Majesty's Armed Forces. He argued strongly for exit from the European Union in 2016, because the EU had failed to live up to its promises and vision, and was for Brexit in the referendum. Irony abounds. Blunt inherited the seat in 1997 after the long, serving MP Sir George Gardiner had been himself deselected for his Euro-skeptic views. Indeed, Gardiner had stood against Blunt in the general election in Reigate as a Referendum party candidate calling for exactly what Blunt had two decades later. Gardiner pulled a live donkey around town with a bright red saddle emblazoned with "Meet Crispin—Who Thinks He Can Be An MP." When challenged that Brexit will place in jeopardy LGBTQ rights in the United Kingdom, Crispin interrupts loudly—"Utter kak!" he says, and then he explains his view. "As the UK has to redefine its role in the world, its attachment to human rights and values is going to be even more important in establishing the kind of nation we are."

I take the train to suburban Surrey two days before the general election of May 2015. The Tories are so unworried about holding Reigate that we spend the morning delivering leaflets in the nearby Liberal Democrat constituency of Kingston-upon-Thames. Twirling his rainbow golf umbrella, Blunt is a chameleon. Without contrivance he is able to appear in different ways to different audiences without losing authenticity. To the stockbroker on the doorstep he is the army son of a major general, but as we say goodbye a little Jack Russell chases us down the garden path and Crispin picks it up and gives it a cuddle. "Now, that's a gay boy's dog," he whispers with a twinkle. A middle-aged Asian man stops us in the street and asks us if we know where he should go to vote. "I'm voting Labour," he volunteers, seemingly not registering Crispin's blue rosette. Crispin asks him where he lives, and realizing he doesn't know where the man's polling booth is, gives the guy the phone number of the local Labour Party. Back in Reigate people often tell him, "Oh, you don't need my vote." He always replies, "I may not need it, but I appreciate it." I grew up hating Tories, but I cannot help but like Crispin Blunt . . . a lot. He is a man happy in his skin. Maybe it's because he is unafraid of losing his safe Tory stockbroker belt seat, but I think it's more. He's a man at peace with himself. He doesn't play games anymore.

He says what he thinks, and damns the consequences. For example, he fell out with Prime Minister David Cameron over intervention in Syria, and argues forcefully that government needs to engage with Hamas and Hezbollah in the Middle East—something that the British government is too precious to do (let alone the US government).

In January 2016 the House of Commons was debating the Psychoactive Substances Bill, which would have banned a host of recreational drugs. Included were alkyl nitrites—party drugs known as poppers—sometimes taken by gay and bisexual men to enhance sex. Blunt got up in the House and said, "I use poppers. I out myself as a user of poppers. I am astonished to find it [the government] is proposing it to be banned and frankly so would many other gay men." He went on to say the ban would be "fantastically stupid," as it would "drive supply underground into the hands of criminals and increase the use of Class A and Class B drugs." Six months later Blunt was the only Conservative MP to vote against renewing the four Vanguard submarines fitted with Trident nuclear warheads. He argued that at a price of £180 billion over the next decade, or one-third of the defense budget, the cost just didn't make sense: "This is a colossal investment in a weapons system that will become increasingly vulnerable and for whose security we will have to throw good money after bad—in fact, tens of billions of it more than already estimated—to try to keep it safe in the decades to come." Of his Tory colleagues, 322 disagreed and went into the other voting lobby. Crispin was left to mingle with Labour, Scottish National Party (SNP), and a few Liberal Democrats. I ask him whether coming out changed his political views. "You have to remember that my starting point was growing up in a military family," he says. "It was always within me, but I think coming out sped up my journey to becoming more aware of those who are marginalized."

There were, of course, gay men in British politics long before Chris Smith, Crispin Blunt, and the tidal wave of lesbian and gay newbies in the twenty-first century. Tom Driberg, the fabled MP and ontime chair of the British Labour Party, spiced up political life from the 1940s to 1970s. He was as out as one could be without publically being so. His exploits were legendary. In his book *Tom Driberg: His Life and Indiscretions,* Francis Wheen recites the Westminster folk law of salacious incidents featuring Driberg and senior members of the Labour government, including a remarkable episode of sexual banter between him and then–Prime Minister James Callaghan. Winston Churchill, master of the ironic put-down, called Driberg "the sort of man who gives sodomy a bad name." But Driberg spent forty years in the public eye in a large closet, only coming out in his posthumously published biography, *Ruling Passions.*

At its core was a century and a half of deep sadness of same-sex-loving politicians who were not allowed to be out and were constantly afraid of discovery: the future home secretary, Roy Jenkins; his lover, the future foreign secretary Tony Crosland; the bachelor prime minister edward heath; the famed economist John Maynard Keynes. In many cases the closet led to unfulfilled lives and to dangerous choices. These were men at the highest levels of British government who played fast and loose with social mores of the day. The Tory MP Sir Paul Latham was imprisoned for homosexuality in 1941, and Labour MP William Field was arrested and convicted of "cottaging" (soliciting sex in public toilets) in 1953. Many others skated on the edge. Michael Bloch notes that three junior members in Harold Macmillan's Tory cabinet of 1957–1963 resigned after scandals. Ian Harvey was caught with a guardsman in St James's Park; Charles Fletcher-Cooke was found living with a young man; and Denzil Freeth was discovered to have "attended a party of a homosexual character and there engaged in homosexual conduct."

Then there were the powerful gay men of a quite different hue. Perhaps the most infamous closeted Tory MP was Peter Morrison, who became Margaret Thatcher's last parliamentary private secretary in 1990 before his early death in 1995. In Lord Hayward's description, Morrison was "most outrageously camp." Stories of cottaging with teenaged boys, the rape of a fourteen-year-old, police cover-ups, and his involvement in a child abuse ring swirled around Morrison even while he was alive. Michael McManus, who wrote the definitive history of homosexuality in the Conservative party, *Tory Pride and Prejudice*, says that for decades the party was "the corporate equivalent of the self-loathing homosexual." Nor were other political parties immune. The Liberal leader from 1967 to 1976, Jeremy Thorpe, was described by Bloch as leading "a hair-raising promiscuous gay life behind the scenes"—a life that ended with him on trial for conspiracy to murder a lover.

For every public scandal there were thousands of other closeted gay men and lesbian women just navigating life the best they could. In 2017 Clare Blading discovered evidence of love letters between her great-grandfather, Captain Sir Malcolm Bullock, First Baronet, soldier, and MP for Waterloo for twenty-seven years, and the artist Rex Whistler—letters that had been burned by Sir Malcolm's daughter.

Hiding in Plain Sight

Before 1990 the majority of lesbian, gay, or bisexual elected officials came out after they had been elected to office. The stereotypes of the 1980s and 1990s were too pernicious to overcome, and not being out when first elected was a way for local voters to get to know them without the baggage of a label. But since 2000 the majority of elected LGBT MPs have been out when elected, and a smaller, though not insignificant, number came out while in office. For many, coming out while in office is traumatic on both a personal and a political level. Nigel Evans came out eighteen years and 253 days after he was elected in the rural Lancashire constituency of Ribble Valley—the longest period between any British MP being elected and then coming out voluntarily. Evans also holds the less than celebratory record of being defeated in three different seats in the same Parliament, losing to Labour in Swansea West in the 1987 general election, the Pontypridd by-election of 1989, and then to the Liberal Democrats in the

Ribble Valley by-election of 1991. But Evans stuck at it and finally took back the traditionally Tory Ribble Valley seat in the General Election of 1992.

About the time that he was elected as a deputy speaker of the house—a position of esteem—Evans spoke to Simon Walters from right-wing *Mail on Sunday* about his intention to come out. Walters kept the secret and then was rewarded with the story in December 2010. I asked Evans why it had taken so long. Was there a triggering moment to his coming out? "Thirty-five years of accumulation," Evans said with a sigh. "The question 'Why am I doing this?' just became louder in my head." Evans says he was tired of living a lie, and the space to be open was safer. "In 1992 when I got elected, things were seismically different." Indeed, Evans was first selected the Ribble Valley Conservative Party was the opposite of queer-friendly. The former MP David Waddington had been Margaret Thatcher's last home secretary before her retirement in 1990. Waddington deplored "gay triumphalism in public life" in a Lords speech, arguing for the retention of the banning of the teaching of homosexuality in schools. Children must be "brought up knowing what is right and what is wrong, understanding that sodomy is not the moral equivalent of sexual intercourse between a man and a wife," he said. Nigel was also weary of the unstated (and sometimes stated) threats of blackmail by opponents, including an unnamed Labour MP. But ultimately he was reassured by the experience of Gareth Thomas, the Welsh rugby star who had come out a year earlier, in 2009.

A weight was lifted from his shoulders, and the reaction was more positive than he ever imagined. Evans's young researcher, Alexander Cruz Vidal, interjects: "We received just shy of 1,000 letters and emails. Ninety-nine-point-five percent were positive—straight and gay—there were only the odd few religious objections." Evans agrees. "I had huge support; the association chairman and agent were perfect. One or two people said, 'Why can't you just carry on as you were?' I said, 'I don't want to.'" Evans says that the speaker John Bercow and Tory prime minister David Cameron were "amazingly supportive. David was far ahead of the curve, his leadership qualities, motives are unquestionable. If he wanted an easy option he would not have done this," a reference to marriage equality, which Cameron brought to the House in 2013. Presiding over that iconic debate in February 2013 was Nigel Evans, the openly gay man from Wales. I asked him how he came to sit in the speakers' chair for the debate, with the speaker and two other deputies available. The speaker, John Bercow, "wanted to make absolutely certain that I was in the chair," reveals Evans. He notes that his presence did not eliminate homophobia in the debate or in the House, but "the presence of so many colleagues that are out has changed the tone—we have moved so far forward as a society." He was particularly moved by Mike Freer's speech and shocked by animosity shown by his Tory colleague Matthew Offerd.

After coming out Evans felt free to speak up on gay rights. He had been particularly shaken by the execution of two teenaged boys in Iran in 2005: "It stuck with me." The Iranian government claimed the boys had been convicted of sodomy rape, while Peter Tatchell claimed they were murdered for engaging in consensual homosexual acts. Evans thought it was pure bigotry. "I thought, I can't let this pass. When I got up to speak on the issue I was almost crying. What that country, that regime, had done to those two lads in the name of the state." But only months after marriage equality was passed in the House of Commons, Evans was charged with multiple counts of rape and sexual assault. Put in a holding cell at the local police station, he felt like he was repeatedly being hit by a truck. Not one of the MP's accusers had gone to the police; another Tory MP had brought the allegations to the attention of Palace of Westminster police.

Evans was reeling. He resigned his position as deputy speaker and party whip. He contemplated suicide: "At the darkest, most loneliest moment you think my god, there is only one thing worse and that's being accused of murder." But the case collapsed as soon as the alleged victims testified in court. "One by one, the young men trooped into Preston crown court and said they did not consider themselves victims of any criminal offense, nor had they wanted to complain to police," noted *The Guardian*. Evans was quickly cleared by the jury on all charges. But the trials did not end. The following year Evans faced de-selection as an MP by his local Tory party, and the *Daily Telegraph* reported that a third of rank-and-file local members and several executive officers of the association had "taken a dim view of allegations made in court about his lifestyle in Westminster, including heavy drinking and sex with younger men." One party official was quoted as saying, "What he does behind closed doors is nothing to do with me, but when it comes out in the press then it's to do with the association and it is something to do with me." However, Evans survived the de-selection attempt and in the general election of May 2015 he retained his massive majority.

Evans has become the norm rather than an aberration. The association between being openly gay and being on the Left of politics is an example of American exceptionalism. It is true that the first adopters of gay rights in most of the world were on the Left, but even then somewhat grudgingly. But today the momentum is with the Right. For the most part conservative parties in democracies, including quite extreme right-wing parties, have remained steadfast in their conservative economic principles while evolving into socially liberal and libertarian movements. In the summer of 2016 the number of out LGBT MPs in office globally from right-of-center parties actually outstripped the number from left-wing parties for the first time. At the start of 2017 there were seventy incumbent right-of-center LGBT parliamentarians from twenty-three countries, only sixty-three left-wing MPs in twenty-two nations. The trend is clear: while gay rights have not become the sole province of right-wing parties they have become a nonpartisan issue in the developed world.

Right-of-center politicians who identify as LGB are members of parliaments in Denmark, Estonia, France, Germany, Ireland, Israel, Lithuania, Luxembourg, Netherlands, New Zealand, Norway, Peru, Slovakia, Sweden, Switzerland, and the United Kingdom. In Scandinavia, this trend has gone on for a while; in fact, openly gay Per-Kristian Foss was briefly the Conservative Party's acting prime minister of Norway in 2002. In Scandinavia as a whole most out MPs are from right-of-center parties. The British Parliament is emblematic. Twenty-seven of the sixty-six out lesbian, gay, and bisexual MPs and Lords in Parliament as of 2018 are Conservatives. Conservative parties in much of the democratic world have become more socially liberal, while maintaining their fiscally conservative bona fides. A Conservative prime minister drove the legislative charge for marriage equality in Britain in 2013, in the face of considerable hostility from a large portion of his own supporters. In return, British LGBT voters were as likely to vote Conservative in the 2015 general election as they were Labour. Every major party in Ireland, including the conservative ones, campaigned for a yes vote on its marriage equality referendum. Tony Abbott, the right-wing prime minister of Australia, was effectively dropped from his own MPs because of his intractable opposition to marriage equality. The April 2013 New Zealand vote was unusual for giving rise to the only openly gay national legislator to vote *against* gay marriage. Chris Finlayson, the National Party attorney general of New Zealand and a man who describes himself as "gay, Catholic, and celibate," said he was voting no because "you register unions and you leave marriage to the church, temples, mosques."

The 2013 marriage equality debate starkly illustrated the changing landscape of social values in Britain. Homophobic rants were seen as the dying gasps of a waning generation. Marriage equality was carried along with the votes of conservative MPs and Lords who a generation before had blanched at even the words "gay rights." Prime Minster David Cameron was unequivocal when he said in October 2011 in front of the party faithful: "I don't support gay marriage despite being a Conservative, I support gay marriage *because* I am a conservative." On the day the law went into effect Cameron, referring to his spouse, Samantha, told *Pink News*, "This is something that has been very important to me. I have been so lucky to find the most incredible lifelong partner in Sam and our marriage has been a very special part of the commitment we have made to each other. That is not something that the state should ever deny someone on the basis of their sexuality. When people's love is divided by law, it is the law that needs to change." He went on to acknowledge that the law spoke to more than just nuptials; "the introduction of same-sex civil marriage says something about the sort of country we are."

The price for Cameron's moral crusade was significant. Writing in the *Daily Mail*, Michael Ashcroft and Isabel Oakeshott reported that Cameron's own mother thought that the costs to the Conservatives were too high, saying, "I know, but David just won't be told." They also quoted the influential chair of the Tory 1922 Committee, long-serving MP Graham Brady, who said, "Pretty much the universal advice of any colleague who spoke to [Cameron] on the subject was to drop it, whatever their personal view." Brady believed the PM was in danger of being ousted over gay marriage as Tory MPs in the shires saw their marginal seats going under water. Indeed, Conor Burns MP stresses that while homophobia in the Tory party maybe on life support, it is not dead yet. "Listen for ten minutes to my older colleagues in the smoking room," he says.

Was Cameron driven by some unknown yet powerful personal reason to expend all this political capital on a nontraditional and highly divisive issue? He had voted against gay rights in the past. All evidence suggests not. Instead, he just had evolved to a point where he believed marriage equality was fundamentally a moral imperative—and the people around him also believed it was the right thing to do. Burns muses, "I suspect Mrs. Cameron had a big influence." Mike Freer sees Cameron's commitment as both principle and pragmatism. "Britain is broadly fiscally conservative and socially liberal," he tells me. You have to "govern Britain as it is, not as you might want it to be."

Crispin Blunt says that while the fallout caused upheavals within the party, "Cameron wanted to establish his credentials as a modernizer—maybe he could have managed it better—but privately he will be thrilled to bits that he did it." One man may have had some outsize influence behind the scenes. Lord Waheed Alli revealed to me that he only really knows one Tory MP well enough to consider a close friend—David Cameron. In 1994 the future prime minister went to work at the largest part of ITV, Carlton television. He stayed for seven years until he was selected to run for the safe Tory seat of Whitney in Oxfordshire. Ironically, Cameron replaced Shaun Woodward, who defected from the Tories to Labour after being sacked for his pro-gay views in 1999. Woodward came out six months after leaving Parliament as a Labour MP in 2015. Alli's TV production company Planet 24 was deeply involved with Carlton, so much so that Carlton bought Alli's company in 1999 and Waheed briefly became a Carlton director—in a sense becoming Cameron's boss. Waheed told me that even back then Cameron "got it"; his acceptance of gay people was "inbuilt into his DNA." The way Cameron interacted with Alli and his partner Charlie Parson demonstrated "acknowledgement, acceptance, and understanding." Indeed, Samantha Cameron's stepfather, Viscount Astor, is today the deputy chairman of Alli's Silvergate Media company.

David Cameron left office after the Brexit vote in the summer of 2016, and his legacy is dominated by marriage equality and the way in which he dragged, kicking and screaming, the British Conservative Party into the twenty-first century. He also can be credited for creating the space in which a record number of openly gay, bisexual, and lesbian Tory MPs could be elected, come out, and be appointed to the highest of offices. Cameron highlighted the legacy at his very last Prime Minister's Question Time. Noting that there were now 30,000 gay people in the country who in the last few years had been able to get married, he said: "I think that is real progress. I'll never forget the day at Number 10 when someone who works very close to the front door said to me 'I'm not that interested in politics, Mr. Cameron, but because of something your lot have done, I'm able to marry the person I love this week' . . . There are many amazing moments in this job, but that was one of my favorites." Lord Robert Hayward sees the evolution as entirely in keeping with the genetics of the Conservative Party. "The Tory party is like the British Constitution. It evolves and then they annex the new as theirs," he says. But political evolution happens slowly, and not without bold moral leadership. Even in 2017, four years after marriage equality was introduced, only 41 percent of Conservative Party members supported gay marriage, with between 81 percent and 85 percent of other partys' members being in favor.

If people have a picture in their minds of a "gay leader," Conor Burns is not it. Burns was elected as the Conservative MP for the sleepy and retiring seaside town of Bournemouth in the general election that brought the Tories back to power in 2010. He is a no-nonsense power-dresser with a quiet, calm self-confidence. Photos of him with Margaret Thatcher, Pope John Paul II, and someone who looked suspiciously like Chilean dictator Augusto Pinochet adorn his bookshelves. As a practicing Catholic, born and raised in Belfast, Northern Ireland, Burns told me that growing up amid violent sectarianism had made him "intolerant of intolerance." His own rejection in the 1970s led him to empathize with other marginalized communities. But he goes out of his way to *not* be defined by the way he was born. "I'm a Catholic, a product of my school, I'm a Thatcherite, and I'm gay," he says.

Like Crispin Blunt, Burns's presence carries additional weight because he shatters stereotypes. His motto was always, "I want to be a Tory MP, not be like a Tory MP." Far from the typical Young Conservative reared in Thatcher's Britain, Burns became a close friend of the iconic prime minister in her waning years as she withdrew further and further into a small world revolving around her Belgravia apartment. Burns would visit her every Sunday, regarding her as his "mentor, protectress, friend." Upon her death in April 2013 Burns told *Pink News*, "Margaret Thatcher is one of these people who carried a sort of force field around with her she was incredibly charismatic and exuded power. When I was growing up in the 80s she was at the height of her powers then and the country was equally enthralled to her and petrified of her."

How could the woman who famously forced through Section 28, banning the teaching of homosexuality in schools, and refused to equalize the age of consent for straight and gay sex, take under her wing an openly gay man at the end of her life? Burns claims that Thatcher was never herself homophobic, and that she merely operated within the context of her time and the pressures of a deeply homophobic party membership. Homophobia was "not a central tenet of Thatcher's philosophy," he argues. He saw her as a product of early-twentieth-century Britain—especially the provinces. "The thing that people don't know about Lady T was that she was completely and utterly un-censorious. She was very naïve about the issue of homosexuality as someone who was born in 1920s Grantham would have been. She was always very surprised to learn that people are gay," he told Scott Roberts, "but once she did know she was fine with it." To support his claim he pointed not just to their friendship at the end of her life but the fact that she surrounded herself with advisors she knew to be gay and appointed cabinet ministers whose homosexuality was an open secret, such as her powerful private secretary, Stephen (now Lord) Sherbourne and Norman St. John Stevens. "In her early years as an MP she had a good narrative voting record on gay rights," says Burns. Along with other right-wing libertarians like Enoch Powell, Keith Joseph, and Iain Macleod, she was strongly in favor of the decriminalization of homosexuality in the 1960s. He recuses Thatcher from responsiblility for Section 28, arguing that it was a back-bench amendment to a tedious local government bill that the notoriously homophobic Jill Knight foisted upon the party. He does, however, credit Tony Blair's Labour government for the "audacious way they Labour changed attitudes within the country. So much faster than we (the Tory Party) would ever have managed."

Burns began his association with the south coast of England as a student at the University of Southampton in the early 1990s. He was blooded by standing twice for the Southampton constituency of Eastleigh, losing the second time in 2005 to Chris Huhne of the Liberal Democrats by only 568 votes. Huhne's downfall amid scandal seven years later seems to give him some pleasure. When first selected as a Tory candidate in 1998 Burns was out to some friends and family but not to a broader circle. After eighteen months he had built good enough relationships with the local party that he was no longer reticent about being open. In effect, like many, he came out by osmosis—never a major announcement, but rather a slow drip. He agrees that coming out becomes easier as attitudes change in government and in society. But he also became internally comfortable enough to say, "If anyone else has a problem they can fuck off." In 2001 the Conservatives, led by William Hague, made a manifesto commitment to keep the vilified Section 28. Burns had the chutzpah to write to Hague, telling him that as someone who had grown up in Northern Ireland, he would not be bound by his party's commitment.

In 2013 Burns was poised to vote against the introduction of state-sanctioned same-sex marriage. He would have been the only out British MP to do so. A practicing Catholic, he was concerned about the robustness of exemptions granted to religious organizations to exempt themselves from not just the ceremonies but trappings of marriage as a whole. However, as he sat on the fence, the vitriol of some of his constituent letters in their opposition to gay marriage, to him, and homosexuality more broadly made him vote for the legislation almost in spite. He reacted viscerally to views which he felt were "fundamentally unchristian and inhumane." As we sit in his Westminster office he insists on reading out a highlight reel of the nastiest notes he received.

> Though we must have the deepest compassion and sympathy for the person afflicted with this condition, nay curse, and must do all in our power to lift this person out of the pit, we are not to tolerate for one moment those who would aggressively promote this in society— especially on to our children—or attempt to keep them in this sexual bondage. This is called abuse, corruption, and grooming.
>
> "Get David Cameron to read his bible, Leviticus, Chapter 20, Verse 13. This applies to gays. They are detestable in God's eyes."
>
> "For two gay men, presenting one another to Christ in this way will be an abomination in the nostrils of God. Gay partners appropriating the name 'husband' is leading them both to sin, the wages of which is death."
>
> "It is abundantly evident that virulent forces are at work, intent on dragging our nation down into the pit of paganism."
>
> "Fathers and mothers who do not sign up to homosexuality will be put into prison and have their children removed and placed in the hands of social services."
>
> "When I was a serving police officer, I arrested men for the very act of kissing and causing public concern; to me nothing changes."

In a letter to his constituents Burns asked the voters to "understand that I could just not align myself with the intolerance, hatred, and bigotry that these views represented." As a prelude to citing Edmund Burke's 1774 *Speech to the Electors of Bristol*, Burns wrote, "As my friend the late Margaret Thatcher once advised me, 'You should aspire to be respected rather than liked.'"

Conor Burns also had a Harvey Milk–like experience that fundamentally shook him. He went to speak at a school in Bournemouth. The next day he received an email from one of the pupils: "You have no idea how proud I was that you were able to say in front of my schoolmates that you are gay. I think I'm gay and I'm being bullied for it. The fact that my MP was able to say that—in front of two of the people who were bullying me—made me greatly confident." The note moved Conor deeply. "I realized I had a duty to use the accidental leadership role I have to help young people, so they wouldn't have to feel the insecurity, doubt, and loneliness that I felt growing up in a climate that was significantly more hostile than today," he reflects. Burns touches on the consequences of being present and seen. He knows of at least three of his colleagues who abstained on the marriage vote of 2013 rather than vote no because of their friendship with him. I told them, "This is going to be one of those seminal votes. It's a defining moment. When you look back at the end of your twenty-five-year parliamentary career, won't you regret that you voted against this?"

The history of the Tory party dramatically illustrates the different effects between being gay and in hiding and being gay and fully out of the closet. Michael McManus quotes Guy Black, the former director of the Conservative Research Department. "It was one of those strange phenomena that when the Conservative party appeared nationally to be at its most homophobic, at the very heart of the organization were all these influential gay men." But their lack of visibility and openness allowed the homophobes to push through legislation that would demonize gay men and lesbians. In 2013 the former Tory MP Jerry Hayes wrote in *The Guardian*: "The Conservative party has always been a riddle within an enigma regarding homosexuality. It has been rather strange that those who have been intolerant of homosexuals and who think that gays have hijacked 'their' party seem blissfully unaware that the friends of Dorothy were very much the friends of Margaret. Most insiders are of the view that when her influential (and gay) private secretary left No.10 the slide to her destruction had begun."

Burns is just one of a number of gay, lesbian, and bisexual conservatives who occupy a newly opened space where they can be out. They have been coming out in a steady stream. After marriage equality was passed in 2013 six more Conservative MPs felt able to come out while in office. They collectively had endured seventy-five years as MPs in the closet. At 6 feet 8 inches, Polish-born Daniel Kawczynski's previous claim to fame was as the tallest British MP and the representative for picture-postcard Shrewsbury on the border of England and Wales, but that was trumped when he came out as bisexual. After splitting from his wife of eleven years in 2011, Kawczynski told his local Conservative association in June 2013, "It is very important to show the youngsters that it is perfectly acceptable and normal to be open about your sexual preferences. I have always been with women. Now, I have met a guy."

On June 6, 2015, Nick Gibb, the minister for schools in the newly minted Conservative government of Prime Minister David Cameron, came out. He did so first to his family and then to the gossip-hungry British media, so that he could marry his partner of almost thirty years, pollster Michael Simmonds. After he made the announcement in *The Times* he was showered with praise and affection from constituents, colleagues, and opponents alike. He told his local newspaper, the *Chichester Observer:* "In the House of Commons colleagues have been hugely warm and supportive in offering their congratulations. It's been overwhelming actually; I didn't think people would be so emotional about it." The symbolism was powerful. A generation before, Gibb's party, led by Margaret Thatcher, had systematically demonized lesbian and gay Britons and outlawed the teaching of the "acceptability of homosexuality as a pretended family relationship" through the much-reviled Section 28 of the Local Government Act. Now the Tory government had an openly gay man in charge of teaching children.

Every Tory MP coming out seemed to beget another—a domino effect of one act of courage prompting another. In November 2016 the Tory back-bencher William Wragg tweeted: "Contacted by someone compiling a database of LGBT politicians. No, I don't want to go on a database, but yes I'm gay. It isn't everything"—which I can only presume was in response to what I thought was a very respectful email I had sent to him asking if he wanted to be included in the list of out MPs (because his colleague had insisted he should be on the list). His agitated tone reflected the understandable fear that anyone asking about sexual orientation might be hostile. Hopefully his own supporters' comments made him feel better: "Well done, coming out. Very brave decision & honest, well worth it. All best wishes," and "Go on the database, you might give someone confidence." Following Wragg, David Mundell, the secretary of state for Scotland, came out on New Year's Day 2016. Mundell—known as "Fluffy" to his friends in Westminster—hardly had the luxury of a safe seat to indulge his soul-baring. The only Tory MP in all of Scotland, he clung to a wafer-thin majority of 798 over the resurgent SNP at the 2015 election. Like a number of MPs before him— Greg Barker, Ron Davis, Crispin Blunt, and Daniel Kawczynski—Mundell had a wife and children before coming out, a vivid illustration of the way in which homophobia had trapped gay and bisexual men in the straitjacket of conforming to traditional views of masculinity and marriage. While these men were able to break free from the straitjacket, countless others drowned under the suffocation, or continue to struggle in the closet because society told them they could not be who they were.

At the end of June 2016, the day after Britain voted to leave the European Union and on the day of London Pride, the 16th incumbent Conservative MP came out via the thoroughly modern method of Twitter. The international development cabinet minister Justine Greening tweeted her 35,000 followers: "I campaigned for Stronger In but sometimes you're better off out!" The following day Greening opened up about her longtime partner Tess, a university lecturer, in the *London Evening Standard.* Now the Conservative government had two out ministers. One more Tory was to follow: Mark Menzies, the MP for the Lancashire constituency of Fylde, which is famous for the Open Championship

Lytham St. Annes golf course. A month after coming out Greening became the education secretary, leaving both senior education portfolios in the hands of openly gay Tories. In March 2017 Greening announced that all children in England would receive effective and age-appropriate relationships and sex education, including education about LGBTQ issues. Greening had been nineteen when her party had banned all discussion of homosexuality in schools under the notorious Section 28 of the Local Government Act.

What's Wrong with the Grand Old Party?

The juxtaposition between the British Conservative Party and the US Republican Party could not be more stark. Since 2015 the British Conservative party has won as great a proportion of the LGBTQ vote as any other party. But in 2016 Donald Trump and the GOP won the votes of less than 15 percent of LGBT Americans. As of 2017 a battle rages for the heart and soul of the Republican party: a battle that the equality movement, for now, is losing. Vice President Mike Pence says that discrimination against those who "choose" to be gay is merely enforcement of "god's idea." Attorney General Jeff Sessions consistently scored zero on his voting support for LGBT equality when in the Senate, and former presidential chief adviser Steve Bannon specialized in demonizing gay people as editor at Breibart. Education Secretary Betsy DeVos has invested huge amounts of money in anti-gay groups, and Housing Secretary Ben Carson once compared marriage equality to bestiality. That the stream of high-profile Trump appointees are avowed homophobes is not a shock; what is striking is how out of step the Trump administration is with the rest of the global conservative movement when it comes to sexual orientation. The GOP is one of a small and dwindling band of right-of-center parties who cling to the creed that straight is normal and anything else is an aberration.

Indeed, the Trump administration's retreat to the politics of fear and loathing also appears to fly in the face of what we know about the evolving American voter. Support for same-sex marriage has more than doubled over the past two decades, to nearly two-thirds of the population. Younger voters as a whole favor LGBT rights by a massive 83 percent, but even two-thirds of Republicans under the age of thirty support marriage equality. Being anti-gay in much of America today is a vote loser and there is no evidence that voters become more homophobic as they age, so the GOP will have to deal with a core base that gets more gay-friendly year by year. This is why some GOP strategists recoil at seeing their leaders expressing views that seem angry, unfair, and out of touch with modern values.

But there are also GOP bigwigs who see gay rights more as a moral touchstone than part of an electoral calculus. Paul Singer, the conservative hedge fund billionaire, has channeled over $17 million of his money over the last ten years to gay rights activism: to Republican candidates who support gay rights, to groups lobbying for employment non-discrimination and gay marriage, and in 2013, $1.5 million to a new initiative led by the Human Rights Campaign to combat homophobia and discrimination overseas. Singer told the *New York Times* columnist Frank Bruni that to him gay rights were consistent with a Republican philosophy of individual liberty, social stability, and stability in raising kids. Singer's son is married to a man. Indeed, most senior Republicans who support gay rights—for example, Dick Cheney and Rob Portman—have a family member who is gay. Where is the Republican party going? Former Washington State Republican governor Daniel Evans despairs for his party. "In the South there are the remnants of old, very conservative people who couldn't get over losing the Civil War, for goodness sake," he says. "What used to be the Dixiecrats are the same people; they just changed parties."

North Carolina highlighted the electoral consequences in 2016 when Republican governor Pat McCrory lost precisely because of his passion for his transphobic HB2 bathroom bill. Donald Trump won the state by 4 percent and the Republican Senator Richard Burr won by 6 percent, but McCrory managed to lose to the Democrat Roy Cooper. Only 30 percent of North Carolina voters approved of the bathroom bill, and they held McCrory responsible.

The GOP is not merely out of step with the mainstream Right of the democratic world, but even the far Right. Over the last few years the extreme Right in Europe has presented a clutch of openly gay leaders—and garnered significant chunks of the LGBT vote, with sufficient consistency to make the phenomenon more of a trend than an aberration. The new prime minister of Serbia, Ana Brnabic, is an apparatchik of the Serbian president Aleksandar Vučić, who started his political life in the ultranationalist Serbian Radical party. Zoe Gudovic told the *New York Times*: "The only thing I share with Ana Brnabic is that we are both lesbians. I find it impossible to accept that she is willing to be part of the nationalist, authoritarian regime that will ruin our economy, sell our country to foreigners and abolish whatever is left of a social state."

Pim Fortuyn began the gay nationalist xenophobic trend in the Netherlands in the early 2000s. French National Front leader Marine Le Pen's closest advisor is the openly gay man Florian Philippot. Alice Weidel, the leader of the Alternative for Germany (AfD), is married to a woman and has two children. She and the party are anti-immigration, anti-EU, and anti-Islamization of German society. She accused Germany's Central Council of Muslims of "never having distanced itself credibly from Stone Age Shariah." In 2016 the party launched a billboard campaign with a photo of a same-sex couple saying, "My partner and I don't want to get to meet Muslim immigrants who believe that our love is a deadly sin." The most right-wing party in the Swedish Parliament, the Swedish Democrats, have organized a provocative Järva Pride march through largely immigrant Muslim areas of Stockholm. In 2016 the organizer, Jan Sjunnesson, proudly wore a "Trump 2016" hat. The Swedish Democrats have an out bisexual MP in the twenty-six-year-old Cassandra Sundin. As of August 2017, a year out from the next general election, the Swedish Democrats had doubled their share of the national vote in polls and were on track to be the largest party in the next Parliament. Three of the candidates running to be leader of the UK Independence Party (UKIP) in 2017 were gay or lesbian: Anne Marie Waters, Scottish MEP David Coburn, and the incumbent Deputy Leader Peter Whittle. Waters had been a leader of the British branch of the extreme anti-Islam movement Pegida, and at the time of the campaign was director of the self-styled Sharia Watch UK.

Some see high-profile right-wing lesbian and gay leaders as merely fig leaves of respectability for unpleasant parties, but there is more to it than that. LGBT voters are increasingly gravitating to such parties with their mix of gay rights policies, xenophobia, and anti-Muslim rhetoric. The French National Front has steadily increased its share of the LGBT vote. It was up to 15 percent in 2013. Four years later Le Pen won 21 percent of the gay male vote in the first round of the presidential election and 36 percent in the second. Her support among gay men under the age of thirty was 44 percent. In 2017 surveys found that 17 per-cent of LGBT Germans support the extremist AfD. The German press called them "homonationalists."

While there have not been scientific studies of whether gay people feel more confident and empowered when they see gay people in office, there are studies showing how embracing one's sexual orientation does appear to trans-form values and voting behavior, at least in the United States. Patrick Egan and Ken Sherrill both note the remarkable robustness of progressive views among LGBT voters in America. Lesbians, gays, and bisexuals are much more likely to be Democrats, liberals, and hold strong progressive views on a whole range of policy issues far beyond those focused on gay rights. In 2007 88 percent of LGBs identified as Democrats, against a general population of 50 percent. Sixty-three percent of LGBs defined themselves as liberal against 26 percent overall. In 2012 self-identified LGBs (5% of the electorate) voted by a 76 percent to 22 percent margin for Obama over Romney, while straights were split equally 49–49 per-cent. In some states this made the difference between winning and losing.

This finding is actually something of a puzzle given that gay Americans are drawn randomly from the population—across class, ethnicity, gender, and geog-raphy. For decades studies have shown how voting behavior is overwhelmingly driven by these factors. The strongest predictor of who you will vote for is for whom your parents voted. But time and time again, Egan and Sherrill find that LGB voters are generally far to the left of their families (and the voting popula-tion as a whole) on questions where sexual orientation is far from the central issue. Sixty-three percent of LGB American say that abortion is a matter of personal choice, while only 36 percent of the at-large population agrees. In 2007, 62 percent of LGBs said that protecting the environment was more important than protecting jobs, against 45 percent overall. Eighty-six percent of LGBs wanted all US troops withdrawn from Iraq within twelve months, while only 58 percent of Americans overall shared that view.

The LGB population is also more likely to be political active, outstripping their straight neighbors in their likelihood of contacting a government official, attending a protest, writing a letter to the editor, joining a community group, or giving money to or working for a political campaign. Ironically, the only form of political activity LGBs are less likely to partake in is elective office. Egan and Sherrill identify coming out as a transformative time not just for family and religion, but for political views as well. When individuals admit to themselves and others they are gay they re-evaluate their deepest-held beliefs and convictions; they become more politically interested, active, and liberal. And this isn't just a phenomenon of the young. The changes are significant, if not quite as large, when coming out in older age. They are more liberal after coming out. The idea that "Democrats are just better on gay rights" does not account for views gay people have on nongay issues.

Sherrill says that realizing you are gay is a shock to the system at any age: "You are not the person you expected to be at your core. It forces you to reconsider every aspect of identity and you begin to act more in line with having a minority status—that of being an outsider." Irish entertainer Rory O'Neill notes that "my gayness made me question everything around me, everything I'd been told, everything I'd taken for granted, because if everything I'd been told about being gay had been wrong—and it had—then couldn't everything else I'd ever been told be wrong? Being gay made me think." Clay Aiken, the US congressional candidate for the 2nd district of North Carolina, tells me he was quite different: "As a student I was far more liberal than I am today." Nevertheless, Aiken is clear about where his politics came from. "I think one of the reasons why I am a Democrat is because I am gay. Recognizing in school that something was different about me and I was being left out, even when I did not understand why. This made me empathize with people who were being left out, [who] were on the fringes of society, and I wanted to look out for them."

Figure 14.1 Sir Simon Hughes, the author, and Cara Gillingham, election canvassing, Bermondsey. Credit: Paul Buckley.

14

Britain Goes Gay at the Polls

While the transformation of British law in the area of gay rights has been pronounced over the last two decades (most notably the equalization of the age of consent in 2000, the abolition of Section 28 of the Local Government Act in 2003, and the introduction of civil unions in 2004 and of marriage equality in 2013), there remains much homophobia in British society. A 2013 report by Stonewall, *Gay in Britain,* found that the vast majority of lesbian and gay people in Britain expected their child to be bullied in school, that they faced prejudice in becoming a school governor, that they would be treated worse than straight people by the police and prison service, and that they would face barriers if they wanted to adopt or foster a child. One in five had experienced verbal bullying from colleagues or customers in the previous five years. Indeed, pernicious legal discrimination has left a legacy in many social realms and in some regions (most notably Northern Ireland) legal discrimination remains.

The UK general election of May 2015 was a ready-made laboratory to explore these questions. A modern democracy had undergone a momentous change from systematic and state-sponsored homophobia, which dominated public policy up until the late 1990s, to the adoption of a raft of sexual orientation equality laws. This legal progress tracked a dramatic transformation in the British public's view of homosexuality and support for LGBT rights. In 2004, 52 percent of UK voters approved of marriage equality, but by 2015 it had increased to 71 percent. However, the prevailing assumption among the gatekeepers to candidacy—and, indeed, the voters themselves—was that no matter how much Britain had changed, running an openly gay or lesbian candidate remained a gamble and such candidates would almost inevitably struggle against homophobia in the campaign whether it was sponsored by the media, competing parties, or the electorate themselves. Nor was it just the establishment gatekeepers who perceived being gay as a challenge to be overcome. Lesbian, gay, and bisexual people also expected to be discriminated against. In the Stonewall survey three-quarters of LGB Britons felt they would face barriers from the Tories if they wanted to stand as an MP, more than a third would expect to face barriers from the Labour Party, and more than a quarter from the Liberal Democrats. Putting up an out transgender candidate was perceived to be less of a gamble than throwing in the towel completely.

The great thing about the 2015 UK general election was that it provided the data to allow for a large-scale quantitative analysis of the impact of sexual orientation on candidate vote share. The number of openly gay, lesbian, bisexual, and transgender candidates was unprecedented. There were 155 out LGBT candidates, from all main parties, standing in 140 of the 650 parliamentary constituencies across all regions of the United Kingdom. In 2018, we used comprehensive demographic, personal, and electoral data to control for the varying characteristics of both districts and candidates. The United Kingdom was unique in its suitability to be a laboratory for this question. While other developed democracies have experienced fundamental legal change and seismic shifts in social views about the acceptability of homosexuality, none have revealed the same high levels of out candidates and elected parliamentarians. For example, in Canada marriage equality was instituted in 2005; there have been openly gay members of Parliament for twenty-six years, and over 80 percent of Canadians say society should accept homosexuality. But the number of out LGBT candidates actually declined from twenty-two to twenty-one between 2004 and 2015, and the number of out LGB MPs has remained static at six through four federal elections since 2006. In the United States the number of out LGBT candidates for Congress has hovered at around ten since 2012, and the number of victors has never risen above seven. Unlike the United States and Canada, the number of out LGBT candidates and elected MPs in the United Kingdom has grown rapidly.

By 2015 all the main parties and party leaders were committed to the recently enacted marriage equality law and anti-discrimination legislation. Among the Conservatives, Liberal Democrats, Labour, and Green parties there was something of an out-bidding race to claim the most gay-friendly platform and history. All save for the Conservatives published LGBT-focused manifestos, while the Tories committed themselves to tackling homophobic and transphobic abuse, pardoning men convicted of homosexuality before 1967, and a transgender action plan. Labour promised action in the areas of health and education, and to appoint a new international envoy on LGBTQ rights.

Part of David Cameron's modernization agenda for the Conservative Party upon taking the leadership in 2005 was to incorporate the faces of modern Britain into his candidate ranks. An effort to signal a new type of Tory party, an "A list" promoted women, ethnic minority, and openly gay candidates (although Lord Robert Hayward says that the A list was never really about gay candidates). More crucially, there was a cultural shift in the top echelons of the Tory Party. Hayward tells me that by the mid-1990s if you went to a Tory party meeting in

London, "Everybody under forty was gay. You might as well have convened it in the gay bar Halfway to Heaven." Between 2005 and 2010 the vast majority of candidate selections were chaired by one of four senior Conservatives who all happened to be high-profile out gay men: Hayward, Matthew Parris, Iain Dales, and Michael Brown. These chairs did not get to influence the vote per se, but they set the tone and parameters of the meeting and local luminaries, often socially conservative, did not interfere with the selection. Hayward tells me that "the reason I was used so much is that I produced more women and BME [black and ethnic minority] candidates than anyone else."

Hayward has had a unique vantage point to watch the changing landscape of British politics. For the first half of his life in politics—as a Conservative candidate in 1974 and as an MP from 1983 to 1992—he was in the closet. A few years after his defeat he came out, and passionately embraced LGBTQ rights causes. In 2015 he was elevated to the Lords, thus becoming one of the few parliamentarians with the experience of being in the closet and then returning to office as an out gay man after a gap of over twenty years. I asked him how he navigated being a Tory MP in the 1980s. His story is very human and familiar, echoing many of the stories in this book. Hayward grew up on a farm west of Oxford; he went to grammar school in Maidenhead, then Rhodesia for university. His mother was a headmistress, passionate about addressing inequality in education, and his parents put into practice what they preached by adopting and fostering children. His upbringing left him as a "very hard right economist but socially liberal," he says. The farm, grammar school, and University of Rhodesia was a life of "no bars, no gay life. I got married because I believed I loved the woman I married, but had I lived in this day and age I probably would not have because I would have greater experience of gay life," he offers. "Society was completely different."

In 1983 Hayward won the Bristol constituency of Kingswood at the summit of Thatcher's popularity. It was the most working-class constituency in the country held by a Tory. By 1987 he had separated from his wife, but there were no role models of out gay Tory MPs. His friends and role models, such as Michael Cashman, were in the Labour Party. He doubled his majority in 1987, and "over next few years wanted to live a gay lifestyle," he says. He voted for clause 28 in early 1988 because he "didn't believe it would cause any problems," but he was getting closer to coming out and worried about being outed. Indeed, he met with a gay group in Bristol to hear their concerns, which "horrified" his agent and local party leadership. "I cottaged," or cruised for sex, he tells me matter-of-factly as we drink tea in the British Museum. "I was pretty sure I was going to lose in 1992, but even if I'd won I'd decided I was going to come out." He would have been the first fully out Tory (Michael Brown came out in 1994), but it was not to be. When Thatcher was ousted by her own parliamentary party, the Kingswood seat returned to Labour.

In 1995 Hayward helped found the first gay rugby club in the world, the Kings Cross Steelers, and was asked to join the board of Stonewall—at the time the only Tory on the board. There was some question of how out he was, but Hayward says that he was openly going to gay bars and that seting up the world's first gay rugby club was highly visible. "I wasn't sure what they wanted me to say," he says of Stonewall; he felt that coming out by megaphone was no longer the way society was heading. Like many other conservatives I've spoken to, Hayward sees his growing awareness of his sexuality as a fillip to his empathy for other marginalized groups. He has a form of multiple sclerosis that affects his eyesight: "I literally see things in a different way," he says. Hayward's rugby club is a weather vane for the progress that has been made. When photographs were first taken twenty years ago of the players they would have to check to see if people were comfortable to be included the picture. They might get fired at work, or be outed against their will. "But now no one cares," Hayward says, smiling.

Ultimately twenty out LGB Tory candidates were selected and twelve won in the elections that brought to power a Tory–Liberal Democrat coalition government in 2010. Despite his relationship with the rank-and-file of the Conservative party being strained over the same-sex marriage bill, Cameron soldiered on. Indeed, a majority of Conservative MPs voted against the bill in 2013 (128 to 117 on the final vote) and there was a fear of voter backlash in the constituencies—especially the rural shires that had elected traditional Tories for centuries. In 2015 many back-bench Tories openly expressed fears that their voters would punish the party for being too socially liberal, and LGB activists worried that local selection committees would back away from installing candidates who were outside of the mainstream. The A list was shelved for candidate selections for the 2015 election, but this did not stop Conservative central office from crafting space for candidates from marginalized communities in more subtle ways. Each local party selection meeting chose from between three and six candidates offered by headquarters; those meetings, often public, which ended with a vote of party members, were chaired by a figure sent by the central office.

Across the aisle, the Labour Party had claimed advocacy of the LGBT community as their bailiwick since the mid-1980s. Despite Labour having fewer out MPs in 2010, even the Conservatives credited Tony Blair's Labour government for transforming the law between 2003 and 2010 and laying the ground for marriage equality in 2013. Figures at the center of parliamentary debates across partisan divides were often quick to credit the Labour peer Lord Waheed Alli as one of the most influential, if unsung, agents behind all the major legal reforms on gay rights that had occurred since his elevation in 1998. The Liberal Democrats had four out gay or bisexual MPs in the 2010–2015 Parliament, and they trumpeted the role of their junior minister, Lynne Featherstone, in shepherding through marriage equality.

In 2010 LGBT voters had been split between all the main parties, but a plurality said they were voting for the Labour Party. By 2015 the Conservatives had moved up to match Labour's share of the LGBT vote, and the Liberal Democrats had dropped back just behind the Greens.

Compared to previous elections, in 2015 there was a striking reduction of overarching and personalized homophobia in the election campaign. The only notable exception occurred in Margaret Thatcher's old constituency of Finchley and Golders Green in north London. There, sitting Tory MP Mike Freer, who was openly gay when selected and elected for the seat in 2010, complained of Labour Party canvassers raising the issue of his sexual orientation with orthodox Jews in the area. A poll a couple of weeks before election day had Freer down a couple of points to his Labour challenger, but ultimately he increased his vote by 4,000 and enjoyed as comfortable a majority as he had in 2010. At the national level, the United Kingdom Independence Party (UKIP) leader Nigel Farage made a series of comments about migrants with HIV/AIDS burdening the British National Health Service, but these statements were broadly condemned by all other parties and viewed as emblematic of outdated prejudices that characterized both UKIP's limited appeal and its unfitness for government. The mere fact that UKIP was condemned for being homophobic by all other mainstream parties illustrated how little homophobia resonated with the electorate. Indeed, UKIP itself sought to counter the criticism by pointing to its six openly gay parliamentary candidates. Finally, Jim Wells, the Democratic Unionist Party Health Minister in the government of Northern Ireland, was forced to step down after making homophobic remarks to a lesbian couple while campaigning.

In 2015 the Conservatives put up more openly gay candidates than any other party: thirty-nine men and three women. Of their thirteen incumbent out MPs twelve stood for re-election and only one lost (Eric Ollerenshaw in Lancaster and Fleetwood), but his loss was made up for by the election of Ben Howlett in Bath. Howlett overcame a huge Liberal Democrat majority in what had been a Liberal Democrat seat since 1992. A quick analysis of the fifty races where there were competitive LGBT candidates shows that Tory LGBT candidates performed better than their straight colleagues: 72 percent of them had larger vote share increases than the national trend, and on average their gains were three times the Tory average. The ranks of LGB-identifying Tory MPs swelled when five more came out between the election and March 2017.

Labour did not take many seats from the Tories in 2015, but of the ten they did win, three were won by gay or bisexual candidates. Wes Streeting and Peter Kyle generated two of the biggest swings to Labour in Ilford North and Hove, respectively, and Cat Smith's victory in Lancaster and Fleetwood was one of the five head-to-heads where both major parties ran out LGB candidates. The nine incumbent Labour lesbian and gay MPs held on comfortably, and the party stood Gerald Jones in the safe seat of Merthyr Tydfil in Wales. In a slap in the face of stereotypes, Wales and Scotland were the UK areas with the highest proportions of out gay MPs. The nine Scots and four Welsh were not concentrated in the green valleys and shimmering lochs; rather, they were predominantly returned from working-class constituencies struggling after mining and industrial decline. The Labour MP Nia Griffith came out in February 2016. Griffith revealed a very sad but very human trigger for her coming out. After many years she split up with her long-term partner. "I couldn't cope with the grief," she told the SNP MP Hannah Bardell on the BBC, of "not being able to tell somebody. Bizarrely, that was the moment I came out."

It is true that all four gay and bisexual Liberal Democrat MPs were ousted: David Laws (Yeovil), Simon Hughes (Bermondsey), Stephen Williams (Bristol West), and Stephen Gilbert (St. Austell and Newquay), but they were swept away on a tide which had little or nothing to do with their work as constituency MPs. The Scottish National Party sent shock waves through British politics in May 2015 by winning almost every seat they contested, and on that wave rode in seven new LGB-identifying Members of Parliament. They exemplify the demographic diversity that is LGBT Britain, ranging from the high-profile Edinburgh Queen's Council Joanna Cherry to the twenty-year-old Glasgow University politics student Mhairi Black. It meant that the SNP had the highest proportion of LGBT MPs anywhere in the world, alongside their five members of the Scottish Parliament and one member of the European Parliament. That number was further increased when Hannah Bardell came out in February 2016. A year later Bardell wrote an op-ed for the Huffington Post explaining her decision.

> Before I took the step to make any public comment about my sexuality I thought long and hard about whether, given how far we've come in terms of LGBT rights, there was a need for me to speak openly about my sexuality. I sought lots of advice from many places; some felt there wasn't a need to comment and it was nobody else's business, whilst others felt it was really important that as an elected representative I spoke out. Ultimately, though, I had to accept that as a female MP and a member of the LGBT community I am a role model. I also contemplated how I felt growing up having very few role models who were openly gay and for the sake of my younger self I felt it was important to speak out.
>
> I often reflect and think how few gay role models there were for me growing up, on reflection I realise there were actually one or two, but

in my fear of being different I rejected any association or exploration of LGBT culture.

Ultimately, it was standing for election and becoming a politician that tipped the balance for me. I realised that I could not, in all conscience, be an authentic politician if I wasn't honest with myself about who I really was. However, coming out also nearly stopped me from standing for election. I was simply terrified what would befall me if I had to come out publicly. I grossly underestimated how far LGBT rights and perceptions of LGBT people had come. After I had indicated I would stand for selection to be an SNP MP, I actually pulled out of candidacy, fear and anxiety gripped me and I cited "personal reasons" to the party. Then I got a call from my former boss and friend Alex Salmond. When I did finally come out publicly (some ten months after I told my family and friends) he, like all of my friends and colleagues, was there to give support and advice.

My analysis with Gabriele Magni showed that on average, sexual orientation did not have a negative impact on candidates' vote share. In other words, the electorate did not punish LGBT candidates over straight ones because of their sexual orientation. Indeed, we found that LGBT candidates had a positive impact in mainly rural and largely rural districts. LGBT candidates increase the vote share by about 2 percent, a substantial contribution in times in which election results are often close and the average vote share across all parties is just slightly less than 20 percent. At first we were puzzled, since one may expect that urban settings are more welcoming of sexual minorities. However, rural districts in the United Kingdom tend to be socioeconomically wealthier and ethnically less diversified than urban areas. Indeed, they display lower levels of deprivation and lower shares of Muslim residents, two factors than can negatively affect the results of LGBT candidates.

But we found that LGBT candidates did not have a significantly negative impact until the percentage of Muslims living in the district becomes relatively large, representing around 18 percent of the population. In Great Britain, only thirty-two out of 632 constituencies had a proportion of Muslims larger than this threshold. When Muslims represent about a fifth of the residents, sexual minority candidates are expected to decrease the vote share on average by about 1.5 percent. Interestingly, gay candidates from the Labour Party—Wes Streeting and Steve Reed—were elected in the districts of Ilford North and Croydon North, where the share of Muslim residents equals 15 percent and 13 percent. There was also a party dimension to the effect. LGBT candidates had a positive impact for the Labour Party, for which they increased the vote share on average by 1 percent. Their impact was instead negative for the Conservative Party, where LGBT identity decreased the electoral result by 0.6 percent. But LGBT Tories—compared to straight Conservative candidates—faced conditions arguably more hostile to the Conservative party: they ran in districts where the Tories gained a smaller percentage of votes in 2010, where Muslim residents were more numerous, and where there were more deprived households.

We were also interested to see if, while adopting LGBT candidates, the British parties were more likely to place them in unwinnable seats. We were glad to find that LGBT candidates are not substantially more likely to be selected in either marginal or safe constituencies, nor to be placed in unwinnable seats, for purely presentational value. Indeed, when we look at just Tories in marginal districts, they did not do any worse than their straight colleagues. LGBT candidates do not decrease the vote of the Conservative Party in competitive districts, while LGBT Tory candidates in no-hoper seats do see a minor reduction in their vote share. Hence, the overall suppression of Tory LGBT vote found above is being driven by the vote share of candidates who have no chance. Overall, LGBT candidates in the 2015 election did not depress the vote share of their party. In some contexts, such as wealthier and ethnically more homogeneous rural areas, they actually improve the electoral results of their party. While some resistance still remains among supporters of the Conservative Party, this negative effect is limited to noncompetitive districts in which LGBT candidates did not enjoy a real chance of winning the seat.

What might explain this? We believe that we need to consider a divide existing between three groups: political parties and their leaders, straight voters (who are the vast majority), and LGBT voters. As noted earlier, the main UK parties were united in their strong support for LGBT rights in their manifestos and public statements. This drove LGBT voters to fragment between the four main UK-wide parties, and presumably between five in Scotland and Wales (when one includes the pro-LGBT Scottish Nationalists and Plaid Cymru). However, despite the radical transformation of the Conservative party under David Cameron, the legacy of state-sponsored homophobia under Tory governments led by Margaret Thatcher and her predecessors remained resonant in the electorate's minds. Therefore, straight voters who supported Labour were likely more inclined to see their party as the historic guardians of gay rights, and voting for an LGBT candidate could be a symbolic statement about what they wanted their party and country to be, and who they wanted to be. Labour voters in 2015 were more likely to be left-of-center progressives who celebrated marriage equality and the transformation of Britain's legal and social attitudes toward gay people. If there was suspicion of Labour's leftist bona fides, then having an LGBT candidate to support may have motivated voters who were initially ambivalent about voting to turnout. An alternative possibility is that Labour LGBT candidates were more able to reach out to voters who had supported other parties previously. This is plausible in the case of Liberal Democrats, who may have been disenchanted with the right-ward turn of their party and defected to Labour in 2015—especially if their progressive values were demonstrated by Labour running an LGBT candidate.

The "gay boost" in personal vote was confirmed in the snap UK election of June 2017. The Tories only made eight gains outside of Scotland, and two of them were by LGBTQ Tory candidates. Two of the new Scottish Conservative MPs are also gay. LGBTQ SNP MPs were more likely to hold their seats than their straight colleagues, and their ten LGBTQ candidates outperformed their straight colleagues by 1.2 percent. LGBTQ Labour made four seat gains. Nationally, the Labour vote was up by 9.5 percent and the Tories by 5.5 percent, but the 42 LGBTQ Labour candidates increased their vote by 10.9 percent and the 42 Tories by 6.3 percent. Remarkably, British voters returned 45 out lesbian, gay, and bisexual MPs to Parliament—7 percent of the 650 members. All but two of the 39 incumbents were re-elected, and they were joined by eight new faces from both the Tory and Labour parties. The all-party (barring the Democratic Unionist Party) consensus on gay rights was illustrated by the fact that there are now 19 Tories, 19 Labour LGBT MPs, and seven Scottish Nationalists. There were 159 LGBT candidates in the elections from every party outside of the Irish Unionists and Sinn Fein (although Sinn Fein have Northern Ireland Assembly candidates and are fundamentally committed to equality).

After an analysis of abusive tweets sent during the 2017 election campaign, Amnesty International noted, "What is especially worrying is that some groups are disproportionately likely to be the targets of intimidation and abuse both online and offline. Candidates who are female, BAME, or LGBT are disproportionately targeted in terms of scale, intensity, and vitriol. The intimidation experienced by those who are in more than one of these groups can be even worse." But the strong evidence cited focused on ethnicity and gender, not sexual orientation or gender identity.

The deep irony was that Theresa May's government, eight seats shy of a majority, was beholden to the most homophobic party in the United Kingdom—the Northern Irish DUP—for its survival. The DUP vetoed marriage equality in Northern Ireland five times despite there being a majority of Northern Irish voters, and the Assembly itself, in favor of gay marriage. The party once launched a campaign called "Save Ulster from Sodomy." The son of the party's founder, Ian Paisley Jr., said he was "repulsed" by gays and lesbians and called homosexuality "immoral, offensive and obnoxious." In 2015 DUP health minister Jim Wells said that children raised by gay parents were more likely to be abused or neglected. In 2017 one of the DUP Assembly members, Trevor Clarke, said that only gay people could get HIV/AIDS. While the ten DUP MPs were essential to Theresa May's survival, so were the nineteen LGB members of her own parliamentary party, and they had been steadfast in their commitment to gay rights in both Britain and overseas.

But the most important gay Tory does not even sit in the House of Commons. Ruth Davidson is the leader of the Scottish Conservative Party, a Member of the Scottish Parliament, and the woman credited for the dramatic reversal of Tory fortunes north of the border. Her party's twelve gains in the election saved the Conservative government. Davidson is talked of as a future leader of the Tory party, and, as a lesbian and protestant unionist who was about to marry her Irish Catholic partner, Jenn Wilson. She demanded that Prime Minister May give assurances that gay rights would be strongly protected in any deal with the Democratic Unionists. Two days after the election in 2017, Davidson said that she had received such assurances from the prime minister. In April 2018 Ruth announced that she and Wilson were expecting their first child.

Has Britain reached a posthomophobic state of grace, or do the better angels of our nature just come out at election time? This is not a thesis which is often proposed. While barely disguised homophobia continues to blight British schools, streets, and screens, electoral politics seems to have reached a point where being a gay or straight barely registers on the hustings. The 2010–2015 Parliament was defined by the fight for marriage equality and its aftermath—but any fear that Tory voters would punish the party for being too socially liberal proved to be unfounded in 2015. If there were votes withheld for candidates because they happened to be LGBT, they were more than made up for with votes won *because* the candidate was LGBT. The experience of candidates on the doorsteps confirmed this. Crispin Blunt couldn't recall a single person bringing the issue up in Reigate, while Simon Hughes was mobbed by adoring black British voters in London untroubled by long-forgotten tabloid headlines about his sexual orientation.

An identity—whether ethnicity, gender, or sexual orientation—is a useful shortcut for voters to assess candidate appeal: what you know, what you like, what you fear, and what you aspire to be. Up until a decade ago, when law and society vilified homosexuality, a gay candidate signaled rebelliousness, deviance, and being out of the mainstream: the very essence of abnormality. Thus, a gay candidate would attract votes if the voter, gay or straight, shared that otherness, that rebelliousness, a yearning *not* to be part of the mainstream. But by 2017 British homosexuals were no longer deviants with diseases. They were embraced by the establishment and society. A gay or lesbian candidate signaled something new to the voter: a sense of progress and empathy, the un-derdog with a heartwarming story. The rough right-wing edges of a Tory were smoothed, and the progressive bona fides of a Labour candidate were bolstered if they identified as LGBTQ. It is our supposition that traditional Labour, Liberal Democrat, and Green voters were, all else being equal, more likely to vote Tory if the candidate identified as LGBT, while Liberal Democrat, Green, and disillusioned Labour voters were more likely to vote Labour if the local candidate was LGBT. When the numbers of Britons who say they know, like, love, and respect someone who is LGBT are at an all-time high, the fact that on balance they are inclined—all else being equal—to vote for an identifying LGBT candidate makes perfect sense.

Scotland the Gay

The transformation in Scottish politics and society have, if anything, been more seismic than even that seen in England and Wales. The last execution in Britain for consensual gay sex took place in Scotland in 1836. Scotland did not decriminalize homosexuality until 1980—a full thirteen years after England and Wales—and it was the last jurisdiction in Europe to abolish the death penalty for same-sex relations, doing so in 1889. From crofting villages on windswept islands to gritty city streets, gayness in Scotland was seen as a sickness. But by early 2017 the nation had a higher proportion of out LGBT politicians and party leaders than anywhere else in the world. The Scottish Parliament in Edinburgh had become, as the *New York Times* noted, "the gayest parliament in the world." Ten of 129 Members of the Holyrood Parliament identified as gay, lesbian, or bisexual, and nine of the fifty-nine Scottish MPs in Westminster were lesbian or gay. In Westminster all but one of those out Scots MPs were Scottish Nationalists, and with over 14 percent that made the SNP the most LGBT-inclusive parliamentary party in the world. The visibility didn't end there. Three of the six major party leaders in Scotland were lesbian, gay, or bisexual: the Tory Ruth Davidson, Labour's Kezia Dugdale, and Patrick Harvie of the Greens. Half of Scotland's six member delegation to the European Parliament were gay. In total that meant that twenty-two out politicians of 194 elected representatives in a country of five million people were gay—a significant voice in a nation where being gay had been taboo for centuries.

The Deputy SNP Leader in Westminster, Edinburgh MP Joanna Cherry, recalled being so terrified of the homophobia of the Bermondsey by-election in 1983 that as a young lawyer who was a lesbian, she knew she could "never be involved in politics." Thirty years on she had switched from Labour to SNP, and her society had shifted to a place where being gay was no hindrance to her election at all. In 2015 Scotland topped the Rainbow Europe Index as the fairest nation in terms of legal protections for lesbian, gay, bisexual, transgender, and intersex people. In the general election of 2017 Scotland confirmed again its pole position for including the voices of the LGBT community. The number of out MPs increased by one to ten (17%), cementing the nation's place as the most politically inclusive country in the world.

The first out Scottish MP who was *not* from the Scottish National Party is perhaps the most curious of them all. In January 2016 David Mundell was the only Conservative MP in Scotland, and thus unsurprisingly the Tory government's secretary of state for Scotland. He came out in a New Year's post on his website. Mundell was first elected to the border constituency of Dumfriesshire, Clydesdale, and Tweeddale in 2005 with a slim majority of less than 2,000 votes. The district embodies and mixes deep traditions of Conservative, Labour, and Liberal politics. Rural and disposed to be anti-establishment, it runs on cattle, horses, tartan, and whisky. The one time the area penetrated global consciousness was when Pan Am 107 was blown from the sky and fell on the tiny village of Lockerbie in the western part of the constituency. As a boy David Mundell attended the Lockerbie Academy, graduating in 1980—eight years later the fuselage of the doomed Pan Am flight would fall on Sherwood Crescent, 1,400 yards from his school, killing eleven Lockerbie residents along with the 259 passengers and crew.

When Mundell first won his seat it was against the tide of anti-conservatism in Scotland; his personal popularity upended what should have been an easy Labour victory. His grip on the district strengthened in 2010 when his majority doubled, but in 2015 the SNP tsunami seemed poised to sweep all away in its wake. As the election approached it would be catastrophic for the only Tory MP in Scotland to do anything to jeopardize the personal vote that sent him to Westminster. In 2015 there were only three seats in Scotland that the SNP failed to win. Their candidate increased the SNP vote by almost 30 percent in Dumfriesshire, Clydesdale, and Tweeddale, but against the tide Mundell held on—by the smallest of margins, of 798 votes. Eight months later Mundell came out as gay. He says the timing was not driven by fear of electoral defeat: "I did not come out before the election because of the huge emotional energy required. We had just had the Scottish independence referendum, my son was getting married, and I did not want my coming out to overshadow his wedding. There was no bearing about whether it would affect my ability to win the seat." Indeed, Mundell is candid about not indulging residual bigotry. "If it did, I'd rather not be an MP," he says.

I sit next to Mundell on leather couches in his palatial office in Dover House, the home of the Scottish Office, a few doors down from Downing Street where the clatter of the horses' hoofs on the cobblestones of Horse Guard's parade is audible. I joke that the secretary of state for Scotland's office is as big as Wales. Mundell's coming out was unusual, although not unique. He had been married to a woman for over twenty years and had three grown children. "It was a personal decision, not a strategy to be a front-line campaigner," he tells me. "I came to understand that the only way for me to be truly happy on a personal level was to acknowledge who I am." But the personal inevitably became political. "Things have moved on, but not as far as you would hope. If I am able to be a role model and give confidence, and confirm that all these things are possible, that's great." Mundell notes that his coming out would not have been possible in earlier times. "I'm very lucky," he tells me. "Ten years ago I'd have to have resigned from the cabinet, twenty years ago as an MP." Indeed, in his village "growing up there weren't any visible gays at all. Of course some people were speculated about," he says. This makes the positive reactions from constituents all the more validating. "Not just the young but older people, perhaps in similar circumstances as I— married with children."

I ask him if there is a palpable effect of having two openly gay Conservative government cabinet ministers for the first time. "In some ways I hope there is not," he says. "I'm pleased we don't say, 'let's go to the gay man and ask him about gay things.'" But clearly the tone is very different. "My son Oliver [who is the spitting image of Mundell the elder] stood for election in Dumfriesshire for the Scottish Parliament. We only encountered one doorstep where they said they weren't voting for him because of me. Just one." In 2017 Mundell the elder massively increased his majority to nearly 10,000 votes.

While the record number of British lesbian, gay, and bisexual British MPs is triumph for diversity, internally the Westminster club is less diverse. There were only two lesbians in the 2010–2015 Parliament, and while the number of women had increased to nine in early 2017, they were still outnumbered by thirty men. In 2017 the nine women were re-elected and they were joined by thirty-six men. In 2015 all the out LGB MPs were white, and a full 152 of the 155 candidates were white. In 2017 the same held true and 157 of the 159 LGBT candidates were white. There were four out transgender candidates in 2015. Emily Brothers for Labour in Sutton and Cheam increased the Labour vote by over 4 percent, as did Zoe O'Connell the Liberal Democrat in Maldon, whose vote actually declined less than the national and regional average, and Greens Stella Gardiner (Bexleyheath) and Charlie Kiss (Islington South), who both increased their party share of the vote. Kiss, the only trans man in the election, actually increased the Green vote by 6 percent, which was twice the national and regional average.

In 2017 there were seven trangender candidates and two who identified as nonbinary. Sophie Cook produced the best performance of any trans candidate in British history by polling an impressive 20,000 votes in East Worthing and Shoreham, but it was far from enough to beat the incumbent transphobic Tory. When the much-loved comedian Eddie Izzard announced his intention to run for the House of Commons at the general election scheduled for 2012, it felt like the ceiling for transgender Brits could now be broken. During a thirty-year career as actor, comedian, and author Izzard had generated more acceptance of gender-nonconforming people than any other person in Britain, and his standing in the Labour Party looked likely to provide him a winnable path to the House of Commons.

The change in Britain can feel jarringly quick, but the reality is that it was a long struggle—over centuries—to reach a point where not being straight is no longer the death knell to a political career. First and foremost, change rests on those brave individuals who made the footholds to the top of the mountain for others to climb. Chris Smith reflects that "the fact that so many can now feel so free to be candid and honest about their sexual orientation does show how far we have travelled as a country in the last thirty years. Not only in terms of statute, but in the attitudes and expectations of society too. Indeed, I suspect that the changes in society came before the changes in legislation." Despite being known for his modesty, Smith allows himself to enjoy the moment a little: "I have to say it makes me a little proud to see so many openly out LGB MPs, following the election on May 7, 2015. This all helped a little bit to erase the acute pain of the overall election result!" The evolution is also testament to those inside and outside politics who were initially beaten down. Peter Tatchell is largely correct in saying that "after the Bermondsey by-election, mainstream parties dared not use homophobia again as a campaign weapon."

Our findings appear to have been confirmed in the snap election of June 8, 2017. Forty-five (7%) out LGBTQ MPs were elected, a net gain of six over the numbers at dissolution. Those forty-five represented 7 percent of the new House and is the highest level of representation ever in the world. There were eight new LGBTQ faces—all men—five new gay Labour MPs and three Tories. The two big parties were once again tied at nineteen members each, with the SNP falling by one to seven. New out candidates were successful in the inner cities of Liverpool and the suburbs of Glasgow; in the seaside towns of Southport, Brighton, and Plymouth; in the rural shires and county market towns. LGBTQ MPs now are found in every part of the British Isles. Only two incumbent gay MPs were ousted: John Nicolson of the SNP in East Dunbartonshire and Tory Ben Howlett in Bath, and while Howlett approached the election with a whiff of sexual scandal, both losses were more about party label than sexual identity. As in 2015 out LGBTQ candidates again looked to have outpolled their straight colleagues. The Tories made only eight gains outside of Scotland, and two of them were by LGBTQ Tory candidates. Two of the new Scottish Conservative MPs were also gay. LGBTQ MPs from the Scottish Nationalist Party were more likely to hold their seats than their straight colleagues, and their ten LGBTQ candidates outperformed their straight colleagues by 1.2 percent. In the Labour Party, LGBTQ MPs made four seat gains (12.5% of their total gains). Nationally, the Labour vote was up by 9.5 percent and the Tories by 5.5 percent, but the forty-two LGBTQ Labour candidates increased their vote by 10.9 percent and the forty-two Tories by 6.3 percent.

The skewing of LGBTQ representation by ethnicity and gender molds the issues that are prioritized and highlighted. For many white middle-class gay men marriage equality became a significant talisman, but lesbians and minority gay men, not to mention transgender and gender-variant communities, often have different priorities and aspirations. Even with a relatively huge group of forty-five out MPs, the cohort remains heavily dominated by highly educated gay white men.

Figure 15.1 The moment of victory: from left Ann Louise Gilligan, Darragh Genockey, and Katherine Zappone, Dublin, February 27, 2016. Credit: Andrew Reynolds.

15

You Win Some, You Lose Some

Peter and Simon: The Party's Over

Peter Tatchell's relationship with the Labour Party was never smooth. In 2000 he resigned his Labour membership and stood as an Independent "Green–Left" candidate in the London Assembly elections, securing 1.4 percent of the vote. In 2004 he formally joined the Green Party. He argues that the Conservative–Liberal Democrat coalition government of 2010–2015 was actually better on promoting gay rights overseas than the previous Labour governments had been. The coalition was also more open to LGBT rights organizations in the United Kingdom. He feels resentment toward himself and on behalf of the organizations he works with. "The Blair government's policy was: Stonewall is the only organization we will meet with," Tatchell says. "All the rest of you can go to hell. They never consulted anyone apart from Stonewall and this led to huge resentment and big mistakes. In 1998 the Labour Party whipped their MPs three times to block legislation to protect gay people in employment and Stonewall colluded with that. In 2010 Labour passed the Equality Act, and it was written into key clauses that these protections do not apply to sexual orientation or gender identity—Stonewall colluded with that."

True to form, in December 2016 Tatchell interrupted the Labour leader Jeremy Corbyn's public speech to commemorate the UN universal declaration of human rights in 1948 to protest Corbyn's perceived inaction on the humanitarian crisis in Syria. Thirty years after his electoral defeat, sitting in his study packed to the rafters with protest paraphernalia, Tatchell told me that ultimately his loss proved his making. He was able to have a much greater impact as the agent provocateur than an elected back-bencher in a straightjacket of party discipline.

By 2015 the coalition government was on the ropes, the Liberal Democrats had collapsed in the opinion polls, and Labour looked like they were poised to retake government. Simon Hughes had made it to the heart of the establishment. Since December 2013 he had been the minister for justice and civil liberties in the British government—his dream job, the one he had prepared for since primary school. The day before the general election of May 2015, the streets of Bermondsey were alive with Africans, Afro-Caribbeans, Asians, Latin Americans, Eastern Europeans, Jews, Spaniards, and working-class whites scurrying from place to place, a human collage straight out of a Peter Spier picture book. Simon is still Simon: Simon our MP, not Hughes the Liberal Democrat. His Day-Glo orange diamond posters are strange flowers blooming everywhere—on trees, lampposts, doors, and brick walls. "Vote Simon Hughes—Fighting for Us," they declare. No mention of a party.

We knock on a peeling green door on a public housing estate. A ruffled gray-haired man ambles to the door. Before Simon can speak the man mumbles "Simon" out of the corner of his mouth. I brace myself. "Can I count on your support?" Simon asks. "Too fucking right," the man replies in a thick Scottish accent, and smiles a crooked smile. As parents pick up their toddlers at the primary school, Simon is surrounded by smiling black faces. Everyone knows him, everyone seems to love him. But the Liberal Democrats have fallen from 23 percent to 8 percent in the national polls since the last election, and Labour have gone up by 5 percent. That magnitude of swing would see Hughes lose his seat.

As we traverse concrete courtyards, from housing block to housing block, away from the rest of the team, I tell Hughes about my conversations with Chris Smith and Peter Tatchell. Despite the awfulness of the 1983 by-election—and there are few people with more right to be aggrieved about that particular Labour defeat—Smith had told me that history would record that the two principal characters ended up where they were meant to be in life: Simon the people's politician working the corridors of power, Peter the grit in the oyster keeping the insiders honest. I tell Hughes that I put Smith's view to Tatchell and asked him whether he achieved more as an outsider. He had answered firmly "probably," and went on to say, "I was never going to be a typical MP. I always envisioned working both inside and outside of Parliament. There would have been the constraints of being a party caucus member and the huge constituency workload." Hughes put his hand on my shoulder and told me that made him glad. I felt like I was witnessing a moment of closure.

Simon arrived at the election count well after midnight on May 7. He looked stoic but devastated. No one needed the returning officer's announcement to know that after nine elections over a span of three decades, he could no longer hold back the tide. "Neil Coyle, the Labour Party, twenty-two thousand, one hundred and forty-six . . . Simon Henry Ward Hughes, Liberal Democrat, seventeen thousand, six hundred and fifty-seven." It was over. The day after Simon lost the seat I wrote to Peter to ask how he felt. "I was more happy that Labour had regained Bermondsey than Simon had lost it," he replied. "I did not rejoice that he had been defeated. Immediately after the by-election in 1983, I put that behind me and moved on."

On paper Simon Hughes was the consummate insider, but something inside him compelled him to stand apart—the righteous rebel. His curse was to be viewed as part of the establishment no matter how many rules he broke. "I always felt that I was a rebel—my family said I was the rebellious one. Ming Campbell [the former leader of the Liberal Democrats] once told me the best way for people outside the establishment to change things is to appear to be inside the establishment. 'Dress right, think left,' he would say. I think it was my Welsh education, which is more egalitarian and anti-establishment than the English, which deep down reinforced my desire to be the champion of the minorities and the underdog." Even as a fully paid-up member of the LGBT caucus between 2013 and 2015, he was still the rebel. He was the only out MP in Britain to not vote for the same-sex marriage bill by refusing to go through either voting lobby. I ask him if after two years of reflection he would still abstain if the vote was today. "No," he says without hesitation. "I would vote for it." A former justice minister with thirty-five years of service as an MP in the Westminster bank would be expected to take a seat in the House of Lords, but Simon refused. Was turning down the peerage in any way leaving open the door for another run in Bermondsey? "The only circumstance in which I would go into the upper house was if we had elected senators for London," he tells me. "I don't rule out going back into politics. I'm enjoying being one step away from the front lines—but never say never." But the next elections would be in 2020, when Simon was approaching seventy—too old for a comeback.

In contrast, Peter Tatchell is the born outsider who demands to be part of the mainstream. He doesn't want to assimilate or be accepted as "normal"; rather, he believes that his sexuality and views of human rights should be the mainstream. To a large degree Tatchell has won his personal battle: the mainstream has come to him. Those in power may still see him as a member of the "awkward squad," but he is now more often attacked from the Left than the Right—mostly because he calls out bigotry irrespective of where it emanates from. Criticism from the Left is the thing that irks him most. "Criticism from the Right is entirely predictable and it is water off a duck's back. It doesn't faze me, I respond to it calmly and without any great emotional passion," he says. "But when it comes from the Left, it's often sometimes even more vicious than from the Right. And it's more dishonest. I'll often be smeared from the Left as a racist, a neo-imperialist, a transphobe, etc. When I ask these people where's your evidence, of course they have none or they concoct something out of thin air. And that's quite tough for me to deal with that, because I know in my heart what I've said and done. When you go around making those kinds of false allegations and smears, that's just indulging in a form of McCarthyism. Not all the Left is like this, there are many honorable people, but there is a strand on the Left, mostly on the far left, who take the view, the Stalinist view, that the ends justify the means. And they'll resort to anything to win a point or to win advantage, including downright lies and fabrication. And this is sadly one of the reasons why the Left is constantly on the back foot. Because the public see through it. They see the inconsistency."

Tatchell tells me with a touch of mischief in his voice, "I was sounded out a few years back about a peerage (and previously a knighthood and before that an OBE), but I can't be certain that it was genuine. It sounded genuine, but the person refused to give their name. Perhaps so there could be an official denial that it had been offered if I turned it down—which I did." His radicalism is undimmed with age. If anything he regrets he wasn't more confrontational in the early years of the movement. "I wish I had the campaign skills then that I have now. I would have been more effective. I also wish I had used ethical outing in the 1970s to expose homophobic public figures who were hypocritically condemning LGBT people despite their own homosexuality. This might have hastened the demise of many homophobes, as it did when I used the outing tactic in the 1990s," he says. I asked Peter if he ever regretted standing in Bermondsey. "No . . . there were lots of things I would have done differently in hindsight . . . but at the time I did my best."

I am left feeling that the traits that make Simon and Peter larger-than-life characters are shared. They are mirrors of each other, and they are both most alive when challenging injustice. Their highly developed empathy genes are coupled with a sensitivity that can make a public life exhausting. If their lives had intersected at the different time, in a difference place, they might have ended up being great friends. For Simon and Peter the very personal has been very political and public. Did the *Sun's* exposure of his private life in 2006 lift a weight for Simon? "Yes," he says. "It lifted a huge burden and made life easier, but it remained an issue, albeit with declining importance." I nervously pose the obvious question. "Were you ever close to coming out?" I feel as if I should turn off the recorder, but I don't. "It was always an option, but you want to protect other people more than yourself he says. "My concern was immediate family, [my] mother and brothers. My mother was loving and caring but would have found it difficult." His faith was also a barrier. He says coming out would have caused "a lot of grief to my friends in the evangelical part of the church." He also acknowledges that the infamous by-election made it much more difficult to be honest in the years after. "Because of 1983, for me to have gratuitously reopened that, well, it risked reopening a whole lot of criticism," he says. "I was conscious that it would have caused difficulties for my colleagues locally. On balance it was better to not gratuitously come out in the public domain when we were just getting on with our lives."

"During the time of the by-election would you have identified as bisexual?" I ask. There is a long pause. "Only to one or two of my very closest friends," he says.

Simon realizes he didn't think through the implications of winning on his personal life. "I didn't expect to win," he says. I ask him whether he had to sacrifice your personal life, to which he replies, "Yes." One of the most pernicious aspects of the closet is that it leaves you alone. No one to confide in, no one to think and talk through the tough choices.

Three and a half decades of highs and lows in the public eye has given Simon ample time to reflect. He confides that looking back, the events are clearer than they were in the fog of battle. I asked him if he ever felt uncomfortable with the tone of the 1983 campaign. "It became uncomfortable for me when Peter was adopted as the candidate," he says. "A very brave candidate would have spoken out publically [against the homophobia directed against Tatchell]—the legacy that I accept is that clearly I was uncomfortable that during the campaign issues were made about Peter's sexuality when I was aware that there were issues about mine which were not in the open. If I'd been stronger I could have said we can't do that, it's not appropriate."

In February 2013—the thirtieth anniversary of the by-election—the Rotherhithe and Bermondsey Local History Society put on an event where Peter and Simon shared the stage with their recollections. To raised eyebrows, not least from Simon, Peter said, "I knew at the time that Simon was gay." He went on to say that some in the Labour Party called for him to expose Simon in retaliation for the dirty tricks. "I decided that we would not do that. We did not, and would never, exploit Simon's sexuality." The irony of the personal and public highs and lows of the characters of the Bermondsey by-election are overlain with pathos.

In 2002 Tatchell made an unplanned revelation on the BBC radio program "They Fought and Lost" with the political journalist Steve Roberts. Bob Mellish, the "Boss of Bermondsey" for forty years—the man who despised all that Peter stood for—had a secret gay life and had propositioned Peter multiple times—even when he was the parliamentary candidate. "Although I was always polite and gracious in turning him down, my rejection of his sexual advances contributed to the animosity he felt towards me," Peter said. "Bob was quite persistent. He didn't take no for an answer. Mellish's subsequent hostility was not just political. As well as hating my grassroots left politics, he also seemed unable to accept that I didn't fancy him. At the time I was in my late twenties and he was in his sixties." Peter described Mellish as the classic repressed married gay man. "He did not seem to have any close gay friends, apart from a couple of other MPs. Most of his sexual encounters with men were brief and furtive. I felt sorry for him. Despite his marriage, he seemed quite lonely. Several times, I asked Bob to table legislation for gay equality in Parliament. But he was only interested in having sex with men, not in supporting the gay community . . . Although I was tempted to out him, I decided not to stoop to his level."

After his devastating election loss of 2015, the government asked Simon if he wanted to be a Lord. He said no thank you. He had never been seduced by the red ermine robes, but he did not begrudge others their romantic moment. At dinner years ago I asked Chris Smith if his socialist principles had given him pause before being ennobled. Simon rolled his eyes at me—a father communicating to his son what a crass question that was. But who would begrudge a man a little pomp and prestige? The queen tapped Simon's shoulders three times with her sword and he became a knight.

Simon Hughes said that if an early election happened within eighteen months he would stand again, but there was really no chance of that. Britain now had fixed-term parliaments, and the Conservatives would shepherd their majority through the five years and then look to bolster it in 2020. They had power, so why roll the dice? But then, on April 18, 2017, the new prime minister, Teresa May shocked everyone and called a general election for June 8. Across the river from Big Ben, it would be a rematch between Labour and Simon. Liberals poured in to help: hundreds of party members from all over the country, and scores of others who were just there for Simon. Could Hughes pull off the comeback of Lazarus? Neil Coyle's majority was only 2,000 and Jeremy Corbyn had been weak on Brexit, which had been very unpopular in the district. But it was not to be. Labour defied expectations and increased their vote share in London. The voters of Bermondsey had become younger, and fewer had grown up south of the river. They did not know who Simon was, and tribal party labels meant more than three decades of service.

It is significant that the three central characters of the Shakespearean play that is Bermondsey were all men who loved men: that the constituency was represented from seventy years and nineteen elections by a bisexual man, but only for nine of those years was the MP out, and in only one of the elections was the out bisexual man victorious. Half a lifetime later Peter and Simon are the odd couple of British politics. Hughes says, "Peter has been generous to me. Things that happened to him were completely unacceptable. I pay tribute to him and his fantastic human rights activism."

Tatchell sees change being driven by insiders and outsiders: "Direct action to highlight discrimination and insider lobbying to change minds of politicians. The combination of the two wins hearts and minds." Is he surprised by the speed of change? "Law reform of the 2000s was the culmination of a half-century battle. In 1969, at the age of seventeen, based on my analysis of the black civil rights movement in the United States, I calculated that it would take fifty years to win legal equality in Britain and other Western countries." But Tatchell is surprised at the slow pace of progress in his country of birth, Australia. "It's astonishing, it's bizarre. How can any modern democracy go to such extraordinary lengths to block equality for its citizens?" After his emigration it took half a century for Australia to elect an openly gay member of their people's lower house. Bob Brown (in 1996) and Penny Wong (in 2002) had made history by being elected to the Australian Senate, but that chamber is weaker and less prestigious than the dominant lower house. The people's house was without an LGBT voice until Trent Zimmerman won a by-election in Sydney for the conservative Liberal Party in 2015.

So who is the evangelical? If you sat down with the two of them, you might mistake them. Simon is the churchgoer, the former member of the Church of England general synod, the man of avowed evangelical faith. But he doesn't come across that way. He strikes one as open, moderate, easy to get along with, a pleaser, a bridge-builder. Ironically Peter, the atheist, feels more like the evangelical—the true believer. Only a man with that level of righteous faith in the absolute truth of his convictions could navigate through the storms that life has sent him. He has the self-confidence of a preacher. Gay liberation is his religion, and he is consumed by it. "Do you ever take a moment to enjoy the victories?" I ask. "I savor the moment, but very briefly," he replies. "We've done that—now on to the next battle. I'm not one who sits back and luxuriates on their laurels with self- satisfaction."

"But how do you recharge?" I press him.

"In terms of rejuvenation—I'm not very good at it," he laughs.

Tatchell is inundated with desperate pleas for help every day. His foundation has received over a thousand messages on a single day. "It is totally and utterly overwhelming . . . to carry on . . . so every now and then I take a few seconds," he tells me. A few seconds, I ask? "I could follow my friends' advice, 'just ignore the emails,' but I don't have the heart."

But there is an essential and jarring dichotomy with Peter Tatchell. He commits the acts of a radical firebrand but in conversation he comes across as measured, constrained, and unfailingly polite. He could be an Old World diplomat, rather than the revolutionary that he is.

I ask whether he has plans to retire, anticipating the answer. "I have no plans to retire . . . it would be very boring," he says. When we most recently spoke Peter was sixty-five. His grandfather was active into his nineties and lived to ninety-seven. "Maybe ninety-five would be a good year to retire," Peter chuckles.

What made this evangelical, a man driven by taking care of others and personally made complete by that passion? He seems never satisfied—there is never a moment when it's done, and it's a constant escalation of the challenge of giving care and changing the world. The surplus of empathy is in his muscle memory. "It's true that I had a pretty tough childhood and had many battles to fight. I suppose that made me have a rather keen sense of right and wrong, of not putting up with injustice. I experienced that as a kid, I didn't want to experience it anymore . . . looking back on it, I suppose my first sense of injustice was the harsh brutality of my stepfather, who was a very right-wing evangelical Christian. I can remember him forcing me to dig the trench and gigantic hole for the septic tank even in the middle of winter, when I was up to my knees in water. And this was really heavy soil, really tough, and he would make me go out into the pouring rain to do it . . . then on top of that my mother had life-threatening asthma; she nearly died several times throughout my childhood, [and] through periods when she was bedridden or in hospital, it fell to me to look after my younger brother and two sisters. That was from the age of about eight onwards . . . initially I didn't know what to do, I remembered what my mother did and sort of copied it best I could. Eventually I learned how to cook and sew, and heat the baby's bottle and feed my sister, and you know I didn't have much play time.

But it also made me sort of feel quite proud, because I was doing at the age of eight something that an adult does. Although initially it was rather chaotic and not very effective, I learned it. And did do the job well. And my brothers and sisters to this day say that I was a great surrogate parent. I also felt that it was terribly unjust that because of my mother's illness we suffered a great deal of financial hardship. As my consciousness expanded, I realized lots of other people were going through other forms of injustice. So, just as I didn't like being sort of left behind, or excluded, or having family traumas, I didn't want other people to go through that either."

The Irish General Election of 2016

Tallaght is the borderland between old and new Ireland: a village of workman houses atop cobblestone streets, surrounded by the glass boxes that housed a burgeoning service industry when Ireland was the emerald tiger of the 1990s. West of the housing estates, the Dublin mountains frame the horizon. They are mini-mountains, green rolling hills of sheep farms and dry-stone walls— what Americans picture when they think of Ireland. Country pubs alive with soaring fiddles, thick-knit jumpers, and pints of Guinness, looking back down on modern Ireland.

Decades before, building on the work of the Shanty, Katherine Zappone and Ann Louise Gilligan had established an adult education and childcare center for lower-income women in the Jobstown area of Tallaght and called, An Cosán, (The Path). Tallaght is the pulsing heart of the Dublin South West constituency. As we speed between narrow hedges on country roads, Katherine tells me that An Cosán is all about breaking the cycle of poverty, and living testimonials surround her: campaign volunteers who grew up on the housing estates but made it out to the city and farther, to college, good jobs, and better lives. One of her success stories, Lynn Ruane, is a thirty-one-year-old single mother of two from the Killinarden estate who grew up on drugs, shoplifting, and despondency. She had her first daughter at age fifteen. But An Cosán helped her get back on track, educating her and her daughter. After finishing up her secondary education at An Cosán she was accepted into Trinity College, Dublin. A year later she upended convention by being elected student body president, and in March 2016 she was elected to the Irish Senate from the Trinity College constituency.

Zappone was a candidate in the general election in 2016. In her favor, she had a reputation as an adopted local who had done great things for impoverished families in the area. The marriage equality referendum had given her a national profile, and as an independent she could ride the wave of anti-establishment that was sweeping the electorate. Against her was the fact that she had no party machine behind her and relied on a passionate but inexperienced group of young volunteers. For many it was their first election campaign after being energized by the marriage referendum. Others had grown up in Zappone and Gilligan's afterschool and child care programs. No independent had been elected in Dublin South West for forty years. No out lesbian had ever been elected in Ireland.

The election was like the district—at the borderlands between Ireland of the future and Ireland of the past, old traditions versus a new style. And it was to be as up and down emotionally as the mountains in the distance. At election time you can tell which part of Dublin you are in by the posters on the lampposts. Large smiling faces of Sean, Dermot, and Finian; Clare, Róisín, and Josepha—the candidates hoping to lodge themselves in the voter's mind to get that second, or third, or even tenth preference vote. As we drive into the Dublin South West constituency we start to see new faces: John, Colm, Sean . . . Katherine, Sandra, and Ann-Marie.

The taxi drops me on the high street. I'm looking for No. 3 Main Street, but every street seems to be named Main Street. The glass shop front of No. 4 is plastered with Anti-Austerity Alliance posters. This is a left-wing party—they must be sympathetic to Katherine, I think? Ever the naïve foreigner, I step in and address the busy room. "Hi, I'm looking for No. 3 Main Street," I say. A shaven-headed man turns to me. "Well, we are No. 4," he says with a smile. I pause. "Who are you looking for?" he asks. "Katherine Zappone," I reply. All heads turn to stare at me. There is silence. The smile disappears. It was exactly the feeling I got when I naively stepped into a pub in Dundalk when driving from Belfast to Dublin in 1998. At the time Dundalk was the home of the "real" IRA, the armed nationalists who had broken with the Provisional IRA over the Northern Irish peace process. An Englishman in Dundalk in 1998 was asking for trouble. At No. 4 I am given terse directions: it turns out the Anti-Austerity Alliance see Katherine as a threat to them in the housing estates, and have been smearing her to constituents for a supposed lack of radical bona fides.

Darragh, Zappone's campaign manager, has the wired look of a man who hasn't slept for a long while. But his energy is high on the thrill of chasing down an unlikely victory. A music agent in real life, he literally grew up around Katherine—his mother took him to the An Cosán day care when he was a baby. Another volunteer, Mike, is an ER doctor in his thirties who grew up in a seaside village in County Clare on the West Coast. When Mike was a gay kid coming of age in the late 1980s, rural Ireland told him that he was not welcome. He spent eleven years treating the sick in Australia. The marriage equality referendum told Mike he could come home—"that I was welcome home now," he smiled. Conor is a grad student in statistics at Trinity; he knew Darragh, and Darragh asked him to do the vote targeting analysis. They are the archetypical motley crew of appealing underdogs—the school kids attempting to put on a show.

The voting ends at 10 p.m. on Friday and the count starts at 9 a.m. the next day. Twenty-one candidates appear on a ballot that is over two feet long: faces that will become imprinted on the minds of the counters over the next three days. Under the Irish voting system voters are free to rank-order candidates with numbers. Five TDs (MPs) will be elected from this district. The big players are the two historic "civil war" parties—Fine Gael, who are running three candidates, and Fianna Fáil, who are strategically running just one. The junior government coalition party, Labour, are running two candidates, Sinn Fein two, Anti-Austerity two, the Greens one, and the small Renua party one. Of the rest, local health campaigner Peter Fitzpatrick looks to be the most competitive independent apart from Katherine Zappone.

The count involves redistributing the ballots of losing and winning candidates to ensure that the fewest votes possible are wasted. In effect, an Irish voter is writing a letter to the returning officer: one might say "I would like my vote to go to Katherine, if she has too many votes (a surplus) or has no chance of winning, then please give my vote to Daniel. If then Daniel wins with more votes than he needs or is knocked out because he has too few, please give me vote to Siobhan. If Siobhan doesn't need my vote . . ." and so on. You can rank as many or as few candidates as you wish. What this gives rise to is a long, fascinating, emotional roller-coaster of a count where votes are moved around by hand by scores of counters until all seats are filled. The quota for election is effectively one-sixth of the total vote (the number of seats plus one), as that is the figure only five candidates can reach. As 67,271 valid votes were cast in Dublin South West, the quota was 11,212. It is quite possible to computerize the vote and count and save oneself a day or more of work. (The Irish did so in 2002 but found it diminished the fun, and so they stuck their nose up at modernity and went back to counting by hand.)

Tradition has it that the first tally of votes—to purely count the total number cast—is observed closely by the candidate's supporters. They collaborate in pairs: a Fianna Fáil man would call out who the first preference was for as the ballot was unfolded and Dr. Mike would make a mark on his tally sheet. A runner would pick up completed sheets from over fifty teams and sprint them over to a bank of computers staffed by party agents. From this, a highly accurate estimate of first preferences votes began to emerge over the morning. I wandered the perimeter looking over the shoulders of the tallymen and women who lent on the metal railings separating them from the ballots in motion. Katherine seemed to be somewhere between fourth and eighth on each sheet—a long way behind the main Fianna Fáil, Fine Gael, Sinn Fein, and Anti-Austerity candidates, but maintaining her position above the rest. If she could be sixth or seventh on the first count she had a chance—*if* the gap between her and the fifth place was not too great to surmount.

Katherine arrived in the hall and I went over to tell her that based on what I was seeing she was in the top seven. "How do you feel?" I asked. She leaned in conspiratorially. "Feckin' nervous," she said, smiling her big smile. It turned out the tally was pretty much spot-on. When the first preferences were announced at 3 p.m., John Lahart of Fianna Fáil had taken 9,647 votes (14.3%), followed by the Anti-Austerity's Paul Murphy with 9,005 (13.4%). Fine Gael's Colm Murphy was third with 7,195 (10.7%), and Sinn Fein's Sean Crowe picked up 6,974 (10.3%). Fine Gael had done a good job of getting their voters to split their votes and their second candidate, Ann-Marie Dermody, came in next with 6,463 (9.6%). Farther back in the tally was Katherine Zappone, one out of the elected places with 4,463 (6.3%).

It was going to be an uphill struggle and a long night, but she was in with a shot. She was in the game on the first count but picking up two thousand votes was, as Darragh noted, "a big ask." It all depended on transfers, but Katherine was known to be transfer-friendly: she might pick up several second- and third-preference votes because of her broad popularity across parties and communities. After the also-ran independents had been eliminated, it became clear that the battle for the last seat was going to be between Zappone and Dermody of Fine Gael. Eight candidates had gone, no one had been elected, and Katherine was still 1,817 votes behind Dermody. At this rate she stood no chance of making up the difference. But next was the redistribution of 2,120 votes one of the Labour candidates had received. Katherine had always been close to Labour, and indeed the party leader had been the one to nominate her to the Senate in 2011. Could this round of transfers give her a big boost and improve our mood? The returning officer went to the microphone—Dermody had picked up 139 votes, with 131 for Katherine. She was even further behind. A wave of tiredness swept over Team Zappone. After excluding three more candidates over three more hours, the gap was still 1,600 votes. John Lahart made it over the quota and was the first declared elected. The independent health campaigner Peter Fitzpatrick was staying in the race, having moved up from ninth to eighth position.

Then came the elimination of the second Anti-Austerity candidate Sandra Fay, which pushed her running mate Sean Murphy over the top with a surplus of 2,300 votes. These votes now had to be redistributed back to the six candidates left standing. Anti-Austerity had been the most hostile party to Zappone during the campaign, but ironically Katherine closed the gap to less than 1,200 in this round, picking up close to 400 more votes than Dermody. There was hope. If Katherine could do much better in the final two transfers—from the Labour candidate Pamela Kearns and the independent Peter Fitzpatrick—then she just might pull victory from the jaws of defeat. But the Kearns transfer was a disaster; Dermody actually took around 400 more votes than Zappone.

At 4 a.m. the writing seemed to be on the wall: it was too much to make up. Fitzpatrick had just over 4,900 votes to transfer and Zappone was over 1,500 votes behind Dermody. That meant that Katherine had to take more than four times as many of Fitzpatrick's ballots as Dermody. And some of his votes would likely go to the other Fine Gael candidate Brophy, who remained in the count as he had still not been elected, while lots of ballots would go into the nontransferable pile at this stage of the count. None of these would help Katherine catch up. She would have to massacre Dermody in this stage—it was beyond the realm of possibility.

The team sat exhausted and despondent, waiting for the axe to fall and Dermody to be elected. The Fine Gaelers were dancing and singing in a circle. The returning officer walked over to Dermody, about ten feet away. She was facing away, but I could see her body shrink in a palpable deflation in mood. "What's going on?" Conor asked me. "I don't know," I said as I moved a little closer to the whispering group, which had grown to include Dermody's campaign manager and husband. Her husband put a supporting arm around Dermody's waist. "It must be closer than we thought," I told Conor. "Maybe he thinks we might call for a recount and he's letting her know." "Where's Darragh?" I found him over by the food truck. "Go speak to the returning officer," I told him. I walked over with him and stood just out of earshot. Darragh walked back to me. "It's close, but he's not telling me who is in front," he said.

We gathered alongside the Fine Gael crowd to face the lectern. The weary returning officer took his place. Katherine steeled herself for the blow.

"On the sixteenth count the transfers from excluded candidate Fitzpatrick were as follows: Brophy, five hundred and thirteen; Dermody, four hundred and twenty-four; nontransferables, one thousand eight hundred and eighty-six"—Katherine gripped Ann Louise's hand—"Zappone, two thousand two hundred and thirteen."

A huge disbelieving roar came from the mouths of the dozen Zappone supporters left in the hall. There was stunned silence from the scores of Fine Gael members. Katherine threw her head back and yelled with unvarnished joy.

"Did I win? Did I win?" she asked no one in particular. Conor was bouncing like Tigger—his face flushed, tears in his eyes. I shouted at him above the hullaballoo, "What was the majority?" "What?" he asked. "How far was she ahead?" I yelled. Conor came down to earth, clutched his chest, and said, "I don't know."

Zappone had won by 152 votes. In all the noise it was easy to miss the returning officer say, "a recount of counts stages 16 and 15 has been called for by Fine Gael which we will start at 10 a.m. tomorrow morning."

Darragh turned to me. "I knew we'd won, but I didn't want it to get out before the announcement." "Good poker face," I said, and slapped him on the back. It suddenly didn't seem like 4 a.m.

The recount began six hours later at 10 a.m. the next morning. All the actors were back in their places. After the review of the sixteenth stage (the allocation of Fitzpatrick's vote) had been completed, Zappone's lead had gone from 152 to 125. After they looked again at the transfer of Crowe's surplus (stage 15), it was down to 122. In the last seventy years a recount had never caused a change in the outcome in an Irish election but Fine Gael—deeply wounded by their crushing defeat at the national polls—were lawyering up. Seven men in suits and clipboards appeared as if from nowhere, led by Fine Gael's chief counsel, Kevin Higgins. The elephant versus the mouse. Fine Gael were ready to throw their weight around to do all they could to stop the upstart taking away what they felt was rightfully theirs. The returning officer had little ability to resist; a full check, of every ballot and every stage of the count would commence Tuesday morning. All the candidates needed to come back, because this meant none of the five had been formally elected.

At the end of Tuesday nothing had changed: Katherine still held about the same lead she had the first time, and despite the blustering of Fine Gael the returning officer declared Katherine Zappone duly elected. She became the first out lesbian elected to the Dail, the 250th out LGBT MP ever in national office, the thirty-second LBT woman MP incumbent as of March 2016, and the first Irish MP from Spokane, Washington. The honeymoon had produced a child.

The election results produced a smorgasbord of old and new parties, with no group easily able to put together a government. After weeks of negotiations Zappone agreed to support the outgoing Fine Gael prime minister Enda Kenny's efforts to put together a minority government. On May 6, 2016, the woman from Spokane was appointed minister for children and youth in the government of Ireland. She was not merely the first lesbian cabinet minister in Ireland (and only the twelfth-ever in the world), but the first American in Irish government since Éamon de Valera.

Less than a year into Katherine's tenure as minister, Ann Louise suffered a catastrophic brain hemorrhage, leaving her without sight. On June 14, 2017, Leo Varadkar was elected by the Dail as the Thirteenth Taoiseach of Ireland. The next morning, less than a mile away, Ann Louise passed away in Katherine's arms, her enormous role in transforming Irish society noted and celebrated. Katherine may have been the lead actor, but few people aside from Ann Louise had been more responsible for building a foundation of respect that enabled Varadkar's triumph. Katherine was devastated. She had lost her lodestar. At the funeral Katherine said, "The evening after her medical team told Ann Louise that she would not recover, she looked at me and said: 'I am just thinking again about the conversation. Did Joe [her doctor] say that I was going to die?' And I responded, 'Yes, Ann Louise.' And then I asked her, 'Are you afraid?' and she said, 'No. I was not afraid before entering the world and I am not afraid to leave it.'" Ann Louise was never afraid; she told friends that if she hadn't entered religious life she would have been a racing car driver, and she was not joking.

The island of Ireland's struggle for equality continues. A couple of hours to the north of Dublin are the six Ulster counties (out of nine) that remained part of the United Kingdom in 1922. As the Republic of Ireland moved toward the light, deeply tribal Northern Ireland grasped for its conservative doctrines and remained mired in homophobia and inequality. While Katherine Zappone was being elevated to the Irish government, the Northern Irish Assembly was left as the only parliament in the British Isles that had never elected an openly LGBT person to office and the only part of the United Kingdom where it was illegal for same-sex couples to marry.

There had in fact been a majority in favor of marriage equality in the Northern Irish Assembly in November 2015—by a vote of 53 to 51—but the bill was vetoed by the majority partner in the power-sharing executive: the protestant Democratic Ulster Unionists. The DUP had enough votes to call a "petition of concern." The Good Friday agreement of 1998 installed this mechanism to re-assure both communities, unionist and nationalist, that "culturally sensitive" laws would not be enacted without their agreement. Thus, a motion needs the support of a majority of both nationalist and unionist members. It was ironic that an instrument meant to protect minority rights was used to restrain a minority's equality. In the reduced 2017 Northern Irish Assembly, only thirty members was enough to call a petition.

On March 2, 2017, just over two hundred candidates competed for ninety Assembly positions in eighteen districts. The snap Northern Irish Assembly election of March 2017 was driven by, of all things, a heating subsidy scandal, but the Irish nationalist Sinn Fein and Social and Liberal Democratic Party (SDLP) parties, the centrist Alliance Party, and the Greens all campaigned on bringing marriage equality to the six counties. Counting for the four Belfast constituencies began at 8 a.m. on a Friday morning in the Titanic Exhibition Center, a cavernous hangar of a building alongside the scrubland of what was once the jewel of the Harland and Wolff shipbuilding yard. Massive steel cranes loomed like dead, rusted dinosaurs of a bygone era. The cold rain pelted me as

I walked past the police with machine guns—nothing could have been bleaker in the world. There were eight out LGBT candidates running in the elections, hoping to break the ceiling and give the emerging youthful Northern Irish LGBTQ population a voice in politics. Six were gay men, one a lesbian, and one a crusading trans woman. Four were standing for the Green Party, two for the moderate nationalist SDLP, and one for the Alliance Party of Northern Ireland.

The last, Julie-Anne Corr-Johnson, was emblematic of the growth of LGBT candidates in unexpected parties. A Belfast North councilor who had married her wife Kerry in a civil ceremony (not recognized by the state), she was standing for the Progressive Unionist Party (PUP), which was the political wing of the defunct unionist paramilitary Ulster Volunteer Force. Corr-Johnson had been recruited into the PUP by the infamous paramilitary Billy Hutchinson, who had served time for the murders of Catholics but come to support the peace process and a brand of socialist class-based unionism by the time he came into contact with the local teenager. Ironically, Corr-Johnson was the only LGBT candidate who stood a hope of being elected—but standing for the third-largest party on the unionist side, she was a long shot.

When the first preferences were counted by midday, it became clear that Corr-Johnson was not going to have a Harvey Milk moment in Belfast and that Northern Ireland would remain without any LGBT voices in government. But as the night wore on, and votes were transferred under the single transferable vote (STV), it became apparent that the real race to watch for signs of progress in LGBT rights was twenty yards away from me at the Belfast South count. At midnight there were four candidates left in the race for the last two seats. Clare Bailey, the coleader of the Green Party, was a couple of thousand votes ahead of her three rivals, but the others were all unionists almost guaranteed to transfer their votes to each other. This final stage was not just important to Belfast South but to the dynamics of the whole Assembly. The Greens had led the fight for marriage equality, and the DUP had led opposition. With just these two seats remaining to be declared, the DUP were on twenty-seven seats and they could rely on one independent unionist, but they still needed both to give them enough for a "petition of concern" veto of marriage equality.

At midnight, next to where the *Titanic* had been born and berthed, with no openly gay candidates left in the race, a few thousand votes might determine the fate of LGBT rights in Northern Ireland. Between them Chris Stalford and Emma Little-Pengelly of the DUP and Michael Henderson of the Ulster Unionist Party (UUP) had 14,000 votes to pass around. The unfortunate Little-Pengelly was 25 votes behind her colleague Stalford and was eliminated, and her 4,700 votes were distributed back to the three remaining candidates. As expected, her DUP colleague won the lion's share—4,000 votes—and was elected four of five. Would there be enough votes for the last anti-LGBT unionist to go ahead of the

Green leader? No. Clare Bailey held on, and a slightly greater space for LGBT people seemed to open.

Fintan Warfield of Sinn Fein was elected to the Irish Senate at the age of twenty-four in 2016—the youngest parliamentarian and the first openly gay man to represent the hardline republican party at the national level. Warfield did not take the sign-posted path to political office. By his own testimony he was not politicized by gay rights. As a teen he was engaged by Irish republicanism, anti-establishment politics, and music. A guitarist and singer, he joined his cousins in the Irish rebel folk band the Wolfe Tones and toured the United States. "You wouldn't believe how many politicians don't know how to use a mic," he laughs.

He was elected to the South Dublin council and became mayor at twenty-two. By then he had connected the dots between his brand of republicanism and the broad marginalization of the "other." Upon being elected mayor he said, "Maybe it's the girl with the funny name or unusual accent. Maybe it's the boy who wants to wear makeup in school. Maybe it's the single mother struggling to make ends meet. Maybe it's the unemployed man ashamed that he can't put food on the table. Maybe it's the older person who goes to the Square to keep warm or whom no one has visited in weeks. These are the people who I as mayor want to stand with." Warfield takes long thoughtful pauses and considers his answers. His honesty, empathy, and sincerity are mesmerizing. You can see why he topped the culture and education poll for the Senate.

In the presidential election of 2011 that saw the implosion of David Norris's candidacy, then–eighteen-year-old Fintan dutifully supported the candidacy of Sinn Fein's, Martin McGuiness. "I canvassed for McGuiness but my heart was for David," he confides, and when Norris pulled out Warfield was left "angry and bitterly disappointed."

Sinn Fein, and nationalist politics writ large, are not usually associated with LGBTQ politics or politicians, but Warfield sees a natural connection. "I don't think it's opportunist to remind ourselves that Stonewall happened three months before British soldiers were deployed to Ireland," he says. "That history reaffirmed my commitment to Sinn Fein. Sometimes I think there is more relevance in the rainbow flag being the national flag of a united Ireland. A united Ireland will naturally be a secular state—a state free from both churches—[and] any new constitution will separate the church from the state and that's a reason to support it." But have you always felt welcome in Sinn Fein, I ask. "Most nationalist movements split before they achieve their aims. Social issues—gay rights, gender equity, abortion, are our fault line," Fintan argues. He notes that Gerry Adams, Sinn Fein's longtime president, was the force behind Sinn Fein's embrace of an equalities agenda. On the day of the marriage equality referendum party in Dublin Castle, Fintan did not have a ticket, so he stood next to Gerry Adams and got in.

There is great pressure on any national politician—and that pressure is magnified when you are young, gay, and visible. Warfield embraced the importance of his, and others', visibility in the marriage referendum campaign: "That was the representative I wanted to be, the most effective way to get things done is to talk personally," he says, but now he fears that he has lost some balance. "I should have kept more private," he tells me. He is somewhat shy and more introverted than you might expect. "It's easier to speak to a big group than small group . . . just as it is with music. There is stuff I have said to journalists that I haven't told mum and dad."

But my assumption is that the multiple gay men and lesbians in the Irish Parliament who came before him have laid a trail for him. Fintan only partially agrees. "It's a safe place for gay men, [but] I don't think it's a safe place for many people." While he values his LGBTQ visibility, "now I feel a little pigeonholed," he says. "I'm concerned that I talk about LGBTQ issues too often—you see in the corner of your eye certain people switch off when I talk about it again." Warfield feels the weight of expectations. "Sometimes I just want to be an ordinary citizen. I'm worried that I'm going to fuck up at some point."

Is that about being gay, or just human? I ask. "I'm a young gay man who is on the scene and the scene can be all sorts of things," he replies. "It's different from being a straight young man in politics. For all of us your reputation is on the line if you fuck up." Nevertheless, he recognizes the value of being at the table. "Yes, I have spent my few years in public life talking about LGBTQ issues, but I'm still working on them because we haven't moved the state to a position of accepting trans people, access to PREP, positive sex education. The issues [are] maybe lessening but are still there." He also seeks to address the things that he argues were "hugely problematic" about the marriage equality referendum campaign, such as the presentation of an "acceptable" gay avatar—"almost as if we are straight but we are gay. It closeted lots of people," Fintan says. His unease over the exclusionary elements of the campaign spurred his efforts to address trans inclusion. Warfield tabled the gender recognition bill soon after being seated.

Above all else, Fintan Warfield gives Irish families the space to heal. He tells me he was leaving a meeting with a "hardened republican." As they walked, Warfield mentioned he was going to meet a gay friend in The George—the famously gay pub of Dublin. Warfield says his colleague was "awkwardly talking, beating around the bush; in a whisper, he said, 'my son frequents the George as well.'" It was a powerful confessional moment. "How's it going for you?" Warfield asked, knowing exactly what the man was saying. The man shared that when his son had first come out it had been really hard for him, "but I'm getting the right language," he said. "Don't worry about the language," Warfield reassured him. "He will love you." Warfield values his role within Sinn Fein and traditional Republican families, and those are the moments which make the pressure worthwhile.

Figure 16.1 Coos Huijsen and Lank Bos. Credit: From the collection of Coos Huijsen.

Conclusion

Be Gay, Just Not Queer

When is the battle for gay rights won? Is it when gay politicians are just as likely to be conservative as liberal, urban as rural? Is it when no one knows or cares who you sleep with or marry? When gay people are as "normal" as everyone else? Many of the gay elected officials who have had the most impact strive for assimilation. Lord Waheed Alli told me that when being gay becomes "normalized" in society, "that's it . . . it's done . . . the victory is won." Similarly, Louisa Wall argued that what she wanted to achieve was "the normalization of the LGBTI identity." But a debate is gathering within the LGBT community over strategy and philosophy. Is assimilation the answer, or should LGBT people demand inclusion on their own terms? A young Oxbridge-educated Tory Party researcher laughed as he told me, "You can be gay, just don't be queer." Indeed, the Tory MP Conor Burns took umbrage at Liberal Democrat leader Nick Clegg saying "it's now normal for people to get married": "What an offensive pejorative way of putting it," says Burns.

The classic leaflet photo for a suburban politician in England is the candidate holding hands with his wife in a field of daisies while their golden Labrador frolics at their feet. Iain Stewart, the openly gay Conservative MP for Milton Keynes South, told me that they used the photo of him in the field with the lab (borrowed) . . . just no wife. Political operatives are selling the message: "Why are you afraid of Sharon? She is married, has three kids, drives a Subaru, chairs the PTA, and shops at Wholefoods. She is *just* like you." But some gay people don't want to be just like straight people. Noah Berlatsky of the *Atlantic* writes that "the very topic of marriage equality foregrounds assimilation; [television presents] LGBT people as typical middle-Americans, working middle-class jobs, raising kids, living the American dream. The half-naked Pride paraders were carefully pushed off center-stage."

In a March 2014 *New Yorker* article, Malcolm Gladwell noted that assimilation has a much brighter track record than acceptance of difference in US history. He was writing about the Branch Dravidian sect, led by David Koresh, which came to a fiery end in 1993. Gladwell noted that "mainstream American society finds it easiest to be tolerant when the outsider chooses to minimize the differences that separate him from the majority. The country club opens its doors to Jews. The university welcomes African Americans. Heterosexuals extend the privilege of marriage to the gay community. Whenever these liberal feats are accomplished, we congratulate ourselves. But it is not exactly a major moral accomplishment for Waspy golfers to accept Jews who have decided that they, too, wish to play golf. It is a much harder form of tolerance to accept an outsider group that chooses to maximize its differences from the broader culture."

In *The Battle Over Marriage: Gay Rights Activism Through the Media*, Leigh Moscowitz argues that "in selling one particular version of gay and lesbian life, the movement risks unintentionally casting other forms of gay identity (not being part of a monogamous, married, child-rearing couple) to the margins." Clay Aiken believes that the tension is overblown. He told me that "in every great cause there have to be normalizers and marginalizers . . . if somebody doesn't stir the turd, nobody gonna smell it."

Working from within has long been a controversial strategy. As David Rayside notes, "there is substantial disagreement in gay/lesbian political communities about the utility of operating within established political institutions . . . there have always been tensions between activists who use traditional lobbying tactics and those in stand in radical opposition to the frameworks, and goals of mainstream politics. They distrust the politics of compromise that so permeates legislative environments; many also resent what they see as the precedence of party loyalty over principle among all parliamentarians." But the founder of Freedom to Marry, Evan Wolfson, argues change happens through the movement of many pieces, and social and political movements are ultimately complementary. When history is written, the "tendency is to think that the world began the day you arrived." That is true of the political realm as much as the activist world. But the reality is that there is credit to be shared out broadly. Wolfson is measured in the credit he gives to out elected officials: "In many places they were very important, the engines of the conversations that change hearts and minds," he says, literally being the good representative—"an example, an exhibit" of why equality is fair.

While out gay and lesbian MPs may be reliable on gay rights, not all are hewn from the Left, and this rankles some. In Washington, DC, two out House Democrats, Krysten Sinema (Arizona) and Sean Patrick Maloney (New York), voted with Republicans against Obamacare. This infuriated the radio talk show host Michaelangelo Signorile, who eviscerated Sinema and Maloney as being "queer conservaDems" promenading their gayness to raise money from gay donors but then selling out their core supporters. Maloney, who represents part of the Hudson Valley in New York State, stressed in a 2014 *National Journal* interview that he was no different from the standard guy in his district: "I get my kids ready for school just like every other parent in the Hudson Valley, dragging them out of bed, making them breakfast, and double checking to ensure that left shoes end up on left feet. At night, I pick them up at soccer practice and basketball games. Trust me: no matter the family, morning tantrums are all the same . . . folks care much more about protecting Medicare and making sure their neighbors can put food on the table than fighting over gay marriage."

Running in the neighboring 19th district of New York in 2014, encompassing the site of the Woodstock music festival, was Sean Eldridge, the twenty-seven-year-old multimillionaire husband of Chris Hughes, the cofounder of Facebook. Eldridge presents a similar image to Maloney, accused of being a Democrat of and for the wealthy liberals who commute into the city. He gives few interviews, and being a gay man is far from the central message of his campaign. Nevertheless, in a fundraising appeal to Victory Fund supporters to coincide with LGBT Pride month, he said: "Growing up in northwest Ohio there were no Pride celebrations in my community, no gay–straight alliances, and no openly gay officials. In fact, there were no openly gay people I knew of. Today life is very different. My husband Chris and I live in a welcoming and supportive community and were able to get married here in New York, and I have the incredible honor of running as an openly gay, married candidate for the United States Congress."

Krysten Sinema built an even more conservative voting record in the House, voting with Repubicans almost half the time. In 2017 alone she took conservative positions on health care, immigration, the death penalty, policing, and disability rights. In 2015 she supported tighter regulations on Syrian and Iraqi refugees being admitted to the United States, and was one of only six Democrats to vote to punish US cities that had vowed to give sanctuary to refugees. In mid-2017 she entered the race for the Senate seat in her native Arizona. With the incumbent senator retiring, Trump's dismal approval ratings, and Sinema's right-of-center positioning, the 2018 race looked like it might produce the first Democratic senator from Arizona since 1990. Sinema studiously avoided making her campaign about her sexual orientation or progressive bona fides.

Up until a decade or so ago, marriage was not the issue bringing activists to the barricades. Patrick Egan and Ken Sherrill note that for decades marriage equality was far down on the list of LGB voters, priorities. Indeed, many LGBT activists remain sanguine about the focus on marriage. Moscowitz notes that activists began to win the battle for marriage by repossessing the images lodged in the public's mind when they thought of gay people. She notes that up until the last decade the media used images of the marginal and illicit: gay bars and seminaked parades and drag queens. The debate over gay rights was between the radical Left and the traditional religious. But activists today have done a great job of making gay people look "normal." Wolfson argues that the leadership of the

LGBT rights community was not prioritizing marriage in the 1980s and 1990s not because it was unimportant to them, but rather because they were fighting on so many other fronts. Wolfson's call was to "stop fighting to be left alone, and start fighting to be let in." He believed that exclusion from institutions was very costly to gay people in both tangible and intangible ways. Marriage was both symbolic and substantive. The very fight would reclaim the language of love and relationship that would transform straight people's views of gay people. In essence, the thirty-year battle that Wolfson waged was not just about the win but the fight itself. The way the argument was advocated would be an engine of transformation—enhancing shared values and assimilating. There was resistance within the LGBTQ movement against focusing on marriage. Wolfson says part of it was ideological: "Marriage is patriarchal and oppressive and we should redefine the family, not emulate straight people," he says, and part was strategic. "It was too difficult a challenge, the movement was not ready, too much of a mountain to climb."

Has the attention on marriage retarded efforts on other fronts, such as passing anti-employment discrimination legislation (ENDA), addressing the devastating issues of LGBT youth suicide and homelessness, bullying in school, or public health concerns? Some, including the British campaigner Peter Tatchell, say yes, but others say that marriage equality has trickle-down effects—it normalizes the community further, making progress on other issues easier. Once a conservative legislator votes yes on gay marriage they are more likely to vote for employment nondiscrimination, for example. Once you have a same-sex family in the school car pool, you are more likely to see homophobic bullying in the classroom as a problem worthy of action. Wolfson notes the indisputable fact that "in the American marriage chapter we have made substantive gains on many other fronts."

Something Gained, Something Lost

When it comes to LGBT rights globally, the 2010s were the best of times and worst of times. One year after the United States introduced nationwide marriage equality in June 2016, one million adults in America were in same-sex marriages—a 33 percent increase over twelve months. Eleven percent of gay men and 9 percent of lesbians were in same-sex marriages, and nearly half of all LGBT couples living together were married. But across the established democracies where progress seemed inevitable just a year ago, complacency masks creeping danger: what Michaelangelo Signorile calls "victory blindness." The middle-class gays with jobs, families, personal security, comfortable lives, and newfound acceptance are enjoying the best of times, but the less fortunate, not so much.

The NYU Professor Kenji Yoshino has written about the phenomenon of "covering" in the Asian American community, which can usefully be applied to the LGBT community. Signorile notes that "for queer people, covering is when we tone down or assimilate in, or try to show cultural tastes that are more in line with the mainstream, and downplay our own culture." Rory O'Neill says that in the early 2000s, before the Irish LGBTQ rights movement had been reborn, "gay culture was being stripped of everything that made it interesting, dangerous and offensive. Plucked, emasculated and disembowelled. Shaved and polished, infantilized til it was neutered . . . It was no longer a rejection of the status quo, it was embracing the status quo and adding a few cushions."

The struggle for equality is a long way from finished. Yes, gay and lesbian people have substantially more legal rights and social respect than ever before, but employment and health discrimination continues to rear their ugly heads, homelessness disproportionately targets LGBTQ youth, and a fear of homophobia keeps many LGBTQ people deep in the closet. Even lesbian, gay, and bisexual Americans are incarcerated at much higher proportions: 9 percent of men in prison, 6 percent of men in jail, 42 percent of women in prison, and 36 percent of women in jail are LGB. Compared with straight inmates, LGB prisoners were more likely to have been sexually victimized as children, to have been sexually victimized while incarcerated, to have experienced solitary confinement and other sanctions, and to report psychological distress. There are 2.5 million LGBT adults over the age of fifty in the United States, and this number will double by 2030. Older lesbians, bisexuals, and gay men have higher susceptibility to mental health problems, disability, and disease and physical limitations than do older heterosexual people. Aging transgender folks are also at higher risk for poor physical health, disability, and depression.

About 8 percent or 1.3 million US high schoolers say they are gay, lesbian, or bisexual. A national Centers for Disease Control survey in 2016 found that these kids were three times more likely than straight students to have been raped, at least a third had been bullied on school property, and they were twice as likely as heterosexual students to have been threatened or injured with a weapon. More than 29 percent had made suicide attempts in the previous year. While 1 percent of straight students said they had used heroin, 6 percent of LGB students reported having done so. These challenges track new waves of discriminatory laws. As Kerry Eleveld noted in 2016, "LGBTQ Americans are now the clear target of a nationwide campaign being waged by religious zealots to systematically lock in discrimination in every state that hasn't already enacted nondiscrimination protections. This could very well lead to a divided nation where most blue states outlaw discrimination on the basis of gender identity and sexual orientation, while most red states explicitly give it their blessing." Activist Cleve Jones sees the compartmentalization of identity politics as a key misstep. "We're increasingly putting each other in these silos where there's just this circular firing squad," he told Alexander Sammon of *Mother Jones* in 2016. "What's missing from so much of it is a class analysis. A whole lot of the way identity politics has gone seems to me to deny empathy. If you tell me I can't understand you because of my color or you can't understand me because of your sexual orientation or she can't understand us because of her faith, well, if you can't have empathy how will you ever have solidarity? I work mostly today in the labor movement."

At the age of eighty-two, having outlived most of his enemies—both human and viral—Larry Kramer, the author, playwright, and scourge of the complacent, is still frightened. In June 2016 he told *Esquire*, "I am frightened that everything gay people have fought for could disappear in an instant. There will be new attacks against us in courts and all across the country every single day. I am frightened we're not strong enough to fight back to save ourselves. There were so few activists fighting for the HIV meds, compared with our total numbers. I have never been able to satisfactorily answer the question I once asked all of the time: Why isn't every gay man in America fighting to save his own life? Our lives will be filled with jeopardy, much of it quite ruthless. We have never lacked for enemies, and they are not going away . . . We must battle not only against our enemies but also against the straightjackets many of us still wear, which interfere with our ability to fight these enemies in full, free, and in-your-face unity. We must have a stronger presence in Washington." Harvey Milk said "keep hope alive," and Kramer remains hopeful "because I can now see so many of us and we can all see more and more of us. Closets are disappearing everywhere. Some gays fear that legal marriage will assimilate us, but I predict just the opposite. Our culture will flourish mightily and even more imaginatively. It's no wonder our enemies are worried by such potential power. This hope excites me. But hope has a way of disguising, if not downright obliterating, the realities of the moment. There is much work to attend to as we enter a new era." Bathroom bills, antitransgender edicts, religious exemptions: Eleveld laments that the movement is "now in a total defensive crouch—dodging anti-equality bullets month after month, year after year, as our entire agenda is effectively dictated by the Right."

When it comes to normalizing the role of LGBTQ people in politics, visibility is the key driver. Indeed, LGBTQ elected officials are often the canary in the coal mine for a whole host of civil rights issues. One cannot rely on straight allies alone to sound the alarm when progress is challenged and curtailed. When it comes to making law, if you are not at the table, you are on the menu. But these crucial agents of change are on the decline. The number of out gay and lesbian elected officials has fallen from already low levels. In 1975 there were two out state legislators, Elaine Nobel in Massachusetts and Alan Spear in Minnesota. By 1985 there were still two, but by 1995 the number had increased to 20 from 14 states. The high-water mark was 117 (119 if you include the two Washington,

DC, council members) in 2014. But by 2017 the number had declined to 109. Even at their peak, LGBT legislators still only constituted less than 1 percent of the members of the fifty state houses. Less than a dozen eleven transgender candidates have ever run for a state house position in the United States. As of August 2017, 45 million Americans living in ten states and the District of Columbia were without a single LGBT representative in their capital—not a single person to pay witness when legislation is debated that determines the rights and opportunities of the LGBT community. Representation in the US Congress has plateaued as well.

This is not American exceptionalism; it is a global phenomenon. After modest gains, growth in the number of out lesbian, gay, bisexual, or transgender national MPs in office stalled. If you set aside the anomaly that is the United Kingdom, the global numbers declined from 2015 to 2018. LGBT-identifying politicians constitute only 0.002 percent of the world's 46,000 parliamentarians.

What explains the decline in representation: A public turn against gay candidates over the last few years? Political parties no longer willing to select LGBTQ candidates? Or, perhaps most troubling of all, complacency within the LGBTQ community and their allies? There is no evidence to support the first two explanations. Popular acceptance of homosexuality and voter support for gay rights has increased the world over. Similarly, political parties are more and more prone to disregard the sexual orientation of their candidates—indeed, many parties celebrate the diversity that an inclusive candidate slate demonstrates. The marriage equality fight in the West was long and tiring. Thirty years ago marriage was a low priority on the wish list of American gays and lesbians; indeed, in 1972 Ken Sherrill found that marriage was the lowest priority for activists. "The movement originated in the desire for sex, not for marriage," he notes—but it became a symbolic talisman, the moment when justice would be served. When the Supreme Court finally ruled in favor of same-sex marriage in June 2015, the battle was won.

Whether through exhaustion or complacency, the urgency to elect representatives has waned. Donors aren't donating and, even more troubling, candidates aren't coming forward. Former Massachusetts State Representative Carl Sciortini's story demonstrates that the problem began even before the same-sex marriage fight was settled. In 2013 he ran in the Democratic primary for the Massachusetts 5th in the US House. He was told by a number of potential donors that they liked him but that they were putting their time and money elsewhere. Electing openly gay leaders was no longer a top priority. Sciortini told me that there was misplaced feeling that the war had been won. Prospective supporters said, "We're not fully done but we're almost there, so we can move on to other issues and priorities." In 2014 Ed Murray was elected mayor of Seattle and was at the time the most powerful gay man in elective office in America, but he told me that when he was elected there was something of a "ho-hum" feeling. "A large part of the gay community said, 'We're over that.' That was a very odd experience."

Tellingly, incumbent LGBT elected officials are not losing—the fact is that they are stepping down and not being replaced. Of the forty US state legislators who left office between 2014 and 2017, only eleven were defeated in re-election bids. The rest either ran for higher office, retired, or were termed out. It is the same story globally—between 2015 and 2017 only seven of the twenty-three LGBT MPs leaving office were given their marching orders by the voters. Rather, the politicians who were so important to progress over the last decade are not being replaced. A new generation of aspirant Harvey Milks is not coming forward.

While the numbers of newly elected openly LGBT MPs has remained fairly static (apart from a large blip caused by the UK), the number of politicians coming out while in office and the closet has slowly increased. Three people came out in 2010 and 2012, two in 2011, four in 2014, five each in 2013 and 2015, a record eight in 2016, and two more in 2017. Closet parliamentarians are feeling emboldened to be open about their sexual identity as society's values evolve. Indeed, before 2000 most MPs were forced, pushed, and exposed out of the closet, but today that has become a rarity. Canada is a case in point: over a decade since marriage equality, nearly thirty years since the first openly gay MP was elected, a popular and respected current cohort of LGBT MPs who cut across party lines—yet there were only fourteen LGBTQ-identifying candidates in the 2015 federal election out of close to 1,500 running for office. After the winning and losing was summed up, the Canadian House of Commons was frozen at six out LGB MPs.

The Irish Prime Minister Leo Varadkar became the seventh lesbian or gay politician to lead their nation in 2017, but how close are other countries to such a breakthrough? In a 2016 survey Pew found that while 69 percent of American voters say a candidate's sexuality would not affect their support of a presidential candidate, 26 percent said they would be less likely to support a hypothetical LGBT candidate and only 4 percent said they would be more likely. At the same time a Canadian poll found that 56 percent of voters thought it was likely Canada would have a gay prime minister within the next decade, and 58 percent predicted it would happen within twenty years.

Ken Sherrill worries that the "obsession with marriage" diverted the movement's electoral politics. "The false sense of great victory ignores the fact that we can be denied jobs, homes, credit, even admission to restaurants, in most jurisdictions in the country," he says. "I think groups like Victory Fund will have trouble recruiting candidates until there is a renewed sense that we need to be in the room on these other issues. This requires a renewed sense of injustice, of insult, of anger. An awful lot of our elected were self-starters. We lack a local infrastructure for recruitment—the equivalents of political clubs, labor unions, chambers of commerce, etc. This is a cost of the nationalization and bureaucratization of the movement. The loss of opportunities for democratic participation has great costs in terms of representation. As we have transformed from a mass movement to a group of organized interest groups, opportunities are for moving up a bureaucratic career ladder and there is less and less motivation to run for public office."

The Heisenberg Principle

As a Londoner, even one who has now lived half his life in the United States, and who was heavily involved in politics as a student, I feel a membership of the British political club which can sometimes blur the detachment of scholarly observer. The distance of time has moved my pendulum toward that of the neutral, but thirty years ago I shivered outside the South African embassy at anti-apartheid protests as rain lashed Trafalgar Square, cruised around inner London in the big yellow taxi of "our" radical hero Simon Hughes, and held the august title of political vicechair of the National League of Young Liberals, which to a twenty-year-old felt very important indeed (suffice to say, it was not). I am no longer a party animal, but London remains the place where I am from and Westminster my Shangri-la. As I have dug more deeply into the work of identifying and analyzing out LGBTQ elected officials I have noticed that my research is sometimes infected by the Heisenberg uncertainty principle.

In the 1920s Werner Heisenberg, a German physicist, realized that just by observing things, in his case particles, we affect their behavior. To know we must measure and in the very act of measuring, we affect. Simply measuring the velocity and position of say, a quark, we affect its velocity and position. In my case, when politicians learn an academic is keeping a list of gay quarks, they start to come out of the quark closet. My guess is that coming out to an academic who is perceived to be sympathetic to gay politicians and gay rights is a friendlier route than being outed by a scandal rag or the unknowns of coming out to a fickle electorate at election time.

Themba Bwalya was uncertain. By April 2013 he was four years into his term as a Member of Parliament for an unnamed constituency in an unnamed African country. There had never been an out black African member of Parliament and no gay MPs at all in Africa outside of idiosyncratic South Africa. A politician coming out in Africa risked more than his seat—he risked his life. On a trip to Washington, DC, Bwalya was exploring his options. He emailed me and a related NGO in Washington. "Should I come out?" he asked. "Perhaps, after you are re-elected" was the considered answer, safety being paramount. As we've seen, Bwalya lost.

The UK general election of May 2015 saw the Heisenberg principle on over-drive. A few weeks before the election I noticed that the constituency of Cardiff South and Penarth was included in a tweet listing where the LGBT section of the Labour Party had candidates standing. The sitting MP, Stephen Doughty, elected in a 2012 by-election, had never been on a list of gay MPs before. Indeed, at dissolution it was widely reported that there were twenty-five out LGB MPs—thirteen Tories, eight Labour, and four Liberal Democrats. If Doughty had been recognized as out, how could the Tories keep on making the claim that they had more out LGBT MPs than all other parties combined? So what was Stephen doing on the list? I tweeted Doughty: "LGBT Labour tweets that they support you as an out LGBT candidate—is that how you identify?" His reply was quick and short: "Yep." "When did you come out?" I replied. "There's no specific date—never worked like that for me!" he tweeted back. It was a sixty-second electronic conversation, but it was huge. That meant twenty-five of the twenty-six out LGBT MPs were restanding for election.

I needed to know who else was standing among the nearly 4,000 candidates across the United Kingdom in 2015. The main parties proudly listed their LGBT candidates on designated web pages, but as I began to collect and release the data I would receive messages saying that I'd missed someone. A Tory activist emailed to suggest that I talk to his good friend from university who was standing for the Liberal Democrats in the Scottish constituency of Banff and Buchan. David Evans was not on the Liberal Democrat list, but I emailed him anyway: "Dear Mr. Evans. We received an email yesterday saying our data was incomplete as we had omitted your name. We are very keen to ensure the accuracy of our data. If you *do* identify as a publicly out gay man we shall of course include you, if not then I apologise for the intrusion. Should we include you?" Fifty minutes later Evans replied with a frankness that is emblematic of many in his position. "Dear Mr. Reynolds. That would be correct however I've not been singing from the rooftops nor am I naturally flamboyant so it's not surprising that you perhaps missed me. I don't feel my sexuality should be a selling point as a candidate; I've preferred to talk about personal attributes. However I have no issue with you including me."

More confusing was the omission of Gerald Vernon-Jackson from the Liberal Democrat LGBT candidate list. Vernon-Jackson was standing in Portsmouth South, the seat held on and off since 1984 by the disgraced former Liberal Democrat MP Mike Hancock. As the candidate of the party holding the seat, Vernon-Jackson was the most likely new gay Liberal Democrat MP. He was not on the list of candidates, but in a separate section the Liberal Democrats said that six of their eleven candidates replacing incumbent MPs were women, one was an ethnic minority, and one identified as LGBT. Who else could it be? The other ten MPs were being replaced by clearly straight-identifying candidates. I called the Liberal Democrat headquarters and got through to their candidates office. "Is the LGBT candidate in a seat with a retiring Liberal Democratic MP Gerald Vernon in Portsmouth South?" "Yes," came the reply. "Then why isn't he listed?" "Errrr . . ." mumbled the LibDem diversity officer.

The Greens did not have their list of LGBT candidates up, but their equalities spokesperson sent me a series of emails naming their out gay, lesbian, bisexual, or transgender-identifying candidates across England and Wales. Soon after, the election preview was published and the full data appeared on the UNC LGBTQ Representation and Rights website. Almost immediately I received an angry email from one of the candidates who was on the list that I had been sent, threatening legal action if they were not removed immediately and demanding to know from where I had got their name.

The big story of the 2015 UK general election was the dramatic surge of the Scottish National Party, who went from having six MPs to sweeping all but three of the constituencies in Scotland. The polls predicted SNP victories almost everywhere in Scotland, so I knew that any out LGBT SNP candidates had a very good chance of being elected. But the party did not produce a list, nor were they responsive when I called their Edinburgh headquarters. Two of their candidates, Stewart MacDonald in Glasgow and John Nicolson in Dumbartonshire, were out in the press and had been for a fair while. The LGBTQ group Kaleidoscope Scotland said in a news report that there were five out SNP candidates, but they didn't name names. The election happened, and 56 SNP MPs were elected.

Our summary election report was about to be released. I emailed the most prominent gay SNP member of the Scottish Parliament, Marco Biagi, to ask if he could offer any help. He said he knew of six new SNP MPs who were lesbian or gay and would ask who wished to be included in our data set. Thus ensued an exciting day of updates and report rewrites. Between 11:23 a.m. and 5:56 p.m. on May 11, 2015, Biagi confirmed Martin Docherty, Joanna Cherry, Angela Crawley, and Stuart MacDonald ("yes, the other one"). Then came the seventh and the biggest surprise—Mhairi Black, whom Biagi was not even aware of. Black was already a controversial figure. At twenty years of age she was the youngest MP elected since the Great Reform Act of 1832. She had been mocked in the tabloid press for off-color tweets made when she was a teenaged university student. I asked Biagi if he was sure about Black. I knew it would be red meat to the right-wing press if we said she was a lesbian. He said he was. Mhairi Black had told Joanna Cherry directly that she wanted to be on the list. A week later, as all the out SNP MPs offered their support to the Irish "Yes to Marriage Equality" campaign, Black was asked when she came out. "I've never been in," she responded.

Biagi told me he was very proud. "Seven from fifty-six, I think that's rather impressive, even if I do say so myself." Add in five members of the Scottish Parliament and one Euro MP and there were now thirteen LGBT SNP parliamentarians out of 112. Not bad going in the representation stakes." Marco Biagi continued, "I've always considered visibility to be so important. While no one has a responsibility to come out, it certainly helps build role models."

The Voice Was Quite Young:
It Was from Altoona, Pennsylvania

What will it mean to be a "gay politician" in the future? Will that label become irrelevant in those countries where gay rights are becoming the norm? Will LGBT leaders begin to find space to exist in the dangerous places in Africa, Asia, and Eastern Europe, and by their presence transform views? Or will the global disjuncture between progress and retreat on gay rights widen even further? The value of visibility goes way beyond legal change. The out LGBTQ elected officials in the book have been powerful role models to future generations. They truly are the offspring of Harvey Milk. In the midst of his campaign for election to the California State Assembly in the mid-1970s, Milk received a late-night phone call from a teenager in conservative small-town America. A young voice on the other end of the line simply said "Thanks." Milk wove this call into the crescendo of his famous "Hope" speech.

> Somewhere in Des Moines or San Antonio there is a young gay person who all of a sudden realizes that he or she is gay. Knows that if the parents find out they could be tossed out of the house. The classmates would torture the child. And the Anita Bryants and John Briggs are doing their bit on TV. That child has several options: staying in the closet or suicide. And then one day that child may open a paper that says "homosexual elected in San Francisco" and there are two new options. One option is to go to California. Or stay in San Antonio and fight!
>
> Two days after I was elected I got a phone call. The voice was quite young. It was from Altoona, Pennsylvania. And the person said, "Thanks."
>
> And you've got to elect gay people. So that young child and the thousands like that child know that there is hope for a better world. Know that there's hope for a better tomorrow. Without hope, not only gays, but those blacks, and the Asians. The disabled. The seniors. The Us's. Without hope, the Us's give up. I know that you cannot live on hope alone but without it life is not worth living. And you.

And you.
And you. Gotta give them hope.

Every high-profile celebrity and openly gay and lesbian elected official has their Altoona, Pennsylvania, moments. Halfway through asking the British Tory MP Crispin Blunt the Altoona question, he stopped me and pulled out a folded letter from his jacket pocket. "Is this your Altoona letter?" I asked. "Yes," he said. It was from an old friend who had written about his gay son and how much Blunt's bravery in coming out meant to him. "How does that make you it feel?" I ask. "Terrific" was his reply. "It makes it all worthwhile." After Carl Sciortino's "Father and Son" TV ad went viral, he received an email from a teenager in Tennessee. His father was not dealing well with his homosexuality, and they were estranged. He had arranged to watch the advert with parents. He told Carl that "That's us" was a bonding moment: "You gave us space to have a conversation that we never had before."

For the surviving members of the Seattle five—Mayor Ed Murray, State Senator Jamie Pedersen, and State Representatives Brady Walkinshaw and Nicole Macri—the kid from Altoona is always present. Jamie Pedersen told me that before marriage equality he carried his civil union card with him wherever he went. Strangers would come up to him and pull out their cards with tears in their eyes. For years people would get out their domestic partnership card and just say thank you. Brady Walkinshaw welled up when he told me about returning to Nooksack Valley High to accept a distinguished alumni award—the town where he'd never met someone else who was gay. He told the teenagers about being gay and being in politics. Kids took him aside after to share their private stories. His mother, who is a teacher at the school, has people stop her in the hallways to talk about her son. When I asked Mayor Ed Murray, his eyes reddened and looked down. He caught his breath. "Sorry, I'm going to cry . . . it's fleeting things that happen. It will be the teenaged page in the legislature saying, 'Thank you for working on gay stuff.' The state patrol officer stopping me on the steps of the capitol thanking me for enabling him to marry his husband. The weddings really make me emotional. People are so appreciative that I'm almost embarrassed by it at times." Cal Anderson kept a diary while in office. Gary Atkins read it for his book *Gay Seattle*. On January 28, 1988, Anderson wrote, "This morning I went to the Washington Cattleman's Association breakfast. A cowboy sits down and says, 'What about this gay legislation?' It turns out he's a gay rancher! He came by and said how wonderful it was to have someone in the legislature."

Barney Frank recalls that "when I came out, I outed my mother as the mother of a gay man. She made a commercial in 1982 for an elderly organization. Women would come up to her in the street and say 'Oh Mrs. Frank, I'm so happy with the way you are supportive of your son. I said to my husband, if Mrs. Frank can be proud of her son, you can be too.' " Rory O'Neill in Dublin gets thousands of Altoona letters, "from twelve-year-old girls and fifty-year-old bus drivers, from lesbians in Denmark, grandmothers in Australia and straight guys in Scotland."

If anything, the Altoona call is even more powerful for out transgender figures. Their rarity makes their visibility even more visceral for those left in the shadows. For a number of years Sarah McBride crossed paths with a kid back in Delaware. The high schooler who would volunteer for anything, just as Sarah had. Now a freshman in college, "she always worried about me, wanted to take pictures with me, was interested in my presence more than anyone." McBride paused and looked up. "She just told me she is coming out as transgender and it was strikingly similar to the things I felt. She said I was the biggest influence on her life and it was so powerful for me because it resembled my own story—and I was struck by how different my life could have been if I'd had that role model. Just living our trans lives is a powerful force—you never know who is sitting in the closet struggling. But it is frightening to me that she is going into the firing zone. I am worried that she won't have as positive experience as me. Now I feel responsible."

The night before election day in Virginia, November 2017, Danica Roem spoke to volunteers in solemn tones, her voice breaking: "I'm scared. I've been scared my whole life. I was scared to transition. I was scared to get into this race." But Roem had received a letter from the mother of Klara, a local ten-year-old transgirl. Klara was being terribly bullied. "Imagine how scared that girl was to go to school after Trump's election last year," Roem said to the assembled volunteers. "She did it anyway. Now I'm going to try and make it a little bit easier for her. How amazing it will be (if we win) after what happened last year."

At the election night party Klara's mother told Diana Tourjée of *Broadly News* that Klara was so despondent after being bullied at school that she tried to jump out of a second-floor window. "She kept telling me there is nobody like her. She's too different. No one would ever understand her." But then the mother saw an article about Danica in the local paper. She thought, "There is hope in this." Klara's mother told her daughter she *must* read it. Klara read the article over and over and her jaw dropped. "She looked at me with a smile I hadn't seen for months," the mother recalled.

"She's just like me," Klara said.

"She's just like you," her mother agreed.

"How does she do it?" Klara asked her mother. "How does she put herself out in front of everybody and do that?"

"Because she knows who she is."

Klara thought for a moment.

"If Danica can do that I can do that."

"That must have changed your life?" Tourjée asked the mother.

"She gave me my daughter back" was the reply.

Out LGBT legislators influence not only their colleagues but also the conversation in courtrooms, media outlets, national government offices, and family dining tables. They are a highly visible part of the tapestry of out gay people in society, alongside the gay son, the lesbian coworker, the transgender classmate. For every individual who acknowledges publicly that his or her views on homosexuality have been transformed by having a gay friend, family member, or colleague, there are countless others who have spoken to the elected official privately about how much their election meant to them and their loved ones.

Harvey Milk's legacy lives on around the world. In the 2013 debate on whether to introduce same-sex marriage in New Zealand the deputy leader of the Labour Party, Grant Robertson, began his remarks by telling the story of Milk, his "Hope" speech, and the phone call from the kid from Altoona. "Well, in New Zealand, in 1986 there was a fourteen-year-old young man sitting in Dunedin who read the newspaper about the law to decriminalize homosexuality, and he cut out of the newspaper the names of those who had voted for and those who voted against the Homosexuality Law Reform Bill. And that gave him—me—hope that maybe his life would be all right." Since the vote the mother of marriage equality in New Zealand, Louisa Wall, has been inundated with Altoona moments. A mother hugged her in the street and said "thank you, my son is getting married." A seventeen-year-old in Christchurch had come out to her unsupportive parents, but she had not told her friends. Louisa gave her a hug and asked people she knew in the girls' community to keep an eye on her. Another girl came to Louisa and told her that her grandmother had vehemently disapproved of her sexual orientation, but after the bill she told her she loved her. For Mike Michaud, a candidate for the governor of Maine and the last US congressman to come out while in office, it was the woman from East Millinocket who told him that her son was gay but had never met anyone else who was openly gay in their little town. "Now I can tell him there is someone else from our neck of the woods," Michaud said at a Victory Fund conference in 2015.

Where Are They Now?

Harvey Milk's children are as active as ever, and now his grandchildren are making waves. When Barney Frank is not curling up with his husband Jim in their cottage in Maine he is teaching, writing, and being wise and blunt. He chaired the Democratic National Convention in 2016, which nominated Hillary Clinton as the first female presidential nominee of any major party.

After fifty years Peter Tatchell remains on the front lines: the last few years have seen him protest arms sales to Saudi Arabia, the abuse of gays in Chechnya, environmental degradation in Iran, pensions, sex education, and the slow pace of change in the Church of England. Tatchell defines intersectionality: "One of the lodestars has been to make the connection between different struggles. Never fight the battle for LGBTQ rights in isolation from the battle for women's rights, black rights, and other human rights. A gigantic thread of diverse struggles united by a common goal of ending injustice and suffering."

David Norris is the longest-serving member and grand old man of the Irish Senate. He is as active as he was thirty years ago.

Leo Varadkar made the cover of *Time* magazine after being elected Taoiseach in July 2017. Panti Bliss tweeted, "I still call him Leo, because in the gay world I still outrank him."

Katherine Zappone is the minister for children in the Irish government. She now serves at the pleasure of her openly gay colleague Taoiseach Leo Varadkar.

Louisa Wall married Prue Kapua in December 2015 at their house in Auckland. Louisa still fights the good fight in the Parliament of New Zealand in Wellington.

Beth Bye stepped down from chairing the Connecticut Senate Appropriations Committee after her wife, Tracey, was diagnosed with cancer in 2016.

Ken Sherrill lives with his husband, Gerald, in the Upper West Side house they bought forty years ago. The neighborhood has changed, but Ken hasn't. He writes, comments, and publishes as he ever did. There are scholarly prizes named for him—and there will surely be more.

Crispin Blunt was chair of House of Commons Foreign Affairs select committee from 2015 to 2017. He continues to be an awkward bugger.

Nigel Evans was re-elected in 2017 in his Lancashire constituency of Ribble Valley with more votes than any candidate had ever received before in the district.

Since leaving office Georgina Beyer has struggled with illness and unemployment. She entered chronic end stage liver failure in 2013. Nevertheless, in 2014 she ran for Parliament for the Mana Party, receiving 1,996 votes and coming in fourth. In November 2015 her friend Grant Pittams, a gay man working in the Health Ministry, offered her one of his kidneys. But two months later it was found that she had cardiomyopathy and her heart was only pumping at 22 percent capacity. The prognosis was bleak. She started making preparations for her funeral. Months of hemo-dialysis followed the years of dialysis. Surprising the doctors, her heart function improved and in April 2017 she successful received Pittams's kidney.

Waheed Alli continues to be both a business mogul and human rights activist, working on the inside and out. He is still the most important gay rights activist you have never heard of.

Sarah McBride has returned to her home state of Delaware and is considering a run for office. She is now the present, rather than the future, of transgender politics.

Michael Cashman has spent a large amount of his time since 2015 in arguing for Britain's role in Europe. He has also returned to acting on occasion.

Annise Parker was termed out as mayor of Houston in 2016. In December 2017 she became the CEO of the Gay and Lesbian Victory Fund. The turtle won the race and now was coaching hatchlings.

Evan Wolfson is a global evangelical for marriage, taking his unique skill set around the world. Since he won at the US Supreme Court, same-sex marriage has become the law of the land in Puerto Rico, Ireland, Greenland, Colombia, the Isle of Man, Gibraltar, the Channel Islands, Bermuda, Germany, Malta, Taiwan, and among many Native American tribes.

Brady Walkinshaw lost his race to be the first out gay Latino man elected to the US Congress to fellow Democrat Pramila Jayapal. He now is the CEO of the company that publishes the environmental magazine *Grist*. He is biding his time.

Coos Huijsen and his husband, Lank, spend their summers in the South of France and the rest of the year in Amsterdam. In 2016 he published his memoir, *Homo Politicus: The First MP Worldwide Who Came Out of the Closet,* and later that year he hosted King Willem-Alexander at a celebration of the seventieth anniversary of the Dutch gay rights movement. Forty years after being the first out gay MP in the world, he was knighted by the King.

The first public accusation of sexual misconduct came in April 2017 in the midst of Seattle mayor Ed Murray's re-election campaign. Delvonn Heckard filed a lawsuit accusing Murray of rape and molestation in 1986. Jeff Simpson had gone to the Seattle police with similar claims in 1984, but after an investigation the police had brought no charges. In July 2017 it was revealed that an Oregon Child Protective Services investigator had written in 1984, "In the professional judgement of this caseworker who has interviewed numerous children of all ages and of all levels of emotional disturbance regarding sexual abuse, Jeff Simpson has been sexually abused by Edward Murray." In 2008 a second man, Lloyd Anderson, along with Simpson, approached the *Seattle Times*, but the paper refused to print their stories. On May 2, 2017, a fourth man, Maurice Jones, accused Murray of paying him for sex when he was underage in the 1980s. On May 9, Murray dropped out of his race to be re-elected mayor. On September 12, Murray's cousin, Joseph Dyer, became the fifth accuser. Dyer said he was thirteen when Murray forced him into sex when the two shared a bedroom at Dyer's mother's home in Medford, New York, in the mid-1970s. Ed Murray resigned from office the next day. He was replaced as mayor of Seattle by Jenny Durkan, a former US prosecutor, mother of two, and a lesbian.

As I have traveled around the world to interview members of Parliament I have taken a dog-eared copy of a report I authored which details all the LGBT people who have been in national office globally. Each interviewee has signed by their name in the table at the back of the book or by their photo. Stuart

Milk, Harvey Milk's nephew and founder of the Harvey Milk Foundation, has scrawled on the back cover under Harvey's photo, "Thank you for keeping hope alive." It is a whisper to the hundreds of gay and transgender trailblazers who made it into elective office, and the many thousands of others who fell along the way. The children of Harvey Milk do not dwell in his shadow; they reflect and magnify his light.

Late at night, the day after the British election of June 2017, I met Simon Hughes and the local councilor David Noakes for a drink in the Lord Clyde Pub, just around the corner from the site of the Borough Market terrorist attacks a week earlier. In 1999 another Lord Clyde—the Scottish Law Lord—wrote the ruling that affirmed that same-sex couples in a stable relationship were a family and warranted legal rights: "It seems to me that essentially the bond must be one of love and affection, not of a casual or transitory nature, but in a relationship which is permanent, or at least intended to be so," Clyde wrote. David tells me he, as a gay man, represents perhaps the highest proportion of gay people anywhere in Britain. As we walk back to Simon's bright yellow taxi, David points out the building where Dustin Lance Black, the Oscar-winning screenwriter of the movie *Milk*, lives with his husband, Tom Daley. Harvey's children are scattered around the globe, but they are bound together by a man who knew who he was—and what he had to become.

They Shall Grow Not Old

On an overcast day in November, Lord Smith of Finsbury, the Master of Pembroke College, Cambridge, takes his place in the rear pulpit of the ornate chapel, consecrated 350 years before. During his two-decades-long imprisonment in the Tower of London, Bishop Matthew Wren, the Pembroke Master four centuries before Smith, had vowed to pay for the building of a new chapel if ever released. Wren gave the charge to his nephew, an aspiring architect. This was the height of serendipitous nepotism: his nephew was the one-and-only Christopher, who used Pembroke as a dry run before rebuilding St. Paul's Cathedral.

The modern Christopher Robert Smith became Master of Pembroke after the retirement of "M"—Sir Richard Dearlove, the former head of MI6. The gay son of Gladys and Colin of Edinburgh, Smith came to Pembroke College in 1969 and spent six years studying for his undergraduate degree and then a PhD in Wordsworth and the English poets of the eighteenth century. "I was not out, but I was happy here," he tells me as we walk through the walled secret gardens with wet autumn leaves strewn over the manicured lawns. "To be able to be out when returning as Master speaks volumes." During the service, the choristers perform

Faure's Messe de Requiem. These modern-day teenagers sit where famed former Pembroke youth perched: the future prime minister William Pitt, comedians Peter Cook and Eric Idle, the writer Clive James, the sound magician Ray Dolby. John Maynard Keynes played the stock market for the college as its bursar in the 1910s. The chapel whispers "British establishment" from every crack in the plaster. The Master embodies that tradition.

Smith tells me that becoming Master in October 2015 felt like coming home, as it did when he first arrived in the late 1960s. As Master he is the public face of the college, fundraising for a £100 million extension across Trumpington Street. The fact that the Master's Lodge is his home says more about the transformation of Britain's attitude to homosexuality than any law ever could. This is the man who was the first British MP ever to come out, the first openly gay British cabinet minister, and the first MP in the world to identify as HIV positive. Healthy and happy, he tells me he doesn't regret coming out in 1984 for a minute—the more challenging leap of faith was in 2005, when he announced to the world that he was HIV positive and had been since the mid-1980s. After the weekend his boyfriend will be coming up to stay; a generation younger, he works in advertising in London and plays the cello. Smith is attempting to recall his childhood piano lessons so he can play the grand piano in the study—perhaps even duet with his lover. Thirty years on, Smith is still touched by those Altoona moments—the activists and politicians who remember how brave he was in 1984 and what it meant to them. He is a man at peace.

As we drink tea in the lodge I outline the evidence of how, in the general election of 2015, being a Labour candidate who happened to be gay actually increased one's personal vote share. Chris Smith gazes through the window to the walled garden below, ruefully smiles, and says: "Thirty-one years."

It is remembrance Sunday, 101 years after the outbreak of the Great War in which one-third of Pembroke's students died horrific and preventable deaths. Resplendent in his robes and surrounded by professors and students in the cloisters, Lord Smith bows his head and intones Laurence Binyon's words:

> They shall grow not old.
> As we that are left grow old.
> Age shall not weary them.
> Nor the years condemn.
> At the going down of the sun.
> And in the morning.
> We will remember them.

Eli Weisel wrote in his novel *The Town Beyond the Wall* that "sometimes it happens that we travel for a long time without knowing that we have made the long journey solely to pronounce a certain word, a certain phrase, in a certain place. The meeting of the place and the word is a rare accomplishment." As I listen to Smith's words echo off the seventeenth-century flagstones, I think of them as a requiem for all those young gay men who died in secret in uniform on the fields of France; a requiem for Chris's ebullient friends whose bodies were ravaged by AIDS in the 1980s; for the queer folks cut down by hate; for the teens who even in the twenty-first century still see suicide as the only way to escape their shame.

> They shall grow not old.
> As we that are left grow old.
> Age shall not weary them.
> Nor the years condemn.
> At the going down of the sun.
> And in the morning.
> We will remember them.

. . . Cal Anderson, Gilbert Baker, Justin Fashanu, Ann Louise Gilligan, Frank Kameny, David Kato, Randy Shilts, Rachael Webb . . . for Harvey Milk . . . and for all his children.

Appendix A

INTERVIEWS CONDUCTED

All interviews were conducted in person unless otherwise indicated.

Legislators

Lord Waheed Alli (UK), London, November 26, 2013
Martin Andreasson, MP (Sweden), Stockholm, March 14, 2013
Stuart Andrew, MP (UK), Birmingham, October 9, 2012
Senator Ivana Bacik (Ireland), Dublin, July 4, 2017 (via email)
Baroness Liz Barker (UK), London, November 2015; November 21, 2017
Marianne Berg, MP (Sweden), Stockholm, March 13, 2013
Clive Betts, MP (UK), London, November 21, 2013
Marco Biagi, MSP (Scotland), May 11–13, 2015 (via email)
Crispin Blunt, MP (UK), London, November 26, 2013; November 21, 2017
Ben Bradshaw, MP (UK), London, March 11, 2013
Conor Burns, MP (UK), London, November 21, 2013
Jerry Buttimer, MP (Ireland), Dublin, October 15, 2014
Themba Bwalya (pseudonym), MP, 2015 (via multiple emails and Skype)
Lord Michael Cashman (UK), London, January 19, 2015
Lord Ray Collins (UK), London, November 26, 2013
Angela Eagle, MP (UK), London, November 21, 2013
Barney Frank (US), Washington, DC, February 18, 2014
Mike Freer, MP (UK), London, March 12, 2013
Nigel Evans, MP (UK), London, March 12, 2013
Kai Gehring, MP (Germany), Berlin, December 6, 2017
Steven Gilbert, MP (UK), London, March 11, 2013
Dominic Hannigan, MP (Ireland), Dublin, October 14, 2014
Lord Robert Hayward (UK), London, November 5, 2015

Ben Howlett, MP (UK), London, November 2, 2015

Sir Simon Hughes, MP (UK), London, November 23, 2012; May 2015; June and November 20, 2017 (additional emails and phone)

Coos Huijsen, MP (Netherlands), Amsterdam, November 25, 2013

Stefan Kaufmann, MP (Germany), Berlin, October 18, 2017

Hans Linde, MP (Sweden), Stockholm, March 13, 2013

Angelica Lozano, MP (Colombia), Chapel Hill, NC, April 24, 2015

John Lyons, MP (Ireland), Dublin, October 15, 2014

Zakhele Mbhele, MP (South Africa), June 4, 2014 (via Skype)

David Mundell, MP (UK), London, March 6, 2017

Henk Nijboer, MP (Netherlands), The Hague, November 25, 2013

David Noakes, Cllr. (Southwark, UK), London, June 9, 2017

David Norris, Senator (Ireland), Dublin, October 15, 2014; 2015 (email)

Lord Oates (UK), London, November 3, 2015

Eric Ollerenshaw, MP (UK), London, November 21, 2013

Astrid Ossenbrug, MP (Netherlands), The Hague, November 25, 2013

Sunil Babu Pant, MP (Nepal), February 7, 2014 (via Skype)

Lord Chris Smith (UK), London, November 16, 2012; November 21, 2013; November 6, 2015

Iain Stewart, MP (UK), London, March 12, 2013

Stephen Twigg, MP (UK), London, March 11, 2013

Boris van der Ham, MP (Netherlands), Amsterdam, November 25, 2013

Louisa Wall, MP (New Zealand), Wellington, November 6, 2013 (via Skype)

Fintan Warfield, Senator (Ireland), Dublin, November 22, 2017

Katherine Zappone, Senator and MP (Ireland), Dublin, October 15, 2014; February 25–28, 2016

Candidates

Clay Aiken (US, North Carolina), Chapel Hill, NC, June 2, 2014; January 29, 2015

Danni Askini (US, Washington), Seattle, August 2, 2016

Bemz Benedito (Philippines), London, November 2015 (multiple days)

Jowelle de Souza (Trinidad and Tobago), August 26, 2015 (via Skype)

Bob Poe (US, Florida), August 17, 2016 (via Skype)

Sameer Ranade (US, Washington), March 12, 2016 (via email)

Dan Shih (US, Washington), Seattle, August 1, 2016

Mel Wymore (US, New York), October 16, 2016; March 17, 2017 (in Chapel Hill, NC)

US State Legislators/Mayors/Governors

Beth Bye, Representative (Connecticut), Denver, December 5, 2013
Frank Chopp, Representative (Washington), August 15, 2015 (via phone)
Daniel J. Evans, Governor (Washington), August 2015 (via phone)
Mark Ferrandino, Representative (Colorado), Denver, December 6, 2013
Mark Kleinschmidt, Mayor (North Carolina), Chapel Hill, NC, 2012–2018
Nicole Macri (US, Washington), Seattle, August 2, 2016
Jack Markell, Governor (Delaware), June 9, 2016 (via phone)
Ed Murray, Mayor (Washington), Seattle, August 6, 2014; July 28, 2015
Jamie Pedersen, Senator (Washington), Seattle, July 28, 2015
Carl Sciortino, Representative (Massachusetts), Boston, September 18, 2015
Brady Walkinshaw, Representative (Washington), Seattle, July 28, 2015; August 2, 2016
Mary Washington, Delegate (Maryland), Denver, December 5, 2013

Activists and Academics

Mark Burstein (US), Appleton, WI, August 10, 2015 (by phone)
Paisley Currah (US), New York, May 27, 2014
Patrick Egan (US), New York, May 27, 2014
Roddy Flynn (US), August 3, 2016 (via email)
Sharita Gruberg (US), August 4, 2016 (via email)
Sally and David McBride (US), July 1, 2016 (via Skype)
Sarah McBride (US), Washington, DC, December 9, 2015
Dave McDonald (US), August 2015 (via emails)
Rory O'Neill, aka Panti Bliss (Ireland), Dublin, November 22, 2017
Harry Prance (UK), London, November 26, 2013
Lance Price (UK), London, November 22, 2013
Ken Sherrill (US), New York, May 28, 2014; additional emails
Peter Tatchell (UK), London, October 17, 2014; November 21, 2017; additional emails
Alexander Cruz Vidal (UK), London, March 12, 2013
Evan Wolfson (US), October 16, 2013 (via phone); New York, May 28, 2014

Appendix B

OUT LGBTQ PARLIAMENTARIANS 1976–2017

	IN OFFICE (Year Out) if not out when first elected	**PARTY/Portfolio**
ARUBA		
Lower House		
Desiree Croes	2011–	Aruban People's Party
AUSTRALIA		
Lower House		
Trent Zimmerman	2015–	Liberal Party
Tim Wilson	2016–	Liberal Party
Trevor Evans	2016–	Liberal Party
Julian Hill	2016	Labour Party
Upper House		
Bob Brown	1996–2012	Green Party
Brian Greig	1999–2005	Australian Democrats
Penny Wong	2002–	Labour Party
Louise Pratt	2008–2014, 2016–	Labour Party
Dean Smith	2012–	Liberal Party
Janet Rice	2014–	Green Party
Robert Simms	2015–2016	Green Party
Cabinet Ministers		
Penny Wong	2007–	Climate Change
Penny Wong	2010–2013	Finance and Deregulation

AUSTRIA

Lower House
Ulrike Lunacek	1999–2009	Green Party
Ewa Dziedzic	2015–2017	Green Party

Upper House
Ewa Dziedzic	2017–	Green Party

European Parliament
Ulrike Lunacek	2009–	Green Party

ARGENTINA

Lower House
Analuz Carol	2015–	Front for Victory

Upper House
Osvaldo López	2011–	Fresh Encounter

BELGIUM

Lower House
Elio Di Rupo	1987–1989, 2003–2005, 2010–2014 (1996)	Socialist Party
Jean-Jacques Flahaux	2007–2010	Reform Movement
Xavier Baeselen	2008–2016	Reform Movement

Upper House	2014–	
Petra de Sutter		Green Party

Cabinet Ministers	2011–2014	
Elio di Rupo		Prime Minister

BOLIVIA

Lower House
Manuel Canelas	2015–	Movement for Socialism

BRAZIL

Lower House
Clodovil Hernandez	2007–2009	Christian Labor Party
Jean Wyllys	2011–	Socialism and Freedom

CANADA
Lower House

Svend Robinson	1979–2004 (1988)	New Democratic Party
Réal Ménard	1993–2009 (1994)	Bloc Québécois
Libby Davies	1997–2015 (2001)	New Democratic Party
Scott Brison	1997– (2002)	Liberal Party
Bill Siksay	2004–2011	New Democratic Party
Mario Silva	2004–2011 (2004)	Liberal Party
Raymond Gravel	2006–2008	Bloc Québécois
Rob Oliphant	2008–2011, 2015–	Liberal Party
Randall Garrison	2011–	New Democratic Party
Dany Morin	2011–2015	New Democratic Party
Philip Toone	2011–2015	New Democratic Party
Craig Scott	2012–2015	New Democratic Party
Sheri Benson	2015–	New Democratic Party
Randy Boissonnault	2015–	Liberal Party
Seamus O'Reagan	2015–	Liberal Party

Upper House

Laurier LaPierre	2001–2004	Liberal Party
Nancy Ruth	2005–	Conservative Party

Cabinet Ministers

Scott Brison	2004–2006	Public Works
Scott Brison	2016–	Treasury
Seamus O'Regan	2017–	Veterans

CHILE

Lower House

Claudio Arriagada	2013–	Christian Democrats
Guillermo Ceroni	1993– (2015)	Party for Democracy

COLOMBIA

Lower House

Angèlica Lozano Correa	2014–	Green Alliance

Upper House

Claudia Lopez	2014–	Green Alliance

Cabinet Ministers

Gina Parody	2014–2016	Education
Cecilia Alvarez	2014–	Commerce

COSTA RICA

Lower House

Carmen Muñoz	2010–2014	Citizen Action

CZECH REPUBLIC

Lower House

Karla Šlechtová	2017–	Independent

Upper House

Vaclav Fischer	1999–2002	Independent

Cabinet Ministers

Gustáv Slamečka	2009–2010	Transport

DENMARK

Lower House

Yvonne Herlov Andersen	1977–1979, 1981–1984, 1987–1988, 1998–2001 (1998)	Centre Party
Torben Lund	1981–1998 (1998)	Social Democrats
Louise Frevert	2001–2007	People's Party
Simon Emil Ammitzbøll	2005–	Liberal Party
Mogens Jensen	2007–	Social Democrats
Flemming Møller Mortensen	2007–	Social Democrats
Uffe Elbæk	2011–	Social Liberal/The Alternative
Søren Pape Poulsen	2015–	Conservative Party

Cabinet Ministers

Uffe Elbæk	2011–2012	Culture
Mogens Jensen	2014–2015	Trade

European Parliament

Torben Lund	1999–2004	Social Democrats

ECUADOR

Lower House

Diane Rodríguez Zambrano	2017–	PAIS Alliance

Cabinet Ministers

Carina Mafla	2012–	Public Health

ESTONIA

Lower House

Imre Sooäär	2011– (2014)	Reform Party

FINLAND
Lower House

Oras Tynkkynen	2004–2015	Green Party
Pekka Haavisto	1987–1995, 2007– (2007)	Green Party
Jani Petteri Toivola	2011–	Green Party
Silvia Modig	2011–	Left Party
Markku Rossi	1991–1995, 2003– (2015)	Center Party

Cabinet Ministers

Pekka Haavisto	1995–1999	Environment

FRANCE

Lower House

André Labarrère	1967–1968, 1973–2001 (1998)	Socialist Party
Franck Riester	2007– (2011)	Union for a Popular Movement
Sergio Coronado	2012– (2012)	Green Party

Upper House

Corrine Bouchoux	2011–	Green Party
Luc Carvounas	2011–	Socialist Party

Cabinet Ministers

Roger Karoutchi	2007–2009	Parliamentary Relations
Jean-Jacques Aillagon	2002–2004	Culture
Frederic Mitterrand	2009–2011	Culture

European Parliament

Michel Teychenné	2008–2009	Socialist Party
Steeve Briois	2014–	National Front

GERMANY

Lower House

Jutta Oesterle-Schwerin	1987–1990	Green Party
Herbert Rusche	1985–1987	Green Party
Christina Schenk	1990–2002	Green Party/Democratic Socialists
Volker Beck	1994–2017	Green Party
Birgitt Bender	2002–2013	Green Party
Jorg van Essen	1990–2013	Free Democrats
Guido Westerwelle	1996–2013 (2004)	Free Democrats
Kai Gehring	2005–	Green Party
Gerhard Schick	2005–	Green Party
Patrick Meinhardt	2005–2013	Free Democrats
Lutz Heilmann	2005–2009	Democratic Socialists
Anja Hajduk	2002–2008, 2013–	Green Party
Bettina Herlitzius	2007–2013	Green Party
Sabine Jünger	1998–2002	Democratic Socialists
Johannes Kahrs	1998–	Social Democrats
Jens Spahn	2002– (2012)	Christian Democrats
Michael Kauch	2003–2013	Free Democrats
Jan Mücke	2005–2013	Free Democrats
Sebastian Körber	2009–2013	Free Democrats
Stefan Kaufmann	2009–	Christian Democrats
Ulle Schauws	2013–	Green Party
Barbara Hendricks	1994– (2013)	Social Democrats
Harald Petzold	2013–2017	Left Party
Bernd Fabritius	2013–2017	Christian Social Union
Alice Weidel	2017–	Alliance for Germany
Sven Lehmann	2017–	Green Party
Thomas Sattelberger	2017–	Free Democrats
Matthias Höhn	2017–	Left Party

Upper House

Klaus Wowereit	2001–2002	Social Democrats

Cabinet Ministers

Guido Westerwelle	2009–2013	Foreign Minister
Barbara Hendricks	2013–	Environment

European Parliament

Lissy Gröner	1989–	Social Democrats
Holger Krahmer	2004–	Free Democrats
Cornelia Ernst	2009–	Left Party

GUAM

Lower House

Benjamin Cruz	2005–2006, 2008–2017	Democratic Party

GUATEMALA

Lower House

Sandra Moran	2015–	Convergence

HONG KONG

Lower House

Raymond Chan Chi-chuen	2012–	People Power

HUNGARY

Lower House

Klára Ungár	1990–1998	Liberal Party

Cabinet Ministers

Gábor Szetey	2006–2008	Human Resources

ICELAND

Lower House

Jóhanna Sigurðardóttir	1978–2013 (1987)	Social Democrats
Árni Steinar Jóhannsson	1999–2003	Left Green Party
Guðfríður Lilja Grétarsdóttir	2009–2011	Left Green Party
Hanna Katrín Friðriksson	2016–	Reform Party

Cabinet Ministers

Jóhanna Sigurðardóttir	2007–2009	Social Affairs
Jóhanna Sigurðardóttir	2009–2014	Prime Minister

ISLE OF MAN

Lower House

Allan Bell	1984– (2015)	Independent

Cabinet Ministers

Allan Bell	2015–	Chief Minister

IRELAND

Lower House

Leo Varadkar	2007– (2014)	Fine Gael
Dominic Hannigan	2011–2016	Labour Party
John Lyons	2011–2016	Labour Party
Jerry Buttimer	2011–2016 (2012)	Fine Gael
Katherine Zappone	2016–	Independent

Upper House

David Norris	1987–	Independent
Colm O'Gorman	2007	Progressive Democrats
Katherine Zappone	2011–2016	Independent
Jerry Buttimer	2016–	Fine Gael
Fintan Warfield	2016–	Sinn Fein

Cabinet Ministers

Leo Varadkar	2011–2014	Transport and Tourism
Leo Varadkar	2014–2016	Health
Leo Varadkar	2016–2017	Social Protection
Leo Varadkar	2017–	Prime Minister
Katherine Zappone	2017–	Children

ISRAEL

Lower House

Uzi Even	2002–2003	Meretz
Nitzan Horowitz	2009–2014	Meretz
Itzak Shmuli	2013– (2015)	Labour
Amir Ohana	2015–	Likud

ITALY

Lower House

Alfonso Pecoraro Scanio	1992–2013 (2000)	Green Party
Paola Concia	2008–2013	Democratic Party
Vladimir Luxuria	2006–2008	Communists
Nichi Vendola	1992–2006	Left Party
Daniele Capezzone	2006–2008	Italian Radicals
Franco Gillini	2001–2007	Left Democrats
Titti de Simone	2001–2013	Communist Reformation
Angelo Pezzana	1979	Italian Radicals
Ivan Scalfarotto	2013–	Democratic Party
Alessandro Zan	2013–	Democratic Party

Upper House

Franco Zeffirelli	1994–2001	Forward Italy
Emilio Colombo	2003–2013	Union of the Center
Giampaolo Silvestri	2006–2008	Forward Italy
Paolo Galimberti	2013–	Democratic Party
Sergio Lo Giudice	2013–	Green Party

Cabinet Ministers

Alfonso Pecoraro Scanio	2000–2001	Agriculture
Alfonso Pecoraro Scanio	2006–2008	Environment

European Parliament

Gianni Vattimo	1999–	Liberal Party
Marco Cappato	2004–2009	List Emma Bonino
Rosario Crocetta	2009–2014	Democratic Party
Daniele Viotti	2014–	Democratic Party

LIECHTENSTEIN

Lower House

Patrick Risch	2013–	Free List
Daniel Seger	2017–	Progressive Citizens

JAPAN

Lower House

Kanako Otsuji	2017–	Constitutional Democrats

Upper House

Kanako Otsuji	2013	Constitutional Democrats

LATVIA

Cabinet Ministers

Edgars Rinkēvičs	2011–	Foreign Affairs

LITHUANIA

Lower House

Rokas Žilinskas	2008– (2009)	National Resurrection Party/Homeland

LUXEMBOURG

Lower House

Xavier Bettel	1999–2011, 2013–	Democratic Party

Cabinet Ministers

Etienne Schneider	2012–2013	Economy and Trade
Etienne Schneider	2013–	Deputy Prime Minister
Xavier Bettel	2013–	Prime Minister

MALTA

Lower House

Karl Gouder	2016–	Nationalist Party

MEXICO

Lower House

Patria Jimenez	1997–2000	Party of the Democratic Revolution
David Sanchez Camacho	2006–2009	Party of the Democratic Revolution
Enoé Uranga	2009–	Party of the Democratic Revolution
Benjamín Medrano	2015–	Institutional Revolutionary Party

Upper House

Patria Jimenez	2006	Party of the Democratic Revolution

NEPAL

Lower House

Sunil Babu Pant	2008–2012	Communist Party Nepal-U

NETHERLANDS

Lower House

Coos Huijsen	1972, 1976–1977 (1976)	Christian Historical Union
Peter Lankhorst	1981–1994	Political Party of Radicals
Jan Franssen	1982–1994	People's Party for Freedom and Democracy
Evelien Eshuis	1982–1986	Communist Party
Wim van de Camp	1986–2009	Christian Democratic Appeal
Clemens Cornielje	1994–2005	People's Party for Freedom and Democracy
Boris Dittrich	1994–2006	Democrats 66
Anne Lize van der Stoel	1994–1998	People's Party for Freedom and Democracy
Peter Rehwinkel	1995–2002	Labour Party
Jose Smits	1998–2006	Labour Party
Boris van der Ham	2002–2012	Democrats 66
Ger Koopmans	2002–2012	Christian Democratic Appeal
Gerda Verburg	1998–2007, 2010–2011	Christian Democratic Appeal
Joop Wijn	1998–2002, 2003, 2006–2007	Christian Democratic Appeal
Mark Harbers	2009–	People's Party for Freedom and Democracy
Henk Krol	2012–	50 Plus
Vera Bergkamp	2012–	Democrats 66
Henk Nijboer	2012–	Labour Party
Hanke Bruins-Slot	2010–	Christian Democratic Appeal

Manon Fokke	2012–2017	Labour Party
Gerard Schouw	2010–2015	Democrats 66
Astrid Oosenbrug	2012–2017	Labour Party
Krista van Velzen	2002–2010	Socialist Party
Jan Kees de Jager	2010	Christian Democratic Appeal
Eric Smaling	2013–2017	Socialist Party
Jeroen Van Wijngaarden	2014–2017	People's Party for Freedom and Democracy
Sjoerd Potters	2017–	People's Party for Freedom and Democracy
Rob Jetten	2017–	Democrats 66

Upper House

| Gerard Schouw | 2003–2010 | Democrats 66 |
| Kim Putters | 2003–2013 | Labour Party |

Cabinet Ministers

Joop Wijn	2002–2003	Economy
Joop Wijn	2006–2007	Finance
Gerda Verburg	2007–2010	Agriculture, Nature, Food
Jan Kees de Jager	2010–2012	Finance

European Parliament

Herman Verbeek	1989–	Political Party of Radicals
Dennis de Jong	2009–	Socialist Party
Wim van der Camp	2009–	Christian Democratic Appeal

NEW ZEALAND

Lower House

Tim Barnett	1996–2008	Labour Party
Chris Carter	1993–2011	Labour Party
Charles Chauvel	2006–2013	Labour Party
Georgina Beyer	1999–2007	Labour Party
Chris Finlayson	2005–	National Party
Louisa Wall	2008, 2011–	Labour Party
Grant Robertson	2008–	Labour Party
Kevin Hague	2008–2016	Green Party
Jan Logie	2011–	Green Party
Maryan Street	2005–2014	Labour Party
Claudette Hauiti	2013–2014	National Party

Meka Whaitiri	2013–	Labour Party
Paul Foster-Bell	2013–2017 (2016)	National Party
Tamati Coffey	2017–	Labour Party
Kiri Allan	2017–	Labour Party

Cabinet Ministers

Chris Carter	2004–2005	Housing
Chris Carter	2005–2007	Building
Chris Carter	2007–2008	Education
Maryan Street	2007–2008	Housing
Chris Finlayson	2008–2017	Attorney General
Chris Finlayson	2008–2017	Arts and Culture
Grant Robertson	2017–	Finance

NORWAY

Lower House

Wenche Lowzow	1977–1985 (1979)	Conservative Party
Anders Hornslien	1993–2001	Labor Party
Bent Hoie	2001–	Conservative Party
Andre Kvakkestad	2001–2005 (2002)	Progress Party
Siri Hall Arnoy	2001–2005	Socialist Left
Per Kristian Foss	1981–2013	Conservative Party
Anette Trettebergstuen	2005–	Labor Party
Andre Dahl	2005–2013	Conservative Party
Ole Henrik Grønn	2005–2009 (2008)	Christian Democratic

Cabinet Ministers

Anne Holt	1996–1997	Justice
Per-Kristian Foss	2001–2005	Finance
Per-Kristian Foss	2002	Acting Prime Minister
Bent Høie	2013–	Health
Knut Olav Åmås	2013–	Culture and Church

PERU

Lower House

Carlos Bruce	2006– (2014)	Possible Peru Alliance
Alberto de Belaunde	2016– (2016)	PPK

PHILIPPINES

Lower House

Geraldine Roman	2016–	Liberal Party

POLAND

Lower House

Robert Biedron	2011–2015	Palikot
Anna Grodzka	2011–2015	Palikot/Greens

PORTUGAL

Lower House

Miguel Vale de Almeida	2009–2011	Socialist
Alexandre Quintanilha	2015–	Socialist

SCOTLAND

Lower House

Iain Smith	1999–2011	Liberal Democratic Party
Margaret Smith	1999–2011	Liberal Democratic Party
Patrick Harvey	2003–	Green Party
Joe FitzPatrick	2007–	Scottish National Party
Derek Mackay	2011–	Scottish National Party
Marco Biagi	2011–2016	Scottish National Party
Kevin Stewart	2011–	Scottish National Party
Kezia Dugdale	2011– (2016)	Labour Party
Jim Eadie	2011–2016	Scottish National Party
Ruth Davidson	2011–	Conservative Party
Jeane Freeman	2016–	Scottish National Party
Annie Wells	2016–	Conservative Party
Jamie Green	2016–	Conservative Party
Ross Thomson	2016–	Conservative Party

SERBIA

Cabinet Ministers

Ana Brnabić	2016–2017	Public Administration
Ana Brnabić	2017–	Prime Minister

SLOVAKIA

Lower House

Stanislav Fořt	2010– (2011)	Freedom and Solidarity

SOUTH AFRICA

Lower House

Mike Waters	1999–	Democratic Alliance
Ian Davidson	1999–2014	Democratic Alliance
Dion George	2008–2015	Democratic Alliance
Manny de Fritas	2009–	Democratic Alliance
Ian Ollis	2009–	Democratic Alliance
Lynne Brown	2014–	African National Congress
Marius Redelinghuys	2014–	Democratic Alliance
Zakhele Mbhele	2014–	Democratic Alliance
Gordon Mackay	2014–	Democratic Alliance
Patrick Atkinson	2014–	Democratic Alliance
Michael Cardo	2014–	Democratic Alliance
Dean MacPherson	2014–	Democratic Alliance

Upper House

Beyers Smit	2014–	Democratic Alliance

Cabinet Ministers

Lynne Brown	2014–	Public Enterprises

SPAIN

Lower House

Miquel Iceta Llorens	1996–1999 (1999)	Socialist Workers Party
Antonio Hurtado	2008– (2014)	Socialist Workers Party
Ángeles Álvarez	2011–2015, 2015– (2013)	Socialist Workers Party
Jose Manuel Girela de la Fuente	2011–2016	Socialist Workers Party
Ricardo Sixto Iglesias	2011–	United Left of the Valencian Country
Maria Such	2015–2015	Socialist Workers Party

Upper House

Jerónimo Saavedra Acevedo	1996–2003	Socialist Workers Party
Iñaki Oyarzabal de Miguel	2015–	People's Party
María Vanessa Angustia Gómez	2015–	United Left

European Parliament

José María Mendiluce Pereiro	1999–2004 (2003)	Socialist Workers Party

SWEDEN

Lower House

Kent Carlsson	1991–1993 (1991)	Social Democrats
Andreas Carlgren	1994–1998 1998)	Center Party
Elisabeht Markstrom	1995–2010 (2006)	Social Democrats
Tasso Stafilidis	1998–2006	Left Party
Tobias Billström	2002–	Moderate Party
Martin Andreasson	2002–2006, 2012	Liberal Party
Ulf Holm	2002–2014	Green Party
Borje Vestlund	2002–	Social Democrats
Fredrick Federley	2006–2014	Center Party
Olof Lavesson	2006–	Moderate Party
Tomas Tobe	2006–	Moderate Party
Marianne Berg	2006–2014	Left Party
Josefin Brink	2006–2014	Left Party
Hans Linde	2006–	Left Party
Hans Ekström	2010–	Social Democrats
Hannah Bergstedt	2010–	Social Democrats
Jonas Gunnarsson	2011–	Social Democrats
Robert Hannah	2014–	Liberal Party
Christian Holm	2006– (2013)	Moderate Party
Cassandra Sundin	2014–	Swedish Democrats
Maria Ferm	2010–	Green Party
Niklas Wykman	2014–	Moderate Party

Cabinet Ministers

Andreas Carlgren	2006–2011	Environment
Tobias Billström	2006–2014	Migration

European Parliament

Malin Björk	2014–	Left Party
Fredrick Federley	2014–	Center Party

SWITZERLAND

Lower House

Doris Stump	2003–2011	Social Democrats
Marianne Huguenin	2003–2007 (2004)	Labor Party
Claude Janiak	1999–2007	Social Democrats
Martin Naef	2011–	Social Democrats
Hans-Peter Portmann	2014–	Free Democratic Party
Daniel Stolz	2012–2015	Free Democratic Party

Angelo Barrile	2015–	Social Democrats
Hans Ueli Vogt	2015–	Swiss People's Party

Upper House
Claude Janiak	2007–	Social Democrats

Cabinet Ministers
Claude Janiak	2005–2006	President

TAIWAN

Cabinet Ministers
Audrey Tang	2016–	Digital

UNITED KINGDOM

Lower House
Chris Smith	1983–2005 (1984)	Labour Party
Matthew Parris	1979–1986 (1984)	Conservative Party
Simon Hughes	1983–2015 (2006)	Liberal/Liberal Democratic Party
Michael Brown	1983–1997 (1994)	Conservative Party
Nick Brown	1983– (1998)	Labour Party
Ron Davies	1983–2001 (1999)	Labour Party
Clive Betts	1992– (2003)	Labour Party
Angela Eagle	1992– (1997)	Labour Party
Alan Duncan	1992– (2002)	Conservative Party
Nigel Evans	1992– (2010)	Conservative Party
Peter Mandelson	1992–2004 (2000)	Labour Party
Stephen Twigg	1997–2005, 2010–	Labour Party
David Borrow	1997–2010 (1998)	Labour Party
Ben Bradshaw	1997–	Labour Party
Gordon Marsden	1997– (1998)	Labour Party
Mark Oaten	1997–2010 (2006)	Liberal Democratic Party
Crispin Blunt	1997– (2010)	Conservative Party
Nick Gibb	1997– (2015)	Conservative Party
Adam Price	2001–2010	Plaid Cymru
Gregory Barker	2001–2015 (2007)	Conservative Party
Chris Bryant	2001–	Labour Party
David Laws	2001–2015 (2010)	Liberal Democratic Party
David Cairns	2001–2011	Labour Party
Stephen Williams	2005–2015	Liberal Democratic Party
Nick Herbert	2005–	Conservative Party

Daniel Kawczynski	2005– (2013)	Conservative Party
David Mundell	2005– (2016)	Conservative Party
Nia Griffith	2005– (2016)	Labour Party
Margot James	2010–	Conservative Party
Iain Stewart	2010–	Conservative Party
Nick Boles	2010–	Conservative Party
Mike Freer	2010–	Conservative Party
Stuart Andrew	2010–	Conservative Party
Conor Burns	2010–	Conservative Party
Eric Ollerenshaw	2010–2015	Conservative Party
Stephen Gilbert	2010–2015	Liberal Democratic Party
Mark Menzies	2010– (2017)	Conservative Party
Steve Reed	2012–	Labour Party
Stephen Doughty	2012– (2015)	Labour Party
Ben Howlett	2015–2017	Conservative Party
Stuart McDonald	2015–	Scottish National Party
Stewart McDonald	2015–	Scottish National Party
Martin Docherty	2015–	Scottish National Party
John Nicolson	2015–2017	Scottish National Party
Joanna Cherry	2015–	Scottish National Party
Peter Kyle	2015–	Labour Party
Wes Streeting	2015–	Labour Party
Angela Crawley	2015–	Scottish National Party
Cat Smith	2015–	Labour Party
Gerald Jones	2015–	Labour Party
Mhairi Black	2015–	Scottish National Party
Hannah Bardell	2015– (2016)	Scottish National Party
William Wragg	2005– (2016)	Conservative Party
Justine Greening	2015– (2016)	Conservative Party
Dan Carden	2017–	Labour Party
Gerard Killen	2017–	Labour Party
Sandy Martin	2017–	Labour Party
Luke Pollard	2017–	Labour Party
Lloyd Russell-Moyle	2017–	Labour Party
Damien Moore	2017–	Conservative Party
Lee Rowley	2017–	Conservative Party
Ross Thomson	2017–	Conservative Party

Upper House

3rd Baron Montagu of Beaulieu	1945–2015 (2000)	Conservative Party
2nd Viscount Maugham	1958–1981	Independent
Lord Allen of Kensington	1991–	Labour Party

Baroness Hilton of Eggardon	1991–	Labour Party
Lord Mandelson of Foy	1998–	Labour Party
Lord Alli	1998–	Labour Party
Lord Browne of Madingley	2001–	Independent
Lord Smith of Finsbury	2005–	Labour Party
Lord Justice Etherton	2008–2009	Law Lord
Baroness Barker	2009– (2013)	Liberal Democratic Party
Baroness Stedman-Scott	2010–	Conservative Party
Lord Lexden	2010–	Conservative Party
Lord Black of Brentwood	2010–	Conservative Party
Lord Gold	2010–	Conservative Party
Lord Glendonbrook	2011–	Conservative Party
Lord Collins of Highbury	2011–	Labour Party
Lord Paddick of Brixton	2013–	Liberal Democratic Party
Lord Cashman	2014–	Labour Party
Lord Scriven	2014–	Liberal Democratic Party
Lord Oates	2015–	Liberal Democratic Party
Lord Livermore	2015–	Labour Party
Lord Barker of Battle	2015–	Conservative Party
Lord Hayward	2015–	Conservative Party
Lord Gilbert of Panteg	2015–	Conservative Party

Cabinet Ministers

Chris Smith	1997–2001	Culture
Peter Mandelson	1998–1999	Trade and Industry
Nick Brown	1998–2001	Agriculture
Peter Mandelson	1999–2001	Northern Ireland
Peter Mandelson	2008–2009	Business
Ben Bradshaw	2009–2010	Culture, Media, Sport
Angela Eagle	2009–2010	Pensions
David Laws	2010–2012	Chief Treasury Secretary
Nick Gibb	2010–2012, 2015–	Schools
Justine Greening	2011–2012	Transport
David Laws	2012–2015	Schools
Justine Greening	2012–2016	International Development
David Mundell	2015–	Scotland
Justine Greening	2016–2017	Education, Women, Equalities

European Parliament

Michael Cashman	1999–2014	Labour Party
Alyn Smith	2004–	Scottish National Party
Nikki Sinclaire	2009–2014	UK Independence Party
Seb Dance	2014–	Labour Party
David Coburn	2014–	UK Independence Party
Ian Duncan	2014–	Conservative Party

URUGUAY

Lower House

Martín Couto	2014– (2017)	Broad Front

Upper House

Michelle Suarez	2017–	Communist Party

UNITED STATES

Lower House

Gerry Studds	1972–1987 (1983)	Democratic Party
Steve Gunderson	1980–1997 (1994)	Republican Party
Barney Frank	1982–2012 (1987)	Democratic Party
Jim Kolbe	1984–2007 (1996)	Republican Party
Tammy Baldwin	1998–2012	Democratic Party
Michael Michaud	2003–2014 (2013)	Democratic Party
Jared Polis	2008–	Democratic Party
David Cicilline	2010–	Democratic Party
Sean Patrick Maloney	2012–	Democratic Party
Kyrsten Sinema	2012–	Democratic Party
Mark Pocan	2012–	Democratic Party
Mark Takano	2012–	Democratic Party

Upper House

Tammy Baldwin	2012–	Democratic Party

VENEZUELA

Lower House

Tamara Adrian	2015–	Popular Will
Rosmit Mantilla	2015–	Popular Will

WALES

Lower House

Ron Davies	1999–2003	Labour Party
Hannah Blythyn	2016–	Labour Party
Jeremy Miles	2016–	Labour Party
Adam Price	2016–	Plaid Cymru

BIBLIOGRAPHY

Prologue

Damon, Anjeanette. 2013. "In Split Vote, Nevada Senate Passes Measure to Begin Repeal of Gay Marriage Ban." Las Vegas Sun, https://lasvegassun.com/news/2013/apr/22/split-vote-nevada-senate-passes-measure-begin-repe/#ixzz2RlfYvO6b.

San Francisco Travel. "A Brief History of the Rainbow Flag." http://www.sftravel.com/article/brief-history-rainbow-flag.

1: The Milk Principle

Aston, Martin. 2016. Breaking Down the Walls of Heartache: How Music Came Out. London: Constable.

BBC News. 2017. "Australian Parliament Approves Same-Sex Marriage." http://www.bbc.com/news/world-australia-42260548.

Beech, Alexandra. 2017. "Keeping the Faith: Andrew Wallace on the Priesthood, Carpentry and Same-Sex Marriage." ABC News, http://mobile.abc.net.au/news/2017-05-04/keeping-the-faith-andrew-wallace/8461122.

Beilock, Sian. 2011. Choke: What the Secrets of the Brain Reveal About Getting It Right When You Have To. New York: Atria Books.

Bell, Alex, Raj Chetty, Xavier Jaravel, Neviana Petkova, and John Van Reenen. 2017. "Who Becomes an Inventor in America? The Importance of Exposure to Innovation." The Equality of Opportunity Project, http://www.equality-of-opportunity.org/assets/documents/inventors_summary.pdf.

Bian, Lin, Sarah-Jane Leslie, Andrei Cimpian. 2017. "Gender Stereotypes about Intellectual Ability Emerge Early and Influence Children's Interests." Science Magazine, http://science.sciencemag.org/content/355/6323/389.

Black, Dustin Lawrence. 2015. "How 'Story' Is the Most Effective Way to Change Hearts and Minds." Speech to University College Dublin Law Society. https://www.youtube.com/watch?v=1m-ELWr8dRo.

Butterworth, Benjamin. 2017. "Australian Parliament Spontaneously Breaks Into Song as Same-Sex Marriage Legalized." Pink News, http://www.pinknews.co.uk/2017/12/07/australian-parliament-spontaneously-breaks-into-song-as-same-sex-marriage-legalised.

Butterworth, Benjamin. 2017. "This MP's Son Died Weeks Ago—She Returned to Work to Vote for Same-Sex Marriage." Pink News, http://www.pinknews.co.uk/2017/12/07/this-mps-son-died-weeks-ago-she-returned-to-work-to-vote-for-same-sex-marriage/.

Campbell, David E., and Christina Wolbrecht. 2006. "See Jane Run: Women Politicians as Role Models for Adolescents." *Journal of Politics* 68, no. 2: 233–247.

Clarke, Allan. 2015. "Here's What It's Like to Grow Up Gay and Indigenous in Australia." *Buzzfeed*, https://www.buzzfeed.com/allanclarke/these-indigenous-people-open-up-about-their-struggles-with-t?utm_term=.otAoXgdar#.tmXMq5a6K.

Cohen, Jennie. 2010. "The Mother Who Saved Suffrage: Passing the 19th Amendment." *History*, http://www.history.com/news/the-mother-who-saved-suffrage-passing-the-19th-amendment.

Cook, Tim. 2014. "Tim Cook Speaks Up." *Bloomberg Business*. https://www.bloomberg.com/news/articles/2014-10-30/tim-cook-speaks-up.

Evershed, Nick. 2017. "Full Results of Australia's vote for Same-Sex Marriage, Electorate by Electorate—Interactive." *The Guardian*, https://www.theguardian.com/australia-news/datablog/ng-interactive/2017/nov/15/same-sex-marriage-survey-how-australia-voted-electorate-by-electorate?CMP=Share_iOSApp_Other.

Farber, Jim. 2017. "The Gay Architects of Rock." *New York Times*, https://www.nytimes.com/2017/10/17/style/the-gay-architects-of-classic-rock.html?smprod=nytcore-ipad&smid=nytcore-ipad-share.

Frontiers Media. 2011. "National Coming Out Day." YouTube, https://www.youtube.com/watch?v=wYgAp7j53q4&feature=youtu.be.

Gillig, Traci and Erica Rosenthal, Sheila Murphy, Kate Langrall Folb. 2017. "More Than a Media Moment: The Influence of Televised Storylines on Viewers' Attitudes toward Transgender People and Policies." *Sex Roles*, https://link.springer.com/epdf/10.1007/s11199-017-0816-1?author_access_token=GB-FEOsJxkioP_ivCgMTZve4RwlQNchNByi7wbcMAY49ZyzVMpMhbJSjvG6wJ2mfqJJYCJ6LJybXPZzkeIoDgeAgyJ8YC3IeWa_y--Zsu4WG3ccMYjBHnjy_p-jxOA0joDFDDU21MZPLcjwya1wHJw%3D%3D.

Glynn, Adam, and Maya Sen. 2015. "Identifying Judicial Empathy: Does Having Daughters Cause Judges to Rule for Women's Issues?" *American Journal of Political Science* 59, no. 1: 37–54.

Haider-Markel, Donald P. 2007. "Representation and Backlash: The Positive and Negative Influence of Descriptive Representation." *Legislative Studies Quarterly* 32, no. 1: 107–134.

Haider-Markel, Donald P., Mark R. Joslyn, and Chad J. Kniss. 2000. "Minority Group Interests and Political Representation: Gay Elected Officials in the Policy Process." *Journal of Politics* 62, no. 2: 568–577.

Harris, Sarah. 2018. "Elizabeth Kerekere Speaks on Maori LGBTQ Term Takatāpui." *New Zealand Herald*. http://www.nzherald.co.nz/nz/news/article.cfm?c_id=1&objectid=11879651.

Herrick, Rebekah. 2009. "The Effect of Sexual Orientation on State Legislators' Behavior and Priorities." *Journal of Homosexuality* 56, no. 8: 1117–1133.

Herrick, Rebekah. 2010. "Legislators' Positions on Gay and Lesbian Rights: The Personal and Political." *Journal of Homosexuality* 57, no. 7: 928–943.

Herrick, Rebekah. 2010. "The Legislative Effectiveness of Gay and Lesbian Legislators." *Journal of Women, Politics & Policy* 31, no. 3: 243–259.

International Lesbian and Gay Association. 2017. "Minorities Report 2017: Attitudes to Sexual and Gender Minorities Around the World." http://ilga.org/ilga-riwi-new-results-research-attitudes-sexual-gender-sex-minorities/.

Jackman, Josh. 2017. "The Majority of Australian Christians Support Same-Sex Marriage, Poll Reveals." *Pink News*, http://www.pinknews.co.uk/2017/07/21/the-majority-of-australian-christians-support-same-sex-marriage-poll-reveals/.

Kliff, Sarah. 2017. "The Research Is Clear: Electing More Women Changes How Government Works." Vox, https://www.vox.com/2016/7/27/12266378/electing-women-congress-hillary-clinton.

Lee, Steve. 2017. "New Research Shows Transgender TV Characters Have the Power to Shape Audience Attitudes." *LGBT Weekly*, http://lgbtweekly.com/2017/08/10/new-research-shows-transgender-tv-characters-have-the-power-to-shape-audience-attitudes/.

Lewis, Gregory B. 2011. "The Friends and Family Plan: Contact with Gays and Support for Gay Rights." *Policy Studies Journal* 39: 217–238.

Masters, Jeffrey. 2017. Podcast, April 24. LGBTQ Interview Podcast, https://www.lgbtqpodcast.com

New Zealand Parliament. "Marriage (Definition of Marriage) Amendment Bill—Third Reading." Transcript. https://www.parliament.nz/en/pb/hansard-debates/rhr/document/50HansD_20130417_00000020/ marriage-definition-of-marriage-amendment-bill-third.

Ocamb, Karen. 2017. Facebook post.

Raifman, Julia, Ellen Moscoe, S. Bryn Austin, Margaret McConnell. 2017. "Difference-in-Differences Analysis of the Association Between State Same-Sex Marriage Policies and Adolescent Suicide Attempts." *JAMA Pedriatrics* 171, no. 4: 350–356.

Reynolds, Andrew. 2013. "Representation and Rights: The Impact of LGBT Legislators in Comparative Perspective." *American Political Science Review* 107, no. 2: 259–274.

Rosen, Jill. 2017. "Black Students Who Have at Least One Black Teacher Are More Likely to Graduate." *The HUB,* John Hopkins University magazine. http://hub.jhu.edu/2017/04/05/black-teachers-improve-student-graduation-college-access/.

Rosenblum, Nancy L. 2016. *Good Neighbors: The Democracy of Everyday Life in America.* Princeton, NJ: Princeton University Press.

Roy, Ujjainee. 2017. "Australian MP Proposes to Partner During Gay Marriage Debate in Parliament." *T2 Online,* http://t2online.com/lifestyle/australian-mp-proposes-partner-gay-marriage-debate-parliament/cid/1.88998.

Singal, Jesse. 2017. "The Contact Hypothesis Offers Hope for the World." *The Cut,* http://nymag.com/scienceofus/2017/02/the-contact-hypothesis-offers-hope-for-the-world.html?mid=twitter-share-scienceofus.

Smith, Fiona. 2017. "Gay Leaders and the Power of Role Models." *Bluenotes,* https://bluenotes.anz.com/posts/2017/05/gay-leaders-and-the-power-of-role-models#.

Swers, Michele L. 2013. *Women in the Club: Gender and Policy Making in the Senate.* Chicago: University of Chicago Press.

Tanner, Lindsey. 2017. "Teen Suicide Attempts Fell as Same-Sex Marriage Became Legal." Associated Press, https://www.apnews.com/46e523cd23f84f549cf2cce0add510ff/Teen-suicide-attempts-fell-as-same-sex-marriage-became-legal.

Tropp Linda. and Thomas Pettigrew.2006. "A Meta-Analytic Test of Intergroup Contact Theory." *Journal of Personality and Social Psychology* 90, no. 5: 751–783.

Williams, Robin. 1947. *The Reduction of Intergroup Tensions: A Survey of Research on Problems of Ethnic, Racial, and Religious Group Relations.* New York: Social Science Research Council.

Wolbrecht, Christina, and David Campbell. 2007. "Leading by Example: Female Members of Parliament as Political Role Models." *American Journal of Political Science* 51, no. 4: 921–939.

2: The Ballad of Peter and Simon

Badash, David. 2017. "Three Out of Ten Young People Are Gay or Bisexual." The New Civil Rights Movement, http://www.thenewcivilrightsmovement.com/davidbadash/one_third_of_16_22_year_olds_say_they_re_not_only_attracted_to_the_opposite_sex.

Blow, Charles. M. 2015. *Fire Shut Up in My Bones.* Boston: Houghton Mifflin Harcourt.

Blow, Charles. M. 2015. "Sexual Attraction and Fluidity." *New York Times,* http://www.nytimes.com/2015/09/07/opinion/charles-m-blow-sexual-attraction-and-fluidity.html?smprod=nytcore-ipad&smid=nytcore-ipad-share.

Brown, Anna. 2016. "Despite Oregon Governor's Win, Candidates of Different Sexual Orientations Could Face Resistance in a Presidential Run." Pew Research Center, http://www.pewresearch.org/fact-tank/2016/11/16/despite-oregon-governors-win-lgbt-candidates-could-face-some-resistance-in-a-presidential-run.

Center for Disease Control. 2010. *The National Intimate Partner and Sexual Violence Survey*. National Center for Injury Prevention and Control. https://www.cdc.gov/violenceprevention/nisvs/index.html.

Dahlgreen, Will, and Anna-Elizabeth Shakespeare. 2015. "1 in 2 Young People Say They Are Not 100% Heterosexual." *YouGov*, https://yougov.co.uk/news/2015/08/16/half-young-not-heterosexual/

Eysenck, H. J. 1971. *Race, Intelligence and Education*. London: Temple Smith.

Gates, Gary. 2011. "How Many People Are Lesbian, Gay, Bisexual, and Transgender?" Los Angeles: Williams Institute.

Gremore, Graham. 2016. "Research Confirms Bisexual Men Make the Best Lovers." *LGBTQNation*, http://www.lgbtqnation.com/2016/08/research-confirms-bisexual-men-make-best-lovers/?utm_sour ce=LGBTQ+Nation+Subscribers&utm_campaign=a171f841f6-20160829_LGBTQ_Nation_ Newsletter&utm_medium=email&utm_term=0_c4eab596bd-a171f841f6-429470973.

Harris Poll. 2017. "Accelerating Acceptance." GLAAD, http://www.glaad.org/files/aa/2017_ GLAAD_Accelerating_Acceptance.pdf.

Jackman, Josh. 2017. "Bisexual People Are 80 Percent More Likely to Feel Anxiety Than the Average Person." *Pink News*, http://www.pinknews.co.uk/2017/07/05/bisexual-people-are-80-percent-more-likely-to-feel-anxiety-than-the-average-person/#.

Johnson, Nicole L., and MaryBeth Grove. 2017. "Why Us? Toward an Understanding of Bisexual Women's Vulnerability for and Negative Consequences of Sexual Violence." *Journal of Bisexuality* 17, no. 4: 435–450.

Jones, Maddie. 2017. "Why Do Bisexuals Get Such a Hard Time?" *Pink News*, http://www.pinknews.co.uk/2017/11/27/feature-why-do-bisexuals-get-such-a-hard-time.

Kinsey, Alfred. 1948. "Sexual Behaviour in the Human Male." *American Journal of Physical Anthropology* 6, no. 1: 127–129.

Kinsey, Alfred. 1953. *Sexual Behaviour in The Human Female*. Indianapolis: Indiana University Press.

Kirkham, Lindsey. 2015. "Here's Why We Need a Bisexual Awareness Week." *The Advocate*, http://www.advocate.com/commentary/2015/9/21/heres-why-we-need-bisexual-awareness-week.

Movement Advancement Project. n.d. "Snapshot: Bisexual in America." http://www.lgbtmap.org/bisexual-snapshot-graphic?utm_source=Snapshot%3Abi+eblast&utm_campaign=Unfair+Price&utm_medium=email.

Movement Advancement Project. 2016. "Invisible Majority: The Disparities Facing Bisexual People and How to Remedy Them." http://lgbtmap.org/policy-and-issue-analysis/invisible-majority.

Rentoul, John. 2014. *The Indpendent*. "Michael Cashman: The Rainbow Warrior." https://www.independent.co.uk/news/people/michael-cashman-the-rainbow-warrior-9863411.html.

Tatchell, Peter. 1983. *The Battle for Bermondsey*. London: Heretic Books.

Tatchell, Peter. 2013. "My Defeat in Bermondsey 30 Years Ago Was a Defeat for the Whole Left." *The Guardian*, http://www.theguardian.com/commentisfree/2013/feb/22/defeat-in-bermondsey-defeat-for-left.

Whyte, Nicholas. 2001. 'The 1995 North Down By-Election.' http://www.ark.ac.uk/elections/fnd95.htm

3: I Have Quite a Powerful and Carrying Voice

Bardon, Sarah. 2017. "Leo Varadkar: The Man Who Evolved Into a Taoiseach." *Irish Times*, https://www.irishtimes.com/news/politics/leo-varadkar-the-man-who-evolved-into-a-taoiseach-1.3106073?mode=amp.

Boland, Rosita. 2017. "David Norris: 'I Have Already Recorded My Own Eulogy.'" *Irish Times*, http://www.irishtimes.com/life-and-style/people/david-norris-i-have-already-recorded-my-own-eulogy-1.3112488.

Elkink, Johan A., David M. Farrell, Theresa Reidy, and Jane Suiter. 2015. "Understanding the 2015 Marriage Referendum in Ireland: Constitutional Convention, Campaign, and Conservative Ireland." Dublin: UCD Geary Institute for Public Policy Discussion Paper Series. https://ideas.repec.org/p/ucd/wpaper/201521.html#.

Gilligan, Ann Louise, and Katherine Zappone. 2008. *Our Lives Out Loud: In Pursuit of Justice and Equality,* Dublin: O'Brien Press.

Hennessy, Michelle. 2014. "New Mayor of South Dublin Says He's Proud to be 'An Openly LGBT Mayor.'" June 6. *thejournal.* http://www.thejournal.ie/lgbt-mayor-south-dublin-1503819-Jun2014.

Kelly, Fiach. 2017. "Campaign for Leo: The Inside Story of How Varadkar Beat Simon Coveney." *Irish Times,* https://www.irishtimes.com/news/ireland/irish-news/campaign-for-leo-the-inside-story-of-how-varadkar-beat-simon-coveney-1.3106066?mode=amp#.WTJpJcnhdjI. twitter.

Mazlow, Abraham. 1943. "A Theory of Human Motivation." *Psychological Review* 50, no. 4: 370–396.

McGreevy, Ronan. 2017. "Leo Varadkar's Indian Relatives Express Pride at His Election." *Irish Times,* https://www.irishtimes.com/news/ireland/irish-news/leo-varadkar-s-indian-relatives-express-pride-at-his-election-1.3106055?mode=amp.

Mullally, Una. 2013. "Panti Unstitched." *Irish Times,* http://www.irishtimes.com/blogs/poplife/2013/07/15/panti-unstitched.

Murray, Pauli. Papers of Pauli Murray. Cambridge, MA: Schlesinger Library, Radcliffe Institute for Advanced Study, Harvard University.

Norris, David. 2012. *A Kick Against the Pricks.* Ireland: Transworld Ireland.

4: I Have Never Come Across a Homo in This House

Gay Times. 2015. "GT Heroes—Michael Cashman." https://www.gaytimes.co.uk/life/19947/gt-heroes-michael-cashman.

Geen, Jessica. 2011. "Gay MEP Michael Cashman Was Abused as a Child." *Pink News,* http://www.pinknews.co.uk/2011/03/07/gay-mep-michael-cashman-was-abused-as-a-child.

Hansard. House of Commons. 2013. Marriage (Same Sex Couples) Bill, February 5. https://publications.parliament.uk/pa/cm201213/cmhansrd/cm130205/debtext/130205 0001. htm.

Hansard. House of Lords. 2013. Marriage (Same Sex Couples) Bill, June 4. https://publications.parliament.uk/pa/ld201314/ldhansrd/text/130603-0001.htm#13060312000364.

Hayes, Jerry. 2012. "Gay Pride." *The Spectator.* https://blogs.spectator.co.uk/2012/01/gay-pride.

Kellaway, Kate. 2017. "Glad to be Gay: Leading Figures on 50 Years of Liberation." *The Guardian,* https://www.theguardian.com/society/2017/may/21/glad-to-be-gay-50-years-liberation-mens-lives-hollinghurst-antony-sher-waheed-alli?utm_source=dlvr.it&utm_medium=twitter.

McCormick, Joseph. 2016. "Would You Be Able to 'Spot a Homo' Using This 1962 Newspaper Column?" *Pink News,* http://www.pinknews.co.uk/2016/01/23/would-you-be-able-to-spot-a-homo-using-this-1962-newspaper-column.

McNeilly, Claire. 2017. "Welsh MP Battered Unconscious for Being Gay Set for His First Belfast Pride." *Belfast Telegraph,* https://www.belfasttelegraph.co.uk/news/northern-ireland/welsh-mp-battered-unconscious-for-being-gay-set-for-his-first-belfast-pride-36001611. html.

McSmith, Andy. 2013. "A Gay Tory MP on Why He Went Public." *Independent,* http://www.independent.co.uk/news/uk/politics/mike-freer-a-gay-tory-mp-on-why-he-went-public-8484017.html.

Peter Tatchell Foundation. "Alan Turing & the Medical Abuse of Gay Men." http://www.petertatchellfoundation.org/health/alan-turing-medical-abuse-gay-men.

Pinfold, Corinne. 2013. "Lib Dem Peer Baroness Barker Comes Out During Equal Marriage Debate." *Pink News,* http://www.pinknews.co.uk/2013/06/04/lib-dem-peer-baroness-barker-comes-out-during-equal-marriage-debate.

UK National Survey of Sexual Attitudes and Lifestyles. 2000. http://www.natsal.ac.uk/home. aspx.

US General Social Survey. 1990. http://gss.norc.org.

Wright, Oliver. 2013. "Lord Alli: 'I Was Called Sinful and Dirty. And That Was in a Lords Debate.'"
    Independent,   http://www.independent.co.uk/news/uk/politics/lord-alli-i-was-called-
    sinful-and-dirty-and-that-was-in-a-lords-debate-8641318.html.

5: From Mississippi to Marriage

Associated Press. 2013. "Minnesota Legalizes Same-Sex Marriage." http://www.nydailynews.
    com/news/politics/minnesota-legalizes-same-sex-marriage-article-1.1344070.
Ball, Molly. 2015. "How Gay Marriage Became a Constitutional Right." *The Atlantic*, https://www.
    theatlantic.com/politics/archive/2015/07/gay-marriage-supreme-court-politics-activism/
    397052.
Duane, Thomas. 1999. "From Stonewall to the Capitol." *The Advocate*, https://books.google.com/
    books?id=rWQEAAAAMBAJ&pg=PA11&lpg=PA11&dq=HIV+positive+elected+offici
    als&source=bl&ots=r0_nW8WcYV&sig=k40gewBLy1iKU8rRBd3IBXX33vc&hl=en&sa
    =X&ved=0ahUKEwj4wKHDzLzOAhWCJsAKHYXDBo8Q6AEISTAH#v=onepage&q=
    HIV%20positive%20elected%20officials&f=false.
Flores, Andrew R., and Scott Barclay. 2013. *Public Support for Marriage for Same-Sex Couples by
    State*. Los Angeles: The Williams Institute, UCLA.
Gallup Poll. 2014. "Marriage." http://www.gallup.com/poll/117328/marriage.aspx.
Gates, Gary. 2017. "Vermont Leads States in LGBT Identification." *Gallup*, http://www.gallup.
    com/poll/203513/vermont-leads-states-lgbt-identification.aspx.
Harvard Law School. 2016. "Evan Wolfson and Ron Suskind: 'Hand in Hand: Equality, Marriage,
    and the Future of LGBT Rights.'" YouTube, https://www.youtube.com/watch?v=B7v7BX7
    G39g&app=desktop.
Hough, Lory. 2013. "Holding Court." *Ed. Magazine*. Harvard Graduate School of Education,
    https://www.gse.harvard.edu/news/ed/13/01/holding-court.
Lavers, Michael K. 2012. "Gay NH Lawmaker Seeks to Become First Out Candidate Elected
    to State Senate." *Washington Blade*, http://www.washingtonblade.com/2012/10/25/
    gay-n-h-lawmaker-seeks-to-become-first-out-candidate-elected-to-state-senate.
Pew Research Center. 2013. "In Gay Marriage Debate, Both Supporters and Opponents
    See Legal Recognition as 'Inevitable.'" http://www.people-press.org/2013/06/06/
    in-gay-marriage-debate-both-supporters-and-opponents-see-legal-recognition-as-inevitable.
Pew Research Center. 2014. "Blacks Are Lukewarm to Gay Marriage, But Most Say Businesses
    Must Provide Wedding Services to Gay Couples." http://www.pewresearch.org/fact-tank/
    2014/10/07/blacks-are-lukewarm-to-gay-marriage-but-most-say-businesses-must-pro-
    vide-wedding-services-to-gay-couples/ft_14-10-1_marriage.
Pew Research Center. 2017. "Changing Attitudes on Gay Marriage." http://www.pewforum.org/
    fact-sheet/changing-attitudes-on-gay-marriage.
Post-ABC National Poll. 2014. "Gay Issues Find Increasing Acceptance." http://www.
    washingtonpost.com/page/2010-2019/WashingtonPost/2014/03/05/National-Politics/
    Polling/release_301.xml.
Rifkin, Jesse. 2016. "Four Times Mediocre Grades Changed America." *Azcentral*, http://www.
    azcentral.com/story/opinion/2016/09/16/mediocre-bad-grades-america-gay-marriage-
    flag-vietnam-memorial-27th-amendment-college-column/90366382.
Silver, Nate. 2013. "How Opinion on Same-Sex Marriage Is Changing, and What It Means."
    FiveThirtyEight, http://fivethirtyeight.blogs.nytimes.com/2013/03/26/how-opinion-on-
    same-sex-marriage-is-changing-and-what-it-means/?_php=true&_type=blogs&_r=0.
Socarides, Charles. 1995. *Homosexuality: A Freedom Too Far*. Phoenix, AZ: Adam
    Margrave Books.
Solomon, Marc. 2014. *Winning Marriage: The Inside Story of How Same-Sex Couples Took On the
    Politicians and Pundits—and Won*. Lebanon, NH: ForeEdge.
The Advocates. 1974. "Advocates; Should Marriage Between Homosexuals Be Permitted?"
    WGBH Media Library & Archives, http://openvault.wgbh.org/catalog/V_57993D38129
    A433AAD10C7B04D019EF.

Tomasky, Michael. 2015. "The Cross-Generational Politics of Barney Frank." *The Atlantic*, http://www.theatlantic.com/magazine/archive/2015/04/the-cross-generational-politics-of-barney-frank/386234.

6: Being First

Allen, Samantha. 2017. "America Needs Another 21,307 LGBT Elected Officials to Achieve True Equality." *The Daily Beast*, https://www.thedailybeast.com/america-needs-another-21307-lgbt-elected-officials-to-achieve-true-equality.

Andersen, Robert, and Tina Fetner. 2008. "Cohort Differences in Tolerance of Homosexuality Attitudinal Change in Canada and the United States 1981–2000." *Public Opinion Quarterly* 72, no. 2: 311–330.

Appel, Madeline. 2010. "Mayor Annise Parker." Houston Oral History Project, Houston Public Library. http://digital.houstonlibrary.net/oral-history/annise-parker.php.

Asthana, Anushka. 2016. "Angela Eagle: 'There's No Point Being Sore.'" *The Guardian*, https://www.theguardian.com/politics/2016/jul/29/angela-eagle-theres-no-point-being-sore-labour-leadership.

Bollinger, Alex. 2017. "New Poll Shows 12 Percent of Americans Identify as LGBTQ." *LGBTQ Nation*, https://www.lgbtqnation.com/2017/04/poll-younger-people-getting-queer-accepting/?utm_source=LGBTQ+Nation+Subscribers&utm_campaign=4f185f82ce-20170403_LGBTQ_Nation_Newsletter&utm_medium=email&utm_term=0_c4eab596bd-4f185f82ce-429470973.

Bridges, Tristan. 2017. "Shifts in the U.S. LGBT Population." *The Society Pages*, https://thesocietypages.org/socimages/2017/01/16/shifts-in-the-us-lgbt-population.

Bruni, Frank. 2017. "It's a Gay, Gay, Gay Government." *New York Times*, https://www.nytimes.com/2017/12/01/opinion/palm-springs-gay-government.html?action=click&pgtype=Homepage&clickSource=story-heading&module=opinion-c-col-right-region&region=opinion-c-col-right-region&WT.nav=opinion-c-col-right-region&_r=0&referer=http://m.facebook.com.

Bushak, Lecia. 2015. "Millennials Are the 'Gayest Generation': 7% of Young Adults Identify As LGBT." *Medical Daily*, http://www.medicaldaily.com/millennials-are-gayest-generation-7-young-adults-identify-lgbt-327956.

Centers for Disease Control and Prevention. 2017. "Heath Risks Among Sexual Minority Youth." https://www.cdc.gov/healthyyouth/disparities/smy.htm.

Cook, Tim. 2015. "Tim Cook Speaks Up." *Bloomberg*, https://www.bloomberg.com/news/articles/2014-10-30/tim-cook-speaks-up.

Duffy, Nick. 2015. "Isle of Man Chief Opens Up About Sexuality as Equal Marriage Discussions Begin." *Pink News*, http://www.pinknews.co.uk/2015/10/07/isle-of-man-chief-opens-up-about-sexuality-as-equal-marriage-discussions-begin.

Duffy, Nick. 2016. "Angela Eagle: Jeremy Corbyn Has Failed to Challenge Homophobic Abuse Against Me." *Pink News*, http://www.pinknews.co.uk/2016/08/08/angela-eagle-jeremy-corbyn-has-failed-to-challenge-homophobic-abuse-against-me.

Duffy, Nick. 2016. "Angela Eagle Was Mocked as 'Angie the Dyke' at Local Party Meeting, Members Say." *Pink News*, http://www.pinknews.co.uk/2016/08/03/angela-eagle-was-mocked-as-angie-the-dyke-at-local-party-meeting-members-say.

Duffy, Nick. 2016. "Record Numbers of Young People Are Coming Out." *Pink News*, http://www.pinknews.co.uk/2016/10/05/record-numbers-of-young-people-are-coming-out.

Feltman, Rachel. 2016. "Study: Same-Sex Experiences Are on the Rise, and Americans Are Increasingly Chill About It." *Washington Post*, https://www.washingtonpost.com/news/speaking-of-science/wp/2016/06/01/study-same-sex-experiences-are-on-the-rise-and-americans-are-increasingly-chill-about-it/?postshare=3821464816211328&tid=ss_mail&utm_term=.94d28535d6a9.

Friess, Steve. 2015. "The First Openly Gay Person to Win an Election in America Was Not Harvey Milk." *Bloomberg*, http://www.bloomberg.com/politics/features/2015-12-11/the-first-openly-gay-person-to-win-an-election-in-america-was-not-harvey-milk.

Gates, Gary. 2017. "In U.S., More Adults Identifying as LGBT." Gallup, http://www.gallup.com/poll/201731/lgbt-identification-rises.aspx.

Grant, Japhy. 2009. "Think Harvey Milk Was the First Openly-Gay Politician? Think Again." Queerty, http://www.queerty.com/think-harvey-milk-was-the-first-openly-gay-politician-think-again-20090121.

Haider-Markel, Donald P. 2010. *Out and Running: Gay and Lesbian Candidates, Elections, and Policy Representation*, Washington, DC: Georgetown University Press.

John, Tara. 2016. "Everything You Need to Know About Angela Eagle, the Challenger for the Leadership of the U.K. Labour Party." *Time*, http://time.com/4400771/angela-eagle-labour-party-leader-corbyn.

Moore, Suzanne. 1997. "'I Need to Get Things Sorted.'" *Independent*, http://www.independent.co.uk/voices/i-need-to-get-things-sorted-1238559.html.

Perraudin, Frances. 2016. "Angela Eagle's Constituency Office Vandalized After Leadership Bid Lunch." *The Guardian*, http://www.theguardian.com/politics/2016/jul/12/angela-eagles-constituency-office-vandalised-after-leadership-bid-launch.

Pidd, Helen. 2015. "Isle of Man Leader Draws Line Under 'Dark Days' and Aims to Legalise Gay Marriage." *The Guardian*, https://www.theguardian.com/society/2015/oct/05/isle-of-man-legalise-gay-marriage.

Preston, Dominic. 2016. "Labour Party Report Confirms Angela Eagle Was Targeted By Homophobic Abuse." *Pink News*, http://www.pinknews.co.uk/2016/10/19/labour-party-report-confirms-angela-eagle-was-targeted-by-homophobic-abuse.

Smith, Raymond A., and Donald P. Haider-Markel. 2002. *Gay and Lesbian Americans and Political Participation*. Denver: ABC-CLIO Publishers.

Williams, Joe. 2016. "Brick Thrown Through Angela Eagle's Office Window Following Labour Leadership Bid." *Pink News*, http://www.pinknews.co.uk/2016/07/12/brick-thrown-to-angela-eagles-office-window-following-labour-leadership-bid-video.

7: St. Christopher

Altman, Lawrence. 1981. "Rare Cancer Seen in 41 Homosexuals." *New York Times*, http://www.nytimes.com/1981/07/03/us/rare-cancer-seen-in-41-homosexuals.html.

Bellafante, Ginia. 2013. "Out, But Not About That." *New York Times*, http://www.nytimes.com/2013/05/05/nyregion/the-lingering-stigma-of-hiv.html?emc=tnt&tntemail1=y&_r=0.

Bollinger, Alex. 2017. "Out New York City Council Member Corey Johnson Will Be Next Speaker." *LGBTQ Nation*, https://www.lgbtqnation.com/2017/12/new-york-city-city-council-member-corey-johnson-will-next-speaker/?utm_source=LGBTQ+Nation+Subscribers&utm_campaign=212260fadf-20171222_LGBTQ_Nation_Newsletter&utm_medium=email&utm_term=0_c4eab596bd-212260fadf-429470973.

Boniface, Susie. 2011. "AIDS 30 Years On: Labour Peer Chris Smith Speaks for the First Time About Living with HIV." *Mirror*, http://www.mirror.co.uk/news/technology-science/aids-30-years-on-labour-107460.

Duffy, Nick. 2015. "Thatcher Claimed AIDS Awareness Campaign Could 'Harm Morals.'" *Pink News*, http://www.pinknews.co.uk/2015/12/30/thatcher-claimed-aids-awareness-campaign-could-harm-morals.

Duffy, Nick. 2017. "Men With HIV Are Twice as Likely to Die by Suicide." *Pink News*, http://www.pinknews.co.uk/2017/04/07/men-with-hiv-are-twice-as-likely-to-die-by-suicide.

Dyer, Tom. 2012. "Gay Democrat Bob Poe Changed the LGBT Political Landscape in Orlando." *South Florida Gay News*, http://southfloridagaynews.com/Local/gay-democrat-bob-poe-changed-the-lgbt-political-landscape-in-orlando.html.

Dyer, Tom. 2016. "Bob Poe Wants to Put a Face on HIV in Congress." *Watermark Online*, http://www.watermarkonline.com/2016/06/09/positive-message-bob-poe-wants-put-face-hiv-congress.

Gallagher, Ian. 2005. "MP Chris Smith: I've Had HIV for 17 Years." *Daily Mail*, http://www.dailymail.co.uk/news/article-335920/MP-Chris-Smith-Ive-HIV-17-years.html.

Halter, Casey. 2014. "Elected Officials Openly Living with HIV/AIDS Remain Few Nationwide." *Poz*, https://www.poz.com/article/hiv-positive-politics-26343-5691.

Hays, Matthew. 2015. "How The Screen Legend's Death Changed Public Perception of AIDS." *Queerty*, https://www.queerty.com/reflections-of-rock-how-the-screen-legends-death-changed-public-perception-of-aids-20151130.

Heitz, David. 2015. "A Quiet Activist: HIV-Positive Former Lawmaker Making Change for People with HIV." *HIV Equal*, http://www.hivequal.org/hiv-equal-online/a-quiet-activist-hiv-positive-former-lawmaker-making-change-for-people-with-hiv.

Hess, K. L. et al. 2017. *Lifetime Risk of a Diagnosis of HIV Infection in the United States*. US National Library of Medicine. https://www.ncbi.nlm.nih.gov/pubmed/28325538? MERMIN0003.

Lipsyte, Richard. 2000. "Icon Recast: Support for a Gay Athlete." *New York Times,* http://www.nytimes.com/2000/04/30/sports/icon-recast-support-for-a-gay-athlete.html?pagewanted=all&src=pm.

Reardon, Sara. 2016. "HIV's Patient Zero Exonerated." https://www.nature.com/news/hiv-s-patient-zero-exonerated-1.20877.

Ring, Trudy. 2014. "Amazing HIV+ Gay Men: John D'Amico, John Duran, Larry Forester." *HIVPlus Magazine*, https://www.hivplusmag.com/people/2014/09/23/amazing-hiv-gay-men-john-damico-john-duran-larry-forester.

Strudwick, Patrick. 2015. "Meet Britain's First HIV-Positive Parliamentary Candidate." Buzzfeed, https://www.buzzfeed.com/patrickstrudwick/meet-britains-first-hiv-positive-parliamentary-candidate?utm_term=.ljXQ57A3M#.nk9VzdybO.

Taylor, Jeff. 2017. "CDC Officially Admits People Who Are Positive but Undetectable Cannot Transmit HIV." *LGBTQ Nation*, https://www.lgbtqnation.com/2017/09/cdc-officially-admits-people-positive-undetectable-cannot-transmit-hiv/?utm_source=LGBTQ+Nation+Subscribers&utm_campaign=9f5fc7da79-20170928_LGBTQ_Nation_Newsletter&utm_medium=email&utm_term=0_c4eab596bd-9f5fc7da79-429470973.

8: More Like Hell Than Heaven

Adams, Rebecca. 2015. "Americans Become More Accepting of Gays Every Day, Study Suggests." *Huffington Post.* http://www.huffingtonpost.com/entry/americans-more-accepting-gays_55b1296ee4b07af29d57c740.

Alimi, Bisi. 2015. "If You Say Being Gay Is Not African, You Don't Know Your History." *The Guardian.* http://www.theguardian.com/commentisfree/2015/sep/09/being-gay-african-history-homosexuality-christianity?CMP=share_btn_fb.

Aspin, Clive. 2017. "Hōkakatanga – Māori sexualities." *Te Ara, the Encyclopedia of New Zealand.* http://www.TeAra.govt.nz/en/hokakatanga-maori-sexualities.

Associated Press. 2016. "Pope Francis Denounces Transgender People as 'Annihilation of Man.'" *LGBTQ Nation.* http://www.lgbtqnation.com/2016/08/pope-francis-denounces-transgender-people-annihilation-man/?utm_source=LGBTQ+Nation+Subscribers&utm_campaign=132aaefffd-20160803_LGBTQ_Nation_Newsletter&utm_medium=email&utm_term=0_c4eab596bd-132aaefffd-429470973.

Associated Press. 2016. "Two Steps Back & One Step Forward for Gays in Asia This Week." *LGBTQ Nation.* https://www.lgbtqnation.com/2017/05/two-steps-back-one-step-forward-gays-asia-week/?utm_source=LGBTQ+Nation+Subscribers&utm_campaign=001983886b-20170526_LGBTQ_Nation_Newsletter&utm_medium=email&utm_term=0_c4eab596bd-001983886b-429470973.

Battell, Andrew. 2015. *The Strange Adventures of Andrew Battell of Leigh, in Angola and the Adjoining Regions*, Andesite Press.

BBC News. 2016. "Gay Bishop: Appointment of Nicholas Chamberlain 'Major Error' Says Gafcon." BBC News, http://www.bbc.com/news/uk-37267148.

BBC News. 2016. "More Anglicans Now Back Gay Marriage Than Oppose It, Poll Suggests." BBC News, http://www.bbc.co.uk/news/uk-35447150.

Beresford, Meka. 2017. "Gay Men Reportedly Detained and Killed by Chechnya Authorities." *Pink News*, http://www.pinknews.co.uk/2017/04/02/gay-men-reportedly-detained-and-killed-by-chechnya-authorities.

Brayboy, Duane. 2017. "Two Spirts, One Heart, Five Genders." *Indian Country Today*, https://indiancountrymedianetwork.com/news/opinions/two-spirits-one-heart-five-genders.

Butterworth, Benjamin. 2017. "Chechnya: Names of 27 Men Slaughtered and Buried in Bloody Night Revealed as Gay Purge Continues." *Pink News*, http://www.pinknews.co.uk/2017/07/11/chechnya-names-of-27-men-slaughtered-and-buried-in-bloody-night-revealed-as-gay-purge-continues.

Center for Muslim Studies. 2009. "A Global Study of Interfaith Relations." Gallup, http://www.olir.it/areetematiche/pagine/documents/News_2150_Gallup2009.pdf.

Duffy, Nick. 2016. "India Arrested Hundreds Last Year Under Colonial-Era Anti-Gay Law." *Pink News*, http://www.pinknews.co.uk/2016/09/29/india-arrested-hundreds- last-year-under-colonial-era-anti-gay-law.

Epprecht, Marc. 2008. *Heterosexual Africa*. Athens: Ohio University Press.

Ford, Clellan, and Frank Beach. 1965. *Patterns of Sexual Behaviour*. London: Methuen Publishing.

Haaretz. 2015. "Israeli Lawmaker 'Comes Out' After Jerusalem Gay Pride Parade Stabbing." August 1. https://www.haaretz.com/mk-comes-out-after-jerusalem-gay-pride-parade-stabbing-1.5381671.

Harris, Sarah. 2017. "Elizabeth Kerekere Speaks on Maori LGBTQ Term Takatāpui." *New Zealand Herald*, http://www.nzherald.co.nz/nz/news/article.cfm?c_id=1&objectid=11879651.

Islamic Education and Research Academy. 2015. "Is Islam the Cause or Solution to Extremism?" YouTube, https://www.youtube.com/watch?v=Jahx01Wo9Gw&app=desktop.

Knight, Kyle. 2015. "How Nepal's Constitution Got Queered." *Human Rights Watch*, https://www.hrw.org/news/2015/10/14/how-nepals-constitution-got-queered.

Lavers, Michael. 2016. "Report: Anti-LGBT Persecution Increased Under Uganda Law." *Washington Blade*, http://www.washingtonblade.com/2016/04/22/report-anti-lgbt-persecution-increased-under-uganda-law.

McKellar, Katie. 2015. "New Beginnings: Biskupski Set to Take Office, Start New Family." *Deseret News*, http://m.deseretnews.com/article/865644075/New-beginnings-Biskupski-set-to-take-office-start-new-family.html?pg=1?ref=http%3A%2F%2Fm.facebook.com.

McManama O'Brien, Kimberly H., Jennifer M. Putney, Nicholas W. Hebert, Amy M. Falk, and Laika D. Aguinaldo. 2016. "Sexual and Gender Minority Youth Suicide: Understanding Subgroup Differences to Inform Interventions." *LGBT Health* 3, no. 4: 248–251.

Murray, Stephen O., and Will Roscoe. 1998. *Boy Wives and Female Husbands*. London: Palgrave Macmillan.

Noronha, Charmaine. 2016. "Anglicans Recount Same-Sex Marriage Votes, Find Love Actually Won." *LGBTQ Nation*, http://www.lgbtqnation.com/2016/07/anglicans-recount-sex-marriage-votes-finds-love-actually-won/?utm_source=LGBTQ+Nation+Subscribers&utm_campaign=90bda12e6d-20160713_LGBTQ_Nation_Newsletter&utm_medium=email&utm_term=0_c4eab596bd-90bda12e6d-429470973.

Orozco, Caleb. 2015. Facebook post.

Penczak, Christopher. 2003. *Gay Witchcraft: Empowering the Tribe*. Newburyport, MA: Weiser.

Pew Research Center. 2014. "Public Sees Religion's Influence Waning, Section 3: Social & Political Issues." http://www.pewforum.org/2014/09/22/section-3-social-political-issues.

The Aswang Project. "The Moon God Libulan/Bulan: Patron Deity of Homosexuals?" https://www.aswangproject.com/the-moon-god-libulan-bulan-patron-deity-of-homosexuals.

Williams, Gareth. 2015. "Israeli MP Comes Out After Pride Stabbings." *Pink News*, http://www.pinknews.co.uk/2015/07/31/we-stayed-silent-no-more-israeli-mp-comes-out-after-pride-stabbings/?utm_source=PNFB&utm_medium=socialFB&utm_campaign=PNFacebook.

Wolpe, David. 2014. "Gay Love and Jewish Tradition." Mosaic Magazine. https://mosaicmagazine.com/response/2014/02/gay-love-and-jewish-tradition.

9: Cinders Goes to the Ball

Adams, Noah, Maaya Hitomi, and Cherie Moody. 2017. "Varied Reports of Adult Transgender Suicidality: Synthesizing and Describing the Peer-Reviewed and Gray Literature." *Transgender Health* 2, no. 1: 60–75.

Allen, Samantha. 2017. "Why a Lot of Americans Don't Want to Befriend a Transgender Person." *The Daily Beast*, http://www.thedailybeast.com/why-a-lot-of-americans-dont-want-to-be-friend-a-transgender-person?via=twitter_page.

Bates, Daniel. 2015. "Meet Tamara Adrián, Venezuela's Crusading Trans Politician." *The Daily Beast*, https://www.thedailybeast.com/meet-tamara-adrian-venezuelas-crusading-trans-politician?source=twitter&via=desktop.

Broadly Staff. 2017. "'This Is How We Win': Inside Danica Roem's Historic Victory." *Broadly*, https://broadly.vice.com/en_us/article/pa3vgb/this-is-how-we-win-inside-danica-roems-historic-victory?utm_source=broadlyfbus.

Bruni, Frank. 2017. "Danica Roem Is Really, Really, Boring." *New York Times*, https://www.nytimes.com/2017/11/14/opinion/danica-roem-virginia-transgender.html.

Buffie, William C. 2011. "Public Health Implications of Same-Sex Marriage." *American Journal of Public Health* 101, no. 6: 986–990.

Choate Hall & Stewart LLP. 2015. "Chief Justice Margaret Marshall on the Same-Sex Marriage Ruling." https://www.choate.com/news/chief-justice-margaret-marshall-on-the-supreme-court-same-sex-marriage-ruling.

Chokshi, Niraj. 2017. "One in Every 137 Teenagers Would Identify as Transgender, Report Says." *New York Times*, https://www.nytimes.com/2017/02/23/us/transgender-teenagers-how-many.html?_r=3.

Duffy, Nick. 2017. "Eddie Izzard Could 'Give Up Comedy' to Become First Transgender MP." *Pink News*, http://www.pinknews.co.uk/2017/09/11/eddie-izzard-could-give-up-comedy-to-become-first-transgender-mp.

Ecarma, Caleb. 2017. "Transgender VA Dem Releases Ad Challenging GOP Opponent: 'This Is Just Who I Am.'" *Mediaite*, https://www.mediaite.com/online/transgender-va-dem-releases-ad-challenging-gop-opponent-this-is-just-who-i-am.

Feder, J., Jeremy Singer-Vine, and Ben King. 2016. "This Is How 23 Countries Feel About Transgender Rights." *Buzzfeed*, https://www.buzzfeed.com/lesterfeder/this-is-how-23-countries-feel-about-transgender-rights?utm_term=.bg1OjM05q&ref=mobile share#.tgVzkqPem.

Flores, Andrew. 2015. *Attitudes Toward Transgender Rights: Perceived Knowledge and Secondary Interpersonal Contact*. Los Angeles: The Williams Institute, UCLA, http://williamsinstitute.law.ucla.edu/research/transgender-issues/attitudes-toward-transgender-rights-perceived-knowledge-and-secondary-interpersonal-contact.

Flores, Andrew R., Taylor N. T. Brown, and Andrew S. Park. 2016. *Public Support for Transgender Rights: A Twenty-Three Country Survey*, Los Angeles: The Williams Institute, UCLA.

Flores, Andrew R., Donald P. Haider-Markel, Daniel C. Lewis, Patrick R. Miller, Barry L. Tadlock, and Jami K. Taylor. 2018. "Challenged Expectations: Mere Exposure Effects on Attitudes About Transgender People and Rights." *Political Psychology* 39, no. 1: 197–216.

Flores, Wilson. 2016. "Geraldine Roman on Being the 1st Transgender in Congress, Beauty Secrets, Love, Duterte, Pope Francis & Pacquiao." *Philstar Global*, http://www.philstar.com/sunday-life/2016/05/29/1587856/geraldine-roman-being-1st-transgender-congress-beauty-secrets-love.

Gay, Lesbian and Straight Education Network. 2013. The 2013 National School Climate Survey. https://www.glsen.org/sites/default/files/2013%20National%20School%20Climate%20Survey%20Full%20Report_0.pdf

Groover, Heidi. 2016. "Trans Activist Danni Askini Is Running for the Washington State Legislature." *Slog*, https://www.thestranger.com/slog/2016/03/01/23637993/trans-activist-danni-askini-is-running-for-the-washington-state-legislature.

Haider-Markel, Donald, Patrick R. Miller, Andrew R. Flores, Daniel C. Lewis, Barry Tadlock, and Jami K. Taylor. 2017. "Bringing 'T' to the Table: Understanding Individual Support of Transgender Candidates for Public Office." *Politics, Groups, and Identities* 5, no. 3: 399–417.

Herman, Jody L., Andrew R. Flores, Taylor N. T. Brown, Bianca D. M. Wilson, and Kerith J. Conron. 2017. *Age of Individuals Who Identify as Transgender in the United States.* Los Angeles: The Williams Institute, UCLA.

Hoffman, Jan. 2016. "Gay and Lesbian High School Students Report 'Heartbreaking' Levels of Violence." *New York Times,* http://www.nytimes.com/2016/08/12/health/gay-lesbian-teenagers-violence.html?smprod=nytcore-ipad&smid=nytcore-ipad-share&_r=0.

Holder, Akilah. 2015. "Don't Vote for Jowelle." *Newsday,* http://newsday.co.tt/news/0,210430.html.

Kaufman, Ellie. 2015. "7 People Under 35 Who Inspire Us to Reconsider the Age Requirement for President." *Mic,* https://mic.com/articles/149069/7-people-under-35-who-inspire-us-to-reconsider-the-age-requirement-for-president#.gRc9yEmJH.

Kelly, Kim. 2017. "This Trans Metalhead Stepmom Is Making a Historic Run for Office in Virginia." *Noisey,* https://noisey.vice.com/en_us/article/ev4gep/this-trans-metalhead-stepmom-is-making-a-historic-run-for-office-in-virginia.

Lavers, Michael. 2015. "Transgender Woman Elected to Venezuelan National Assembly." *Washington Blade,* http://www.washingtonblade.com/2015/12/07/transgender-woman-elected-to-venezuelan-national-assembly.

Lees, Paris. 2017. "The Media Is Obsessed With Trans People—Until We Kill Ourselves." *The Pool,* https://www.the-pool.com/news-views/opinion/2017/30/paris-lees-on-talking-about-trans-suicide-not-toilets.

McBride, Sarah. 2017. "Forever and Ever: Losing My Husband at 24." *Huffington Post,* thttp://www.huffingtonpost.com/sarah-mcbride/forever-and-ever-losing-my-husband-at-24_b_8038600.html.

McCormick, Joseph. 2017. "Post-Presidential Election Youth Survey Paints a Shocking Picture of Bullying." *Pink News,* http://www.pinknews.co.uk/2017/01/25/post-presidential-election-youth-survey-paints-a-shocking-picture-of-bullying.

Milton, Josh. 2017. "China Has Published Its First Study of Transgender People and It's Exactly as Worrying as You'd Expect." *Pink News,* http://www.pinknews.co.uk/2017/11/23/china-has-published-its-first-study-of-transgender-people-and-its-exactly-as-worrying-as-youd-expect.

Morgan, Joe. 2015. "Tamara Adrian Becomes First Elected Trans MP in Venezuela." *Gaystar News,* http://www.gaystarnews.com/article/tamara-adrian-becomes-first-elected-trans-mp-in-venezuela/#gs.RpWFJ5k.

Movement Advancement Project. 2017. "Mapping Transgender Equality in the United States." http://www.lgbtmap.org/mapping-trans-equality.

Newsday. 2015. "TT needs Independents." http://newsday.co.tt/womens_weekly/0,216289.html.

Pew Research Center. 2016. "Where the Public Stands on Religious Liberty vs. Nondiscrimination." http://www.pewforum.org/2016/09/28/5-vast-majority-of-americans-know-someone-who-is-gay-fewer-know-someone-who-is-transgender.

Qnews. 2015. "Americans Are More Likely to Have Seen a Ghost Than to Have Met a Trans Person." http://www.qnews.com.au/americans-are-more-likely-to-have-seen-a-ghost-than-to-have-met-a-trans-person.

Riley, John. 2017. "Transgender Journalist Announces Run for Virginia House of Delegates." *Metro Weekly,* http://www.metroweekly.com/2017/01/transgender-journalist-announces-virginia-house-of-delegates.

Rood, Brian A., Sari L. Reisner, Francisco I. Surace, Jae A. Puckett, Meredith R. Maroney, and David W. Pantalone. 2016. "Expecting Rejection: Understanding the Minority Stress Experiences of Transgender and Gender-Nonconforming Individuals." *Transgender Health* 1, no. 1: 151–164.

Russell, Stephen T., and Jessica N. Fish. 2016. "Mental Health in Lesbian, Gay, Bisexual, and Transgender (LGBT) Youth." *Annual Review of Clinical Psychology* 28, no. 12: 465–487.

Seelman, Kristie. 2016. "Transgender Adults' Access to College Bathrooms and Housing and the Relationship to Suicidality." *Journal of Homosexuality* 63, no. 10: 1378–1399.

Sherfinski, David. 2014. "Virginia Republican Bob Marshall Stands By Remarks That Raise Eyebrows." *Washington Post.* https://www.washingtontimes.com/news/2014/apr/10/virginia-republican-bob-marshall-stands-by-remarks.

Stern, Mark Joseph. 2015. "Biden's True Legacy: He Was Obama's Conscience on LGBTQ Rights." http://www.slate.com/blogs/outward/2015/10/21/joe_biden_s_true_legacy_is_as_obama_s_conscience_on_lgbtq_rights.html.

Talusan, Meredith. 2015. "26 Times Trans People Ruled in 2015." Buzzfeed, http://www.buzzfeed.com/meredithtalusan/26-times-trans-people-slayed-in-2015#.kx0aRg0vl.

Talusan, Meredith. 2016. "Unerased: Counting Transgender Lives." *Mic*, https://mic.com/unerased.

Tiven, 2016. "National Geographic Features Transgender Kid on the Cover." *Attn*, http://www.attn.com/stories/13572/national-geographic-features-transgender-kid-on-cover?utm_source=itgetsbetter&utm_medium=fbpost&utm_campaign=influence.

Tourjée, Diana. 2016. "To Stop Trans Kids from Killing Themselves, Shocking Study Says 'Accept Them.'" *Broadly*, https://broadly.vice.com/en_us/article/pg7nq7/to-stop-trans-kids-from-killing-themselves-shocking-study-says-accept-them.

Zeilinger, Julie. 2015. "Venezuela Just Elected the First Transgender Congresswoman in South America." *Mic*, https://mic.com/articles/129940/venezuela-just-elected-the-first-transgender-congresswoman-in-south-america#.Fox8TR29O.

10: Mel and the Bees

Axler, Abraham. 2015. "An Examination of a Transgender Candidate's Interactions with Media: The Wymore Case." Unpublished manuscript.

Lavers, Michael. 2018. "Danica Roem Comes to Richmond." *Washington Blade*, http://www.washingtonblade.com/2018/01/12/danica-roem-comes-richmond, January 18.

McKeon, Lucy. 2012. "Mel Wymore Chooses People Over Politics." *The Nation*, November 5.

New York Times. 2013. "For New York City Council." August 30. https://www.nytimes.com/2013/08/31/opinion/for-new-york-city-council.html.

Ryle, Gilbert. 1949. *The Concept of Mind.* Chicago: University of Chicago Press.

Weick, Karl E. 1995. *Sensemaking in Organizations: Volume 3 of Foundations for Organizational Science.* Thousand Oaks, CA.: Sage Publications.

11: Southern Queers

D'Addario, Daniel. 2015. "Clay Aiken on a Second Run for Office: 'I Think It'll Happen.'" *Time*, http://time.com/3750959/clay-aiken-esquire-network-the-runner-up.

Jones, H. G., and David Southern. 2014. Miss Mary's Money: Fortune and Misfortune in a North Carolina Plantation Family. Jefferson, NC: McFarland.

Lasswell, Harold. 1948. *Power and Personality.* New York: Norton.

Lasswell, Harold. 1951. *The Political Writings of Harold D. Lasswell.* Glencoe, Ill: Free Press.

Murray, Pauli. 1956. *Proud Shoes: The Story of an American Family.* New York: Harper and Row.

Murray, Pauli. 1970. *Dark Testament and Other Poems.* Norwalk, CT: Silvermine.

Rosenberg, Rosalind. 2017. *Jane Crow: The Life of Pauli Murray.* New York: Oxford University Press.

Schultz, Kathryn. 2017. "The Many Lives of Pauli Murray." *The New Yorker*, http://www.newyorker.com/magazine/2017/04/17/the-many-lives-of-pauli-murray.

Smith, Kim. 2016. "Book of Harriet: The Disambiguation of Five North Carolinian Siblings 1840–1941." *Duke University Graduate Liberal Studies*, Center for Documentary Studies. https://dukespace.lib.duke.edu/dspace/bitstream/handle/10161/11964/Kim%20Smith%20GLS%20Master%27s%20Project%202016%20Book%20of%20Harriet--The%20

Disambiguation%20of%20Five%20North%20Carolinian%20Siblings%201840-1941. pdf?sequence=1.

Stein, Sam. 2016. "Clay Aiken Gained 30 Pounds Eating Bojangles Chicken During His Campaign." *Huffington Post*, http://www.huffingtonpost.com/entry/clay-aiken-30-pounds-eating-bojangles_us_57211401e4b01a5ebde44ddc?section=politicsZbailey,

Williams Institute, UCLA. 2016. LGBT in the South. https://williamsinstitute.law.ucla.edu/research/census-lgbt-demographics-studies/lgbt-in-the-south.

Zaru, Deena. 2017. "Clay Aiken Drops Clinton for Biden, Praises Trump." *CNN*, http://www.cnn.com/2015/10/08/politics/clay-aiken-joe-biden-hillary-clinton-donald-trump/.

Zbailey, Mike. 2016. "Galloway Ridge and the Extraordinary History of Its Land." https://gallowayridge.com/galloway-ridge-and-the-extraordinary-history-of-the-land-it-sits-on.

12: The Washington 43rd

Atkins, Gary L. 2013. *Gay Seattle: Stories of Exile and Belonging*, Seattle: University of Washington Press.

Feit, Josh. 2012. "Is McKenna Still a Dan Evans Republican?" *Seattle Met*, https://www.seattlemet.com/articles/2012/11/1/is-mckenna-still-a-dan-evans-republican.

Groover, Heidi. 2015. "State Rep. Brady Walkinshaw Will Challenge US Rep. Jim McDermott in 2016." *The Stranger*, http://www.thestranger.com/blogs/slog/2015/12/03/23226181/state-rep-brady-walkinshaw-will-challenge-us-rep-jim-mcdermott-in-2016.

Kelety, Josh. 2016. "In 43rd Legislative District Race, Nobody Has Really Had a Chance to Get to Know the Candidates." Capitol Hill Seattle Blog. http://www.capitolhillseattle.com/2016/06/in-43rd-legislative-district-race-nobody-has-really-had-a-chance-to-get-to-know-the-candidates.

Kershner, Kate. 2012. "Anderson, Cal (1948–1995)." *HistoryLink*, http://www.historylink.org/index.cfm?DisplayPage=output.cfm&file_id=10265.

King, Marsha. 1990. "Concerned About Privacy as Well as Hypocrisy, Gays and Lesbians Debate the Practice of Outing." *Seattle Times*, June 22.

King County Young Democrats. 43rd Legislative District Debate. 2016. YouTube, https://www.youtube.com/watch?v=ABQznkmj4Qw&feature=youtu.be.

Out History. "Out and Elected in the USA: 1974–2004." http://outhistory.org/exhibits/show/out-and-elected/late-1980s/cal-anderson.

Savage, Dan. 2006. "Murray vs. Thibaudeau." *The Stranger*, http://slog.thestranger.com/2006/04/murray_vs_thiba.

Seattle Times Editorial Board. 2016. "The Times Recommends: Dan Shih for 43rd Legislative District Position No. 1." *Seattle Times*, http://www.seattletimes.com/opinion/editorials/the-times-recommends-dan-shih-for-43rd-legislative-district-position-no-1.

Spencer, Hal.1992."Lawmakers Clash Amid Hate-crimes Testimony." *Seattle Times*, February 27.

Stranger Election Control Board. 2016. "*The Stranger*'s Endorsements for the August 2016 Primary Election." *The Stranger*, http://www.thestranger.com/news/2016/07/13/24336905/the-strangers-endorsements-for-the-august-2016-primary-election#Macri.

Wang, Deborah. 2014. "Seattle Sends a New Face to Olympia—Brady Walkinshaw, 29." *Kuow*, http://kuow.org/post/seattle-sends-new-face-olympia-brady-walkinshaw-29.

13: The Right Gays

Ashcroft, Michael, and Isabel Oakeshott. 2016. *Call Me Dave: The Unauthorised Biography of David Cameron*. London: Biteback.

Bale, Tim, Paul Webb, and Monica Poletti. 2017. *Grassroots. Britain's Party Members: Who They Are, What They Think and What They Do*. London: Mile End Institute, Queen Mary College, University of London.

Bloch, Michael. 2015. "Double Lives—A History of Sex and Secrecy at Westminster." *The Guardian*, http://www.theguardian.com/books/2015/may/16/double-lives-a-history-of-sex-and-secrecy-at-westminster.

Bloch, Michael. 2016. *Closet Queens: Some 20th Century British Politicians,* London: Abacus.

Bollinger, Alex. 2017. "Lesbian Named Leader of Germany's Fascist Party." *LGBTQ Nation,* https://www.lgbtqnation.com/2017/04/lesbian-named-leader-germanys-fascist-party/?utm_source=LGBTQ+Nation+Subscribers&utm_campaign=da3e04a9bd-20170425_LGBTQ_Nation_Newsletter&utm_medium=email&utm_term=0_c4eab596bd-da3e04a9bd-429470973.

Borjas, Weronika. 2016. "Rainbows and Racism Marched Together in Sweden During LGBT Pride Week." *Vice,* https://www.vice.com/sv/article/pp4k58/sweden-jarva-pride-parade-immigration-protest.

Burns, Conor. 2013. "My Fondest Farewells to Margaret Thatcher." *The Telegraph,* http://www.telegraph.co.uk/news/politics/margaret-thatcher/9991815/Conor-Burns-MP-My-fondest-farewell-to-Margaret-Thatcher.html.

Butterworth, Benjamin. 2017. "Lesbian Ally of the EDL's Tommy Robinson Standing to Be UKIP Leader." *Pink News,* http://www.pinknews.co.uk/2017/06/14/lesbian-ally-of-the-edls-tommy-robinson-standing-to-be-ukip-leader.

Butterworth, Benjamin. 2017. "Meet the Gay Man Masterminding Marine Le Pen's Bid to Be French President." *Pink News,* http://www.pinknews.co.uk/2017/04/26/this-is-the-gay-man-masterminding-marine-le-pens-bid-to-be-french-president.

Cameron, David. 2014. "When People's Love Is Divided By Law, It Is the Law That Needs to Change." http://www.pinknews.co.uk/2014/03/28/david-cameron.

Campbell, John. 2014. "Passionate Letters Roy Jenkins' Male Lover Wrote to Try to Halt His Marriage: More Startling Revelations About the VERY Permissive Love Life of Labour's Father of the Permissive Society." *The Daily Mail,* http://www.dailymail.co.uk/news/article-2577080/Passionate-letters-Roy-Jenkins-male-lover-wrote-try-halt-marriage-More-startling-revelations-VERY-permissive-love-life-Labours-father-permissive-society.html.

Chalk, Will. 2017. "White Gay French Men Are Voting Far Right." *BBC,* http://www.bbc.co.uk/newsbeat/article/39641822/why-gay-french-men-are-voting-far-right.

CNN. 2016. "Exit Polls." http://www.cnn.com/election/results/exit-polls.

Duffy, Nick. 2015. "Too Many Are Denied Chances Because of Who They Love." *Pink News,* http://www.pinknews.co.uk/2015/10/22/david-cameron-tells-pinknews-awards-too-many-are-denied-chances-because-of-who-they-love.

Duffy, Nick. 2017. "1 in 5 French Gays Are Voting for Anti-Gay Marriage Marine Le Pen." *Pink News,* http://www.pinknews.co.uk/2017/03/01/1-in-5-french-gays-are-voting-for-anti-gay-marriage-marine-le-pen.

Duffy, Nick. 2017. "Sir Vince Cable: My Liberal Hero Roy Jenkins Was a Bisexual Man." *Pink News,* http://www.pinknews.co.uk/2017/10/19/sir-vince-cable-my-liberal-hero-roy-jenkins-was-a-bisexual-man.

Egan, Patrick J., and Kenneth Sherrill. 2005. "Marriage and the Shifting Priorities of a New Generation of Lesbians and Gays." *PS: Political Science & Politics,*38, no. 2: 229–232.

Elliott, Francis, and James Hanning. 2007. *Cameron: The Rise of the New Conservative,* London: Fourth Estate.

Hayes, Jerry. 2013. "Gay Marriage Vote: Why It's Groundhog Day for the Tories." *The Guardian.* May 21. https://www.theguardian.com/commentisfree/2013/may/21/gay-marriage-groundhog-day-tories.

Holehouse, Matthew. 2014. "Nigel Evans Fights to Save Seat After Tory Activist Revolt." *Telegraph,* http://www.telegraph.co.uk/news/politics/conservative/10918020/Nigel-Evans-fights-to-save-seat-after-Tory-activist-revolt.html.

McManus, Michael. 2011. *Tory Pride and Prejudice.* London: Biteback.

Mowlabocus, Sharif. 2016. "Crispin Blunt's Poppers Speech: A Brave Acknowledgment of Awkward Truths." *Pink News,* http://www.pinknews.co.uk/2016/01/22/crispin-blunts-poppers-speech-a-brave-acknowledgment-of-awkward-truths.

O'Grady, Sean. 2015. "John Maynard Keynes: New Biography Reveals Shocking Details About the Economist's Sex Life." *Independent,* http://www.independent.co.uk/news/business/

analysis-and-features/john-maynard-keynes-new-biography-reveals-shocking-details-about-the-economists-sex-life-10101971.html.

Pickthall, Stephen. 2015. "MP 'Overwhelmed' With Support After Coming Out as Gay." *Chichester Observer,* http://www.chichester.co.uk/news/local/nick-gibb-interview-mp-overwhelmed-with-support-after-coming-out-as-gay-1-6796354.

Roberts, Scott. 2013. "Gay Tory MP Conor Burns: 'Lady Thatcher Did Not Have a Problem with Gay People.' " *Pink News,* http://www.pinknews.co.uk/2013/06/24/gay-tory-mp-conor-burns-lady-thatcher-did-not-have-a-problem-with-gay-people.

Rogers, Thomas. 2017. "Gays Really Love Germany's Racist, Homophobic Far Right Party."*Vice,*https://www.vice.com/en_ca/article/53ndzd/gays-really-love-germanys-racist-homophobic-far-right-party.

Shubert, Atika, Nadine Schmidt, and Judith Vonberg. 2017. "The Gay Men Turning to the Far Right in Germany." *CNN,* http://edition.cnn.com/2017/09/14/europe/germany-far-right-lgbt-support/index.html?ofs=fbia.

Surk, Barbara. 2017. "Serbia Gets Its First Female, and First Openly Gay, Premier." *New York Times.* June 28.
https://www.nytimes.com/2017/06/28/world/europe/serbia-ana-brnabic-prime-minister.html.

The Advocate. 2011. "Crispin Blunt's Story: The Evolution of a Gay Conservative in Parliament." *The Advocate,* http://www.advocate.com/news/2011/09/02/crispin-blunt-story-evolution-gay-conservative-parliament.

Urwin, Rosamund. 2016. "My Partner Tess Is Very Pleased I Felt Able to Be Clear About Our Relationship." *Evening Standard,* http://www.standard.co.uk/lifestyle/london-life/putney-mp-justine-greening-says-partner-tess-is-pleased-she-came-out-as-lgbt-a3282641.html.

Waldegrave, William. 2016. " 'Edward Heath' by Michael McManus, Review: 'Portrait of a British Political Ninja.' " *Daily Telegraph,* https://www.telegraph.co.uk/books/what-to-read/edward-heath-by-michael-mcmanus-review-portrait-of-a-british-pol.

Walters, Simon. 2010. "Commons Deputy Speaker Tells Why He Is Fed Up With 'Living a Lie': Growing Up in South Wales, It Was Hard Enough Being a Tory, Let Alone Being a Gay." *Daily Mail,* http://www.dailymail.co.uk/news/article-1339885/Commons-Deputy-Speaker-tells-fed-living-lie-Growing-South-Wales-hard-Tory-let-gay.html.

Williams, Joe. 2015. "David Cameron Refused to Back Down on Equal Marriage—Despite Protests from His Own Mother." *Pink News,* rhttp://www.pinknews.co.uk/2015/09/'25/david-cameron-refused-to-back-down-on-equal-marriage-despite-protests-from-his-own-mothe.

Wheen, Francis. 1992. *Tom Driberg: His Life and Indiscretions.* London: Pan Books.

14: Britain Goes Gay at the Polls

Bardell, Hannah. 2017. "Coming Out as a Politician." *Huffington Post,* http://www.huffingtonpost.co.uk/hannah-bardell/coming-out-as-a-politician_b_17874702.html.

Bennhold, Katrin. 2016. "Scotland Embraces Gay Politicians in a Profound Cultural Shift." *New York Times.* October 23. https://www.nytimes.com/2016/10/23/world/europe/scotland-gay-politicians.html.

Bradlow, Josh, Fay Bartram, April Guasp, and Vasanti Jadva. 2017. *School Report.* Stonewall, http://www.stonewall.org.uk/sites/default/files/the_school_report_2017.pdf.

Committee on Standards in Public Life. 2017. "Intimidation in Public Life." UK Government. https://www.gov.uk/government/uploads/system/uploads/attachment_data/file/666927/6.3637_CO_v6_061217_Web3.1__2_.pdf.

Dhrodia, Azmina. 2017. "We Tracked 25,688 Abusive Tweets Sent to Women MPs—Half Were Directed at Diane Abbott." *New Statesman,* https://www.newstatesman.com/2017/09/we-tracked-25688-abusive-tweets-sent-women-mps-half-were-directed-diane-abbott.

Duffy, Nick. 2016. "Speaker John Bercow Praises 'Most Diverse' House of Commons as He Is Re-Elected." *Pink News,* http://www.pinknews.co.uk/2017/06/13/speaker-john-bercow-praises-most-diverse-house-of-commons-as-he-is-re-elected.

Duffy, Nick. 2016. "Tory Minister Opens Up About Coming Out to PM David Cameron." *Pink News*, http://www.pinknews.co.uk/2016/03/03/tory-minister-opens-up-about-coming-out-to-pm-david-cameron.

Elgot, Jessica. 2017. "'You Are a Danger to Civilization': Gay Politicians Share Their Experiences." *The Guardian*, https://www.theguardian.com/world/2017/aug/31/you-are-a-danger-to-civilisation-gay-mps-share-their-experiences.

Magni, Gabriele, and Andrew Reynolds. 2018. "Candidate Sexual Orientation Didn't Matter (in the Way You Might Think) in the 2015 UK General Election." March 25. *American Political Science Review*. https://www.cambridge.org/core/journals/american-political-science-review/article/candidate-sexual-orientation-didnt-matter-in-the-way-you-might-think-in-the-2015-uk-general-election/752C15E25F17D3A13031A2693E8B7A01.

Park, Alison. 2017. *British Social Attitudes*. The National Centre for Social Research, http://www.bsa.natcen.ac.uk/?_ga=2.151737721.1957783070.1522756310-1562 982721.1522756310

Stambolieva, Ekaterina. 2017. "Detecting Online Abuse against Women MPs on Twitter." Amnesty International. https://drive.google.com/file/d/0B3bg_SJKE9GOenpaekZ4eXRBWk0/view.

Stonewall. 2013. "Gay in Britain." https://www.stonewall.org.uk/sites/default/files/Gay_in_Britain__2013_.pdf.

15: You Win Some, You Lose Some

Duffy, Nick. 2016. "Academics and Activists Condemn 'Bully' Peter Tatchell in Open Letter." *Pink News*, http://www.pinknews.co.uk/2016/02/22/academics-and-activists-condemn-bully-peter-tatchell-in-open-letter.

Tatchell, Peter. 2002. "Sex Harassment by Labour MP Bob Mellish." http://www.petertatchell.net/politics/tatchell-sex-harassment-by-labour-mp-bob-mellish.

Yeates, Alex. 2016. "Former Lib Dem MP Sir Simon Hughes to Run in Bermondsey and Old Southwark if There's a Snap Election." *Southwark News*, http://www.southwarknews.co.uk/news/look-hughes-coming-back.

Conclusion

Berlatsky, Noah. 2013. "Gay Marriage Is Not the Death Knell of the Sexual Revolution." *The Atlantic*.
https://www.theatlantic.com/sexes/archive/2013/03/gay-marriage-is-not-the-death-knell-of-the-sexual-revolution/274436.

Browning, Bill. 2016. "Special Snowflake Syndrome Is Ruining the Progressive LGBTQ Movement." *LGBTQ Nation*, http://www.lgbtqnation.com/2016/01/special-snowflake-syndrome-is-ruining-the-progressive-lgbtq-movement/?utm_source=LGBTQ+Nation+Subscribers&utm_campaign=ee8fbec9d8-20160128_LGBTQ_Nation_Newsletter&utm_medium=email&utm_term=0_c4eab596bd-ee8fbec9d8-429470973.

Brunner, Jim, Danoel Beekman, and Lewis Kamb. 2017. "Seattle Mayor Ed Murray Resigns After Fifth Child Sex-Abuse Allegation." *Seattle Times*, https://www.seattletimes.com/seattle-news/politics/seattle-mayor-ed-murray-resigns-after-fifth-child-sex-abuse-allegation/?utm_source=email&utm_medium=email&utm_campaign=article_title_1.1.

Eleveld, Kerry. 2016. "Some LGBT Movement Leaders Flirt With Strategic Disaster." *Daily Kos*, http://m.dailykos.com/story/2016/10/29/1588113/-View-from-the-Left-LGBT-movement-leaders-flirt-with-strategic-disaster.

Eleveld, Kerry. 2016. "View From the Left: How the LGBTQ Movement Went From Winning to Losing in Nine Months." *Daily Kos*, http://www.dailykos.com/story/2016/3/26/1506236/-View-from-the-left-How-the-LGBTQ-movement-went-from-winning-to-losing-in-nine-months.

Farzan, Antonia Noori. 2017. "Kyrsten Sinema, Allegedly a Democrat, Still Votes With Trump Half the Time." *Phoenix New Times*, http://www.phoenixnewtimes.com/news/kyrsten-sinemas-voting-record-immigration-refugees-health-care-ada-9682545, September 28.

Feder, J. 2015. "Top Rights Court Rules That Same-Sex Partnerships Must Be Treated as a Human Right." Buzzfeed, http://www.buzzfeed.com/lesterfeder/partnership-recognition-a-right-for-same-sex-couples-in-euro#.jkKXO1Na3.

Gladwell, Malcom. 2014. "Sacred And Profane: How Not to Negotiate With Believers." *The New Yorker*. https://www.newyorker.com/magazine/2014/03/31/sacred-and-profane-4.

Graff, E. J. 2013. "What's Next for the Gay-Rights Movement?" *Newsweek*, http://www.newsweek.com/2013/09/27/whats-next-gay-rights-movement-238040.html.

Greenberg, Will. 2016. "Brace Yourselves for an Onslaught of Anti-LGBT Proposals in 2017." *Mother Jones*, http://m.motherjones.com/politics/2016/12/lgbt-advocates-gearing-another-year-fights.

Hansard, New Zeland Parliament. 2013. "Marriage (Definition of Marriage) Amendment Bill, Third Reading." https://www.parliament.nz/en/pb/hansard-debates/rhr/document/50HansD_20130417_00000020/marriage-definition-of-marriage-amendment-bill-third.

Holden, Dominic. 2015. "Why America's Top LGBT Group is Losing an Argument Over Bathrooms." Buzzfeed, http://www.buzzfeed.com/dominicholden/hrc-bathroom-strategy#.ttmalVpLJN.

Holden, Dominic. 2016. "Top LGBT Leaders Are Divided Over Compromising On The Bathroom Fight." Buzzfeed, https://www.buzzfeed.com/dominicholden/lgbt-leaders-divided-bathroom-fight?utm_term=.ps9Lk12OwW#.ccbzDNGmx3.

Jones, Jeffrey. 2017. "In U.S., 10.2% of LGBT Adults Now Married to Same-Sex Spouse." *Gallup*, http://www.gallup.com/poll/212702/lgbt-adults-married-sex-spouse.aspx.

Kramer, Larry. 2016. "Happy. Frightened. Worried Hopeful." *Esquire*, http://www.esquire.com/news-politics/a45907/larry-kramer-speaks-gay-rights.

Maloney, Ryan. 2016. "Most Canadians Say A Gay Prime Minister Is Likely Within 10 Years: Abacus Data Poll." *Huffington Post*, http://www.huffingtonpost.ca/2016/07/26/canada-gay-prime-minister-poll-abacus-data_n_11199482.html.

Miller , Jonathan. 2012. "New York, 18th House District." *National Journal*. http://www.nationaljournal.com/congress-legacy/new-york-18th-house-district-20121105.

Moscowitz, Leigh. 2013. *The Battle Over Marriage: Gay Rights Activism Through the Media*. Champaign: University of Illinois Press.

Movement Advancement Project. 2016. "Unjust: How the Broken Criminal Justice System Fails LGBTQ Youth." http://www.lgbtmap.org/criminal-justice-youth?utm_source=Unjust+Youth&utm_campaign=Youth+CJ+report&utm_medium=email.

Peters, Stephen. 2017. "HRC Previews Anti-LGBTQ Action Anticipated in Statehouses During 2017." *Human Rights Campaign*, http://www.hrc.org/blog/hrc-previews-anti-lgbtq-action-anticipated-in-statehouses-during-2017.

Pew Research Center. 2016. "Faith and the 2016 Campaign." http://www.pewforum.org/2016/01/27/faith-and-the-2016-campaign.

Rayside, David. 1998. *On the Fringe: Gays and Lesbians in Politics*. Ithaca, NY: Cornell University Press.

Reynolds, Andrew. 2015. "The UK Just Elected a Record Number of LGBTQ People to Parliament." *Pink News*. https://www.pinknews.co.uk/2017/06/09/the-uk-just-elected-a-record-number-of-lgbtq-people-to-parliament.

Riggle, Ellen, Robert E. Wickham, Sharon S. Rostosky, Esther D. Rothblum, and Kimberly F. Balsam. 2016. *Impact of Civil Marriage Recognition for Long-Term Same-Sex Couples*. Los Angeles: The Williams Institute, UCLA. http://williamsinstitute.law.ucla.edu/research/marriage-and-couples-rights/impact-of-civil-marriage-recognition-for-long-term-same-sex-couples.

Sammon, Alexander. 2016. "Legendary LGBT Activists Want You to Get Up and Fight." *Mother Jones*, http://m.motherjones.com/media/2016/12/gay-rights-cleve-jones-when-we-rise-my-life-movement.

Sherrill, Kenneth. 1999. "The Youth of the Movement: Gay Activists in 1972–1973."

In *Gays and Lesbians in the Democratic Process: Public Policy, Public Opinion and Political Representation*, edited by Ellen Riggle and Barry Tadlock. New York: Columbia University Press.

Signorile, Michaelangelo. 2015. *It's Not Over: Getting Beyond Tolerance, Defeating Homophobia, and Winning True Equality*. Boston: Houghton Mifflin Harcourt.

Strangio, Chase. 2016. "Legislators Across the Country Set Their Sights on Transgender People." American Civil Liberties Union, https://www.aclu.org/blog/speak-freely/legislators-across-country-set-their-sights-transgender-people.

Taylor, Sarah, and Emily Swanson. 2016. "Poll: Young Americans Overwhelmingly Support LGBT Rights." *LGBTQ Nation*, http://www.lgbtqnation.com/2016/08/poll-young-americans-overwhelmingly-favor-lgbt-rights/?utm_source=LGBTQ+Nation+Subscr ibers&utm_campaign=7a7290dbdf-20160815_LGBTQ_Nation_Newsletter&utm_medium=email&utm_term=0_c4eab596bd-7a7290dbdf-429470973.

Turner, Allison. 2016. "HRC Report Finds Opponents of LGBTQ Equality are Ramping Up State Efforts to Sanction Discrimination." *Human Rights Campaign*, http://www.hrc.org/blog/hrc-report-finds-opponents-of-lgbtq-equality-are-ramping-up-state-efforts-t.

Weisel, Elie. 1995. *The Town Beyond the Wall*. New York: Schocken Books.

Williams, Joe. 2016. "Same-Sex Marriage Up By 33% in Just One Year." *Pink News*, http://www.pinknews.co.uk/2016/06/22/same-sex-marriage-up-by-33-in-just-one-year.

Wright, John. 2016. "Anti-LGBT State Lawmakers to Unleash Another Tsunami of Bigoted Bills in 2016." *Towleroad*, http://www.towleroad.com/2016/01/anti-lgbt-state-lawmakers-unleash-another-tsunami-bigoted-bills-2016.

Yoshino, Kenji. 2006. *Covering: The Hidden Assault on Our Civil Rights*. New York: Random House.

INDEX